NOT ALL FUN AND GAMES

Not All Fun and Games

VIDEOGAME LABOUR, PROJECT-BASED WORKPLACES,
AND THE NEW CITIZENSHIP AT WORK

Marie-Josée Legault and
Johanna Weststar

Concordia University Press
Montreal

Unless otherwise noted, all text and photographs copyright the authors.

Every reasonable effort has been made to acquire permission for copyright material used in this publication, and to acknowledge all such indebtedness accurately. Any errors and omissions called to the publisher's attention will be corrected in future printings.

Design: Garet Markvoort
Copy editing: Correy Baldwin
Index: Alexandra Peace
Proofreading: Saelan Twerdy

Not All Fun and Games is set in Eames Century Modern, designed by Erik van Blokland, Andy Cruz, and Ken Barber in 2010 for House Industries. Inspired by the collaborative work of Charles and Ray Eames, the typeface combines efficiency and playfulness for an exuberantly versatile serif face.

Titles and display text are set in LL Unica77, released by Lineto in 2015 and drawn for digital typesetting by Christian Mengelt of Team'77 in collaboration with Maurice Göldner. Mengelt used the original drawings of Haas Unica, first released for Bobst Graphic/Autologic systems in 1980.

Printed and bound in Canada by Marquis Book Printing

This book is printed on Forest Stewardship Council certified paper and meets the permanence of paper requirements of ANSI/NISO Z39.48-1992.

Concordia University Press's books are available for free on several platforms. Visit www.concordia.ca/press

First English edition published in 2024
10 9 8 7 6 5 4 3 2 1

978-1-988111-49-0 | Paper
978-1-988111-50-6 | E-book

Library and Archives Canada Cataloguing in Publication

Title: Not all fun and games : videogame labour, project-based workplaces, and the new citizenship at work / Marie-Josée Legault and Johanna Weststar.
Names: Legault, Marie-Josée, 1955- author. | Weststar, Johanna, author.
Description: First English edition. | Includes bibliographical references and index.
Identifiers: Canadiana (print) 20240318048 | Canadiana (ebook) 20240318250 | ISBN 9781988111490 (softcover) | ISBN 9781988111506 (EPUB)
Subjects: LCSH: Video games industry—Canada. | LCSH: Video games industry—United States.
Classification: LCC HD9993.E453 C3 2024 | DDC 338.7/6179480971—dc23

Concordia University Press
1455 de Maisonneuve Blvd. W.
Montreal, Quebec H3G 1M8
CANADA

Concordia University Press gratefully acknowledges the generous support of the Birks Family Foundation, the Estate of Linda Kay, and the Estate of Tanneke De Zwart.

This book has been published with the help of a grant from the Federation of the Humanities and Social Sciences through the Awards to Scholarly Publications Program, using funds provided by the Social Sciences and Humanities Research Council of Canada. Support has also been received from The University of Western Ontario's J.B. Smallman Fund.

TABLE OF CONTENTS

Acknowledgements	vi
Introduction	ix

PART ONE: THEORY

1. Citizenship at Work in the Post-Industrial Landscape	3
2. Project Management at the Foreground	23

PART TWO: CONTEXT

3. Videogame Development as an Illustration of Project-Based Work	37
4. The Other Side of the Playful Bunch: Risks Faced by Videogame Developers	63

PART THREE: APPLIED ANALYSIS

5. Are Game Developers Protected against Employment Risks?	105
6. Do Game Developers Have Recourse against Arbitrary Treatment?	129
7. Do Game Developers Participate in the Local Regulation of Work?	167
8. Do Game Developers Participate in the Social Regulation of Work?	193

9. The Regulation of Working Time Is a Citizenship-Free Zone	227
10. Second-Class Citizens in the VGI	253
Conclusion	291
References	307
Data Appendix	355
Index	369

ACKNOWLEDGEMENTS

We first must send a very large thank-you to the many graduate and undergraduate students who worked on critical elements of this project along the way and/or contributed directly or indirectly to our related research: Maria Andrei-Gedja, Pierson Browne, Indranil Chakraborty, Trevor Coppins, Sarah Dashow, Alyssa DeAngelis, Chandell Gosse, Christopher Hurry, Ezgi Inceefe, Daniel Korn, Shruti Kumar, Eva Kwan, Alyssa MacDougall, Elham Marzi, Sarah Mederios, Victoria O'Meara, Marie-Soleil Ouellette, Vishal Sooknanan, John R.J. Thompson, Laurence Tô, Joyce Truong, and Nancy Zenger. We could not have done this without you!

We acknowledge our industry-academic partnership with the International Game Developers Association (IGDA) and the fruitful collaborations we have had with the IGDA and its partners in creating, administering, and analysing the Quality of Life and Developer Satisfaction Surveys which serve as a central component in this book. Thank you to past Executive Director Jason Della Rocca and past Quality of Life SIG Chair Judy Tyrer for establishing our initial partnership and to past Executive Directors Kate Edwards, Jen McLean, and Renee Gittins for keeping it going. Thanks to our collaborators on the 2015 DSS, Wanda Meloni and Celia Pearce.

We thank Greig de Peuter, Sean Gouglas, and Geoffrey Wood for rich feedback on our initial manuscript proposal and our many wonderful colleagues who provided feedback as we presented parts of this book at conferences over the years—thanks especially to our tribe at CIRA and CRIMT, but also to the international game studies community who warmly welcomed us as contributors to the emerging subfield of game-production studies and game-worker labour.

Thank you also to our editor Ryan Van Huijstee, the team at Concordia University Press, and our book indexer Alexandra Peace. We are also very honoured that our book cover features the artwork of Carolyn Jong, a game worker and union activist.

And finally, on a personal ground, we thank our families.

> Over the years I have been engrossed in this book, my partner Marc was always there as a mooring, to listen and either bring up another point of view or provide a peaceful landing to my over-stimulated self. It is not his lesser virtue to ease my daily life when I am anxious!—Marie-Josée Legault

> To my partner Evan, you are a source of inspiration and your expertise and experience has made an important contribution to this book. You were a well of patience, support, and clarity when I struggled. To my kids, Anneke and Merrick, you are fabulous always—independent, organized, adaptable, and splendid. Thank you for being willing to share me with my work...and for making dinner most of the time. Finally, thanks to my parents, for your values and the formative life experiences you provided.—Johanna Weststar

We acknowledge that this work was financially supported in part by the Social Sciences and Humanities Research Council of Canada, the IGDA and the IGDA Foundation, the Dancap Private Equity Research Award in the DAN Department of Management and Organizational Studies at Western University, the J.B. Smallman Publication Fund and the Faculty of Social Science at Western University, and the Federation for the Humanities and Social Sciences Scholarly Book Awards.

INTRODUCTION

Videogame developers (VGDs) are the diverse group of workers who create videogames. They have many roles and job titles, including: artists, animators and modellers; programmers and engineers; game, level, and interaction designers; sound and audio designers; user-experience and localization specialists; writers and narrative designers; testers; and producers. They are emblematic of the rising players of contemporary project-based creative work who are often more committed to their trade and projects than they are to any workplace. VGDs in smaller game studios are often gig workers who move from project to project across employers and workplaces. VGDs in large studios are usually hired and retained on open-ended contracts, but they too are frequently reassigned across projects. Even those with some employment stability tend to move jobs in the pursuit of new challenges. Other VGDs do not have an employment status. They are independent workers who invest significant personal resources and "sweat equity" into their projects before they see external injection of funds (Keogh 2021, 121). Taken as a whole, VGDs share characteristics of cultural creative workers such as performing, recording, and film artists and software workers in the information and communications technology sector (McKinlay and Smith 2009).

In 2022, videogame profits were projected to reach US$200 billion globally (Barbour 2021). As an icon of a promising knowledge economy promoted by the private creative sector, the videogame industry (VGI) is globally sought-after and highly subsidized by governments. The quality of this work is critical to, for instance, the more than 48,000 workers directly and indirectly employed in the industry in Canada (Nordicity 2019) and the more than 276,000 workers in the United States (IBISWorld 2022).

In 2004, the International Game Developers Association (IGDA) surveyed developers about their quality of life, and despite identifying many challenges, concluded they were "overall, a happy bunch" (IGDA 2004, 16). Are they still? Randall Nichols sets out this ideal presentation:

the video games industry is an ideal example of what it means to live and work in an information society. Programming and design jobs require both high skill levels and, in many cases, high levels of creativity. In keeping with this, workers tend be highly educated. Because the jobs often use computers and high-speed Internet connections, greater than usual levels of employee mobility are possible. According to theories about the information society, this combination of skills should grant workers in the video game industry more influence in the labour market. Because their combination of skills is rare, highly sought after, and in demand, video game workers should be more able to switch jobs within the industry and be more secure in their jobs. It would be expected that they would earn higher wages, have better benefits, and experience greater job satisfaction than employees in most other sectors. (Nichols 2005, 189)

In this way, game development is often portrayed as non-work, or work as play. Beginning with its late 1960s to early 1970s creation story of student resistance against the military–industrial complex and "monotonous jobs in industrial plants and offices," the game industry has been described as a space where the lines between work and leisure are blurred (Dyer-Witheford and de Peuter 2009, 12). Indeed, the industry was built and still routinely capitalizes on the "free labour" of hackers, modders, fans, and hobbyists—what Kücklich (2005) called "playbour." Though the industry has grown into large studios and institutionalized some hardcore management practices, the "work as play ethos" is still applied to paid work environments (Dyer-Witheford and de Peuter 2006) in order to promote them.

Notwithstanding their love for their work, VGDs relentlessly use social and professional media to voice work concerns. They face pervasive overtime and unpredictable working time; employment instability; lack of diversity and equity (and ensuing sexism and racism); poor compensation management; unrelenting layoffs and placement processes due to "at-will" employment; health problems; lack of protection when losing employment income (and particularly scarce retirement plans); unexplained dismissals, assessments, assignments, and so forth; and an overall absence of a voice in their work environments. A growing number of VGDs are engaging in direct actions to show their dissatisfaction with their employers and the direction of their companies (Chapters 7 and 8). That said, though they have certain modes of collective action through which to voice their claims, they remain a mostly non-unionized and non-represented group. The broad spectrum of grievances held by VGDs led us to consider the wide-ranging question of their "citizenship at work" as an encompassing expression of the problem and its source.

Citizenship at work is a status that extends the benefits of democracy into work environments. A citizen status allows workers to take part in the regulation of their working conditions and environment, and not be subjected to a unilateral power relationship in the governance of their work or an asymmetrical relationship with authority. It was originally conceived as "industrial citizenship" and was enabled through labour market institutions that, in North America, date back to the mid-twentieth century (Chapter 1). Harry Arthurs (1967) and Thomas Humphrey Marshall (1950, 1964) are acknowledged founding fathers of the concept, though it has been developed over the years by numerous legal and industrial-relations scholars (see Coutu 2004; Coutu and Murray 2010a; Fudge 2005, 2010). Arthurs and Marshall placed differential emphasis on the labour institutions best placed to deliver citizenship to workers. Arthurs championed collective bargaining through labour unions as a means to achieve wage and employment determination, while Marshall emphasized protective policy interventions through universal laws (for example, legislation on minimum wages and employment protection, mandatory social benefits such as employment insurance [EI] and labour market policies, wage setting institutions, enforcement of the legislation). Yet, when taken together, these labour market institutions aim to promote a certain degree of symmetry between the rights and obligations of employers and those of workers. They were celebrated, particularly by jurists, for expanding the boundaries of democracy into the workplace by allowing workers to play a role in the critical question, "Who should govern the workplace?"

However, labour market institutions do not meet the needs of many contemporary workers like they used to (though always imperfectly) for workers in industrial and bureaucratic settings. According to many experts, the profound transformation of the contemporary economic system, as the importance of the industrial sector in Western economies fades away, seriously challenges the assets of what was known as "industrial citizenship."

The Need for Research

In this book we will fill a gap in the knowledge about the working conditions of VGDs. Labour and employment relations scholars have shown little interest in VGDs and thus little is known about their actual working conditions and labour relations. Besides a few contributions—for example, Dyer-Witheford 1999, and the study of gamer "modding" practices (software or programming modification to introduce new experiences or settings) by Postigo 2003—research on videogames showed no great interest in labour before about 2005 (Nichols 2005). Only in recent years have we seen greater attention, such as in-depth studio case studies like the ethnographic account of developers in a medium-sized studio in the United States by Bulut (2020a; see also O'Donnell 2014), but these were not conducted through the lens of labour relations.

There are a growing number of studies into "game production" that are concerned about the working environment. However, these often focus less on working conditions on the shopfloor and more on the politico-economic organization and evolution of the industry and its logistical and value chain (de Peuter 2012; Deuze 2007a; Dyer-Witheford and de Peuter 2009; Engström 2020; Kelly et al. 2021; Kirkpatrick 2013; O'Donnell 2019; Teipen 2008; Woodcock 2016); the creative process (O'Donnell 2014, 2019); the culture of games, gamers and game making, and the meaning, content, and effect of games (Kerr 2011, 2017; Muriel and Crawford 2018; C. Paul 2018; Ruffino 2018); a blend of these (Flew and Smith 2011; Kline, Dyer-Witheford, and de Peuter 2003; Sotamaa and Švelch 2021); or "gender at work" and feminist analyses of game content, gamer communities, and gamer culture (Gray, Voorhees, and Vossen 2018; Kafai et al. 2008; Taylor and Voorhees 2018). Some other studies focus on how the VGI is controlled and policed—such as through the power of states to establish game rating systems, regulate intellectual property (IP), or set downloadable content policy (Conway and deWinter 2016).

Several studies on working conditions do exist that embrace other sectors of creative labour (Cohen and de Peuter 2020; D'Amours 2009; Deuze 2007b; Huws 2011; McKinlay and Smith 2009; McRobbie 2016; Neff 2012; Pérez-Zapata et al. 2016; Ross 2003, 2009). This corpus of research has criticized the much-vaunted flexibility, autonomy, and informality of these jobs. It paints a clear and largely consistent picture of workers who face many problems and a way of life that involves constant striving. Applied to VGDs, our book supports many of these conclusions, despite an enduring discourse that paints a picture of a "playful bunch" of gamers paid to play. However, these studies seldom engage with the theoretical corpus of labour relations—for instance, the management of people and human resource management (HRM) policies, the regulation of work and its institutions, and resistance and collective action taken in response to working conditions.

Over the past twenty years, we have applied the theoretical tools of labour relations to study business-to-business information technology (IT) services (Chasserio and Legault 2005, 2009, 2010; Legault 2005b,

2008, 2013; Legault and Belarbi-Basbous 2006; Legault and Chasserio 2009, 2010, 2012, 2014; Legault and D'Amours 2011; Legault and Ouellet 2012). In this book, we take part in a larger enterprise and apply these tools to study the VGI as a case of highly skilled jobs in the private creative sector. Dyer-Witheford and de Peuter (2009) have argued that the VGI is emblematic of global capitalism and that the behaviours, norms, and history of that industry are important to understand the hegemony of a new regulation of work on a broader scale.

In both the IT and VGI cases, we have observed that the practice of project management has redesigned the organization of work in radical contrast to the mid-twentieth century bureaucratic context of the emergent industrial citizenship.

This has prompted us to theorize whether this phenomenon could account for a similar change in the regulation of work taking place in the broader private creative sector of the knowledge economy, which shares the practice of project management (performing, recording, and screen-based industries, archaeology, architecture, fashion design, news and media, information and communications technology, high-tech specialized and custom design services, research and development, marketing, advertising, public relations, and more). Could the common project-based organizational context across these industries explain the state of working conditions?

Our study of the VGI contributes to answering this question by mapping the influence of project management on working conditions and establishing a general portrait of citizenship at work. For comparative purposes, more research is needed to paint a similar portrait of other jobs in this sector. For instance, while IT services and the VGI share strikingly common project management features that have consequences for the regulation of work (summarized in Chapter 2), they also differ on certain features that may—or may not—be unique to the VGI (summarized in Chapter 3).

This book also contributes to a larger effort to identify the absence of democracy at work in contemporary workplaces and promote a joint governance model of the firm in which capital and labour participate on equal footing. This is the "economic bicameralism" referred to in Isabelle Ferraras and colleagues' call to democratize, decommodify, and environmentally remediate work (Ferraras 2017; Ferraras, Battilana, and Méda 2022). Increasing citizenship at work is a contributory means to achieve those broad, laudable ends. As such, this book can be of interest to scholars and practitioners across many fields such as sociology, law, labour studies, industrial and employment relations, HRM, political economy, game studies, and communication and cultural studies.

A New Post-Bureaucratic Context for Citizenship at Work

Jobs in the private creative sector of the knowledge economy can usually be found usually exist in trendy, project-based organizations that are part of a larger evolution of post-bureaucratic organizational forms. Citing the economic context and the needs of production, new experts of organizational structure have argued that the principles that supported the bureaucratic model and mass production are outdated. The organization of work is markedly different from that in bureaucracies and manufacturing because it is often arranged on a project basis. This means a short-lived and fixed-term employment relationship. With those in the knowledge economy deprived of social entitlements to joint contributory plans and faced with a shrinking welfare state, responsibility for preventing risk is increasingly left up to the individual (McCluskey 2002; O'Malley 2004). Employees are on their own to fill up their portfolio based on accomplishments and know-how, network in order to be ready to move, be informed enough to make important planning decisions about their future, and manage loss of income, when it happens, by means of commercial, personal, family, or community resources.

Inherited structures of the heyday of the industrial age are tailored to conditions that no longer exist (for example, employment stability, long-term commitment). The context of globalization puts pressure on the employment relationship (Budd 2004c). The associated post-bureaucratic managerial model brought in new labour market practices that have weakened the labour market institutions that provided citizenship (D'Amours 2009; Coutu and Murray 2010a). Union membership has dropped, enforcement of labour laws has dwindled (Mueller 2020; Rainey 2020), and pay inequity has widened.[1] This is more evident in the English-speaking democracies that have liberalist regimes,[2] emphasizing market policies favouring competitive individualism over welfare state intervention (Esping-Andersen 1999). Where labour institutions and unions were two pillars of twentieth-century working life, they are now considered a useless hindrance and are seriously challenged (Heckscher et al. 2003b).

The growth of a new globalized economy prompted Arthurs (1999, 2000), among others, to reconsider his belief in the right to collective

---

1. The Gini index, which is used to measure income inequality, reached 0.485 in 2018, from 0.397 in 1967, where the perfect equality score is 0 (Guida 2019).

2. These include Australia, Canada, New Zealand, the United Kingdom, and the United States, in contrast to the coordinated market economies of continental and Northern Europe (Huber and Stephens 2015).

bargaining as an instrument of citizenship. The international opening of markets has led to increased competition and major economic pressure, with significant effects on the social relations of work and downward pressure on the price of labour (Conaghan, Fischl, and Klare 2000; Condon and Philipps 2004; Crouch 1998; Fudge 2005; Hindess 2002). Modes of regulating work have been severely affected by the increased mobility of capital and its operations. This includes drastic reductions in labour rights and in the bargaining power of unions (D'Antona 2000; Klare 2000). The growth of the service economy has pushed aside permanent full-time industrial employment and atypical employment types have mushroomed. Rates of unionization have fallen the world over and an increasingly large share of the labour force can seemingly no longer hope for unionization (Arthurs 1999; Fudge 2005; OECD 2017b, 2019). Knowledge workers who are both nationally and internationally mobile show little interest in mobilizing to improve local working conditions (Coutu and Murray 2010a; Deakin 2000; McKinlay and Smith 2009). Further to this, many have contractor or self-employed worker status and are not "unionizable" within the meaning of the laws. Such workers face many challenges and continually face the risk of losing their source of income, but their only recourse is legal action (Amman, Carpenter, and Neff 2007; Cooper 2008; Legge 2005; Neff 2012; Neff, Wissinger and Zukin 2005).

Some people thought that social states would take responsibility for workers by passing universal labour laws (Marshall 1964; Coutu 2004), but this scenario has not unfolded in its entirety, either. Since the heyday of the welfare state during the 1950s to 1970s, there has been an overall weakening in the scope of social laws to provide universal protection regimes (Fudge 2005; OECD 2017b, 2019). Governments are in a hurry to reduce their spending and the size of their apparatus, thus reducing the labour market institutions associated with the welfare state (for example, occupational health and safety protection and workers' compensation, minimum labour standards, EI, and human rights). Precarious employment allows employers to skirt labour laws. As well, and against the backdrop of increased capital mobility, the bargaining power of multinational corporations has curtailed the regulatory power of the interventionist social state. This threatens the major social progress made through Keynesian policies (Arthurs 2000, 2010; Collins 2000; Coutu and Murray 2010b).

Under the perspectives of both Arthurs and Marshall, the mechanisms for advancing democracy (unions or universal laws, respectively) are only as good as their inclusivity. Both fail to reach some groups, who remain excluded. First, as efficient as unions can be at providing citizenship at work, many workers are not part of a union. Second, universal laws fail to deliver equality in practice due to a lack of surveillance and enforcement, limited complaints due to fear of reprisals, workaround solutions, etc. The effect of distinctions, exclusions, or preferences according to factors such as race, colour, sex, gender identity or expression, and disability may lead members of a social group to be denied full citizenship status in the work environment.

If some labour market institutions can outlive the economic transformation currently underway, we need them to do more than survive. They must also to account for the enormous social changes that have brought about demands for new arrangements between work and life, a diverse workforce, and a larger scope of human rights. In other words, we need to renew the industrial citizenship framework in order to take stock of lifestyle and workforce changes to elaborate a citizenship at work framework adjusted to the contemporary organizational environment of work.

The Grounds of Our Analysis

To take part in this collective effort, we present the case of the VGI to illustrate the transformation of work and its consequences for citizenship. In this we mainly focus on the game development process that can be found in (larger) studios because we are centred on the employment relationship. We focus on the employment context of VGDs, though this requires some analysis of upstream (funding, publishing, production of tools, middleware, engines, software platforms, etc.) and downstream (marketing, distribution, etc.) activities along the value chain (see, for example, Chapters 3 and 8).

Based on more than fifteen years of surveying and interviewing VGDs internationally, our work sheds light on their working environments, conditions, and practices to take stock of their working status. Are VGDs citizens in their workplace?

Quantitative Data

We are independent partners of the IGDA in administrating, processing, and analysing their online surveys of VGDs. The IGDA is a nonprofit, membership-based organization for people who create games. It offers individual and studio-affiliate memberships. It has over twelve thousand members internationally and operates in over 100 cities through a network of relatively autonomous local chapters and a collection of special interest groups (SIGs). Selectively assuming roles typical of both a professional association and a trade association (see Chapter 8), the IGDA's mission is: "To advance the careers and enhance the lives of game developers by connecting members with their peers, promoting professional development, and advocating on issues that affect the developer community."[3] It also provides (largely though our partnership) some detailed quantitative information on the industry, based on regular surveys on employment, demography, industry and market trends, etc.

In 2004, the IGDA launched its initial Quality of Life (QoL) survey to gain understanding of some employment issues—from "crunch time" (overtime) to compensation. In 2009, the IGDA partnered with us to develop a new version of the QoL survey and to process and analyze its results. In 2014, this partnership took a broader scope, including a larger team, and focusing on employment, demography, and the state of the industry, in a more encompassing Developer Satisfaction Survey (DSS). This has continued yearly or biannually.

The terms of our partnership include periodic financial support from the IGDA, which is sourced independently from us and transferred to an audited research account at Western University. In earlier years there was direct funding from the IGDA Foundation through a research grant initiative, which has been discontinued. Since then, the IGDA has allocated funding received from other industry partners (for example, Facebook Gaming) to the DSS. The project operates on a shoestring budget and there is no financial benefit to us. Funding is solely used to pay graduate students to conduct data analysis and write the reports; we do not take a stipend or consulting fee, buy out our teaching, or fund conference travel. The IGDA independently sources in-kind support for translation and data visualization, and exercises limited oversight. The executive director is invited to provide input on changes to the survey each round, to review the industry-facing DSS reports, which are published under the IGDA moniker, and to write an introduction to those reports (see igda.org/dss). The IGDA has official responsibility to publish and broadcast the DSS reports, though we also publicize them through our networks. The terms of the relationship do not interfere with our full academic freedom for analysis and commentary in other outputs such as this book or academic or popular articles.

Our first set of data consists of statistical data collected in eight IGDA surveys:

- 2004 QoL survey (994 respondents)
- 2005 Developer Demographics Survey (DDS) (6,437 respondents)

---

3. IGDA. http://igda.org.

- 2009, 2014, and 2019 DSS (3,362, 2,202, and 1,116 respondents, respectively), which included questions about employment relations
- 2015, 2016, and 2017 Developer Satisfaction Short Survey (DSS short) (2,928, 1,186, and 963 respondents, respectively)

The surveys were pitched broadly and therefore senior managers, project managers, and team leads could provide answers as well as salaried, freelance, and self-employed developers; would-be developers; people who left the industry; students; and others more tangentially related to the industry. We have not used data from all the respondents, except for the (rarely used) 2004 survey, which did not distinguish respondents by job role/discipline. When discussing working conditions, it is important to separate salaried and freelance developers from those who have not worked yet or who hold a management job. Thus, and basically for reasons of consistency and uniformity, we have not systematically analyzed data from managers or team leads. We also have not routinely included quality assurance testers because they tend to be hourly employees and often face quite different conditions relative to salaried developers. Sometimes we do include specific data from these groups to shed light on the position of various groups of VGDs in the logistic value chain and to outline the exclusion and inclusion of citizenship.

Qualitative Data

The second dataset consists of two series of interviews conducted among Canadian VGDs.

This data allows us to learn more about what figures do not tell, that is the detailed, intimate experience of VGDs:

- In 2008, we interviewed fifty-three developers in Montreal.
- In 2013 to 2014, we interviewed ninety-three developers in three important videogame hubs in the provinces that represented the most employment in 2013 (Quebec: 53 percent; British Columbia: 31 percent; Ontario: 11 percent) (ESAC 2013, 23–30):
  - thirty-four in Vancouver, British Columbia
  - thirty-two in Toronto, Ontario
  - twenty-seven in Montreal, Quebec

In both interview datasets, the sample contains roughly equal numbers of men and women, despite the low proportion of women in the industry.

On the Canadian scene, women counted for 14 percent of creative workers and 5 percent of technical workers during the second round of interviews (ESAC 2013). We make no claims about statistical representativeness, as our aim in establishing the sample was to help us make sense of the low numbers of women in the sector.

The in-depth interviews lasted one and a half to two hours and the interview guide was semi-structured. Many questions were posed as standard procedure to everyone, which allows for simple descriptive statistics to be summed up. Data were initially analyzed with the grounded theory procedure (Charmaz 2000) and then revisited for this book under the citizenship at work framework.

Limits of Our Data

The DSS is not statistically representative; it is a self-report, cross-sectional survey conducted at different time periods. The IGDA recruits survey participants through its membership, newsletters and publications, website and social media, and other professional networks. Many of the survey respondents had been IGDA members, active in IGDA chapters in their local areas, or had participated in IGDA events (see Table 0.1 in the Data Appendix). To the extent that the IGDA attracts a certain type of game worker, this may introduce some degree of bias. The stronger presence of the IGDA in the United States relative to other countries also contributes to an overrepresentation of US VGDs in the sample. Survey respondents were also recruited through general word of mouth, social media, notifications through a mailing list of past respondents, and networks of the academic team.

The interview data is also not statistically representative. We recruited interview respondents on a voluntary basis through personal and professional networks and word of mouth, through attendance at industry or community events, and through social media groups. We purposefully oversampled among women VGDs, to get their point of view about working conditions in the context of their longstanding minority status in the industry.

In our quantitative and qualitative data, respondents were quite evenly distributed among publisher-owned AAA (mid-sized or major) studios or their subsidiaries, third-party studios of various sizes, and indie (or independent) studios usually of smaller size. In each survey sample, about 30 percent of respondents worked for indie studios. Survey samples also represented a range of employment types. Across the surveys most respondents worked full-time (70–89%) and smaller numbers worked part-time (10–13%). Most worked as employees (70–81%) while others worked as freelancers (8–15%) or were self-employed (4–19%). That said, our interrogation of citizenship assumes the existence of an organizational context, an employment status, and a minimal hierarchy of authority and decision-making. In our interviews, developers in a small indie context either answered questions based on their previous experience in bigger studios or declined answering based on the irrelevance of the question for them. Freelancers and self-employed developers answered survey questions tailored to their context that were often comparable to those asked of employees, but which were not always identical. In the end, the portrait of citizenship at work that we draw in this book is primarily that of employees in medium and large studios and cannot presume to completely reflect the situation of small indie developers or the self-employed (Keogh 2018, 2021, 2023).

We take a global perspective, when possible, but our analysis is most applicable to the context of Canada and the United States, with reasonable expectations of generalization first to the United Kingdom, Australia, and New Zealand, and with greater caveat to Europe. Our primary data most represents Western countries (with the United States and Canada predominating). The social, legal, and political regimes applicable to our theorization of citizenship at work draw from the traditions of the Western world, and most of the literature on VGDs and the VGI remains rooted in this space.

Overview of the Book

This book is laid out in three parts: theory, context, and applied analysis. The first part of the book provides rich theoretical and contextual grounding in our core concepts of interest and acts as the frame for the analytical work in the remainder of the book.

Chapter 1 introduces the concept of citizenship at work as a status that allows workers to take part in the regulation of their working conditions and environment. We outline the four components of citizenship that represent the progress in workplace democracy made in the mid-twentieth century, as articulated by Arthurs and Marshall. These are: 1) protection against economic insecurity, 2) recourse against arbitrary decisions at work, 3) participation in the local regulation of labour, and 4) participation in the broader social regulation of work. We present the social and economic evolution that has since taken place and stress the need for commensurate revision to the theoretical approach. To this end we draw in the work of Bosniak (2000, 2003) to better articulate the subject, object, and domain of citizenship for each of the four components. This allows us to locate variations in citizenship status over time and space. Moreover, this articulation accounts for the possibility that citizenship gains may vary across workers and studios in the industry, which constitute a heterogeneous whole.

Chapter 2 provides an in-depth review of the features of project management and the project-based workplace that influence the regulation of work. This underlies our subsequent analysis of citizenship at work among the VGDs. Indeed, our supporting premise is that the organizational context of project management is deeply different from bureaucracy and has a major influence on working conditions in project-based organizations. Project management seriously challenges the labour institutions born in the mid-twentieth century, often disregarding HRM and human resources (HR) policies as labour institutions of another era. For that reason, it also challenges citizenship at work as traditionally defined. We must understand the nature, structure, and requirements of the project-based organizational model to understand its organization of work and the HRM practices that will be discussed in the following chapters. Moreover, the link established between project management and citizenship at work in project-based organizations provides a solid generalization power—that is, a basis from which to generalize—from our case of VGDs to the broader private creative sector of the knowledge economy.

The second part of the book provides the essential contextual detail on the VGI and the work of VGDs as our explanatory case for an analysis of citizenship at work.

Chapter 3 extends the theoretical grounding of Chapter 2 to show that the VGI, while sharing the general features of project-based knowledge work, has specific features that may—or may not—be found in other jobs of the private creative sector. We show that the game industry is shaped by the inherent uncertainties of game making and of the resulting organizational (project management) and market-based (financialization) practices intended to minimize that risk for owners and shareholders. These are the grounds over which working conditions take place and assessments of citizenship are made. Over the course of the chapter, we introduce important labour-relations actors and articulate their relative positions in the financialized VGI value chain.

Chapter 4 provides a detailed portrait of the working conditions of VGDs, with specific attention to the employment risks that they face. This chapter provides the necessary context for the remaining chapters of the book, where we assess how VGDs can protect themselves against these risks and measure them against participatory and democratic standards.

The third part of the book assesses whether VGDs are citizens in their workplaces according to the four components outlined in Chapter 1 and across a range of subjects, objects, and domains of citizenship.

Chapter 5 addresses the first component of citizenship at work (protection against economic insecurity). It analyzes how VGDs are coping with the economic uncertainty and risk of lost income identified in Chapter 4. We focus on the policies and programs deemed central to the provision of a social safety net in which risks are shared across employees, employers, and the state (e.g., EI, retirement provision, health insurance and leaves, pregnancy and parental leaves, and training). Using the framing of the "risk society," we conclude that VGDs are highly disadvantaged in the individualization of risk and face a citizenship deficit on that front.

Chapter 6 analyzes the second component of citizenship at work (recourse against arbitrary decisions). We examine the decision-making processes regarding working conditions that are fraught with economic or professional consequences. These include discipline and dismissal, enforcement of non-disclosure and non-compete agreements, IP crediting policies, evaluation and promotion, and compensation. We discuss the arbitrariness embedded in decisions of working time and hiring separately in Chapters 9 and 10, given the importance of this issue.

Chapter 7 takes us to the third component of citizenship at work and examines how VGDs participate in the local regulation of their work—that is, in having a say in the rules that govern their workplaces. Workers can attempt to obtain a meaningful influence through a range of formal and informal means both as individuals and as groups, and these are each examined. The chapter concludes with a significant discussion of unionization as the central means by which to gain this component of citizenship (as per Arthurs).

Chapter 8 presents a wide canvass of the spaces in which VGDs could wish for a voice in the broader social regulation of their work, industry, and sector—the final component of citizenship at work. We challenge the limited interpretation of this component under the traditional definition of industrial citizenship as union representation before the state (that is, through lobbying or legal claims) and acknowledge the range of actors who wish to have a say in the shaping of the global VGI. The change of perspective is big enough to bring out a change in union organizing and a larger scope of union action.

Chapter 9 tackles the critical issue of unlimited, unpaid overtime ("crunch") in a stand-alone interrogation across all four objects of citizenship at work (see Table 1.3). Building from Chapter 6, it is a stark example of arbitrary decision-making processes and a lack of recourse. However, protection against this employment risk and participation in the regulation of working time can also come through procedures in the local workplace and through social laws. Are there domains of citizenship related to working time, and are VGDs subjects to these domains?

Chapter 10 also zeroes in on a specific issue in the VGI: the "elephant in the room" of White masculinity. We profile differential working experiences across groups of VGDs and focus on the subjects of citizenship. Nowhere more than in the highly discretionary decision-making process of hiring and staffing can we identify unequal subjects of citizenship by factors such as gender and ethnicity, whatever the object and the domain. Even when some status of citizenship is achieved for the majority, there are workers who are very much second-class citizens. Framing lack of diversity, inclusivity, and belonging as an employment risk, we interrogate the experiences and protections available to members of underrepresented groups—primarily women, but also people of colour (a discussion of game testers as second-class citizens is included in Chapter 4).

We conclude the book with reflections about the state of citizenship at work among VGDs and the deficits that workers in private sector project-based knowledge work face—either because they are not recognized as citizens in the environment (subjects), because they have no say regarding certain important issues (objects), or because there is no space or territory within which they can exercise a voice (domains). We call for new or renewed systems and institutions to better account for these gaps in the contemporary employment landscape, particularly to account for the crucial influence of funders on working conditions in the context of the growing financialization of enterprises. Yet, even as we acknowledge these deficits, we argue for the need to revise the theoretical construct of citizenship to better account for a fuller range of participatory activities, participating actors, and regulatory spaces.

PART ONE
Theory

CHAPTER 1

Citizenship at Work in the Post-Industrial Landscape

What Is Citizenship at Work?

As outlined in the Introduction, at its best, "citizenship at work" is a status that allows workers to take part in the regulation of their working conditions and environment, and not be subjected to a unilateral power relationship in the governance of their work or to an asymmetrical relationship with authority.[1] It requires two important factors. First, the governance mode of HRM must offer a proper balance between the quest for efficiency, equity, and voice to reconcile between property and labour rights. Second, the state power must enforce laws, institutions, and practices that shape and regulate markets and communities—including workplaces—in the private sphere to maintain this balance.

Industrial Citizenship: A Step Forward in the History of Democracy

Before discussing contemporary working conditions in project-based work generally and in the VGI specifically, it is important to recall what labour conditions were like not too long ago, as a means of providing contrast.

Arthurs (1967) and Marshall (1950, 1964) earmarked four emblematic outcomes of workers' campaigns that gave workers the status of citizens

---

1. The concept must be distinguished from the notion of "organizational citizenship," a normative notion regarding the behaviour of a "good" citizen in the workplace. The disciplines of HRM and industrial/organizational psychology study the concept of organizational citizenship behaviour, which is a deliberate behaviour to give more to an organization or employer than is being asked of you. It describes behaviours that are not required, but appreciated, as they bear witness to a person's personal commitment within an organization that goes beyond their contractual tasks (Organ 1997; Organ, Podsakoff, and MacKenzie 2006; Organ and Ryan, 1995). This is not to say that VGDs never show organizational citizenship behaviours—as we will see further. We are not using this psychological concept. We use the socio-legal framework of citizenship at work, which is quite different.

in their workplace and marked decisive progress in democracy, social governance, and sustainability in the mid-twentieth century: protection against economic insecurity, recourses against arbitrary decisions, participation in the local regulation of labour, and participation in the broader social regulation of labour. According to experts in labour law, these gains allowed workers to achieve both an active and a passive status of citizenship in their workplaces. Active status was provided through workers' participation in the local and broader social regulation of labour in the workplace, industry, or sector, while passive status was conferred through state regulations and social laws.

This is not to say that these scholars presumed that these four gains were the only ones to be won from all the labour movement's campaigns since the beginning of the industrial era; this would fail to provide a fair portrait of the labour movement's successes and the current state of labour. However, we have consolidated under four general components different gains that represent an improvement in material working conditions and have a deeper social meaning according to the foundational approaches of Arthurs and Marshall (see Table 1.1).

These components are sufficiently general to be used as a yardstick to compare the status of workers from different work environments and across different territories and time periods, and thereby estimate the state of citizenship at work. It is important to note that the gains from these reforms have not benefitted all workplaces uniformly and have not been constant over time, but in combination, these gains constitute the essence of citizenship at work if we combine both Arthurs' and Marshall's observations.

An examination of these four components allows us to study the existence and effect of citizenship as separate from the means of citizenship (trade unionism or labour laws). With this approach, we can seek out the characteristic elements of citizenship in non-unionized settings, based on the actual modes of regulation present in the workplace, as well as study unionized settings without taking for granted that all unionized workers have acquired the same level of citizenship status.

For these reasons, the theoretical framework of citizenship at work is appropriate for assessing a work environment in which workers are not unionized, such as the VGI and other project-based workplaces in the private creative sector of the knowledge economy, without assuming a priori that they are deprived of all the characteristics associated with citizenship status. Are there practices that give workers a voice with respect to the regulation of their workplace, their participation, and the delegation of decision-making authority? Do these workers individually

Table 1.1
The Four Components of Gains That Characterize Citizenship at Work

Gains	Form of citizenship
1. Policies and programs to protect against economic insecurity and the risks of lost income (i.e., unemployment, skill obsolescence, birth of a child, illness, injury, layoff, retirement)	A form of *passive* citizenship in that employees make use of a regulation stipulating their rights and obligations, which is already established by the legislative state, without being involved in defining those provisions. Universal social laws can indeed provide remedies against certain managerial decisions, insurance programs against the risk of the loss of employment income under certain circumstances, and so on. Primarily understood as a legal status, this liberal dimension of citizenship is *potentially* inclusive and indefinitely extensible.
2. Recourses against arbitrary decisions (at best) and ways to influence local decisions regarding work and working conditions (at least)	
3. Participation in the local regulation of labour regarding critical issues (i.e., in the case of VGDs: working hours, overtime compensation, quality of life, work–life balance, IP, crediting standards, non-compete and confidentiality clauses, knowledge management, sexism, and discrimination)	A form of *active* citizenship in that employees participate in setting the advocacy priorities for their representing body and take part in drawing up the regulation by negotiating the broad outlines of their rights and obligations in a collective agreement that binds the two parties. The republican model of democracy emphasizes this *political agency* as an essential component of democracy.
4. Participation in the broader social regulation of work, the industry, or the sector (i.e., lobbying the state in support of or in opposition to certain laws or regulatory regimes, carrying an industry- or employment-based legal claim to the state or other relevant social authority, or forming professional bodies)	

assume the risk of losing their employment income? Are they subject to arbitrary managerial decisions? Answering these questions allows for an estimation of the state of citizenship at work in a given environment.

Briefly delving into the history of labour helps to summarize why Arthurs (1967) and Marshall (1950, 1964) praised these gains as progress towards democracy in the workplace. From the beginning to mid-twentieth century, new institutions brought in a certain symmetry between the parties in the employment relationship: workers' right to defend their labour rights and to negotiate their working conditions with their employer, the collection of information on labour markets, the provision of experts and support to govern the certification of these associations, and the enforcement of negotiated collective agreements. The trade union movement also won the status of being a committed institutional player in the development of public policies concerning the economy and employment—in other words, a stakeholder with the same capacity as employers. Those changes were meaningful because they provided a response to the unsustainability—for employers, employees, and society—of a governance mode that relied mostly on utilitarian and libertarian laissez-faire market policies during the first centuries of capitalism. This governance mode singled out efficiency as the core management principle to make use of resources, including human beings. Under such assumptions, a cost–benefit analysis lies at the core of any decision, making property rights sovereign (Budd 2004a, 2004b). The new labour market institutions addressed the clash between two competing human rights: property and labour rights.

At the same time, these governments also enacted social legislation. This legislation applies universally to all workers defined as wage earners, to reduce the imbalance between the rights and obligations of workers and those of employers (for example, minimum wage, workplace accident prevention and workers' compensation, EI, holidays, and vacation time) (Fudge 2005).

This trend was not limited to North America and extended to all Western industrialized countries. It is now commonly known as the welfare state model, defining a "form of government in which the state protects and promotes the economic and social well-being of the citizens, based upon the principles of equal opportunity, equitable distribution of wealth, and public responsibility for citizens unable to avail themselves of the minimal provisions for a good life" (Britannica Online Encyclopedia, nd). However, regarding the protection of employment income, strictly speaking, the state is not the only provider of citizens' compensatory income in the case of lost employability. Across Western industrialized countries, we note various national institutional regimes based on different combinations of three essential means to attain this goal: free-market policies, private contributory insurance plans, and state intervention and support. The relative weight conferred to each of these three is used to distinguish different national regimes (Esping-Andersen 1999).

The same can be said about the form that union organization and labour market institutions would take. The North American system of representing workers' interests differs from its European counterparts

Table 1.2
Developments of Citizenship

Citizenship	Form
Civil citizenship	Universal civil rights are typically the formal equality of all citizens at birth and include the freedom to make one's own decisions, the right to habeas corpus, the freedom to enter contracts, and the right to sue.
Political citizenship	The universal right to vote and stand for election
Social citizenship	The universal right to the resources essential to one's development: education, health, and the job market
Economic and industrial citizenship	Social (and private collective) insurance to protect against the risk of the loss of income and to support workers experiencing job loss or reduced employability
	The right to negotiate working conditions collectively and to take part in regulating the work environment

Sources: Coutu and Murray 2010b; Fudge 2010; Marshall 1964

in that its enterprise-based certification makes sector-based unionization an exception.

The theoretical framework of citizenship gave theoreticians and philosophers of law a perspective for linking labour history to the more general context of the democratization of societies. In such a perspective, labour institutionalization is no longer limited to the acquisition of workers' rights but is part of a bigger inroad into social democracy, a new territory of democracy further reducing the sphere of unilateral, autocratic decision-making. Societies governed by liberal law have gone through four developments of citizenship: civil, political, social, and economic and industrial (see Table 1.2).

Industrial citizenship was also favoured by the Weberian organizational model of bureaucracy, which dominated during the twentieth century. This was linked to both a desire to rationalize management decisions and a democratic concern for the point of view of workers, as well as the need to accommodate these two factors (Heckscher et al. 2003b). Among the emblematic values and norms of industrial citizenship in this regard, there is an explicit preference for the formal decision-making process over the arbitrary (Weber 1921). Bureaucracy is, in fact, "the institutional manifestation of a continuous effort to create responsible, accountable government by ensuring that discretion is not abused, that due process is the norm not the exception, and that undue risks are not taken that undermine the integrity of the ... system" (DuGay 2005, 4).

Improving Job Quality and Balancing the Distribution of Power

By legalizing the right of workers to take collective action, governments recognized workers' right to be involved in the regulation of their own work environment. On this, industrial relations scholarship proposes a reflection on workplace regulation (Budd 2004c, 82). Since the object of industrial relations is the political and economic relationship between the parties in the production process, work regulation is an important indicator of the distribution of power among those parties. It can be defined, painstakingly, as follows:

> The concept of job (or work) regulation refers to the rules that govern the content of the employment relationship and the behaviour and activities of employees, employers, and their representatives. The study of job regulation is therefore the study of the creation, application, and effects of job or employment rules. Employment rules can be classified in a number of different ways. An important distinction can be drawn between those rules that are formal, and written down in company handbooks, collective agreements, and employment statutes, and those that are informal and take the form of customary understandings or norms about appropriate workplace behaviour. A second distinction can be drawn between substantive rules, which govern the content of the employment relationship, and procedural rules, which govern the behaviour of workers, managers, trade unions, employers' associations, and others who become involved in industrial relations. A third distinction relates to the way in which rules are created. Some employment rules are simply inherited from the past and take the form of custom and practice; that is, a taken-for-granted way of behaving or relating to co-workers or managers. Other rules are created through processes of joint regulation, in which employers and employees come together to regulate the employment relationship through collective bargaining, joint consultation, or some other joint mechanism. A third method is unilateral regulation, in which either managers or, more rarely, workers one-sidedly decide what the content of regulation will be. Finally, rules may be generated by the state through the process of legal regulation and the creation of laws that directly determine the content of the employment relationship (for example, through a statutory minimum wage) or regulate the behaviour of employers and trade unions through collective employment law. (Heery and Noon 2008, n.p.)

Through a review of industrial relations research, Budd (2004c) identified six general modes of workplace governance: 1) free markets supported only by common law, 2) free markets coupled with statutory work regulation to provide for failures of the market, 3) unilateral HRM decision-making rooted in a "people concern," 4) HRM with an employer-initiated employee voice (modes three and four are inspired by utilitarian and libertarian laissez-faire ideology in that employers still have full latitude in decision-making), 5) independent employee representation leading to bilateral employer–employee negotiations (inspired by republican democracy), and 6) worker control (inspired by socialism). These depend on the modes of work regulation in use and can cover most of the situations in the contemporary Western world.

Reflecting on the contemporary challenges to democracy in the workplace, industrial relations theorists further contextualized these six modes within a larger framework based on principles of organizational democracy. To better situate this range of workplace governance modes, Budd (2004a, c) proposed a socio-historical framework based on the relative importance of three core principles to the reconciliation of property and labour rights. For proper balance, management should consider not just efficiency, but equity (which entails fairness in wages, hours, health and safety, insurance in the case of lost income, freedom from discrimination, and hiring and firing based on just cause) and a meaningful voice (meaningful employee input based on the ideals of democracy and human dignity) in workplace governance.

The six modes of workplace governance offer different combinations of these three principles, and each one operationalizes an (often unconscious) ethical position in the balance between respective rights. As we move from the first to the sixth, we note a growing blend of the three principles. Not all of the six types of regulation include the three principles; voice is the one that is most often excluded. For instance, the managerialist school (number three) would argue that a practice of equity by management is sufficient to reconcile property and labour rights, and that a formal worker voice is not required. The institutionalist school (number five) would argue that both are necessary, because equity pertains to the distribution of benefits and can be unilaterally provided according to management's preferences and their perception of workers' needs (leaving workers in a passive role), whereas voice involves participation and requires involvement (making workers actors in the exercise of regulation) (Budd 2004a, c; Kaufman 2004).

Data supports the conclusion that Budd's three principles can be complementary. Equitable treatment (equity) and employee participation (voice) can reinforce efficiency in "reducing turnover, increasing commitment and harnessing workers' ideas for improving productivity and quality" (Budd 2004a, 1; 2004d; Budd and Colvin 2005). But they conflict as well. And, despite the short-term cost of enacting and balancing the three principles, they are all required to create sustainable employment relationships in the long term and avoid the social costs related to poor employment conditions.

Now, in light of the economic evolution towards a post-industrial era, how does citizenship at work hold up in the contemporary game development sector and, moreover, in the private creative sector of the knowledge economy? Are we to conclude that citizenship is threatened or dead, and that the market is now the main regulating factor, capriciously giving some workers special bargaining power because of the demand for their specific skills?

The Contemporary Post-Industrial Landscape

If the bureaucratic model still applies, the golden age of its rhetoric is gone. A manifold movement fed by academics[2] and now conveyed by consultants and expert-practitioners challenges its appropriateness in the contemporary knowledge economy. They contend that many constraints of the bureaucratic organizational model need to be removed in order to allow the post-bureaucratic organizational model to adjust to new conditions. In such a framework:

> While bureaucracy may be appropriate and indeed functional to particular economic or political environments, it does not "fit" others, notably where there is a high degree of unpredictability and instability, and innovation and situational adaptiveness are vital parts of work. (Thompson and Alvesson 2005, 90)

Bureaucracy places value on impartial conduct, due process, and accountability to impersonal order rather than to individual people. Yet, opponents of bureaucracy denounce its inefficiency in creative industries. Knowledge work must make room for entrepreneurship and worker responsibility, client-oriented attitudes, simple structures, worker initiative, and the promotion of imagination (Peters and Waterman 1982). The contemporary ideal form of organization favours flexibility over sta-

---

[2]. The first work to emerge would be Burns and Stalker's *Management of Innovation* (1961), while Peters and Waterman's *In Search of Excellence* (1982) would provoke the more popular craze among practitioners for the post-bureaucratic school of thought (Heckscher and Applegate 1994).

bility, empowerment over surveillance, commitment over compliance, and responsiveness over rigidity (Salaman 2005). This program aims to make organizations flexible in order to better face rapid changes (Castells 2000). It also aims to "re-enchant" organizational life (Sennet 1998) in conveying an ideological framework that defines work as part of a "society of enjoyment" in which "lack of enjoyment" counts as a failure and work is disassociated from toil (Bulut 2020a, 23 and 32). In some cases, this is more rhetoric than a revolution of actual organizational structures, with the result being regimes of "soft bureaucracy" (Courpasson 2000; Hodgson 2004). But the post-bureaucratic organizational movement is no less serious for all that.

Far from being a negligible phenomenon, experts have observed this movement across developed economies of North America and Western Europe, promoting not only a new organizational model, but also union avoidance and rollbacks in work regulations (Heckscher et al. 2003a).[3] The development of this movement has seriously challenged industrial citizenship by delegitimizing the institutions that were its cradle: universal labour laws and unionization. It has percolated deep into the work culture of the young generation of students. When asked about their dream jobs, they often reject white-collar work. They report a desire for creative jobs and workplaces where "informality rules," ignoring the fact that informality can result in setbacks to working conditions. Seeking "fun," "glamorous," "lively workplaces" and "transnational connections," students harbour some illusions in their disregard of precariousness, unpredictability of both contracts and working day duration, unlimited unpaid overtime, and unbalanced power relations in daily routines (Bulut 2020a, ix, 30; McRobbie 2016).

English-speaking democracies began ushering in reforms to the welfare states during the 1980s and 1990s to adapt to the new social and economic conditions of the post-industrial era (Deeming 2017, 412). As the world entered a globalized age, states shifted to neoliberalism and away from the prevailing Keynesian economic consensus (Palley 2004). Regimes of institutional protection were challenged and weakened in favour of a resurgence of nineteenth-century ideas associated with economic liberalism and free-market capitalism. This saw a reduction in government spending and state influence in the economy; an increased role of the private sector, especially through privatization and austerity; and the deregulation of capital markets, the elimination of price controls, and lowered trade barriers (Bloom 2017). In matters of social policy, this

---

3. For instance, North American employers like Walmart, Amazon, Home Depot, and FedEx are entirely union-free, but they have not broken with the whole bureaucratic model; they have picked up some features of the model while not adopting it in whole.

"market-oriented revolution" means that workers who lose their income must rely on individual resources or those given by family, religious institutions, and communities. The VGI emerged contiguously with these reforms and was post-industrial and post-bureaucratic from the outset. Its workers have never known access to some important elements of citizenship.

This shift towards individual responsibility and private-sector solutions to insure against risk resulted in more social inequality and socioeconomic polarization (Tòth 2014). The legitimacy of welfare markets, market institutions, and market discipline has also increased, as has the unchecked power of corporations (Crouch 2011). In this, we see convergence in institutional regimes across nations (Deeming 2017, 418), as neoliberal reforms appear to have also undermined social democratic institutions across Europe (Lodemel and Moreira 2014). A shared concern among social policy scholars is that increasing financialization and wealth accumulation, privatization, and marketization of risk can only coalesce to further downsize state welfare (Deeming 2017, 418). This has led citizenship experts to conclude that welfare rights are not genuine rights—insofar as civil or political rights are—but contextual political agreements bound to vary with differing conditions (Edmiston, Patrick, and Garthwaite 2017; Plant 2012).

In the context of globalization and the booming knowledge economy, the new organizational model threatens social progress and challenges past citizenship achievements because an increasing share of the job market no longer falls under protective Keynesian policies (Arthurs 2000, 2010; Coutu and Murray 2010b; Collins 2000). This is grounds for wondering about the future of citizenship at work, based on the four gains in our definition (see Table 1.1).

The Limits of the Industrial Citizenship Concept

We must also draw attention to the binary nature of the studies of industrial citizenship. Some of the assumptions underlying the framework that has been used by legal experts to study the rights of employed workers are problematic in the contemporary world. We outline three limits to this framework.

First, access to the workplace is a blind spot to those focusing on employed workers. Do those who are not employed have an equal opportunity to access the workplace, whatever their ethnic origin, gender, sexual orientation, or class? It is important to recognize that this framework was elaborated in times where the workforce was quite uniformly White, male, and cisgender.

Though they profess the formal equality of all citizens under the laws, liberal nations have never obtained an actual social "equality of facts." Equality of facts is defined by a social reality in which the aggregated statistical data on the working population of a society (or an organization) closely match the demographic data of society as a whole, signifying that the main demographic groups are well represented. After two decades of policies based on simple equality of rights and treatment, the aggregated statistics of underrepresentation, status, and pay inequity among liberal nations have shown considerable inertia. This prompted a general admission of the relative failure of civil citizenship around the end of the 1980s:

> Scepticism towards the universalist model was spurred by concerns that the extension of citizenship rights to groups previously excluded had not translated into equality and full integration ... Critics argued that the model proves exclusionary if one interprets universal citizenship as requiring (a) the transcendence of particular, situated perspectives to achieve a common, general point of view and (b) the formulation of laws and policies that are difference-blind (Young 1989). The first requirement seems particularly odious once generality is exposed as a myth covering the majority's culture and conventions. The call to transcend particularity too often translates into the imposition of the majority perspective on minorities. The second requirement may produce more inequality rather than less since the purported neutrality of difference-blind institutions often belies an implicit bias towards the needs, interests and identities of the majority group. This bias often creates specific burdens for members of minorities, i.e. more inequality. (*Stanford Encyclopedia of Philosophy* 2017)

As citizenship is a legal concept, it calls for a legal response to the acknowledgment of the political relevance of difference (cultural, gender, class, race, etc.). If social barriers can account for inequitable representation, discrimination is the legal concept that points out those barriers.

Direct, explicit discrimination is forbidden by law. However, discrimination can have a collective and societal dimension. It is assumed to be a "system effect," a consequence of diverse actions that are not always intentionally discriminatory. The concept of systemic discrimination captures the notion that some discrimination is not overt or addressed in any specific ban or ruleset. This conceptualization helps to acknowledge a more widespread problem of access to citizenship than the simple idea of direct discrimination. In the matter of employment, discrimination exists where a distinction, exclusion, or preference based on demographic factors has the effect of nullifying or impairing employment-related rights for a given individual or demographic group, regardless of any intention. This includes hiring (selection, recruitment, etc.), apprenticeship, duration of the probationary period, vocational training, promotion, transfer, displacement, layoffs, suspension, dismissal, or conditions of employment (pay, discipline, etc.) or job status (Legault 2017, 62–66). It manifests within HRM decisions. In the VGI, for instance, HRM decisions might be included in the category of systemic discrimination as soon as they produce effects like excluding some groups (women, minority groups of ethnic origin), preferring some groups (White men), or using distinguishing criteria when allocating employment benefits, beginning with access.

This brings us to the second limitation of the concept of industrial citizenship. Beyond the issue of access to the workplace, there are issues of internal mobility and benefits distribution among workers. The original framework carries the assumption that the workplace provides citizenship, or it does not. But a closer examination of work environments challenges the idea that all workers are considered citizens on the same basis, even within individual workplaces. Even if all workers are declared equal, and if the benefits of the citizen status (as usually set down in formal devices like collective agreements or legislative provisions) apply to everyone, the reality may be otherwise.

HRM decisions can be discriminatory in preventing access to the workplace. They can also be discriminatory after the point of hire. Even though they are workers themselves, people in authority may discriminate in their daily interactions. Harassment, whether in person or online, is an example of a practice that can result in systemic discrimination by having an exclusionary effect. Harassment covers a wide range of offensive behaviours that demean, humiliate, or embarrass a person and may be disturbing, upsetting, or threatening. It manifests in words, speeches, gestures, and jokes that are vexatious or spiteful towards a person or a group and is based on general characteristics like race or ethnic origin, gender, sexual orientation, religion, or disability. In the workplace, these behaviours are very serious even if they occur only once. Furthermore, while they are mostly aimed at certain groups, they can become exclusionary or single out certain workers in a way that makes members of a particular group less comfortable, less vocal, and disempowered in their work environment, sometimes to the point of leaving, because power relationships can keep victims from speaking out (Legault 2017, 94–100).

In the absence of a critical mass of members of a minority group (Kanter 1977), harassment is significantly more likely. Research (by Kanter, among others) shows that representational scarcity has the tendency to make individuals stand out as the "token members of groups," whose behaviour remains unknown (or less known) and, thus, unpredictable. This leads to enduring prejudices, scant occasions for promotion, and being excluded from networks. In a minority situation, hostile behaviours not only can go unchecked but can even be "rewarded" (Levchak 2018, 106). Kanter (1977, 966, 987) proposed that "with an increase in relative numbers, minority members can ... form coalitions and affect the culture of the group," and they can also "begin to become individuals differentiated from each other." Yet even the definition of a critical mass must be scrutinized. If, as in the VGI, women are concentrated and isolated in female-dominated areas and subfields, this may not necessarily change the dynamics of a masculine environment across the board. Also, women have been found to "moderat[e] their gender role identity to fit into the industry," and/or adopt "male" or "androgynous" behaviours to fit into the group (Derks et al. 2011; Fine 2010; Hirshfield 2010; G. Powell and Butterfield 2003; Prescott and Bogg 2013, 2011a, 219–20). These problems tend to diminish when the minority group is larger (Legault 2017, 6–7).

In the absence of a critical mass of any minority group, workers from these groups tend to leave organizations in greater proportions than do members of the majority because of work-related problems associated with a hostile environment. This brings together the first two limitations of the industrial citizenship model, which grants access to citizenship only upon hire and then assumes equal citizenship for all hired workers in that workplace.

There is a related third limitation to the industrial citizenship model. When we find some features of citizenship in an industry or a sector, can it be implied that the entire industry offers the same features? Or is it possible to find an uneven distribution of these features among different nation-states, or across an industry with diverse workplaces? These questions are critical to a study of the VGI.

Attaining genuine equality requires actions to rapidly transform formal equality rights into reality, for both individuals and groups. The notion of diversity, in this context, refers to a state that an organization can attain. It is usually the outcome of establishing equality of rights and equity measures. However, discussions of "diversity" within the VGI can portray it as more of an issue of business strategy than a justice concern (Perks and Whitson 2022). For instance, it has been argued that diversity is essential for innovation, openness, and adaptation to different audiences, but such calls can ignore equity issues like access to jobs, equal treatment, fair procedures, and so on.

These important issues are ignored in the industrial citizenship framework and must be dealt with through the renewed study of contemporary citizenship at work. We can no longer ignore the limitations of a universalist citizenship notion or be satisfied with binary notions. We can capture these elements more subtly.

Adding Inclusion for a Contemporary Framework of Citizenship at Work

To help locate the variations in citizenship status over time and space, and overcome some of the limitations of the historical framework, we add a new theoretical lens to this analysis. We borrow three categories of a general notion of citizenship from Bosniak (2000, 2003). For each of the four citizenship-at-work gains that we examine among VGDs, we raise the question of the *subject,* the *object,* and the *domain* to account for the possibility that gains may vary across workers and studios in the industry, which constitute a heterogeneous whole.

The Subject of Citizenship

The subject of citizenship is the person recognized as a citizen in the environment—the one who can aspire to citizenship status. This conceptualization can capture the boundaries of inclusion and exclusion, and the resulting struggles to gain entry. Are all workers in a given work environment citizens on the same level? Are there second-class citizens who do not enjoy all the privileges of citizenship?

The traditional subjects of industrial citizenship were wage earners represented collectively by a union, who were considered fully fledged citizens. These workers were stable enough to have an interest in mobilizing to improve their working conditions. Mass production requires many similar workstations, and resulting collective agreements establish pay scales such that the performance of all workers occupying the same positions and having the same skills and experience are assumed to be of equal value. Non-unionized workers are partly citizens if they are covered by labour laws, but these often fail to protect workers with atypical statuses (Vosko, Noack, and Tucker 2016; Vosko and Closing the Enforcement Gap Research Group 2020).

However, there are exceptions to the enterprise-based union model. For instance, the sector-based model specific to film artists and technicians provides for minimum working conditions that apply to all union members across employers. Enhanced benefits can be added to this minimum. These are negotiated individually based on the demand for specific job-related characteristics. In the context of the knowledge economy, these models could allow collective mobilization despite the constraints of project-based mobility, the focus on creation and innovation, and the importance of individual merit. Indeed, the competence- or seniority-based pay system inherent to the unionized bureaucratic environment is not well-reflected in the "star-system" typical of the unionized movie industry. The "star system" allows for some individuals who enjoy bargaining power due to their role, skills, or status to engage in individual bargaining over working conditions. This approach was adopted to respond to the importance of market value and allows for enormous gaps between what a sought-after star can negotiate compared to a less well known or accomplished actor (D'Amours 2009). But the general outcome is a "built in" unequal status of citizens.

Last, the study of the subject of citizenship raises the question of exclusion; the illegal migrant worker is the best-known example. Are other workers likewise excluded from contemporary citizenship at work? Are independent contractors, freelancers, and self-employed workers, who are all very common in today's economy, citizens of their work environment?

Examining the parameters of inclusion and exclusion affecting the subjects of citizenship at work exposes a problematic assumption of homogeneity that was built into the industrial citizenship model. The increasing demographic diversification of the labour force and the adoption of charters of fundamental rights constitutionalizing minority rights has exposed the limitations of union organization, in which decisions are based on the views of the dominant group or the so-called "median worker" (Fudge 2005; Legault 2005a; Ontiveros 2000). Studies on citizenship at work have presented unions as a place of citizenship for members of the majority and, for the others, of citizenship under the conditions of the majority. Where are the fault lines of exclusion for the subjects of contemporary knowledge work?

The Object (or Substance) of Citizenship

The object of citizenship concerns what is to be regulated or conveyed. It is the substance of citizenship, how it manifests, and over what topics.

The substance of industrial citizenship consists of uniform working conditions for all members of the union through the collective agreement. Unlike legislation on employment standards, the average collective agreement is typically not a minimum plan for conditions that can be enhanced through individual contracts (Murray and Verge 1999, 46–47). Once again, the sector-based regimes specific to workers such as performing artists are already an exception to this rule. As noted above, collective agreements in this context provide for a minimum set of conditions that could be enhanced through better individual agreements. Individual bargaining thus coexists alongside collective bargaining, and rights and obligations may vary. This reflects the understanding that a single collective agreement cannot be expected to govern all specific situations in a context in which performance projects vary just like a person's value on the market. These regimes are good illustrations of the functioning of labour relations issues in the knowledge economy. In creative environments in which work is project-based, hiring is short term and a person's value on the job market fluctuates sharply depending on the demand for their skills.

What are the rights and obligations derived from citizenship? Do the four gains of industrial citizenship have the same substance in different work environments? Are new objects of citizenship emerging and older ones disappearing? Is the demand for citizenship uniform or does it vary?

The Domain of Citizenship

The domain of citizenship is the area of activity or territory within which citizenship is exercised. Is it growing? Is it shrinking? Are some job sectors or certain workers systematically excluded? Are the borders of the territory which is to be regulated clear or blurred? Citizenship status consists of rights and obligations, guarantees and protections that exist only insofar as they can be enforced. Is the domain of citizenship essentially limited to a territory (that is, a single, usually national, legislature)? This is a crucial question in a context of globalized trade. Is an industry that is by definition international condemned to remain bereft of citizenship?

The domain of industrial citizenship was restricted to the employing organization insofar as unionization was concerned, and more generally to a national regulatory framework for both a unionization regime and labour laws. This may have suited stable workers holding lifetime jobs, but it no longer suits workers who frequently change jobs and regions. Non-unionized workers are protected only by whatever universal provisions of labour laws are in force. As an outcome, even in domains of potential citizenship at work, subjects of that citizenship are not in reality equal. While having the same formal rights, some workers face obstacles pertaining to common conditions that distinguish them from the dominant group and make them stand out as second-class citizens. As noted earlier, they are often underrepresented, lack critical mass, and/or face overt discrimination, including harassment.

The notable growth in project-based work environments (which studies refer to as the "projectivization" of society or the "project society"; Ekstedt et al. 1999; Jensen, Thuesen, and Geraldi 2016; Lundin et al. 2015; Wenell, Ekstedt, and Lundin 2017) and the increasing mobility of capital and labour have profoundly changed the nature of the economic environment. Many of the benefits of employer-based unionization are lost in a context of temporary employment. Mobile workers, brought together for a short time for the purpose of a specific project, have less interest in joining together to achieve gains that are meaningless when constrained to a single employer. Moreover, these employers are not even subject to the same legislative system within globalized industries. The priority then becomes one of nationally and internationally portable rights, like the case of performing artists in a sector-based certification system. For instance, an industry-wide pension plan is more relevant to mobile workers than an enterprise plan.

The many contemporary studies on changes in citizenship at work often conclude that there is a lack of citizenship among workers in deskilled jobs or among migrants seeking decent work (Bernstein 2010; Brunelle 2010; Carré 2010). There is an underlying assumption that knowledge workers are not at risk because they have their own individual bargaining power (Thuderoz 2010). VGDs share characteristics with film workers in the unionized creative and cultural industries, and collective interests as well. Many are not deprived and do make use of their own specific modes of advocating for those interests. This could suggest that knowledge workers are well placed to gain meaningful citizenship in their workplaces, but does this presumption stand up to analysis? Do these new modes give them access to a form of citizenship? Or are they all condemned to a lack of citizenship?

To sum up, if the mid-twentieth century made enterprise-based unionization the yardstick of industrial citizenship, the contemporary development of work requires new forms of citizenship. If enterprise-based unionization has been a powerful means for workers to reach for citizenship at work and for the democratization of the workplace, the contemporary transformation is substantial enough to prompt us to re-evaluate the question of citizenship at work.

The new paradigm of citizenship at work must incorporate subjects, objects, and domains that have been ignored up to now or that have recently appeared in contemporary work, such as:

- the gendered division of labour in paid employment and reproductive work, and the demands of reconciling employment and family life;

- the national mobility of labour, multiple employers, employers who are difficult to identify, new employment statuses, and the necessity of lifelong learning;
- the international mobility of labour, concern about transnational citizenship, struggles against local differences between migrant workers and domestic workers, and the protection of rights when it is difficult to define which law actually applies;
- the new social stakeholders wanting to have a say in the regulation of work: organizations that defend the rights of workers with no job security, identity-based advocacy groups, sustainable development or local economy organizations, professional associations, and transborder alliances;
- the new stakeholders who do not wish to feature in labour relations, but who in fact play a determinant role in the working conditions; and
- the inclusion of people engaged in atypical forms of employment to ensure the universal protection of the labour laws that generally protect salaried employees.

We see that not everyone has the same level of citizenship. Workers are not part of a uniform whole; they do not have the same access to protection against economic insecurity and the risks of lost income, recourses against arbitrary decisions and ways to influence local decisions regarding work and working conditions, or participation in the local and broader social institutions of the regulation of labour. Because some are not citizens or are second-class citizens, objects of their citizenship may vary and cover more or less ground, and while some territories are democratic, others are closer to free zones.

A Framework for Studying VGDs, and the Structure of this Book

Observing the mostly White, male workforce of the VGI within a diverse society suggests to us that there may be areas of "uncitizenship." Indeed, the VGI is regularly shaken by scandals and controversies around sexism and the industry's "boys' club" culture regarding the content of games, and in the workplace (see Chapter 10).

We now have a framework to address the question of citizenship at work in the VGI (see Table 1.3) in a way that allows us to reframe the four gains of industrial citizenship as the substance of citizenship and evaluate what has become of them. In what follows, we use the VGI as a case study to reassess the four democratic benefits of industrial citizenship within the new context of the post-industrial era and identify the

Table 1.3
Our Framework

Objects of citizenship	Measures of citizenship for each object	Measures of citizenship for the VGI as a whole
1. Policies and programs to protect against economic insecurity and the risks of lost income (i.e., unemployment, skill obsolescence, birth of a child, illness, injury, layoff, retirement)	Are there *subjects* of citizenship from this point of view, and, if any, who are they?	Subjects, objects, and domains of citizenship (as middle column)
2. Recourses against arbitrary decisions (at best) and ways to influence local decisions regarding work and working conditions (at least)	What are the specific provisions or measures that can cover this *object* of citizenship? Do they totally or partially achieve the objective? Who is touched by these provisions or measures, if any? Where do they work? These places, clusters of jobs, or territories are the *domains* of citizenship.	
3. Participation in the local regulation of labour regarding critical issues (i.e., in the case of VGDs: working hours, overtime compensation, quality of life, work-life balance, IP, crediting standards, non-compete and confidentiality clauses, knowledge management, sexism and discrimination)		
4. Participation in the broader social regulation of work, industry, or sector (i.e., lobbying the state in support of or in opposition to certain laws or regulatory regimes, carrying an industry or employment-based legal claim to the state or other relevant social authority, forming professional bodies)		

subjects, objects, and domains of the resulting citizenship, if any exist. We will use the theoretical concept of citizenship at work to map its features "on the ground" in the VGI and address some practical questions: Who has access to jobs in the VGI? Among those who do have access, do they have even access to every object of citizenship or are some objects unevenly distributed? In this diverse industry, can we observe uniform practices of regulation in the matter of citizenship or are there some territories of citizenship while others remain untouched?

CHAPTER 2

Project Management at the Foreground

After setting out the links between industrial citizenship and work in bureaucratic environments, it is useful to examine post-bureaucratic environments, which raise many questions about the persistence of citizenship at work. In this chapter, we outline the general working conditions in project-based workplaces that are emblematic of post-bureaucratic environments. These conditions are widespread in project-based environments and apply to the VGI as well. However, project management can manifest uniquely across industries and workplaces. In the following chapter, we will set forward some specific features of project management in the VGI that may or may not be shared by other creative project-based workplaces. More research in other sectors is necessary to ascertain the generalization power of our conclusions project management on the VGI.

Workplace relations during the mid-twentieth century stabilized over a trade-off between security and subordination. Salaried workers were granted diverse protections against risk, a voice in the regulating process, and wage policies. Labour laws enhanced working conditions and made many workers passive citizens. In North America, the certification of unions as bargaining agents for employees of a single employer suited a system of stable, long-term employment and provided active citizenship for that group. HRM "best practices" ensued from the ripple effect of both the laws and negotiated collective agreements and were adjusted to the bureaucratic organizations of those times. The result was a stability of organizations and employment; seniority as a principle grounding work benefits; a workforce dedicated to mass production and relieved of responsibility towards the clientele; tight hierarchic supervision and control of workers, who were expected to be obedient; a high commitment among workers to a stable employer; and standardized processes of evaluation and compensation based on discipline and conformity to strict rules.

Jobs in the private creative sector of the knowledge economy usually take place under an organizational model that is part of a larger post-bureaucratic evolution. The organization of work in these jobs is markedly different from that in bureaucracies in that it is often arranged on a project basis. Project-based work requires a flexible structure, the free flow of information, cohesive teamwork, reduced hierarchical layers, entrusted individual employees, teams with a margin of decision-making autonomy, less direct supervision, and more worker accountability.

This chapter briefly outlines the nature, structure, and requirements of the generalized project-based organizational model and sketches the ways in which this model and the mechanisms that historically provided for citizenship at work do not fit. These are essential premises for understanding the organization of work and HRM practices in game studios and that underlie our subsequent analysis of citizenship at work among VGDs.

The Project Management Regime

According to the Project Management Institute (PMI 2019), a "project" is a temporary and progressive endeavour undertaken to create a unique and/or unprecedented product, service, or result. The temporary nature of projects implies a predetermined beginning and end. Usually, each project comes with a contract that binds the supplier organization to a client company to provide a specific item or service.

In general, each project creates a product (for example, constructing a building, developing and setting up an information system), service (for example, organizing a festival, implementing neighbourhood policing in a police department), or result (for example, changing the structure of an organization, holding a jazz festival, sending a mission abroad, or following a court case) that is unique or new.

Project management offers a range of means to organize and manage a discontinuous process, and flexible, fluid roles that can adapt quickly to changes in the planning without sacrificing predictability, managerial control over the work, and discipline in spite of the creativity and esoteric knowledge of expert labour (Hodgson 2004, 85–86; see also Weststar and Dubois, 2022, 13). Moreover, in creative and innovative environments, project management primarily means managing people, who are the main production resource (Gemünden, Lehner, and Kock 2018) and who are interacting in an uncertain and often stressful setting. Relationships and interactions are key to a process in which the human element is everywhere; although the technical apparatus is essential, everything that is done with that apparatus is based on decisions made by people. HR and their management are therefore a prime factor in the success of any project.

However, HRM is discounted in the world of project management. This should come as no surprise, since HRM, as currently conceived and taught, is designed to serve bureaucratic organizations, and is thus perceived as an enemy of the great flexibility needed in a project setting. In the project-based world, project managers try to cut red tape instead of creating procedures that would suit the setting. They attempt to reduce the role of the HR department, giving it a low-profile (Perrons 2002; Pina e Cunha 2002), to ensure that HR comes and goes at the right time and in sufficient numbers, deploying them, complying with labour laws, and contributing to the mandatory insurance and social security plans. When HRM policies are in effect in project-based organizations, they have no great coercive power if they conflict with the interests of the project. The project manager is often free to apply policies with discretion. If expected to set working conditions such as overtime or schedules, or regarding working from home, the manager will essentially make those decisions according to the needs of the project and client (Chasserio and Legault 2009).

Projects are short term. Teams are expected to produce goods or services by a date and at a price pre-established by contract, with penalties in the event of failure (Alvesson 1995). These conditions are a source of pressure because the end result is always ill-defined. The client is the source of the triple constraint—or "iron triangle"—posed by the budget, deadline, and the scope of the order, which is generally stipulated in the contract signed between the client and the supplier of the item, product, or service (PMI 2019). These three conditions also serve as the mandatory evaluation criteria that generally spell success or failure for a project.

The production of an original product or service involves considerable uncertainty, which clearly differentiates projects from mass production. Although the degree of uncertainty varies, what sets projects apart is the essential fact that there is no protocol that sets out all the steps. The project team seldom knows the precise nature of the final product and must create (and constantly re-create through subsequent iterations) its own protocol. Uncertainty involves risk, and managing that risk is a major concern in the project world. The process needs to leave room for the unexpected, with ongoing adjustments and improvisation, as it cannot be based on detailed operational planning (Chasserio and Legault 2010; Legault and Chasserio 2009, 2012). The risk of failure is high, including first and foremost financial risk, since the timeframe, means, and resources needed to complete a project can be difficult to predict.

Pursuing the objective of innovation requires taking risks and therefore frequently involves conflicts, with the objective of reducing uncertainty, as demanded by the client. When in the heat of the moment, it can be hard to remember that innovation needs exploration and unexpected twists, turns, and errors. Ideally, the environment fosters risk-taking and encourages workers to learn from their mistakes (Yahya and Goh 2002). The discipline of project management and its body of knowledge encoded in the *Guide to the Project Management Body of Knowledge* (PMBoK *Guide*) (PMI 2019) involves a planning process that is designed to deal with this uncertainty and necessary risk by creating multiple ways to control the three dimensions of the "iron triangle."

Pervasive Time and Pace

At each project milestone the project manager meets with the client or its representatives. Milestones are mini deadlines within the project for which precursor elements of the final deliverable (that is, the final product or service) are expected to be complete. Clients closely scrutinize projects, monitoring the progress of work and making decisions according to its outcomes. A dissatisfied client may terminate the project and decide not to renew funding.

An approaching milestone is nearly always a source of stress for project managers and team members, even more so if the deadline is tight. Milestones can come quickly and the pace can be relentless. The manager may decide, as a preventive measure or as things become urgent, that all resources must be deployed and many sacrifices made to reach the milestone objective. This model is hard to sustain over the long term.

Planning meetings are held frequently (every day for many projects) and there are constant reminders of delays and problems. These are moments of discipline and control, in that the many micro-decisions required as work progresses represent so many opportunities to deviate from the plan (Hodgson 2004, 87). For example, team members may have to decide whether to sacrifice a test phase to meet a deadline, and thus risk releasing a product with bugs, or to put quality first by taking their time and risk trying the client's patience by running late. These are logistical decisions that ultimately have a significant impact on risk. Effective as it may be, this way of doing things involves daily collective supervision, since everyone reports to the team every day and the slightest daily variation in performance is noticed. These tools are a constant and rich source of information, but also a source of stress for employees who are grappling with complex challenges and are subject to group pressure.

Volatile Funding by Venture Capital

Due to the uncertainty and risk of failure inherent in creative and innovative projects, companies that take on these projects are often funded by venture or risk capital. This is capital invested in equity or quasi-equity in companies that are managed independently, rather than being funded on the public equity market. Those investing in capital from the public stock market is fearful of companies that lack sizeable assets, have not achieved stable returns, and are not able to provide proper financial statements. Innovative firms often do not yet have revenue or profits—or at least, none over the long term.

Venture capital involves focusing on the difficult task of funding new and growing firms knowing that only a few of them will survive. The investor seeks to recognize those that will survive as soon as possible, focus on them, and leave the others. Investors want to play an active role and negotiate the conditions attached to their investment to protect it, meaning, among other things, gaining control over the management of the firm (Gompers and Lerner 2004) by holding frequent meetings or being an active participant in firm activities (Duruflé 2009). External funding brings with it the test of a renewal of terms, which often require the project team to produce results in the (relatively) short term. This leads to a great drive to achieve profitability, which leads to pressure to reduce labour costs, since people are the main production resource.

Throughout the production process, the project manager keeps the client informed of any problems, since the client may decide to change the initial request in the face of obstacles or as they see more of the project shaping up. These requests may lead to extra work for the team. There is constant interaction between the client and the project manager but also with different members of the project team, with or without the project manager's consent (Chasserio and Legault 2005, 2009, 2010; Legault and Chasserio 2009, 2012). The clients' representatives may exceed their powers, without being called to order. Therefore, the client may come to have considerable influence over the organization of work and even to exert influence on the manager to affect various daily HRM decisions, regarding such things as recruitment, days off, vacations, working hours, working from home, discipline and penalties, and hiring and firing.

Flexible Employment Relationships and Nomadic Careers

There is no way for a project-based organization to know ahead of time how many projects will be in the works at any one time, as orders come in at different times. The same can be said of tenders to be accepted and, therefore, of the number and type of workers who will be needed. Even with projects that are already underway, unexpected HR requirements can always come up over the short or long term based on new requests from clients, new constraints, or changes in employment as people leave their positions.

Therefore, it is difficult to plan for labour requirements right from the start. This results in a preference for filling HR requirements "on demand," meaning that project staffing is a house unrelentingly on fire. The sense of crisis and urgency is never far away for managers. When an organization has workers who are only required at specific points in a project, it becomes necessary to manage frequent reassignments and avoid conflicting assignments. Multiple assignments can exhaust a worker who is expected to work at maximum pace on two or more projects and be accountable to the schedules and needs of the team members on those projects. Bottlenecks of work—in which one team member is waiting for the output of another—pose serious logistical problems in a fast-paced environment and may cause conflicts regarding workers' roles. A project-based organization may hire a pool of regular workers but will generally also use a pool of workers whose status is precarious (temporary, contract, or freelance) to adjust to specific needs as projects proceed.

Since projects are temporary, workers are highly mobile. Project-based careers take the form of working on a series of different projects in the shape of a spiral staircase, and lateral changes from client to client are common (Turner, Huemann, and Keegan 2018, 11–24). Instead of "climbing up the ladder up the hierarchical silo," workers take moves that "can be half or even a quarter of a step sideways and upwards," in which projects can be learning opportunities that may—or may not—lead to more prestigious projects, but not necessarily to higher positions along a vertical line (Turner, Huemann, and Keegan 2018, 12–13). The concept of "nomadic careers" reflects this new reality (Arthur and Rousseau 1996). Career progress manifests through the prestige of one's past projects rather than climbing a vertical ladder. Whether nomadic or portfolio, successful careers are up to individuals (Turner, Huemann, and Keegan 2018, 13).

Team members often need to adapt as the makeup of teams changes over different stages in a project, as people come and go or are hired to meet specific needs. Frequent changes in the makeup of teams and strained logistical needs can multiply occasions of conflict. Workers must work together tightly without necessarily having the time to develop bonds of trust. Team spirit is constantly being rebuilt. Though some people find frequent changes to be psychologically challenging (Turner, Huemann, and Keegan 2018, 11–24), they must take part in the team effort and its cohesiveness because colleagues are an important source of recommendation in future job searches. Since the process of job placement and team assemblage for new projects is perpetually ongoing in an unrelenting internal or external job market, workers are subject to constant pressure to uphold their reputation. Project managers, clients, and peers can make or break that reputation by recommending the person—or not. Workers must try their best to please everyone, as recruitment and selection methods in projects rely heavily on networking (Christopherson 2009; O'Riain 2000).

Placement is even more important, as work functions as a privileged training venue. When an organization is not concerned about keeping its best resources over the long term, professional development is left up to individuals, who need to plan, choose, and pay for training, try to find assignments on projects that will allow them to learn new skills, and so on. People are required to take on this responsibility on their own, keeping informed and preparing for moves that will help them achieve their goals.

Consequently, staff assignment to projects is a substantial issue and a contested terrain. Management is interested in the short-term goal of assigning workers based on skills they have already mastered, but employees may wish to be assigned to another project that lets them learn new skills in order to upgrade and refine their portfolio over the longer term. Project managers exert pressure and can engage in internal lobbying that conflicts with professional development objectives.

Initially chosen for their skills and experience, members of project teams are then assigned targeted responsibilities. While workers in bureaucracies have an obligation of means (that is, the obligation to fill the requirements of the protocol they are given), the members of a project team have more autonomy. They are assessed in terms of the contribution they make to the project, which means bringing the process to a successful conclusion. In this, they have an obligation of results. The autonomy granted to knowledge workers in a project setting is an implicit trade-off against a commitment to accomplishing the objectives for which they are held accountable. Their evaluation depends on it (Chasserio and Legault 2010), though they do not necessarily have the needed decision-making leeway to respond to the demands of clients.

Many organizations practice what is known as the "360-degree" assessment, in which the viewpoints of superiors, peers, and subordinates are collected. Client views are also important. Since the satisfaction of the client is the most important factor in the success of a project and the very survival of the organization depends upon it, management naturally has an interest in knowing how the client perceives the product and the project workflow. However, this type of practice raises questions of procedural fairness (see Chapter 6). It is important to bear in mind that the client's objectives are short term. Every delay imposed on the team compromises their success, and there may be a tendency to place blame on the person who has encountered a problem.

All in, this environment gives project workers a powerful lever for self-discipline, as well as peer pressure. If they fail, their reputation, and the reputation of the team and the studio, will suffer.

Unpredictable Working Time

Project management has many advantages over bureaucracy that can account for its major upswing: the ability to respond quickly, an adaptability to change, and a devotion to client requests. However, the price of that flexibility is unlimited and unpredictable working hours that can easily interfere with employees' private lives (Chasserio and Legault 2005; Legault and Ouellet 2012; Legault and Weststar 2017).

Employees are not involved in negotiating the contracts that set the conditions for the "iron triangle," but they must execute the work and respect the contract. This situation is closely linked to the practice of a "closed budget envelope," which is part of the constraining "iron triangle" that has a direct impact on working hours. In a context of high risk of commercial failure, the budget for a project (or a step leading to a milestone) is limited to a known, fixed amount. On the other hand, the time required to produce the desired result cannot be known ahead of time, and working hours are unpredictable. This paradox is enacted along these lines. The success of the project is established as an overriding objective right from the start. Client satisfaction is of great importance for both the employee and the manager because the employee's worth is measured by their last project (Legault 2013). Therefore, each team member puts their individual reputation on the line, which motivates team members to commit to a project "however long it takes." The importance of reputation and putting together a competitive portfolio ensures that workers remain devoted to taking on that responsibility and is a much more effective tool of control than any form of managerial authority (Peticca-Harris, Weststar, and McKenna 2015).

Of the three constraints, the time allotted to work is the only one that has any elasticity, as long as overtime is unpaid. In this type of situation, the project manager has considerable leeway in terms of managing time off, vacations, working hours, and so on. (Chasserio and Legault 2009, 2010). The organization of project work often goes hand in hand with a deregulation of working hours (Legault and Ouellet 2012; Legault and

Weststar 2017; O'Carroll 2015). In fact, this means that the risk related to unexpected events in a project is transferred to the employee, who must work for free (Legault 2013). The more hours a person puts in at work, the less time they have to devote to their private life, placing their health, social, and family life at risk. Over the long term, people have trouble regaining their strength and begin to dip into their reserves. As a result, we see rising presenteeism (people refraining from taking sick leave when needed), psychological problems, stress- and work-related illness, workplace accidents, and even suicide, alcoholism, and drug addiction (Carter et al. 2013; Legault and Belarbi-Basbous 2006; Legault and Chasserio 2014; Pérez-Zapata et al. 2016; Pfeiffer, Sauer, and Ritter 2019; Picq, Asquin, and Garel 2007).

Scarcity of Women

This way of organizing work has an inhospitable effect and affects the diversity of the work environment, since many more women than men want to reduce their working hours, and refuse or reduce overtime, especially if they have children and are affected by gendered divisions of domestic labour (Legault and Chasserio 2009; Lindgren and Packendorff 2006; Perlow and Porter 2009; Perrons 2002, 2003). Because of incompatible pressures to work overtime and assume housework and domestic labour, women's place on project teams is uneven. Women are significantly underrepresented in project-managed, high-technology work environments (Chasserio and Legault 2010; Legault 2005b; Legault and Chasserio 2012; Valenduc et al. 2004, 14–20). In the information and communications technology sector, women barely top the 20-percent mark of workers assigned to projects. Even when women are invited to join projects due to labour shortages, fewer women than men make incursions into this sector, and those who do are more prone to leave than their male counterparts (Ashcraft, McLain, and Eger 2016; Platman and Taylor 2004; Prescott and Bogg 2010, 2011b).

Teamwork, Peer Pressure, and a Client-Oriented Attitude

Project teams are multidisciplinary and require that efforts be made in terms of communication. Employees do not have the shared language that time spent working together or a common training brings, but they still need to get up to speed quickly to deliver. The flattened structure of projects aims to foster collaborative relationships oriented towards problem-solving and reduce supervision and control costs. An important prerequisite of teamwork are a set of skills somewhat disdainfully called "soft skills": solving problems as a group, sharing knowledge, and contributing to collective learning. Depending on a project manager's style, conflicts may become aggravated. Yet these are often casually disregarded by comparison with the importance given to technical skills (Grugulis and Vincent 2009; Thomas and Buckle-Henning 2007).

Overloaded workers get too busy to communicate their different viewpoints. Instead of enjoying the cross-fertilization among people with different background and skills, they can be driven into conflict. There are many different channels of communication, as team members may communicate between themselves and/or through a single project manager; management styles differ, and team members must oblige. Members need to interact constantly in order for the project to progress, as their contributions are interdependent. One missing person sets the rest of the team back, leading to an imperative of working overtime to recoup. As the team's collective performance is evaluated, colleagues may resent someone's refusal to work in a crunch and may exert their own power against a perceived lack of solidarity. They can marginalize a member and, most of all, stain that person's reputation, which will make them less employable (Legault and Chasserio 2009; Scarbrough and Kinnie 2003). Few people want to run that risk. Indeed, the time devoted to work and the many hours of voluntary overtime frequently become the primary indicators of commitment when evaluation comes, followed by remarkable contributions to a project (Chasserio and Legault 2009).

As a result, project management has obvious advantages for the management of labour. Held accountable for the success of the operation, team members exert control over the work and monitor the progress of the work. Peer pressure to extend the workday, speed up performance, and limit absenteeism is at least as powerful, if not more so, as pressure from a hierarchical boss and guarantees an intensity of work, as an individual reputation is conducive to future placement (Bresnen et al. 2003; Legault 2008).

The expected commitment to work is short-lived but very demanding. Whereas in bureaucratic organizations the desire to stay with an employer over the long term indicates a worker's commitment (Mowday, Steers, and Porter 1979; Meyer and Allen 1997), in project-based organizations, the employment relationship is often devoid of long-term reciprocal commitment. Managers favour flexibility. Given rising worker mobility since the turn of the last century, the notion of commitment to work has changed (Alvesson 2000; Barley and Kunda 2004; Baruch 1998; Cappelli 1999; Chasserio and Legault 2009). It could now be defined as the ad-hoc propensity for doing everything possible to ensure the success of a project and satisfy the client, sparing no time or effort when it comes to work, displaying devotion and flexibility without waiting to be prompted, and going well beyond any formal job description (Anderson-Gough, Grey and Robson 2000; Singh and Vinnicombe 2000; Yeuk-Mui May, Korczynski, and Frenkel 2002). As a result, project-based workers have only an ephemeral commitment to their employer, and are primarily committed to the client and the project team in the short term and to their profession and sector in the long term.

This places employees in an unusual position in project-based organizations. Up to a certain level, they share in management's imperative to satisfy the client. When they must bend to extremely high demands from clients, some are inclined to blame it on the client and on competition rather than on their employer, while others blame poor management. The discourse of employees is indeed client-oriented and more of an entrepreneur type of discourse than a salaried worker's type of discourse (Lindgren and Packendorff 2006, 859), which complicates the propensity to unionization.

Compensation Is an Individual Game

Project-based organizations try to keep the regulation of employment to a minimum so that practices remain flexible. HR policies are not coercive, since project managers confer high importance to their ability to exercise discretion, to keep up with the triple constraint. In the absence of unionization, compensation is secretive and generally left to the discretion of managers instead of being regulated by policies. New hires individually negotiate the provisions of their contract, and particularly their pay level, based on market value (that is, the demand for skills on the job market). Highly sought after workers—the "stars"—can also negotiate exemptions from overtime, which enhances the effort/pay balance included in the notion of compensation.

Conclusion

Compared to the age of bureaucracy, the boom of the knowledge economy and the related sphere of project management have profoundly changed the employment scene. The general features of project-based work challenge labour institutions and the entire discipline of HRM, since these were developed to meet the needs of bureaucratic organizations during the twentieth century.

Employment practices common in the context of project management has put workers in an indefinite labour law zone that is verging on entrepreneurship, with all the risks that can ensue. Workers bear greater responsibility, since individuals and teams are assessed based on results—an entrepreneur-like benchmark. The client and the team have a high level of power when it comes to the regulation of work because reputation is critical to job placement in a high flexibility and high mobility staffing environment. Reputation is so important that workers discipline themselves and agree, apparently on their own initiative, to the same type of commitment as an entrepreneur, including unpaid overtime. With highly qualified work gathered around the creation of new and unique objects, we are attending the coming of a neo-artisanal organization of work.

If we look back to the notion of citizenship at work (Table 1.1), we can appreciate how project-based environments and their rules challenge its four assets. First, given the very demanding but short-term commitment between employers and employees, workers oversee their own careers and are responsible for managing the risks related to loss of income: health problems, unemployment, parenting, retirement, professional misconduct, and their skills becoming obsolete. Moreover, the risk related to commercial failure and to unexpected events within a project is transferred to the employee, who must work for free to respect the "closed budget envelope." Second, given the importance that project managers place on having leeway in daily operational decision-making and the application of policies (if any), there is not much room for recourse against arbitrary actions and decisions. Third, project-based workers—who are, so far, a mostly non-unionized group—negotiate individually with the only bargaining power their market value can command. They have very little say in the local regulation of their work and workplaces, and must instead accede in order to stay in the race. They must continue to update their portfolio, expand their network, and upgrade their professional development, as these factors enrich their market value and in turn their individual bargaining power. Fourth, as labour institutions were designed for mass production and bureaucracies, project workers are under-protected in the domain of the social regulation of work. For these reasons, the general features of project-based organizations also present a challenge to citizenship at work.

PART TWO
Context

CHAPTER 3

Videogame Development as an Illustration of Project-Based Work

Game development studios are organizations that manage projects. In this chapter, we present the specific characteristics of game studios that distinguish them from project-based organizations of the general form outlined in Chapter 2. In providing this overview of the political economy and local working conditions of game making, we supply the necessary context for our search for the subjects, objects, and domains of citizenship in the VGI.

The game development aspect of the VGI is a component of a larger value chain. This consists of a pool of diverse studios that vary by size, the nature and range of game projects, the division of work, funding scenario, and their dependency on publishers. Studios range from small start-up companies with a few people working on a single project to large established studios producing AAA titles ("triple-A games"),[1] with hundreds of employees working on multiple projects, sometimes across international borders. Yet the distribution of studios along this spectrum is uneven. According to de Peuter, "There's a vast pool of companies, with just a fraction of them commanding the bulk of revenues and employees" (2012, 82).

Indeed, among the six hundred studios in Canada, for example, only 4 percent are "very large" (with more than 100 employees), but they hire 62 percent of the game development workforce, while 7 percent are "large" and hire 4 percent of the workforce. As a result, two-thirds of VGDs work in 11 percent of the studios in Canada (ESAC 2017). Because the transformation of the employment relationship is our principal interest, except when otherwise specified, we are describing the functioning of medium-large and very large employers, and therefore on studios

---

1. "AAA" is analogous to the film industry term "blockbuster" (ESAC 2017). It is an informal classification for video games produced and distributed by a mid-sized or major publishing company, typically having larger development and marketing budgets (an average budget of $12.5 million for console games) and larger production teams (an average team of forty and up to one thousand developers for console games).

developing medium-sized projects or AAA games. They have existed longer than many start-ups and survived downturns in the industry, so in this regard they can inform us about the long-lasting practices of the industry. This does not mean, however, that they represent the business model of the future, as platform games are on the rise and have a different production process (Kerr 2017, 16).

Great Uncertainty in Game Projects

As we have seen in Chapter 2, projects and their teams are in essence ephemeral, but this qualifier is relative given the diversity among studios and projects. Most personal computer (PC) or console games take from two to five years to complete, whereas a mobile game can be developed in a few months. The duration of development is influenced by several factors, such as genre, scale, development platform, and number of assets.

A literature review aiming to provide a comprehensive overview of contemporary development practices used in the VGI reveals that any timeframe and planning of the production process of a videogame is doomed to failure:

> It is almost impossible to accurately plan a [game] development project in detail, largely due to the soft requirements inherent in game production which emerge mid-process during development projects, when testing is coupled with continuous ideation and refinement. (Marklund et al. 2019, 179)

In game development, project managers are often called *producers*, so we will use these terms interchangeably according to the context. A producer works under the scrutiny of external stakeholders to adhere to the triple constraints. In addition to their own employer, producers are responsible to a publisher and, when working on a game based on another company's intellectual property (IP), a licensor. A producer may also coordinate the process of earning a platform owner's approval (such as Nintendo approving a title for the Switch game console) and the rating of the game from the relevant software ratings board (see Chapter 8), depending on how the final title will be marketed and distributed.

In large projects, producers are seconded by team leads, who:

> are the bridge between their teams of fellow artists/designers/programmers and the producers or the project managers. They communicate the concerns or work schedules of their fellow workers to upper management and vice versa. Producers then ensure that

resources are allocated to team members and that the team is on schedule. Leads remind team members what needs to be done within a given time frame, which might position them as a source of discontent for the creative team. ... When creative disagreements occur, the producer is ultimately in control and makes the final call. (Bulut 2020a, 20)

Technology, Art, and the "Fun Factor"

High uncertainty in the VGI is driven by the need to "find the fun factor" for the user-to-be—that is finding the mixture of elements that will make the game enjoyable to those who will eventually play it. This is mainly the responsibility of the game designers who are the stars of the development process, the ones who are interviewed in magazines and featured at conferences (Bulut 2020a, 19; Kyle and Bryce 2012). Many producers mention the "fun factor" as a key risk and an ongoing concern. This relates to the usability aspects of a product that is present in all software development, but also to the artistic elements that are a unique aspect of entertainment software:

> Testing, design, and ideation may not be exclusively relevant to game development as they, for example, happen in software and information system development as well. They are, however, uniquely approached in game development in that they ... extend beyond functionality and effectivity. (Marklund et al. 2019, 187)

A producer balances technology and art to deliver an original product tailored to a targeted audience: making a game that will appeal to them, calibrating it to be challenging, but not overly so, and designing engaging characters and smooth and intuitive gameplay that will draw the player into the universe of the game. These things must be done within the constraints of the development technology. The focus on the "art form" suggests that game projects may differ from other development projects, in that the quest for creativity is more important than the quest for "effectivity."

Gameplay goals (for example, aesthetic goals, or creating a game that is fun or thrilling) do not easily lend themselves to formalization and definition (Kasurinen and Smolander 2014; Murphy-Hill, Zimmermann, and Nagappan 2014). As has been said, "Even an apparently complete [game design document] is likely to change during the development process" (Alves, Ramalho, and Damasceno 2007, 278). Or, as stated by an interviewee: "When the production started, the specifications went out the window ... There simply is not enough knowledge to develop a full design at the early stage" (Kasurinen, Laine, and Smolander 2013, 14).

While the subjective concept of "fun" is mostly defined by developers themselves in smaller indie projects (Zackariasson, Walfisz, and Wilson 2006), larger studios use identified subjective preferences (whether known or stereotyped) and usability concerns of their target audiences as guiding requirements (Alves, Ramalho, and Damasceno 2007; Bryant, Akerman, and Drell 2010; Murphy-Hill, Zimmermann, and Nagappan 2014). These are a factor of standardization and "stability" in processes:

> Most [AAA] games are not written from scratch; instead they utilize game engines and various kinds of middleware ... In this process, the creative role of designers and developers faces off against the economic imperatives of efficient production for a competitive market, reflected in the demands of publishers and console manufacturers and embodied in technology. ... The introduction of capital-intensive methods [like software development kits] to videogame production has resulted in a number of changes. The most important of these is a concerted attempt at managerial control. At the start of a development cycle, management asserts the "determination to control, in a highly predictable manner, the outcome of a complex, potentially chaotic production process." (Woodcock 2016, 137)

We will see that the use of formalized requirements in development seems to be tied to a game studio's size and maturity.

Uncertainty until a Very Late Stage of Development

The challenge of controlling and standardizing a creative process that is largely unpredictable and open to new input until a very late stage is a common issue in game projects. Among the themes that are prevalent enough to be considered general truisms is a conspicuous wish among developers to avoid strict methods and explicitly unified language. They prefer ad-hoc development driven by subjective experience (Marklund et al. 2019, 192–95).

According to VGDs, game development requires very flexible processes, room for collaboration, and an openness to change (Hagen 2012; Hodgson and Briand 2013; Hotho and Champion 2011; Kirkpatrick 2013; Lê, Massé, and Paris 2013; Llerena, Burger-Helmchen, and Cohendet 2009; Musial, Kauppinen, and Puhakka 2015; O'Donnell 2014; Tschang and Szczypula 2006). This preference of developers often clashes with the standardization practices of big studios described above:

> As companies develop more complex hierarchies of stakeholders and staff, the desired flexibility and autonomy of game development becomes increasingly complicated to maintain, and often necessitates more formalized management processes and company structures. In these cases, the inherent tensions of game development become more pronounced, and continuous creativity is hard to maintain due to a growing need to formalize processes (Marklund et al. 2019, 179).

To plan the "unplannable," the discipline of project management makes use of different methods, such as the Agile programming method, which encourages multiple project phases and continuous improvement, to gain some control over the chaos. Though many software projects formally rely on Agile development philosophy, game developers apply development methods differently from how they are prescribed (Chung and Kwon 2020; Kasurinen, Laine, and Smolander 2013; Kasurinen and Smolander 2014; Lê, Massé, and Paris 2013; Murphy-Hill, Zimmermann, and Nagappan 2014; O'Hagan and O'Connor 2015; Schmalz, Finn, and Taylor 2014; Stacey and Nandhakumar 2008; Walfisz, Zackariasson, and Wilson 2006; Zackariasson, Walfisz, and Wilson 2006). Agile, Scrum, and Extreme Programming methods are applied in an unorthodox manner compared to the "regular" software industry and this gives rise to conflicts between programming teams, who tend to support and promote these methods, and artists. In the words of one programmer: "We have a problem because the artists aren't Agile. They detest it! … That's a problem. There's a dual system happening here" (Hodgson and Briand 2013, 320).

While "Agile" is a term often used as a synonym for flexibility, it remains questionable whether it is actually an apt description of the development model used in game projects (Hodgson and Briand 2013; Murphy-Hill, Zimmermann, and Nagappan 2014; Schmalz, Finn, and Taylor 2014; Stacey and Nandhakumar 2008). Developers' reasons for deviating from established project management and software engineering methods mainly stem from the focus on player experience (Murphy-Hill, Zimmermann, and Nagappan 2014; Walfisz, Zackariasson, and Wilson 2006; Wang and Nordmark 2015), instead of reliability or efficiency (Hodgson and Briand 2013). In other words, the project management tools used to control uncertainty are not universally accepted as helpful devices in game development, unlike environments in which aesthetic goals and the "fun factor" are less important.

Interpersonal relationships in teamwork and the interplay between ideas and the technology used to realize them are important contributors to constant change over the course of a project's ideation (Lê, Massé, and Paris 2013; O'Donnell 2014, 41; Stacey and Nandhakumar 2008, 2009; Tschang and Szczypula 2006; Wang and Nordmark 2015). Innovative technological possibilities, as well as their limitations and "bugs," can give rise to new game concepts through a non-linear process (Marklund et al. 2019, 188; O'Donnell 2014, 41).

The testing of a game may also lead to the identification of new ideas that were impossible to foresee at an early ideation stage (Marklund et al. 2019, 189). Moreover, the testing phase is tightly connected to the goal of "player experience" and provides information about the "fun factor," so play-testing has a central role in all phases of game development. Ultimately, final decisions are made after testing (Kasurinen and Smolander 2014):

> If a tester comes to say that this does not work, there is no fun in it, you really cannot leave that in the game, you have to fix it. (Kasurinen, Laine, and Smolander 2013, 14)

> The game experience rules. [If it fails] change is imperative. (Walfisz, Zackariasson, and Wilson 2006, 492)

Since it is difficult to clearly identify which features will ultimately result in the desired player experience, game developers often remain open to new ideas late into the production process (Petrillo et al. 2009). The main downside of this open-ended ideation is the high risk of "feature or scope creep," in which changes are allowed during all stages of production and project requirements increase during development beyond those originally foreseen. This is a pervasive risk more present in game development than in generic software development (Wang and Nordmark 2015; O'Donnell 2014).

In essence, requirements in game development are determined by end-results. They are a great source of uncertainty, since they are known to be highly subjective and reliant on "informed guesses" (Alves, Ramalho, and Damasceno 2007; Kasurinen, Maglyas, and Smolander 2014; Murphy-Hill, Zimmermann, and Nagappan 2014; O'Hagan and O'Connor 2015), and are unpredictable (Kasurinen, Maglyas, and Smolander 2014; Tran and Biddle 2008) and flexible (Daneva 2014; Schmalz, Finn, and Taylor 2014). All this makes for a perilous combination. Other than with a few specific areas in game development (like software architecture) in which requirements are presented as a list of fixed, objective, necessary goals that developers need to accomplish, elements related to the appreciation of the fun factor distinguish game requirements from other software development practices (Alves, Ramalho, and Damasceno 2007; McAllister and White 2015; Myllärniemi, Raatikainen, and Männistö 2006; Stacey, Brown, and Nandhakumar 2007; Wang and Nordmark 2015). VGDs who have also had other software development experience assert that there are few, if any, transferable requirements from one game to the next (Murphy-Hill et al. 2014; Wang and Nordmark 2015).

Overall, reconciling multiple requirements can necessitate difficult and painful arbitration. Yet, game development teams do not always participate in this arbitration. We will explain below how their involvement in decision-making varies among studios and projects.

Risk of Failure and the Value Chain

The risk of failure, first and foremost the financial risk, is particularly great in game projects, since it is difficult to predict the commercial success of a game, as well as the time, means, and resources required for its production. Industry commentators have made the following observations:

1. 10 percent of published games generate 90 percent of revenue (Dyer-Witheford and Sharman 2005).
2. Only 3 percent of PC games and 15 percent of console games have global sales of US$100,000 or more a year, and even this level is insufficient to make high-budget titles profitable (Laramee 2005).
3. The movie industry's rule of thumb is that just two out of 10 movies make a profit. Videogame executives say their industry now has about the same batting average. A game that costs US$10 million to produce—the industry average—and another $10 million to market must sell a lot more units to make money than games made in the late 1990s, when the average production budget was closer to $3 million. At the videogame publisher Activision, 40 percent of publishing revenue [in 2003] came from two sets of games (Nussenbaum 2004).
4. It can take a team of fifty or more developers between one and three years to produce a title on a budget between US$20 and $100 million—and most games sink without a trace (de Peuter 2012, 83).

5   Only one in twenty-five console games are profitable, and the top twenty games bring in 80 percent of industry revenues (Whitson 2013, 123).

We have seen in Chapter 2 that the triple constraint posed by the budget, deadline, and scope of the order is crucial because missing a deadline, exceeding a budget, or failing to fulfill a client's objectives entails large financial and reputational penalties for the studio. These three conditions are the mandatory evaluation criteria that generally spell success or failure for a project.

As the risk of failure is very high in the VGI, few funders are amenable to supporting game projects, and they set up strict funding frameworks to mitigate uncertainty and commercial risk. Funding providers also transfer part of the risk down the logistical value chain. Game development studios play the dependent part in the chain, as roughly summarized:

- Hardware and software distribution includes providers of the underlying platform, which may be console-based or accessed through mobile devices (that is, smart phones) or software platforms (for example, iOS store, Google Play, or Steam). This is the most concentrated of all groups in the chain, with three dominant firms: Sony with its PlayStation, Nintendo with its Switch, and Microsoft with its Xbox. Asia is the primary site for manufacturing hardware, but also plays a role in the software business and creation of IP, mostly in South Korea, China, and Singapore (Bulut 2020a, 15; Huntemann and Aslinger 2013).
- Production tools include game development middleware (software that allows different applications to communicate with each other), customizable game engines or authoring tools (e.g., Unity and Unreal), and management tools.
- Capital funding and publishing involves paying for the development of new titles and seeking returns through licensing of the titles. This is also a very concentrated group. Some publishers have in-house development studios: "Publishers, sometimes overlapping in ownership with console manufacturers, are the fulcrum of power in the value chain, due to their control of IP and their financing increasingly costly games development" (Thompson, Parker, and Cox 2016, 322). The VGI is, indeed, highly concerned with controlling piracy, as is the software industry more broadly (Nichols 2005).
- Development studios of any size include developers, designers, and artists, who may be working independently or under

piecemeal contracts with publishers or platform owners, as subsidiaries of publishers or platform owners, or as part of in-house development teams. This is the largest and most diffuse group. The United States and Canada (60 percent), Europe (20 percent), and Japan (Asia represents 8 percent) host the main actors in game development (Bulut 2020a, 15; Clement 2019), though the contributions of other countries are being increasingly recognized (Kerr 2017; Huntemann and Aslinger 2013).
- Distribution is involved in generating and marketing catalogues of games for retail in physical and online outlets (de Peuter 2012). They are often involved in film distribution as well (Nichols 2005).

There is complex competition for value capture among console manufacturers, publishers, development studios, and retailers (Johns 2006). Because of their position in the value chain, studios are generally condemned to remain dependent in the uneven distribution of power:

> Here what must be highlighted is the nature of the relationship between developers and publishers. Developers generally create games under contract to publishers. Publishers include the console makers—Microsoft, Nintendo, Sony—as well as third-party companies—such as Capcom, EA, THQ, and Take Two—that usually operate in-house studios and also hire outside studios on a project-by-project basis to make games for their label. The power relationship between developers and publishers is uneven. Publishers finance game development, exercise control over the decisions about which games get made, and market the end product. This asymmetrical arrangement is often justified on the grounds that console game creation is pricey, and risky. ... Typically, a developer receives incremental payments from a publisher as development milestones are reached. Being economically dependent in this way can be quite precarious, as developers are beholden to publishers that can technically pull the plug on a development project at any time. (de Peuter 2012, 83)

In this regard, publishing companies and global hardware producers ... have power over essential resources and entry barriers ... for example financing development staff and controlling access to technical systems in the case of licence fees for certain console types. The Global Value Chain approach ... highlights the development studios' lack of bargaining power in relation to that of publishers and the standard-setting capacity of international hardware producers. (Teipen 2015, 315)

Among studios, independent development studios are therefore highly dependent actors (Thompson, Parker, and Cox 2016, 329). Ultimately, many independent studios are acquired by US publishers or close down (Nichols 2013). Data across the International Game Developers Association (IGDA) surveys shows a dearth of mid-sized studios because viable independent studios are often snatched up by larger players for their valuable IP (see Nieborg 2021, for the illustrative case of Activision Blizzard, and Nieborg and de Kloet 2016, on the European indie scene).

Games and gaming may be a booming business, but this does not mean its workforce is protected from employment insecurity. Of the varied manifestations of precariousness, the most severe are unpredictable contracts and job losses (Bulut 2020a, 144). A console game that fails in the market can lead to a shutdown for a studio whose fate hangs on a single project, or a massive layoff in a big studio. One industry observer counted ninety-nine shutdowns internationally between 2006 and 2012—a nonexhaustive list (Plunkett 2012).

We have seen in Chapter 2 the overwhelming influence of the client on the day-to-day organization of work in projects. In the VGI, the concept of the "client" of a studio's game project can be broken down into many roles:

1. the entity providing capital for the project (financier, investor, or funder)
2. the entity owning the IP used in the project (licensor)
3. the entity distributing the game in electronic and/or physical form (publisher)
4. the entity owning the platform on which the game will be released (e.g., Facebook for Facebook Gaming or the Oculus VR (virtual reality) console, Apple for iOS devices, Valve for Steam, and Microsoft for the Xbox game console and Xbox Live) (platform owner)

Historically, even when more than one stakeholder is involved, publishers have been the ones in relationship with studios, whether independent or dependent. In the new context of casual and mobile game development, there may be a growing division among these roles and a lessening of publisher dominance in favour of the distribution platform as the important intermediary (Kerr 2017), but this shift is seen far less in the development of bigger games and console games. In these, the publisher is the funding provider, the distributor, and the owner of the IP. Despite the early phase of "garage inventiveness" (Kline, Dyer-Witheford, and de Peuter 2003, 81) and the more recently perceived heyday of independent studios, the game industry has shown the same tendency toward consolidation of corporate wealth and power as other cultural industries (Nieborg 2021). A case in point is the recent acquisitions made by Microsoft. In March 2021 the company acquired ZeniMax Media and its successful game publisher Bethesda Softworks (Warren 2021), and in January 2022 Microsoft announced its acquisition of the publisher Activision Blizzard (Chalk 2022). This latter move represents a consolidation of the fourth and sixth largest game companies by revenue (Strickland 2020) and has solidified Microsoft as a global game powerhouse.

In fact, the political economy of games combines the revenue model of TV with new media economics. Giant console producers "sell consoles at or below cost ... but make money on the software thanks to their dominance in the market and the proprietary nature of game platforms they produce." They put "money in the software that is played on the hardware" because "the political economy of video games is platform dependent," which is different from movies, for instance (Bulut 2020a, 21, taking up Dyer-Witheford and de Peuter 2009). This means a great deal in terms of the power relationship between console producers and studios. When the publisher is a publicly listed company whose ownership is organized via shares of stock traded on stock exchange markets, it has easy access to financial markets but is also accountable to shareholders. This means that the publisher can impose some scheduling limits and genre selection on projects (Bulut 2020a, 68–72) and shape a game's form, format, and publishing flow (Nieborg 2021).

Two typical scenarios frame this action. In one, publishers order the development of a precise (and predefined) game. In the other, publishers shop for ongoing game development projects. They may offer to fund some through development, often buying the IP in the bargaining process, or simply buy the IP rights of nearly completed game projects. In some instances, a publisher may buy a studio with promising IP outright and run it as a subsidiary or independent business unit (Nichols 2013; Nieborg 2021; Warren 2021). Publishers fund projects with the income they derive from selling platforms, owning game IP rights, and licensing their use in exchange for royalties or from specific sources adapted to the risk level, like the stock market (Teipen 2015, 324).

There are roughly three principal financing models of studios in the industry. Firstly, in-house financing is when large multinational hardware producers or publishers run their own development studios (first- or second-party studios). This is illustrated in the Nintendo and Ubisoft cases, respectively. Asked about the funding of their projects in the 2021 Game Developers Conference (GDC) State of the Game Industry survey,

51 percent of developers said that their funding came at least in part from the "company's existing funds" (GDC 2021, 9; respondents could choose more than one answer).

Secondly, publishers can finance the projects of independent development studios on a contractual basis and combine financing, production, distribution, and marketing functions (known as "third-party studios"). Multinational console producers, such as Sony, illustrate this type of scenario. They foster medium-sized studios and maintain enduring relationships with them. According to the 2021 GDC survey, 17 percent of game developers said that their projects were funded by an external publisher and 6 percent said that they received funding from a videogame platform holder (e.g., Apple Arcade, Xbox Game Pass) (GDC 2021, 9). This fits with the responses to a separate question on the 2020 GDC survey in which 26 percent of respondents said that they were using the services of a publisher; indeed, 19 percent said the publisher "has paid us an advance and takes a percentage of revenue" and 7 percent said that the publisher "has not paid us an advance but takes a percentage of revenue" (GDC 2020, 14). Publishers can also finance the projects of independent development studios that struggle to make ends meet. Such studios aim to meet funding providers at special events, such as trade fairs. Producers looking for funding promote their games-in-the-making with short pitches. The most fortunate will get "money and service" contracts, which means part of the payment is "in kind" (for example, through skills and expertise, translation services, or IT services). In doing so, funders are able to participate in the development process and garner appreciation when they contribute know-how. Studios can get some funds to finish their games but will often have to sell the IP to the publisher. As Nieborg (2021, 186) outlined, publishers exert their dominance because they have unique access to four essential assets: "1) a large portfolio of content that can be used to cross-promote content; 2) superior marketing skills and assets; 3) a good relationship with game platforms; and 4) having a good track record or reputation."

Even though they are not official venture capital providers, publishers "behave like givers of risk capital" (Teipen 2015). This means that publishers make sure to play an influential role in game development studios to "limit the damage." The following excerpt illustrates the precariousness of independent studios:

> [Under a model in which publishers finance "the projects of independent development studios that struggle to make ends meet," above], it is typical that the studios first develop a self-financed "developer demo" and then present it to a publisher. For major

productions, development studios must finance 20% of their costs in advance. Publishers can issue "letters of intent" without obligation for the pre-production phases, providing financial security for three months of development time, for example. This intent does not, however, promise long-term financing of a game, until the date of completion. As a rule, after four to five months of development time, when the initial prototype is finished, the studio can only receive a commitment of this nature for a big console game. ... Development studios usually receive payments at three points during the process: initially, once the prototype is developed, then in the middle of development, if intermediate results are submitted, and finally at the end, once the product is delivered. In addition, many contracts guarantee publishers an extensive co-decision power on game production, culminating in "direct involvement" in personnel decisions. Developer studios bear both the risks of unforeseeable tasks and the costs for any late delivery of products. The development firms' powerlessness leads to unfavourable contractual terms in the relationship between publishers and developers in this sector. Contracts are said to be a "farce"; as a consequence of their weak financial situation, independent developer studios stated that they have no choice but to sign on the dotted line. If the publisher decides to finance a production, independent developers usually receive 20% of the sum yielded from a game (Teipen 2015, 319–20).

Less fortunate others will get an invitation to submit the game when it is ready to sell, which may be the start of a path leading to the purchase of the studio. These are the many ways that lead to a concentration of means in the hands of the "majors":

> Vanedge Capital is an investment fund that steers capital, or money in search of money, to studios working on promising projects. ... Headquartered in BC with an office in Shanghai, Vanedge taps global investors capable of putting in a minimum of $2 million CAD. Its model is straightforward: finance game firms "with the expectation that we're going to sell them" (and hence be absorbed by conglomerates) "or have them go public" (and hence be listed on a stock exchange open to international participation). (de Peuter 2012, 84)

Thirdly, there is independent financing. This is the rare case in which development studios can obtain (or seek) financing without resorting to publishers. Neither banks nor venture capital firms invest money in independent videogame start-ups that lack institutional support. Game start-ups opt for projects with smaller budgets and are financed mainly by personal investment, government grants or subsidies, crowdfunding, and/or single investors (Teipen 2015, 319–23; Woodcock 2016, 136; see also Chapter 8). Again, according to the 2020 GDC survey, 31 percent of game developers used "personal funds" to support their projects, 11 percent said they received funding from government funds, 10 percent used formal venture capital, 8 percent had "angel investors,"[2] 6 percent used crowdfunding platforms, and 3 percent received Alpha funding (pre-release purchases by consumers) (GDC 2020, 15). All in, 50 percent of respondents to the GDC survey used independent financing in full or in part to support their games.

On smaller projects, game makers often wear multiple hats. A single person can run a game studio as company co-owner, publisher, designer, and artist, and take on the roles of producer (Whitson, Simon, and Parker 2021). These game projects are more likely to be organically organized and exhibit less of a division of tasks and roles. These independent studios bear the entire risk in the case of failure, but if the game becomes a commercial success, the studio will receive purchase offers:

> The key shift in less complex casual games for mobile phones has created new opportunities for small developers. Developers can now upload their games onto retail sites such as the Apple App store, without the involvement of a publisher. This reduces barriers to entry associated with cost and reputation and, therefore, the dependence of developers on publishers. However, here developers assume all the risk of development in the competitive market for mobile devices. The heavy concentration in the retail and phone markets has ensured that developers bear the costs of developing the vast bulk of games that never succeed in the online market. (Thompson, Parker, and Cox 2016, 331)

Providing and controlling developers' access to financing is an essential part of publishers' business strategies for maintaining their dominant position in the value chain, but it is insufficient. Licensing is another part of the funder's protection against risk, because the production cost is very high and the reproduction cost could be very low in technical terms.

2. An "angel investor" is a private investor who provides financial backing for small startup, typically in exchange for ownership equity; they can often be found among an entrepreneur's family and friends to help the business get off the ground or to provide an injection to carry the company through its difficult early stages.

Licensing limits the use of the property of each game to its IP owner and serves to artificially create scarcity in the market (Kerr 2017, 5–6).

In the first and second financing models (in-house financing and publishers financing the projects of independent development studios), each game development project is the object of an agreement between a client and a studio. Even in the first scenario in which entities have a dual publisher-developer status, each game is an individually funded project managed as an independent business unit by corporate headquarters. Many short- or medium-term contracts may overlap in a single development studio. The funding contract includes a high degree of publisher surveillance over daily progress. However, despite the influence the publisher has over working conditions, they are not the legal employer and would not be part of any typical bargaining process. When confronted with workers' requests, claims, or complaints, a studio manager will regularly put the publisher's conditions forward as an obstacle to any alternative course of action and claim their own helplessness. Indeed, project-based workers are often told that "such is the tightly competitive market," "the client won't be back if they are not satisfied," and so on. Producers and team leads often refer to the wishes and constraints handed down from publishers or "corporate headquarters" as the real source of management decisions, including HRM decisions.

Therefore, managerial discretion is decoupled from perceived worker outcomes and workplace dissatisfaction is not attributed to employer actions (Legault and Weststar 2015b). VGDs often share the view that their legal employer is not an autonomous actor in HRM decisions, and that the publisher is a very powerful one. Indeed, more than shareholders having their say in general management decisions, publishers are able to have their say in the day-to-day management of projects.

The Funder's Protection: Client Control over the Development Process

In any project-based organization, the daily work routine is focused on the client's satisfaction, which occupies a central place in the statements and concerns voiced by both management and workers (Anderson-Gough, Grey, and Robson 2000; Singh and Vinnicombe 2000; see also Chapter 2). This makes the client an omnipresent figure, though invisible to workers. We see this clearly in game development through the mechanism of precise project milestones.

To avoid assuming the risk of loss, investors allocate funding over a series of steps (milestones), thereby attaching conditions to each new provision of capital. As such, "Staged capital infusion keeps the owner/

manager on a 'tight leash' and reduces potential losses from bad decisions" (Gompers and Lerner 2001, 155). The game development process is broken into milestones and requirements are established which must be fulfilled within a certain number of months. The parties take stock of the progress made at each checkpoint. Producers are responsible for delivering the product as agreed and (if needed) negotiating with the publisher.

To begin a project, the publishers provide an in-house or external studio with a limited sum, constituting an advance against royalties (after costs are recouped). This sum is restricted to the loss that the investor is willing to cover. The development team must start the project with this sum and use it to accomplish some of the work described in the requirements contract. This confines the studio to its "iron triangle," allocated within this "closed budget envelope." The team is constantly threatened with the possibility of a funding interruption and studios enjoy little bargaining power:

> Developer firms can normally cover their costs during the production period, but nothing remains after that point—unless they can produce a highly successful market hit. Therefore, the studios' ability to finance a development team for the next game from the earnings from the previous one is contingent on success. This contingency leads us to our main observation: independent development studios are the weakest links in the traditional value chain, and they carry the greatest risks. ... Because of the strong power asymmetry between publishers and independent development studios ... switching studios costs the publishers very little. (Teipen 2015, 320–21)

Developers in independent game studios may dream of being acquired by a large international publisher to achieve some financial stability (Bulut 2020a). These publishers have greater access to markets, offering more assurance of at least some commercial success. This allows for bigger budgets up front and more human resource availability (Teipen 2015, 320). However, they give up creative autonomy; game projects are "ordered," and in-house or subsidiary studios are not free to develop their own:

> On the upside, the acquired studios "gain access to their parents' deeper pockets," but this comes at the cost of "a degree of control" when the seat of decision-making power shifts (de Peuter 2012, 84, quoting Hon 2009).

In a telling case study of an acquired studio, Bulut (2020a, 149-50) shows this loss of control while also demonstrating that financial security is not guaranteed in these arrangements:

> To improve the financial standing of the company, [the publisher/parent company] was constantly thinking about how they could boost stock prices and provide more cash flow. The master plan relied on [the studio] to produce an expansion game as part of their biggest franchise, sell it at a cheaper price, remain the focus of attention, and hopefully provide cash for the parent company. ... The smaller team in charge of the expansion game initially thought: "Shit, nobody is gonna buy this." The developers felt like the project was forced upon them. Moreover, when publicly traded companies want to meet specific deadlines to prove growth for the investors and the public, they might force their studios to release games at an earlier time when the developers are not ready or comfortable doing so. In this sense, the requirements dictated by the parent company can be a major source of frustration and lead to crunch periods for developers. ... Stocks present an existential source of anxiety because the very interface on the developers' computers—used for internal communication in the studio—displays the stock ticker of the parent company and other major publishers in the game market. That visual presence of the financial performance of [the parent company] becomes both a warning sign and a disciplinary mechanism.

To avoid conflicts, lost time, and disappointment, the requirements for the milestones should, ideally, be realistic and precise. However, it is hard to strike a balance in an uncertain environment. If a client is too precise, the requirements could turn out to be unattainable or counterproductive. Yet, requirements that are ambiguous enough to accommodate uncertainty can leave room for interpretation and conflict (Bulut 2020a 18; Rollings and Morris 2004, 294-307).

Reconciling multiple requirements is a delicate art in game development, but the role that development teams play in this varies among studios and projects. As capital providers attempt to reduce uncertainty, they tighten up supervisory procedures (Deuze, Chase Bowen, and Allen 2007, 350). VGDs often chafe against the limits of creative autonomy imposed in this context: "Production processes have shifted from one-person craftsmanship to an intricate division of labour" (Izushi and Aoyama 2006, 1,846), in which "workers fulfil narrowly defined roles within a hierarchical production pipeline" (Deuze, Chase Bowen, and

Allen 2007, 342) and are subject to "regular interventions from senior management and also to the persistence of an emphatically hierarchical division of decision-making" (Hodgson and Briand 2013, 309). As an outcome, "the nature of this interaction between the often more creatively concerned developers and the revenue driven publishers reveals a key tension apparent in the video games industry" (Johns 2006, 165). A developer interviewed in Johns' survey bluntly says: "We only deal with them because we have to" (Johns 2006, 165).

Funders also try to reduce uncertainty by emphasizing a flexible and comprehensive early stage of game production (Cohendet and Simon 2007; Schmalz, Finn, and Taylor 2014), followed by a severe screening and elimination process. They allow several potential products through the ideation and pre-production phases and employ early and frequent play-testing of these prototypes to determine which will ultimately go into production, shedding the riskiest projects before too much is invested in them (Schmalz, Finn, and Taylor 2014). However, this strategy still comes at considerable cost, and it remains fallible. Even after this first screening, saved projects remain risky ventures.

Funders also shield themselves from risk and make the production process more predictable by favouring a franchise model, or a series of related games (Bulut 2020a, 38; Kerr 2017, 5–6; O'Donnell 2014, 20–21). Sequels and franchises rely on the past success or proven model of a game or film (Kirkpatrick 2013; Nussenbaum 2004) and allow for the use of more precise, formalized requirements. Technical requirements seem to become more explicit and static in these cases (Cohendet and Simon 2007; Hodgson and Briand 2013; Walfisz, Zackariasson, and Wilson 2006). Any games released on major hardware-specific platforms also need to adhere to rigorous lists of requirements for performance, compatibility, and usability. This contributes to the monopolistic power of developers who are able to meet these standards.

Publishers are also moving to a games-as-a-service or "live games" model to reduce market risk. Players pay as they go, and interest in a game title is maintained for a longer period through periodic releases of new downloadable live content. In this way publishers can extract rent from their existing assets through revenues from a stable and dedicated player base without having to invest in an entirely new game (Dubois and Weststar 2021):

> While video game companies used to make dozens of games a year in the hopes of striking gold once or twice, they are now focused on making a few big hits that will keep players coming back for more

... That's led companies to consolidate operations and shut down some studios. Electronic Arts, for example, used to have 49 titles; it's now down to around 10. (Semuels 2019, n.p.)

When an independent studio is acquired by a publisher, it usually means abandoning the cherished model of (the aforementioned) "flexible processes, room for collaboration, and an openness to change" until "late into the production process." Rather, it entails taking a first step in a "rationalizing" process that emphasizes a new financial approach. Here, creativity and developers' input are streamlined to mitigate market risks and align production with commercial mandates (O'Donnell 2014, 65). In this vein, one of our interview respondents voiced frustration regarding last-minute important changes in a game's plot:

> ▸ Finding out that someone has added an animation to make one of the female characters do something that is sexually suggestive and I only find out when I play the game, and especially when I wrote that character, it's very upsetting ... [many elements] don't get in until right before it goes gold, and then it just goes to the publisher and no one thinks about it and I'm playing the game six months later and I go, "Why did she do that? That is ridiculous, that is completely at odds with her character, I can't believe ... Did you not listen to the dialogue, did you not read the character bio? Do you not know the story? She would not do that, it is not about that." (F-12-20-M-E-03-12-13-16-02)

While gaining some funding stability and comfort, the newly integrated labour force is "at the mercy of financial networks, marketing schemes and investment plans" that are black-boxed and over which they have no control (Bulut 2020a, 4–5). The property transfer is usually a dichotomous experience for developers, described as "a contradictory drama of expropriation" grounded in "antagonistic imperatives" between creative workers and publishers, entailing clashes between creativity and marketing when developers' desire for experimentation collides with corporate demands (Huws 2014, 53–58).

Project-Based Organizations Illustrate the Essence of the Financialized Workplace

We have seen that game-making projects are uncertain and the VGI is a highly competitive environment. We have also seen that capital providers seek to gain control over this risky cocktail by setting precise requirements, arranging regular milestone meetings to take stock of progress, and withdrawing their funding when targeted requirements are not fulfilled.

In this, project-based organizations are a perfect example of the process of financialization of the economy. Financialization involves a cluster of changes to corporate ownership and governance due to the deregulation of financial systems in many advanced capitalist countries since the 1980s. Within this context, states have pursued financial sector liberalization and global integration as an engine of economic growth in its own right (Crotty 2005; Durand 2017; Helleiner 1995; Lapavitsas 2014). To that end, financial corporations designed as external centres for decision-making are superimposed on organizations that they either buy outright or in which they invest via short-term contracts or agreements, the renewal of which is subject to short-term returns criteria (L'Italien 2012). These short-term contracts entail a constant threat of withdrawal of the stakeholders' capital and, consequently, make the payment of dividends the prevailing factor in organizational decisions, instead of investment in production and employment (Appelbaum and Batt 2015; Auvray, Dallery, and Rigot 2016).

The pursuit of short-term returns can affect the management of the financialized organization in two different ways. First, equity investors take a strategic place along the decision-making chain to ensure the representation of their interests. In exercising their own interests, these investors can modify the managers' compensation policy to align with dividend yield to make sure management decisions follow any desired rationale (Auvray, Dallery, and Rigot 2016; Favereau 2016). Second, in the alternative scenario of ownership by an external corporation, financial management and decision-making become oriented toward optimal financial valuation operations—that is, share value instead of the general economic health of the owned corporation (L'Italien 2012).

To ensure optimal financial valuation, firms attempt to reduce the risk of negative return on investment and financial loss. This implies that production costs must be kept under control. Equity investors often seek immediate returns and financial stakeholders request management strategies that reduce labour costs and distribute cost-savings back to them (Kollmeyer and Peters 2018, 2). Since investors can end funding when an enterprise or a project does not provide a positive return on their investment, managers who need this funding comply with investors' demands (Dumenil and Levy 2005).

Project-based knowledge work is labour intensive. Labour constitutes between 70 and 90 percent of game development costs. Studios, especially small ones, seek ways to scale this down, as they depend on publisher contracts (Teipen 2015, 318):

> This cognitive labour is, however, a costly commodity. With industry salaries in Canada in the range of $70–$80,000, payroll is a studio's single greatest expense. It is not surprising that the tax credits for which industry has lobbied mostly apply to labour budgets. (de Peuter 2012, 86)

In its inexorable search for greater returns for financial stakeholders, funding capital is highly mobile so as to be immediately responsive to diverse incentives. This is the case of any industry like the VGI that has limited fixed infrastructures and is based on knowledge and IT (de Peuter 2012). Investors are sensitive to many environmental factors, such as the cost of the relevant labour force, and financial advantages, such as tax laws. In Canada, for instance, tax credits in the digital media industry can help cut labour costs and fuel rapid industry development in a region (see Chapter 8). Studios chase these incentives, and the consequences of "forced mobility" have been considerable in Canada:

> Significantly, some of the new studios springing up in Vancouver are responding to a risky market by substituting short-term, project-based contract workers for the long-term studio employee, ... thereby making precarious employment a more formal part of the business model of game development. Some insiders anticipate the game sector moving to a freelance labour economy like that of film production. ... This model becomes more feasible as the "wealth of talent" grows. (de Peuter 2012, 87)

In this context of financialization, studio managers and producers are cast in the subcontractor or franchisee role in a "fissured workplace" scenario (Weil 2014). Weil depicts a scenario in which big business groups (for instance, Apple or Walmart) subcontract segments of production (for instance, to Foxconn) to break the legal employment chain between employment-relations actors. The contractor funds the process and exercises considerable control over production but is disengaged from the employment relationship. Employment relations are pushed onto the subsidiary organization (subcontractor or franchisee), which must employ or deploy labour to provide the product according to the contractor's strictly defined performance standards. Subsidiary organizations operate under tight margins and strict guidelines that make poor pay and working conditions a precondition to solvency.

In a similar process, financialized activity sectors are divided between capital providers and subsidiaries to form networked organizations. The former disengage from employment relationships and turn to a network of small businesses for production. Game studios are like franchisees in this scenario, as their room for manoeuvre is strictly curtailed (Weil 2014, 174–81). This plays a strategic regulating role in working conditions and employment relationships. For instance, the funding mode of an advance on royalties used in the VGI is like the royalty/fee system in force in retail franchising systems. These systems "make it nearly impossible for a franchise to be profitable without cutting corners in meeting the minimum legislative standards" (O'Brady 2014, 656). Weil "integrates the labour problems associated with subcontracting, franchising, and supply chain management into a cohesive framework" (O'Brady 2014, 656).

An All-Encompassing Flexibility of Employment

As an unavoidable consequence of all we have discussed, we will see in this book that employment in game development—as much as the daily schedule—can be nothing other than "flexible." In other words, the employment relationships, as well as the working time (see Chapter 9), show great variability. Staff varies in quantity and nature, employment relationships can be interrupted on short notice, and crunch-time work can be demanded at the last minute. The project-based structure of the industry also poses a high risk of layoffs and firing (see Chapter 5).

Thus, job stability is not uniformly sought after in the industry. Indeed, some VGDs do not want it, as long as they have general employment stability in their trade. Large or AAA studios tend to offer greater stability than small- to medium-sized studios, but it is not guaranteed:

> ▸ Of course, there are things that turn me off in big studios. But, on the contrary, there are things I appreciate, like stability, although big studios sometimes close down ... Small start-ups have really super cool features I love, but stability in big studios attracts me. ... As I'm 31 and I want kids at a certain point, I have to get some stable compensation. (F-05-08-19-M-G-21-10-13-13-19-15-JL)

In reality, some will get stability while others will not, and it can come and go. VGDs can be let go in a context of layoffs, but they may also wish for a change, for stimulation or to learn new skills (Peticca-Harris, Weststar, and McKenna 2015; Weststar and Legault 2014). Ter Minassian and Zabban (2021, 71) classify four dominant types of job mobility among

French game makers: "going elsewhere; going foreign; going indie; and getting out," and note that game makers can experience all four over the course of a career. Losing your job has many different meanings. It may be an unforeseen and unfortunate experience following a firing, a layoff, or a closure, but it can also be the result of a developer's decision to move to a better position. The industry sees a high degree of turnover as workers move in and out of paid employment; shift across projects and studios; try their hand at different employment forms, such as contract work or self-employment; or leave for other lines of work. The ability to navigate geographical, intra-sectoral, and extra-sectoral mobility is essential to staying in the sector (Ter Minassian and Zabban 2021, 77). We will discuss employability and training more in Chapters 5 and 6.

Developers have been socialized to operate on a very short time horizon, and to think that being around for "five years or so" represents stability. Most are well aware of their employment insecurity and some do not fear it. A female developer at a large studio in Vancouver told us:

> ▶ Right now, I'm fairly confident that the product will get done and that I'll be there for a couple of years. However, I know that sometimes, just the way the industry is, if a product isn't that successful or whatever, a part of the team is laid off. I basically understand that's the circumstance of the industry. (F-03-13-V-R-25-11-13-14-26)

Among the VGDs we interviewed, 33 percent had been unemployed for a time in their careers, and, for 22 percent, this was the result of a layoff rather than leaving voluntarily. Their words provide insight into how developers experience this:

> ▶ [The VGI is] not very stable. The company that I first worked for, you know, they ran out of money and they laid everyone off and I think they're now bankrupt. They had another layoff or two before that. [Another studio] is, I think, quite a bit more stable in that it's been around for five years or so, but even then we could run out of money or whatever. ... as an indie studio, that's the danger. And then in the big corporate studios you are, I feel, pretty disposable. (F-05-19-T-L-19-03-14-04-11-JT)

They rationalize this employment insecurity as an overarching, inescapable trend in the trade. In a hit-driven market, VGDs end up bearing the risk of commercial failures. For those developers who work within increasingly networked organizations made up of subsidiaries to an international parent, the success of a completely different studio in another part of the world can have a direct effect on labour practices and the survival of the studio they work for. Bulut's (2020a) case study of a Midwest US studio and their parent company shows how VGDs can bear the brunt of financial restructuring that has no relation to the effort, performance, or success of their studio. Our interviewees shared similar experiences:

> ▸ Basically, I was working for a company that was employed by the owner of that studio, and they had a bunch of offices all over North America and we were the only Canadian office, so I was laid off because I was affiliated with that sector of it and they abolished the Canadian office. How did I feel about it? I saw it coming; it's a normal aspect of the industry. (F-01-19-V-B-27-11-13-14-26-PB)

In such a context, we may wonder why large studios offer (some) job stability in their demand for labour. Many factors contribute to this. First, large studios are more prone to repeat similar formulae and they have incentives to keep their trained workforce. With such a trump card, they are better able to compete for the most skilled workers (Keune et al. 2018, 19–20). Second, they handle multiple projects concurrently, so they can reassign staff. For example, they have "dispersement policies" when the time comes to wrap up a project (Turner, Huemann, and Keegan 2018, 64). Third, tax credit programs subsidize wages, allowing large studios to retain a bigger workforce (see Chapter 8):

> ▸ Sometimes they'll give you a little time to float between projects. They pay you, so they expect you to study, update your skills. They give you free training. (M-12-16-04-M-W-10-10-13-13-19-15-JL)

> ▸ There were six weeks—they actually called it the "inter-project." It's cool though because other companies would lay people off in between and then rehire them. But [my studio], they know that it's way more costly to do that—it's better to actually just give people time and say, "Listen, you've got nothing to do—until we say so. Just do whatever you want. You can surf the net, play games…" (M-02-13-T-U-02-04-14-04-11-JT)

In this way, large studios can absorb the cost of retaining unassigned workers they will need again soon. These "on the bench" VGDs can be very useful to the studio in performing certain tasks, for example in writing submissions, post-mortem analyses, or audits or evaluations of completed projects, or in furthering their own professional development during this time.

Conclusion

To complete the portrait of project-based work environments drawn up in Chapter 2, we have focussed on the features of the VGI that constitute a necessary backdrop for the rest of the book.

We have noted how financial stakeholders, here taking the form of clients as de facto investors/funders, confront an unusual uncertainty in the production process and a high risk of commercial failure. They are not without means to face this situation, as they sit at the top of the logistic value chain of the game development process. Looking for ways to limit the damage to protect their investment capacity, they exert significant influence over HR strategies, daily HR routines, and decision-making, as labour is the main cost in knowledge work.

Part of an array of networked organizations, development studios exist in a sector that stands out as a quintessential example of the financialized organization in which not only firms but projects are remotely managed by investors. Managerial authority over HR decisions is focussed on the success of the contract and HR policies are therefore often skewed. Managerial discretion may be decoupled from workplace dissatisfaction when producers and/or VGDs view the client as ultimately accountable.

The legal employer is not an autonomous actor in financialized environments in which the client is an omnipresent figure, though invisible and inaccessible to workers. This is not unheard of, as most collective bargaining systems do not include funders as actors in the process of establishing working conditions. Yet this is more important in financialized environments because of their direct influence on working conditions.

These are the grounds over which working conditions take place in project-based game development studios, and over which assessments of citizenship will be made. This environment presents significant risks of lost income and employment to VGDs and shapes the substance of potential citizenship. We will outline these risks in Chapter 4 and then systematically probe the existence of citizenship across the four broad objects (see Table 1.3). Do VGDs have protections against the risk of lost income? Do they have recourse against arbitrary treatment and decision-making? Do they participate in the local regulation of their work regarding key risks and issues? Do they have a voice in the shape and regulation of the VGI as a whole? And, importantly, are all VGDs equal subjects to citizenship across a stable and universal domain?

CHAPTER 4

The Other Side of the Playful Bunch: Risks Faced by Videogame Developers

In Chapter 2 we saw that project-based work presents a challenge to labour institutions and that the constraints of project management have side effects on work. In Chapter 3, we further explored how the case of game development illustrates, and sometimes emphasizes to the point of caricature, the economic relationships among actors in a project-based industry of the private creative sector of the knowledge economy. In this chapter we get to the heart of the topic of citizenship by laying out the risks game developers run, within the context of project management and financialization. We discuss how these economic relationships create a particular cocktail of features in the daily work of game development that is conducive to risks of lost income (see Table 1.1). As noted by Gill and Pratt (2008, 6), "precariousness is a defining feature of cultural labour." Indeed, its contemporaneous workers are "disproportionately affected by risk and insecurity, compared to the previous generation, and with little expectation of work security," and "might make above standard wages but if they lose their job are thrown into poverty" (Gill and Pratt 2008, 18). McRobbie (2018, 146) also critiques what she calls the "creative dispositive"—the new economic discourse focused on creative entrepreneurship—as a form of "labour reform by stealth" in which "a younger generation is being prepared for work in which there is no protection." According to observations made in Korea, the rapid industrial transition to the mobile game market deepened labour precarity, promoted the degradation of skills, and ultimately fragments workers in the digital game industry (C. Kim and Lee 2020). Laying out these risks sets the stage for examination of the first object of citizenship at work: the degree of protection against these risks (see Table 1.1). This is the focus of Chapter 5.

Some important risks will not be discussed in this chapter because they are analyzed later in this book. They include results-based and individualized compensation systems (see Chapter 6); unlimited, unpaid, and unpredictable working time (see Chapter 9); and the exclusionary power of a uniform White male workforce (see Chapter 10).

A Playful Bunch, They Say

According to a widespread preconception, "autonomy is the defining feature of both enterprises and workers" in "creative and cultural industries" (Thompson, Parker, and Cox 2016, 316). Theoretical claims depict work environments, which suggests that it is rather challenging to separate capital or management from labour within a labour process of "collective improvisation," without job descriptions or functions, and in which actors do not confront each other or conflict. Unlike workers in other times, they are said to transcend the "old class struggle." Boundaries in authority are porous, so creative labour comes to lose sight of the very notion of a wage-effort bargain. A combination of social networks and aestheticized studio spaces is said to break down the distinctions between work and play (Thompson, Parker, and Cox 2016, 319), and those between work and free time (Bulut 2020a, 6).

Knowledge workers are purported to be resourceful agents, reliant on their own bargaining power and unfettered from "old world" issues of authority and control. As outlined in the Introduction, there is an ideal view of the VGI as an industry with high compensation, high creativity, high autonomy, desirable mobility, and high job satisfaction (Nichols 2005, 189), and a persistent discourse painting a picture of a "playful bunch" of gamers who are paid to play (Dyer-Witheford and de Peuter 2006). However, there is increasing acknowledgement of the contradictions in the industry's labour processes and contestation of the growing control over creative labour in the VGI:

> The complication is that "playbour"—a hybridized form of work and play (Kücklich 2005)—stems from the traditions of hacker culture and the ethos of open source software. It originates as a response to the Fordist, Taylorized workplaces of the past ... the post-1968 refusal of work has done much to shape video games. Atari even made "this 'refusal of work' its key to commercial success" .... These elements of counterculture combine with corporate capitalism in various ways to gloss over some of the contradictions of the workplace. (Woodcock 2016, 138).

Indeed, recent years have seen a proliferation of conceptual terminology: the creative class, network or immaterial labour, the cognitariat, the cybertariat, the precariat... These are not reducible to each other, and many are bluntly defined, lack accuracy, and collapse different kinds of work and experience. Yet, these concepts share a common theoretical concern for contemporary transformations in the class structure. From very different standpoints, they highlight an emerging complexity in the class structure and stir up debates around the position of knowledge workers within it.

Some researchers embrace the coming of a supposed "creative class" endowed with almost mythical qualities (Florida 2002). Whatever drawbacks these people endure at work, they are presented as self-disciplined and networked workers, many of whom "promote initiative and responsibility as highly motivated self-entrepreneurs" (Moralde 2018), as opposed to "victims of capital or managerial oppression" (O'Doherty and Willmott 2009, 941).

Others adopt a more critical stance. Promoting a "neo-orthodox labour process analysis," they are concerned with accounting for an updated analysis of the wage–effort bargain and capital–labour conflict. They argue that knowledge workers deal with a combination of some prestige and above-average pay levels alongside precariousness and poor working conditions. Instead of putting forward the enduring power of capital, and without denying it, these researchers stress the creativity of powerful, playful, and resistant workers in the face of their exploitation (Gill and Pratt 2008).

Indeed, empirical research on market-structured organizations does not reveal an employee that is empowered and free of being controlled, but a rather *remotely controlled* worker. True, instead of being held to prescribed behaviours from top management, these "empowered" employees are able to select and deploy strategies adapted to the situation at hand. They do not rely on detailed descriptions of action but aim for outputs (Salaman 2005). However, instead of having an obligation of means, these workers have an obligation of results that leaves little room for mistakes in this "government at a distance." The sanctioning of these individually steered choices lies in the focus on market success.

Therefore, when we locate game development within the value chain context and draw on evidence from interviews and surveys with VGDs to examine work conditions and employment trends, a mixed portrait emerges. Studios can be disciplinary spaces and sites for insecurity, long hours, and low pay, as well as lively spaces of creation.

"Flexibility" of Employment Is a Determining Factor in Working Conditions

In Chapter 3, we saw the encompassing character of "flexible" employment that makes it a key factor in explaining the ensuing working conditions. For this, we will first discuss its consequences for VGDs. As Bulut observes, "Although testers experience the most blatant precariousness, the phenomenon is not confined to the *tester pit*, as it stands out as a general feature of the financialized sector" (2020a, 141; see also Ozimek 2019b).

Layoffs, Unemployment, and an Unrelenting Placement Process

The game industry is one of constant churn (or turnover). VGDs have a high risk of losing their income, and time spent under these conditions adds up over a life span in terms of lost experience and revenues. News of layoffs, bankruptcies, and mergers abound and reinforce VGDs' insecurity (Plunkett 2012). The popular game news website Kotaku has a category tag called "layoffs" to help organize all of the articles they publish on the topic (see kotaku.com/tag/layoffs). To raise awareness of the high number of layoffs and their negative effects on communities, one visual effects artist has created a database that catalogued layoffs and their causes at studios around the world since 2004 (Klepek 2020).

Many factors contribute to the instability.

First, there are shifts related to government incentives. Regional and national governments have embraced the "creative city" rhetoric of Richard Florida (2002) which suggests that when you accumulate a critical mass of workers in the creative sectors of a city, that city becomes a magnet for more and more prestigious enterprises of the creative sector and beyond, which then attracts more highly qualified workers. At first, governments have to chase cultural and creative industries as the bulwark of their new economies (McRobbie 2016) to reach the point where the creative sector in a city progresses and thrives on its own momentum. Following this model, governments and intra-state regions compete heavily for game studios (see Chapters 3 and 8). Medium-sized studios are particularly sensitive to financial incentives. This subsidization of the industry by the taxpayer creates a highly volatile job market, since it is subject to political pressure. VGDs engage in daily speculation about whether their studio will stay or go (Bulut 2020a, 122–40).

Second, entertainment industries are vulnerable. Market failure can lead to a shutdown for a studio whose fate hangs on a single project, or a massive layoff in a large studio. Yet game failures are extremely common (see Chapter 3). Though all studios are exposed to the risk of commercial failure, larger companies are able to make use of more risk avoidance strategies. Small studios lead the most precarious existences. Independent studios can hardly absorb the impact of market failures, but even when they succeed, they will often be bought out by a bigger entity. In both cases, they end up laying off some or all of their developers.

Third, exporting game development jobs has been big business for a long time, with specialized companies who help outsource labour to low-cost countries. For instance, programmers and digital artists in India and Eastern Europe cost considerably less than those in the West and have growing capacity (Chebotareva 2019; P. Hyman 2007; Nichols 2005). The threat of outsourcing is much discussed and has a forceful disciplinary impact, effectively lessening individual bargaining power. This contributes to the employment uncertainty of VGDs:

> Studios are exporting an increasing portion of development work to lower-wage locations such as China, India, and Vietnam. Outsourcing has been steadily inching up the value chain, and now affects everything from programming to animation. ... Geographic diffusion of game-making know-how suggests that countries of the Global North are not guaranteed a monopoly in this regard. (de Peuter 2012, 87–88)

Last, the project-based structure of the industry poses a higher firing and layoff risk, as the dynamics of projects proposed, accepted, and completed does not encourage a perfect sequence of job opportunities. Each project requires specific skills depending on its current stage. Moreover, studios do not always take on the same type of projects and therefore do not always require the same technology or competencies. Consequently, a variable rate of turnover is inevitable. Smaller studios cannot absorb the cost of the undefined idle periods between two projects ("inter-project" or "being on the bench"), when the date of closure of one project and the start of another do not coincide. Even in a large studio, teams or individual employees may be let go when a project is over, given up on by the publisher, or reduced under cost pressures. The greater the economic dependency of the studio, the likelier the layoff. This makes it challenging to retain rare, specialized teams and developers (Teipen 2015, 331).

Depending on the IGDA survey year, 15 to 35 percent of developers reported being laid off, with most experiencing permanent job loss. According to the 2004 survey, the biggest reason for layoffs was studio closures, followed by cancelled projects and the completion of projects. We lack survey data on this topic for 2009, and therefore have a gap in our understanding of the downward trend (see Figure 4.1).

Even in unionized environments, unions seem to concede that a certain fluctuation in employment is unavoidable and have a collaborative attitude in this regard. Teipen (2015, 328) outlined the case of a unionized game environment in Sweden in which management gave advance

Figure 4.1
Developers experiencing permanent or temporary layoff (2004–19)

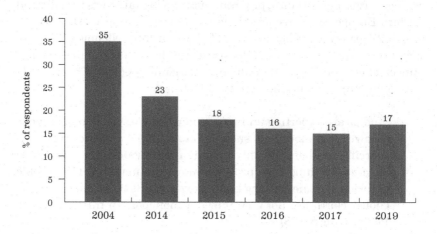

Source: Original data from the IGDA QoL survey 2004, DSS survey 2014, DSS 2015, DSS 2016, DSS 2017, and DSS 2019. The data included employed and currently unemployed respondents.

notice in the case of layoffs and rehired the relevant employees when there was an upturn. Unions appear open to ad hoc flexibility in the application of labour laws when they are not well suited to the constraints of the sector. For instance, they may accede to a lessening of seniority provisions such as the "last in, first out" rule and ease up on protection against firing so that game studios can more flexibly apply broad considerations of merit in strategies to retain the "best" VGDs. In such cases, unions have been found to compromise on the imperative of stable, long-term employment when it is incompatible with the constraints of game projects. In return, 60 percent of VGDs in Germany, Sweden, and Poland are said to have secure employment because management also benefits (Teipen 2015, 328).

In aggregate, the proportion of permanent employees is nearly constant. Our survey data from 2004 to 2019 show that a consistent seventy-one to 74 percent of respondents had permanent status. However, there are no illusions about the true "permanence" of the employment relationship. VGDs know that this status means, in fact, an open-ended contract.

Losing your job has many different meanings in the VGI. It may be an unforeseen and unfortunate experience following a firing, a layoff, or a closure, but, alternatively, it might be the developer's decision to move for a better opportunity. VGDs move in and out of paid employment, shift across projects and studios, try their hand at different employment forms such as contract work or self-employment, or leave for other lines of work. However, this mobility is still risky, as VGDs are exposed to high local and international competition on the labour market. Even internally, they must continually showcase their work, remain up-to-date, and prove their contribution to the studio in order to be retained and assigned to the best projects.

The risk of job loss can be underestimated because the demand for game labour is quite high, and studios face a shortage of experienced developers ready to hit the ground running. A male developer in Montreal said he would be surprised if he was ever out of a job because if a studio "goes belly up, you can just take your résumé over to the others" (M-06-15-M-W-20-11-14-13-15-19-MSO). Indeed, when the market is strong, VGDs with extensive networks and good reputations find jobs.

More accurately, we could say that being cavalier about the risk and displaying confidence is closely tied to one's position in the social hierarchy, based on reputation, occupational role, and track record of past projects, and the economic geography of game development in the region. Demand is not as high for all occupational groups, and some have more trouble finding a job. There seems to be a consensus that it is easier for those in technical jobs, like programming and technical design, than it is for artists and testers, who compete with the reserve army of labour waiting at the gates:

> ▸ The more technical they are, the easier it is to get hired anywhere. ... Programmers, even if they can't get jobs in the industry, they'll get jobs anywhere else for probably twice as much. They never have to worry about that kind of stuff, and they get paid more. It can be pretty tough for artists. At least they can still go into film and do a lot of freelancing. I think that non-technical designers have the worst scenario. (M-02-13-T-U-02-04-14-04-11-JT)

> ▸ I was out of work for about a month and a half, which is an extremely short time for an artist in the industry. It's super hard to get a job as an artist, because there are so many of them, and so many of them want to break into the gaming industry. (M-13-10-T-B-20-01-14-04-11)

Developers are confident because of the balance of probabilities. Given the statistics in Figure 4.1, perhaps layoffs are not a universal concern, because the risk depends on the studio's size and position in the market. Instability of employment does not automatically entail unemployment,

Figure 4.2
How long have you been unemployed in the industry? (2014 and 2019)

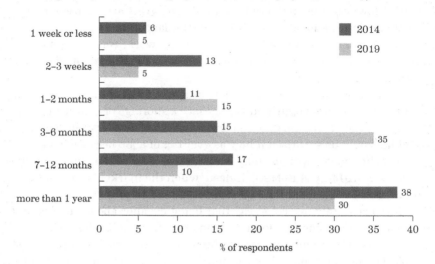

Source: Modified from Weststar and Legault (2014), with original data from IGDA DSS 2019

but it may. Some VGDs reported extended periods of unemployment (see Figure 4.2). As well, in the period of 2009 to 2019, a consistent quarter to a third of respondents said that they worried that their job would not exist in the next month. VGDs were polarized about the job prospects in the industry, with two-thirds expressing negative or uncertain views about job opportunities in 2014 and 2019 (see Figure 4.3 in the Data Appendix). To a question we asked only in 2014, only 53 percent of developers said that they were somewhat or very confident in their ability to find a new job at about the same pay, without having to relocate.

Casualization of Labour and "At-Will" Employment

Ulrich Beck (1992) speaks of the "de-standardization of work," and more specifically of the creation of a risk-fraught system of flexible, pluralized underemployment, in which both the risk and the responsibility for protecting against it are being shifted to workers. A similar logic operates in many sectors of the economy, in which atypical forms of work are multiplying.

In 2019, most of our survey respondents seemed to expect high job mobility: 34 percent expected to be employed for less than three years with their current employer, and 23 percent expected four to six years (Weststar, Kwan, and Kumar 2019, 20–22).

Figure 4.4
Number of game-related employers in the past five years (2019)

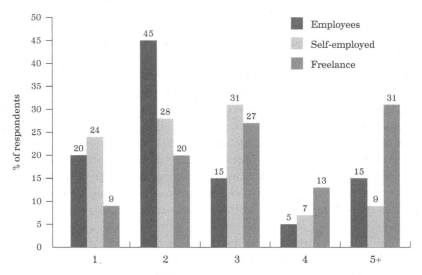

Source: Original data from IGDA DSS 2019

Job hopping sometimes involves moving locally and sometimes internationally, though we note a downward trend in worker mobility. Among the employed in 2014, 56 percent said that they had not had to relocate for work in the past five years, while the remaining 44 percent had to relocate at least once (Weststar and Legault 2014, 71). In 2019, slightly fewer salaried developers reported the need to relocate (61 percent said they had not, but 39 percent had to relocate at least once).

Additional evidence for endemic employment insecurity is the number of past employers. Figure 4.4 shows the 2019 data for developers who were employees, on contract, or freelance and self-employed. This data paints a somewhat counter-intuitive picture. While we could expect that freelancers would have a larger stable of employers or clients as they move from contract to contract, they do not seem to have many more employers than do salaried employees. Even the self-employed reported a high number of other employers in the past five years. We see similar patterns in earlier survey data (Weststar and Legault 2014, 2015, 2016; Weststar, O'Meara, and Legault 2018).

There is much to unpack in this simple figure in terms of the casualization of videogame labour. We would expect employees to report the greatest longevity at a single employer. Instead, we see evidence that being hired as a permanent employee in a non-unionized workplace can mean very little. Each new project and each project milestone represents a distinct moment when developers could lose their jobs. On the other hand, we see freelancers working for long periods of time with the same employer or for repeat contracts with the same employer. This could be a signal that studio managers are dodging employment standards obligations by misclassifying workers as independent contractors when they should instead be deemed employees. Studio managers may also be optimizing their numerical flexibility by hiring on contract when they could make permanent hires (Kalleberg, Reynolds, Marsden 2003).

Though hiring through networks is most common, large studios also turn to temporary hiring agencies to quickly supply workers. The experience of a developer in Montreal highlights the risks of such arrangements for developers. While it might be a common trope to think of the creative artist scraping by in a restaurant to support their career, this is not the typical view of the "glamorous" videogame industry:

> ▶ I was earning peanuts and I was having cash taken off because I was hired through a temp agency, which took a cut. And, of course, I wasn't permanent … I was just on a term contract … So I knew that when it got to be Christmastime, I'd be out of a job, and I didn't know what I'd be doing. And often they'd say to me, "Well, there's no more work. Maybe it'll pick up in April or May," and I said to myself, "Shit! I'm just going to have to scrape by for three or four months." I wound up as a dishwasher in a restaurant for two months. (M-06-15-M-W-20-11-14-13-15-19-MSO)

Is this mobility what VGDs want? In 2014, all respondents who were working full-time or part-time, as employees, freelancers, or self-employed, were asked which would be their preferred status. A considerable majority (70 percent) reported that they would prefer permanent (full-time or part-time) employment and 30 percent said that self-employment would be their preference (Weststar and Legault 2014, 64). In 2019, 49 percent of freelancers said they had that status because they "could not find a permanent job at an established studio" (Weststar, Kwan, and Kumar 2019, 30).

The data from self-employed workers also highlight the porosity of employment relationships in the industry. Most self-employed survey respondents over the years said that they had also worked as employees for studios or in freelance arrangements. Figure 4.4 above shows that for many in the 2019 sample, being self-employed was a recent event—having worked for two, three, or more employers in the past five years. It is a common assumption that experienced game developers splinter from larger studios to start an independent shop or engage in freelance work. Self-employment and indie development can seem a panacea to the issues of IP, creative freedom, and working conditions that workers must deal with when working with larger developers and publishers (Whitson 2013). The high-profile successes and glamorization of select indie titles fuels the myths about indie development. However, it is subjected to the same competitive and financialized forces as the rest of the industry, but with even less legal protection and an uneasy situation with respect to the development of labour solidarity (see, for instance, Keogh and Abraham 2022).

There Is Limited Diversity in the VGI

Even in domains of potential citizenship at work, subjects of that citizenship do not turn out to be equal (see Chapter 1). Some workers face obstacles pertaining to common conditions that make them stand out as second-class citizens. They lack critical mass and can face overt discrimination, including harassment. Such is the case in the VGI.

Snapshot of the Workforce in 2004

The IGDA commissioned an initial study on the composition of the workforce in 2004 and revealed that only sixteen to 17 percent of those working in the game industry were women, in an employment market in which 39 percent of the media workforce were, at that point, women. Most of these women (73 percent) worked in traditionally "female" jobs: managerial, administrative, marketing, and public relations roles, rather than in game development proper. Only 2 percent of programmers, 3 percent of those working in audio and 5 percent in game design were women, while 8 percent of producers and 9 percent of artists were women. There was no obvious relationship between the size of studios and the gendering of the workforce (Haines 2004, 5).

Contrary to stereotypes, 41 percent of freelancers working in games were women, many of them writers. Furthermore, nearly a quarter of all those in senior positions (23 percent) were women, though most often in managerial or marketing roles, rather than in hands-on direction of game development (Haines 2004, 5–6). Studios were accustomed to recruiting:

> entirely from the "usual suspects": people that they already know and unsolicited CVs, of which they get thousands. An already male-dominated workforce and tribes of determined male hardcore gamers wishing to join in means that unless companies make

an effort to look at less traditional sources of recruitment, they may never see many female applicants. (Haines 2004, 9)

While women VGDs enjoyed working in game development, they bemoaned the same obstacles we hear about today: a male-dominated environment, no family-friendly practices, male jargon, patronizing attitudes, sexism and racism, poor and unequal pay, long hours, crunch time/overtime, few women in senior roles, and a glass ceiling (Haines 2004, 10).

At that point in time, the game development sector was not notably concerned about other factors of uniformity in its young, White, masculine, cisgender, and able-bodied workforce.

The Contemporary Workforce

In the snapshot taken in 2019, the contemporary population of VGDs seems to be growing older, showing a distribution much closer than seen in previous IGDA surveys to the general labour force in the United States[1] (with its mean age of forty-two) and other industrialized countries (see Table 4.1).

However, it looks like age distribution is the main demographic change in the landscape.

STILL MASCULINE: GENDER AND SEXUAL ORIENTATION

In 2019, survey respondents still predominately identified as men (71 percent). Only one quarter (24 percent) identified as women, 3 percent as nonbinary, and 2 percent preferred to self-describe. This is a relative increase compared to 2009, when 14 percent identified as women, but since then, the profile has been notably stable (see Table 4.2).

This makes women significantly underrepresented in game development compared to the general population. According to the 2019 United States census (no date), 51 percent of the population was female, and in 2019, women aged sixteen and older represented half (47 percent) of the total labour force (Bureau of Labor Statistics 2020).

Conversely, in 2016 an estimated 0.6 percent of adults in the United States were transgender, which suggests that this population may be overrepresented among VGDs (Flores et al. 2016).

Surveys show stability regarding sexual orientation, with about 20 percent identifying as LGB (see Table 4.3 in the Data Appendix). In this,

---

[1]. As our sample in the IGDA surveys includes mostly North American respondents, mostly from the United States, we refer to the US population as a basis for comparison.

Table 4.1
Distribution of VGDs (% of respondents) according to age, 2009 and 2019

	2009	2019
25-29	30	17
30-34	23	20
35-39	28.5	22
40-49		22
50 years and older		9

Source: Legault and Weststar 2009, 13; Weststar, Kwan, and Kumar 2019, 12

Table 4.2
Distribution of VGDs (% of respondents) according to gender, 2015-19

Gender reported	2015	2019
Men	75	71
Women	22	24
Transgender	1.5	4*
Non-binary or prefer to self-describe	1	5

Source: Weststar and Legault 2015, 11; Weststar, Kwan, and Kumar 2019, 12

* In the 2019 survey, respondents were invited to indicate in a secondary question whether they were transgender; therefore the total for this column exceeds 100%.

representation is a little higher than the general population: 12 percent identified as LGBTQ in a US study in 2017; while 4.5 percent of adults identified as LGBT in a 2017 Gallup poll (Weststar, Kwan, and Kumar 2019, 12-13).

Still White: Ethnicity

There is a similar ethnic homogeneity among the IGDA survey respondents (see Table 4.4 in the Data Appendix). The VGD population (as of 2019) is more dramatically skewed in favour of Caucasians than the general US population, in which 60 percent identified as "white only, non-Hispanic" (United States census, 2018). If we used a similar definitional category for "white only," the 2019 DSS sample would be 69 percent White, and if adding West Asians, it would be 71 percent. The rest of the US population identified as Hispanic or Latinx (of any race) (18 percent), Black (13 percent), Asian (6 percent), and Indigenous (1.5 percent). Relative to this, Indigenous people and Asians are slightly overrepresented in the DSS samples, while those identifying as Black

Table 4.5
Distribution of VGDs (% of respondents) according to disability, 2015–19

Reporting a disability	2015	2019
Psychiatric disability or mental illness	9	12
Visual impairment	7	5
Physical disability	4	4
Intellectual or learning disability	4	4
Neurological disability	4	3
Hearing impairment	3	2

Source: Weststar, Legault, Gosse, and O'Meara 2016, 11; Original data from the IGDA DSS 2019

Note: Totals do not add to 100% because respondents could select multiple categories

and Hispanic/Latinx are largely underrepresented (Weststar, Kwan, and Kumar 2019, 13).

OPEN TO WORKERS WITH DISABILITIES

Our data indicate a similar share of people with disabilities among VGDs as among the US population. In both the 2015 and 2019 DSS, 23 percent of the sample indicated that they had some form of disability (see Table 4.5), while a 2018 report indicates that 26 percent of adults in the United States live with a disability (Okoro et al. 2018).

However, we do not know the nature of the relationship between VGDs' disabilities and their work:

> It is possible that the video game industry, and the type of work done there, accommodates the needs of those with a disability more effectively than other industries. This means that workers who identify as having a disability may gravitate to these spaces. Alternatively, and particularly in the case of mental health and disabilities developed as a result of repetitive strain injuries, it is worth investigating if the working environments of the video game industry contribute to or exacerbate the negative effects of particular disabilities (Weststar, Legault, Gosse, and O'Meara 2016, 11).

A previous report on the 2015 DSS noted some gender differences: "[Women] reported psychiatric disabilities or mental illness at a rate twice as high as [men] (14% compared to 7%)" (Weststar, Legault, Gosse, and O'Meara 2016, 11). Additional research is needed in these areas.

Occupational Segregation

We have seen that women constitute approximately one quarter of the contemporary workforce in the industry, but their representation in "core" game development roles is uneven.

The issue of occupational segregation is very significant when discussing equity and diversity and domains of citizenship because aggregated participation of women in the workforce does not provide the entire picture—far from it. Some occupations show barriers to the entry of women, and this occupational segregation is closely associated with the gender gap in earnings: "When women are segregated into certain jobs, those jobs usually pay less, have fewer opportunities for progression, less job autonomy, and less authority within the organisation" (Prescott and Bogg 2011a, 207). Both men and women workers fear being offered a "female job," which they perceive as being poorly paid and of low status, even when the duties are similar to male-dominated occupations. Worse, this social phenomenon tends to reproduce itself: "people tend to choose occupations where their own gender is represented" (L. Miller et al. 2004, quoted in Prescott and Bogg 2011a, 206) because occupational categories are an important part of a person's sense of self:

> A worker's occupation is imbued with meanings about the identity of the worker and the appropriateness of the worker's role in that occupation—and these meanings can have negative or positive implications for perceptions of interactions and support among workers. (C. Taylor 2010, 190)

In other words, a worker may not be part of a minority in an organization, but still be part of a minority "within their occupation in that particular organization, and they will therefore feel the cultural effects of working in a gender incongruent occupation." (Prescott and Bogg 2011a, 206) This is important to bear in mind when examining research about women working in the VGI that aggregates women of all trades: women in predominantly female trades, such as marketing or HR for instance, may not feel part of a minority if their trade is mostly female.

Classifying the job tasks performed within game development is challenging. There is considerable role overlap or "multitasking" in the daily experience of many game developers and the specificity of a job often varies according to studio or team size. As well, job titles are not consistent across studios and new roles continually evolve. However, it is still useful to obtain a general sense of the demography in broad categories of

Table 4.6
Distribution of VGDs (% of men and women respondents) of primary role according to gender (2015-19)

	2015 Men	2015 Women	2019 Men	2019 Women
Upper/middle management	3	2	7	4
Team lead/producer/project manager	12	17	15	17
Designer/scripter	14	10	17	14
Writer	2	4	2	10
UX/UI research and design	2	3	2	8
Programmer/engineer	27	11	31	10
Hardware engineer	0	0	0.4	0
Art	9	17	5	12
Audio	1	1	2	0
Localization/translation	1	1	0.2	0
QA/testers	4	4	3	3
Operations/IT/support/HR	1	0	0.4	4
Marketing/PR/sales	2	7	1	2
Customer support	1	1	0	1
Consultant	1	1	2	3

Source: Weststar, Legault, Gosse, and O'Meara 2016, 14; Original data from the IGDA DSS 2019

game development jobs. We have compared figures from 2015 and 2019 to see whether the representation of women has changed (see Table 4.6).

Table 4.6 indicates how many women and men are in a given role relative to the total sample of women and men. For instance, 2 percent of all men respondents and 4 percent of all women respondents were writers in 2015. This means that being a writer is a more common role for women than men; but there are still more men writers than women writers in studios because there are simply more men overall.

From this, we see that women reported working in programming and design positions at rates significantly lower than men. Conversely, they reported working in art positions at higher rates than men. Women were also more prevalent in administrative and support roles. So, though more women have entered the industry since 2004, their gains are clustered in more marginal areas of game development. Women seem to hold project manager roles at similar rates to men; however, these roles are at risk of feminization, as job descriptions tend to emphasize "soft skills" and are removed from the core technical work.

We have observed both vertical segregation, concentrating workers in the lower echelons of an organization (the glass ceiling), and horizontal segregation, concentrating workers in particular occupations, making some occupations either "men's" work or "women's" work. Men continue to heavily dominate the core content creative roles, such as design, programming, and senior management roles (Gourdin 2005; Prescott and Bogg 2011a, 210). Consequently, women in the industry have little say in the content, interaction styles, character representation, and reward systems involved in games, and thus in how games are perceived. Women in development roles do feel isolated and poorly represented within their profession, while those in non-development or project management roles agreed significantly more that women were well represented (Prescott and Bogg 2011a, 219).

We conducted a similar analysis to compare White workers with workers of colour,[2] and the results were quite mixed. This may be a result of a low sample size for workers of colour or the inclusion of respondents who were not racialized in their workplaces (for example, Japanese workers working in Japan).

Open-ended comments from the IGDA surveys exemplify some of this gender-based occupational segregation and hint at segregation by race, but more research is needed in this area. In the 2015 DSS, one women manager carefully detailed the demographic makeup of the studio where she worked:

- Our studio leadership team consists of six members. All of them are men.
- On my own team, three out of four leads are men. I am the only woman in a position of authority.

---

2. The term "person of colour" or "worker of colour" is commonly employed in the US and Canada, and emphasizes the common experiences of systemic racism by members of racialized groups. It originated in the context of social justice, civil rights, and human rights, and has spread to academia (Moses 2016). The term is flawed—it reaffirms non-Whiteness against a standard of Whiteness and lumps very different individuals together. The term BIPOC (Black, Indigenous, and people of colour) is a modification of the term, which also faces detractors. Our language continues to reflect our ongoing attempts to grapple with the racialized social and cultural hierarchies in our societies and with decolonization. However, we recognize that members of different racialized groups face differential experiences in society and in the game industry proper, where East Asian game developers are more common and respected. Due to sample size, it was impossible to examine the experiences of each racial or ethnic group separately.

- On the second team, all four leads are men. Only one is of non-White descent.
- On the third team, three out of four leads are men: one woman and one man of non-White descent.
- Most of our women are artists, with production, QA [quality assurance], and support filling the rest.
- Most of our ethnic employees are artists and engineers. (F.M.02635.2015)

In the interviews, women pointed out that certain roles and trades are spontaneously labelled "male" and others "female":

> It's very male dominated and that in itself is kind of like a circle, right? ... My fiancé actually took my resumé and took my name off of it and was talking to someone else about it, just being, like, "Oh, I just want some feedback." Like, [to] another engineer. And so he kept in mind [not to say "she," but to use "they" or "them"], and everything he got back from this co-worker was "he," "he," "he," "he." It's, like, assumed. It's almost a barrier to entry. (F-18-07-T-Z-28-04-14-04-11-JT)

> We do have a lot more women at our company, but most of them work ... in the art department. You know... It's like hiring female artists is a no-brainer but hiring women into producer or design roles is... like, it's just not the same. But nobody really looks at that closely anymore. (F-13-19-T-B-29-05-14-05-13-JT)

Sexism and Racism in Game Development

Sexism and racism seem to be on the rise, at least in terms of the broader public discourse about the industry. Respondents to the DSS were asked to list the factors that they felt were associated with a negative perception of the game industry. Three options for sexism and racism were presented: "among gamers," "in games themselves," and "in the workplace." All increased from 2015 to 2019 (see Table 4.7), but the options for "sexism in the workplace" and "racism in the workplace" were lower than the others, and racism was selected less frequently than sexism in general.

Since the early years, women have been less prone to agree that their environment was diverse. In 2005, they were twice as likely as men to agree that a diverse team had a direct impact on the games produced (34 percent compared to 16 percent) and that diversity in the workforce

Table 4.7
Distribution of answers (% of respondents) to the question: "What factors, either actual or perceived, do you feel create a negative perception of the game industry?" (2015-19)

	2015	2019
Working conditions	58	73
Sexism among gamers	63	72
Sexism in games themselves	57	57
Link to violence	55	56
Racism among gamers	38	55
Sexism in the workforce	42	54
Lack of overall diversity	37	49
Link to obesity or lack of physical activity	41	39
Racism in games themselves	26	30
Racism in the workforce	19	29
Other	16	13
Microtransactions	—	2
Gambling and loot boxes	—	1
I don't think there is a negative perception of the industry.	4	3

Source: Original data from the IGDA DSS 2015 and 2019

was an important factor in the industry's future success (41 percent versus 21 percent). In contrast, workers of colour frequently agreed that their environment was diverse. They also agreed that a diverse workforce had a direct impact on the games produced and that workforce diversity was important (IGDA 2005, 12).

In recent years, most respondents say that diversity is critical in the workplace, in the game industry, and in game content, and this majority has risen over the years (see Table 4.8 in the Data Appendix). Many events, starting with Gamergate, or #gamergate (see Chapters 8 and 10), generated acute tensions that have raised awareness of issues of diversity and equity. Our data suggest that responses have also become more polarized during this period.

Sadly, diversity in the workplace remains the least important factor identified by workers compared to diversity in the industry and game content. This might suggest that, despite a rising awareness of diversity among VGDs, they seem less likely to perceive the negative implications—for themselves or the cultural content of games—of a homogenous team in their own workplaces.

When we delve into details for 2015 and 2019, we find that women were more likely to report that diversity across all three domains was important, compared to men, White men, and workers of colour (Weststar, Legault, Gosse, and O'Meara 2016, 23–24). Workers of colour were the least likely to report that diversity was important across all three domains, even less than men, at both points in time. As an underrepresented group, this is interesting. However, when we isolate the responses for women of colour, we find greater importance accorded to diversity, compared to men of colour. This suggests that the issue of diversity is much more salient in terms of gender than it is of ethnicity (Weststar, Legault, Gosse, and O'Meara 2016, 23–24).

What about Job Status? Testers as Second-Class Citizens

The bulk of the last section has been focused on "second-class citizenship" through the lack of diversity according to socio-demographic characteristics like gender and ethnicity. However, we have alluded to the importance of an informal occupational hierarchy within game studios. For instance, "hard" technical skills, programming, and engineering roles have greater status (and greater pay) than art roles, and, at the same time, are a male preserve in a gendered segregation of roles. Critical research that disentangles occupational roles within the industry (rather than treating "developers" as a homogenous mass) is emerging. Notably, some has focused on the population most at risk of second-class citizenship: those who work in quality assurance (QA) or game testing either within development studios (Briziarelli 2016; Bulut 2015, 2020a) or in outsourcing arrangements (Ozimek 2019b).

Testing can appear to be a dream job of "play working" (Briziarelli 2016), an entry to the industry that requires no formal educational credentials (Bulut 2020a; Sloper 2017). Yet, the labour of testers is marginalized and undervalued relative to "core creative" work and made invisible because "the more effective they are in their job, the more invisible appears their intervention" (Briziarelli 2016, 256). They are not part of the "in-group" who can intervene or voice their opinion in the creative process. They often explicitly feel they have second-class citizenship, because they face poor compensation, a lack of respect, greater surveillance, and harsh working conditions; pay their own health insurance; do not enjoy cheap prices for games; and have poor economic and job security (Bulut 2020a; Ozimek 2019b; Taylor and Parish 2007; Thang 2012).

Although they develop deep expertise in terms of gameplay experience, game mechanics and aesthetics, communication, and often modding, testers have a temporary status within studios because testing is only required sporadically, when projects ramp up (Bulut 2020a). Indeed, many studios outsource their QA and testing work, which reinforces the boundary between testers and "real developers" on the "core team" (Ozimek 2019b). What they experience as harsh treatment is not the layoffs per se, but rather losing their jobs to others who do not have experience but will subsequently be trained to their level. It can seem a "cruel joke" for some (Bulut 2020a, 139–40).

Unlike the autonomy given to most game developers, testers must strictly obey working guidelines and workplace prescriptions in their repetitive tasks. They work under the scrutiny of a software program that measures their productivity. However, they are required to develop analytical and diplomatic skills to accurately convey their gameplay experience to developers, to precisely understand both the nature and the source of any bug, while at the same time offering constructive critiques that don't hurt developers' feelings (Briziarelli 2016; Bulut 2020a). Further reinforcing a boundary, testers have limited interaction with the development team; their contributions are mediated and constrained through written reports (Briziarelli 2016; Ozimek 2019b; Sloper 2017). Their contribution is, nevertheless, noteworthy because they "ensure that a game does not crash and give the studio a good reputation. A good console game without the labor of testers is simply not possible" (Bulut 2020a, 138).

Wages are kept low by an oversized reserve army of would-be testers hoping to get the job (Bulut 2020a, 123). They enjoy some "privileges" from their low status in that they are paid for every hour worked, because they are considered wage-earners non-exempt from labour standards under North American labour laws (Bulut 2020a; Taylor and Parish 2007; see also Chapter 9). However, ambition and a "vocational attitude" (Briziarelli 2016) drive them to devote much more time than formally requested in the hope of upward mobility to a development job (Bulut 2020a, 124). In pointing out the low pay, employment uncertainty, and competition among outsourced testers in Poland, Ozimek (2019b) questions the "voluntary" nature of working overtime. Upward mobility happens more rarely than is hoped for—perhaps particularly for women, as one tester said:

> ▸ It was a bit boys club-y. ... For instance, none of the women in the department were ever officially promoted, even if someone was doing the work. You'd be kept out of conversations. I thought that I witnessed some sort of suspect treatment of different testers than was usual. (F-13-13-T-U-05-05-14-04-11-JT)

Though more research is needed to disambiguate the experiences of workers across different occupational roles, the emerging research on QA and testing shows how the industry has produced "subjects who are keen on the hard work ethos, competitive play and self-surveillance to secure their temporary position both at present and in the future" (Bulut 2020a, 138). However, while they crave being part of development teams and work hard to reach their goal, testers are denied subject status in terms of citizenship at work.

Job Insecurity Presents Risks to Health and Private Life

Work environments that are characterized by job insecurity (such as frequent layoffs, churn, on-demand hiring, and job assignment practices) produce conditions for being overworked as each worker struggles in a competitive environment to retain and advance in their job. Such work environments are marked by physical, social, and psychological poor health (Anonymous 2020; Legault and Belarbi-Basbous 2006; Legault and Chasserio 2014; Peticca-Harris, Weststar, and McKenna 2015), including burnout, exhaustion, musculoskeletal disorders related to the use of computers, social and family conflict, substance abuse, and other behavioural problems:

> ▶ Co-workers with behavioural problems ... often, it's work under pressure. There's a lot of teamwork in the industry. ... So, when there's somebody who really has problems ... when someone has really, really big problems, and becomes toxic to other team members and you can't ask him questions anymore because he's practically psychotic, to me, it's really... (F-05-08-19-M-G-21-10-13-13-19-15-JL)

Mass layoffs can be devastating for the health and well-being of employees left behind. Morale and trust suffer as "survivors" mourn for their colleagues who have lost their jobs, wonder why they themselves have been spared, and are on edge waiting for the next shoe to drop. There is also a great risk of burnout or being overworked now that the team is short-staffed (Grunberg, Anderson-Connolly, and Greenberg 2000; Manson 2014; López-Bohle et al. 2017). Repeated exposure to layoffs results in lower perceptions of job security, higher levels of role ambiguity, intentions of quitting, depression and health problems among those who remain (Moore, Grunberg, and Greenberg 2004), and considerable impact on families and local communities (Feldman 2003).

Many VGDs opt for "presenteeism." In North America, "presenteeism" refers to spending time at work without being normally productive, often because of illness, injury, anxiety, and so on (Monneuse 2013). It can also refer to working unpaid overtime, which is known as "overpresenteeism." According to Vézina et al. (2011), although short-term presenteeism is often voluntary, long-term presenteeism is more likely to be imposed, and it particularly affects workers without job security. Medical studies associate this with pathogenic pressures, great psychological distress, depression, and substance abuse, as well as other serious health problems.

The cycle of burnout and being overworked is enabled through the threat of job loss. Job insecurity is reinforced through the threat of outsourcing to emerging countries, through the mobility of capital, and because of the young workforce of the game industry. These workers are keen to get their foot in the door. The mean age of employees is low but rising: in 2019, 37 percent of workers were between twenty-five and thirty-four years old (Weststar, Kwan, and Kumar 2019, 12), while it was 62 percent in 2014. Only the future can tell whether a large part of those workers will leave the industry as they age, citing the wear and tear on their bodies.

To mitigate against job insecurity, VGDs must have a strong portfolio and a strong reputation, and be willing to be nationally and internationally mobile. Threatening to leave for a rival firm is a known strategy to obtain a wage increase. This threat works best if you have a good reputation, which is based on a portfolio of professional successes, rare and valued skills, promising ideas, technical exploits, and strong personal relationships:

> ▶ One must really pay attention to one's reputation in this field. Because people shift a lot from one firm to another, we all know each other—I know the animators of almost all the companies in Montreal and around, and that's how we find jobs, it's really from contacts, so, you have to be careful. (F-03-18-U-13-06-08-01-07).

However, behaviours that enhance reputation pose risks to health and private life. As we have seen in Chapter 2, reputation is enhanced by a willingness to participate in the team effort and put in crunch time. When recruiting or assigning people to coveted decision-making positions (such as that of lead designer or artistic director), producers take into account that the most prestigious projects often require overtime (see Chapter 9). Developers can be facetious when talking about the downward mobility of people who do not play along—one interviewee joked that refusal to work overtime would soon result in their being assigned to work on a stupid game about dogs—and they know the system of retention and advancement:

> ▶ Absolutely [I can refuse to work overtime]. It's very much frowned upon and, as I say, there are a lot of internal projects and pretty soon I will probably be working on a game of dogs or other things like that. Still, people know each other, and so they'll want to try to get those they know are hard working and all that. (H-06-13-U-19-06-08-01-07)

> ▶ Whether you like it or not ... there are interviews even if you're an insider. For the projects, there is your reputation, and there is a follow-up and references: "I'd like to get him for my project..." I've had a number of interviews on each side of the table, so I see how this works. (H-06-13-U-19-06-08-01-07)

The reputational system also constrains the ability to seek legal redress for overtime pay:

> ▶ We admit that the employer does not have the right to oblige me to work overtime. But ... personally, I want the game to be good. I want this because, after, that gives us and the company a reputation ... if, after, I'm looking for another job. So, even if my employer does not make me, somehow it is almost obligatory. It's good that he doesn't tell me that I have to work overtime but it's rather insinuated or... you know, it's unspoken. (H-05-16-W-09-06-01-07)

> ▶ But you tell yourself all the time: if it's the company against me, you say I would really like to contest it, but, on the other hand, I'm never getting a good reputation because it's surely going to become public. ... It's such a small industry, everyone knows everyone else, so that that company will know that I took action against my [prior] company, that I caused trouble, so maybe they won't want to hire me if they know that. If ever I take action, I might be forced to go and look for work outside the country or outside Montreal. (F-10-12-U-12-05-08-01-07)

In short, working overtime is rewarded, boosts the status of developers, and allows them to succeed in a job market in which mobility is required. Conversely, refusing overtime work can mean that a developer is denied those benefits through informal sanctioning processes. Some referred to the "dark side" of overtime work, a rampant threat of exclusion for those who consider refusing crunch-time work. Some described studios that sent blatant messages that there was an obligation to stay late at the office, for instance, by sending emails during the night blaming those who left work. Others learned through other means:

> ▸ No, there was no disciplinary sanction for refusing overtime; as I say, the worst is peer pressure. When I was refusing to work overtime, they were back asking me again next time to work overtime, and again, and again. I was never set apart. On the other hand, when the time came to fill a job ... I can swear to you that my application was on the bottom of the pile! It's not me who had done the most overtime; that's it. I was not as dedicated, as much "going all out for the company" as others because I had self-respect. (Translated from French) (M-19-10-M-I-17-7-13-13-10-12-MSO)

This is the implicit rule that forbids leaving before the team lead does, because one "leads by example" and cannot let the team down. These observations are wrapped up in an ongoing coercive narrative that is powerful enough to become normative. It fosters self-discipline and makes managerial discipline superfluous. The peer group is a key link in the employment network that is essential to a developer's internal and external mobility, because of the importance of information about available jobs and recommendations for hiring (Legault and Ouellet 2012). It is no less important than one's portfolio and the employer performance appraisal.

In this way, VGDs face collectively constructed workplace norms and symbolic meanings of time that "act as a guide for appropriate behaviours" and do not allow for "free choice" (Rose 2016, 18). If people choose a work-time arrangement that goes against what is socially accepted and expected in the environment, they "demonstrate deviant behaviour in relation to the accepted temporal practices in that workplace" and "may rightly fear negative repercussions as a result" (Rose 2016, 19). As such, VGDs who greatly value family life, or who have already faced health concerns, are often led to re-evaluate their priorities and to envisage less strategic and prestigious positions that allow for a balance of professional and personal objectives. Women are particularly targeted by these informal group cultures since they tend to bear the responsibility for children and more often ask for private/work-time balance (Everingham 2002; Perlow 2012; Perlow and Kelly 2014; Perlow, Mazmanian, and

Hansen 2017; Walby 2011; Watts 2009). In the end, reputational systems play a key role not only in decisions about working time, but also in individual decisions regarding maternity and paternity leave.

The Expected Commitment to Work Is Short-Lived but Very Demanding

de Peuter (2011) captured contemporary project-based knowledge workers in the concept of the "precog," a contracted term for "precarious" and "cognitive" labour:

> *Precogs* are characterized by the following traits: self-driven, passionate, commitment to work; willingness to work for nothing; perpetual and personally financed reskilling; habituation to material insecurity; obsessive networking, bold enterprising behavior ... the *precog* is a pragmatic adjustment to flexploitation. (6)

A commitment to work occupies a central place in the narratives of VGDs, even while it is secretly denounced as detrimental to private and family life. It is praised as ambition by industry proselytes of this normative framework (Bulut 2020a, 31). When reputation is the normative control mechanism, it becomes a priority to avoid the "killjoy" reputation that characterizes "the undesirable, disposable citizen" who wishes to enjoy their private life (Bulut 2020a, 26). The individual responsibilities of workers in a project environment are as great as those of an entrepreneur because they are indeed entrepreneurs of their own careers. In fact, VGDs will never need to satisfy any manager as much as they need the project to succeed: they are client-oriented first.

Because of fierce competition among would-be developers, newcomers are familiar with the need to make a performance of dedication and high commitment from the start. They buy into hard working conditions with the hope that performance under those conditions will lead to better pay, better positions, high profile projects, and so on.

Bulut (2020a, 124) focuses on "cruel optimism" among testers, while Ozimek (2019b) characterizes the work of testers using Kuehn and Corrigan's (2013, 10) similar concept of "hope labour." In truth, these concepts can apply broadly to VGDs who quite rapidly start to offer some "un- or under-compensated work carried out in the present, often for experience or exposure, in the hope that future employment opportunities may follow." They operate as if they are making an investment that will pay off for deserving workers in a meritocracy. The cruelty of such optimism lies in the fact that "hope is such a powerful tool because, cultivated in specific ways, it facilitates identification with exploitative forces rather than the assertion of one's own interests" (Bulut 2020a, 138, quoting Tokumitsu 2015, 960).

The "cruel optimism" of the "hope labour" is the cynical counterpart to the "passionate" rhetoric of game development and its celebratory accounts of people doing their work because they love it, rather than for reward (see Chapter 3), and of the "labour of love" and "playbour" discourses discussed earlier in this chapter and in the Introduction. They highlight the imbalance between commitment and the protections afforded. When the practice of crunch time becomes institutionalized and normalized, what is pictured as self-imposed pressure can be a confusing notion, because what can be explained as a "self-driven" propensity to put in the time might stem from an internalization of the general career progress system enforced in studios:

> ▸ It's full of people who are passionate about their jobs. That's unfortunately taken advantage of by some companies that use that to make you work longer hours, but everyone who wants to be there is there because they love it, because it is a hard job. It takes a lot of you, it takes a lot of time, people burn out. You ... have to really love it, because you can make a lot more money doing the same thing somewhere else. I think as a community, and as a group of people and as an industry that exists, it is the best place to work. (F-12-20-M-E-03-12-13-16-02)

> ▸ I tend to be quite passionate about what I do in life and I'll keep going with that until something dissuades me otherwise. As a result ... it's kind of implied or there's pressure that I should stay at work. I usually stay because I want to advance myself and I will put in the time to show that I'm worth the advancement, you know? And also just because I'm dedicated to projects I work on. (F-18-02-T-G-10-04-14-05-13-LT)

The costs and risks of such a strategy are shifted to the individual, who may be deprived of wages to no avail. VGDs—and testers even more so—struggle on with scarcely any protection, hoping that they will not collapse, burn out, or lose their job, and that they will have enough savings or helpful friends to compensate for any lost income. As developers gain experience, they become more critical of the invasiveness of their work:

> ▸ I have trouble seeing myself working until I'm fifty-five or sixty in this field, a kind of aging adolescent. There's the stress that

comes with it, but I don't know if it's just because we're one of the first generations to do it for a long time. ... Then there's also the fact that now there are people coming in who are five, ten, fifteen years younger than me ... twenty-five-year-olds who are super happy to be in the field because they go home and all they do is play videogames and they have no life, no kids. It's two totally different realities. (M-06-15-M-W-20-11-14-13-15-19-MSO)

Across the surveys, VGDs were asked whether any sacrifices they made for the job were worth it. They seem increasingly less inclined to tolerate the sacrifices asked of them, working against the passion argument, and less prone to stay at work and do overtime of their own free will or initiative.

Working Time as a Source of Physical Health Risk: Where Do We Call for Dinner, Team?

Besides their material insecurity, game developers face considerable health risks that are largely tied to the long hours and the "crunch time" culture (Legault and Ouellet 2012; Legault and Weststar 2017). As we will explore more in Chapter 9, unlimited, unpaid overtime (UUO) is by far the biggest problem mentioned by VGDs. The high-commitment ethos and the "iron triangle" constraint of the "closed budget envelope" created by project management results in extreme working time regimes regarding both the amount of working time and its unpredictability (Blagoev et al. 2018; O'Carroll 2015; O'Riain 2000; Reid 2015). UUO is a risk factor for accidents and disorders attributable to fatigue, from burnout to more serious conditions (Amar 2007; Burke 2009; Burke and Fiskenbaum 2009; I. Campbell 2002a, 2002b; Dembe 2009; Jacobs and Gerson 2001; Kanai 2009; Legault and Belarbi-Basbous 2006; Legault and Chasserio 2014; Pereira 2009).

Research in occupational health has made significant progress based on the demand-control model (Karasek and Theorell 1990), a theoretical apparatus that enables international and intersectoral comparisons of stress-related work problems. In accordance with this model, a greater workload (quantitatively and qualitatively, physical and mental) coupled with less job control leads to an increase in workers' stress, but social support and job recognition can attenuate the pernicious effects (Gonzalez-Mulé and Cockburn 2017; Pinto, Dawood, and Pinto 2014). Job control refers to control over decision-making: the ability to use your skills to solve an issue or technical problem, and the ability to choose how and when to do your work and take part in making decisions about it (Karasek and

Table 4.9
Distribution of answers (% of respondents) to perceptions of job demands and job control (2014 and 2019)

	Agree		Neutral		Disagree	
	2014	2019	2014	2019	2014	2019
I have creative freedom in my work.	58	65	20	18	21	17
I often do not know what is going on outside of my immediate work area.	44	43	22	18	35	38
I never finish one thing before I'm pulled away to do something else.	30	34	25	26	45	40
I have more work to do than time to do it.	49	57	30	19	20	24

Source: Original data from IGDA DSS 2014, 2019

Theorell 1990). Job control is very important to mental health because it can serve as a buffer against a quantitative or qualitative work overload, yet it is cruelly lacking in project situations.

Among VGDs, being overworked has both physical effects, due to long hours, and psychological effects, as developers are encouraged to become subjects who are proactive, individually responsible, passionate, flexible, and good team members. This is both quantitative and qualitative, as you not only have to work your allotted hours, you must also make the project succeed in the end. To meet their obligation of results (see Chapter 2), project employees rely mostly on putting in more working time. It is a powerful pressure towards self-discipline and self-regulation.

As we see in responses to questions about job demands and job control in the 2014 and 2019 surveys, the work of game development is far from the ideal of an open-ended creative sandbox driven by artistic rhythms (see Table 4.9).

Such considerable demands are not always counterbalanced by decision-making power in terms of the organization of the work, and never with respect to attendance at work or arranging work hours. Among professional, technical, and artistic fields, we assume that jobs come with commensurate control over the work process. However, VGDs do not enjoy much job control (Legault and Weststar 2017). Firstly, this is due to the pervasive control of the client, publisher, or funder (see Chapters 2, 3, and 6), and secondly, to constraints of working in often large interdisciplinary teams coordinated from above under the principles of project management, a discipline that has its own provisions to pursue efficiency and control uncertainty (Fournier and Grey 2000; see also Chapters 2 and 3). The game production process is planned by producers and then broken down into tasks, often of very short duration, parcelled out to various workers. As a result, these workers do not generally have an overview of the game design and see themselves, in some ways, as mere "doers." One of our interviewees was blunt about the lack of stimulation, variety, and scope in his current job: "I take the game and I see whether the blue princess was put in the right place. It's pretty passive" (M-12-16-13-M-B-24-10-13-13-19-15-JL).

Some VGDs enjoy some job control in certain postings, but most have more of an alleged and circumscribed control, coupled with a huge responsibility for success. This should not be confused with autonomy. Instead, it is a weapon that can be used against them if a project fails, which increases the stress attributable to feeling powerless.

This risk of "overuse" increases with regular overtime, whether paid or not (Vézina et al. 2011, 97). Researchers in the French school of "psychodynamics of work" have referred to the notion of the "overuse" of workers (Dejours 2000), using it first to explain musculoskeletal disorders in terms of the wear and tear incurred from the excessive use of some biological functions. The concept is now also applied to mental and psychological functions to explain permanent stress, depression, psychosomatic disorders, psychological decompensation, workaholism, and burnout. VGDs suffer from both: musculoskeletal disorders related to the use of computers and psychological overuse. Given the constant pace of work, respondents fear fatigue, and wear and tear:

> ▶ But I don't know how much longer I'm going to be accepted as a legit member of staff. ... You see this old man walking to the door, it's like, "Oh dear." So, that's the sad aspect of it. There's also the burnout aspect. It's like, "Can I keep this up for as long as I am?" ... I actually interviewed this one guy back in the UK, must have been about seven or eight years ago, and his resumé was amazing. It's like, "Oh my God, he's worked on everything that I love. This guy must be an awesome coder..." But he was washed out. He couldn't answer any of my questions. ... I felt like he was tired and just couldn't do it anymore. And shit, is this what's going to happen to me? (M-14-15-V-N-21-10-14-14-26-AD)

Excessive demand may also result from a VGD being given multiple assignments on competing projects. Our data suggest that this is the case for 40 to 60 percent of developers, regardless of whether they are salaried employees, freelancers, or self-employed (Weststar and Legault 2015, 2016; Weststar, O'Meara, and Legault 2018; Weststar, Kwan, and

Kumar 2019). As a result, they end up working longer hours, nights, and weekends, at the office or at home. There is a high risk of role ambiguity and conflict in such a situation in which VGDs are often left on their own with the difficult task of arbitrating between competing responsibilities. Whereas the natural rhythm of a project would normally allow for a break after delivery, professionals working on more than one project do not get a break, because the end of one project may coincide with the critical phase of another. Emerging research also points to the increased risk of being overworked that comes with the new "live" games or games-as-a-service production model, in which there is no defined project end date (Weststar and Dubois 2022).

To sum up, when workers are subject to a constant stream of challenges and the project is understaffed in order to "to eliminate dead periods" and maximize time worked, they suffer from high job demands coupled with limited real job control. This leads to an increase in workers' physiological and psychological stress, which is not always attenuated by job recognition, and which runs the risk of making them ill. Research findings on the specific occupational health risks of VGDs are scarce—most existing health research is focused on young (extreme) gamers (Huard Pelletier et al. 2020) or consists of general studies of high screen use and sedentary occupational tasks. This lack of specific research and advocacy considerably constrains progress on protection.

Working Time as a Source of Social Health Risk: No Country for Parents!

The pressure resulting from long working hours and unpredictable schedules beyond one's control (Legault and Weststar 2015b) jeopardizes social life and creates an imbalance between work and private life that, in turn, has an impact on both mental health (ISQ 2013) and physical health, including life expectancy (Gonzalez-Mulé and Cockburn 2017; K. Powell 2017). Moreover, each pregnancy and parental leave constitutes lost momentum in the constant learning and updating process (more under "Work as a Privileged Training Venue," below).

While we can see that taking time for oneself and for one's social life has gained legitimacy, the pressure to sacrifice one's family life to work in this environment still prevails. The simple fact of having a family is known to be an inconvenience and a disadvantage for VGDs. In 2014, we asked whether VGDs were worried that time spent with their family could hinder their advancement or professional progression. Though half said no, 32 percent did have these worries, and 18 percent selected "neither agree nor disagree." This proportion was slightly lower in the 2019 data, in which 24 percent were worried and 19 percent neither agreed nor disagreed. Studio management demands a level of flexibility from VGDs that is difficult to reconcile with family life:

> ▸ Yeah, [having a family] would definitely be difficult. I mean, I see a lot of people at my studio who are exactly at that point now, where they have kids and spouses. And it does seem to be a bit of a struggle with the hours and the uncertainty of it all. Because, of course, they don't know for sure if they're staying late; that can be hard. And your job sort of depends sometimes on you putting in extra hours, which I think can be very difficult with a family. (F-11-23-V-U-24-09-13-10-23 SM)

Given the fact that those who are not worried might be nulliparous (that is, not having children), this is a rather dramatic finding. Consistently, in 2014, more than half of VGDs surveyed were partnered (22 percent) or married (35 percent), but 38 percent were still single. It can also be seen that throughout the entire study period (2004 to 2019), parents are a minority among a mostly nulliparous group, with a slight increase in 2019 (see Table 4.10 in the Data Appendix). In 2014 and 2019, a minority of the parents had young children (see Table 4.11 in the Data Appendix).

The intensity of work cuts into free time, and VGDs who are parents are unhappy that their personal lives suffer. They do not have enough time for themselves, for everyday living (Legault and Weststar 2015a, 108–16). Their families and friends are frustrated that work takes up all their free time (Peticca-Harris, Weststar, and McKenna 2015). Across the surveys there is a consistent majority who feel that they are always behind, both at work and at home, with never enough time for either (see Table 4.12 in the Data Appendix).

In 2014, we asked VGDs whether they were worried that time spent with family could hinder their advancement or the progress of their careers. Though half said no, 32 percent did have these worries and 18 percent selected "neither agree nor disagree." This proportion was slightly lower in the 2019 data, in which 24 percent were worried and 19 percent neither agreed nor disagreed.

Having a child is an employment risk for women who leave the workforce for pregnancy. The right to parental leave is acknowledged, but in practice it is not a priority because it can get in the way of the needs of the project. Some (larger) studios, offer employment stability in this case. Yet even when maintaining their employment relationship, pregnant women risk the disapproval of producers or peers. It is hard to fit a pregnancy leave around a project, and it is difficult to schedule and plan for a replacement. Depending on the context surrounding the leave, such a decision can diminish the trust of peers, and thus cause a rupture in the their network, limiting their opportunities in the replacement process. We have seen how the "emergency" context of projects requires a high level of commitment, in terms of intensity, personal engagement, and time dedicated to work:

> Structurally, research has also pointed to the preponderance of youthful, able-bodied people in these fields, marked gender inequalities, high levels of educational achievement ... and to the relative lack of caring responsibilities undertaken by people involved in this kind of creative work in ways that might lend support to Beck's arguments about individualization as a "compulsion," the drive in capitalism towards a moment in which subjects can work unfettered by relationships or family. (Gill and Pratt 2008, 21)

The industry is not structured to be supportive of home and family lives, and fosters a working time regime that relies heavily on the domestic and reproductive labour of the partners and spouses of developers (Bulut 2020a; Dyer-Witheford and de Peuter 2009, 63; Peticca-Harris, Weststar, and McKenna 2015). Developers resort to individualized solutions that draw on their positions of privilege—a stay-at-home spouse, paid care, the support of extended family members, negotiated flexible hours, or a progressive employer. It is much more difficult for women than it is for men, as Bulut (2020a) explains, because women are seldom able to count on a stay-at-home spouse, which can be a key factor to maintaining a family life.

Finally, while career advancement often requires a propensity to relocate for work, a worker may refuse employment opportunities out of consideration of their family life. Moving abroad for work while the family stays at home is not an easy solution either. In this, parents face greater mobility hurdles than nulliparous workers. These factors add up to create significant barriers in an industry in which both professional and pay advancement rely on mobility, commitment, and sacrifice. Long and unpredictable working hours push some VGDs—mostly women—to leave the industry as a protective measure when they have children. People who enjoy or need private time, particularly mothers of young children, are often compelled to desert project-based fields (Chasserio and Legault 2009; Legault and Chasserio 2012). This consideration was top of mind for many developers; for one male developer, children were not part of his plan:

> It's a young people's industry, too; I mean, if you have family and children and stuff, and, you know, you think you're going to be working long hours a lot of the time, then that's definitely something to take into consideration. ... I don't really plan on having kids. (M-16-05-V-E-24-09-13-10-23-JT)

The longer they stay in the industry, the more trapped they become because their resumés become too slanted toward games to allow a shift in career, even to a related job. This risk is higher with more specialized jobs:

> There are days when I'd chuck it all in, but the thing is, my experience is really in videogames. I don't know if I'd be able to [transfer] that experience to another field. ... I look into it when I start getting sick of it all. (M-06-15-M-W-20-11-14-13-15-19-MSO)

Having a family can also mean that a worker may not consider filling a higher-level job because of the longer hours of work required. Some seek employment at studios where they know the work is more reasonable, but this choice represents career compromises, as this work is often in less glamorous sectors of the industry—educational games, games for hire, or advertising—or part of studios whose focus is not just on games.

Teamwork Is Not Negotiable

A recurrent theme in contemporary game development practice relates to "knowledge architecture" and the flow of ideas in game production. This includes the inspiration of original game ideas (Hagen 2012), how ideas transform during the process (Tschang and Szczypula 2006), and how ideas are formed in the interplay between different development groups (Cohendet and Simon 2007; Lê, Massé, and Paris 2013; Simon 2006; Wang and Nordmark 2015). The creative endeavours in game development involve collaboration:

> The sources of creativity, as well as efficiency at [the studio], rely on a subtle alchemy among communities of scriptwriters, game-designers, graphic artists, sound designers, software programmers and even testers. The team is important for the creative process. (Cohendet and Simon 2007, 591)

> The auteur tradition, which is strong in the movie industry, has very limited support in the game industry ... the empirical studies on game development provide a relatively uniform picture: that

creativity is achieved through a collaborative, test-driven process. (Marklund et al. 2019, 188)

The unpredictability and changing nature of requirements necessitates iterative working processes (Schmalz, Finn, and Taylor 2014). Constant team communication (Land and Wilson 2006; Tran and Biddle 2008) and testing (Cohendet and Simon 2007; Kasurinen, Maglyas, and Smolander 2014; Tran and Biddle 2008; Walfisz, Zackariasson, and Wilson 2006) are essential—though costly—means of scoping out and identifying requirements as production progresses.

Conflicts may occur among designers, artists, and programmers because game designers and artists, on the *creative* side, generally try to include features that improve the gameplay and the overall look and feel of the game, but that present challenges for the *technical* side to implement. The latter may come to distrust their peers, whose creativity could seem detached from realistic implementation (Alves, Ramalho, and Damasceno 2007; Bulut 2020a: 18; Kasurinen and Smolander 2014; Simon 2006; Stacey and Nandhakumar 2009). The final game is inevitably the result of trade-offs among creative design and technical, budget, and platform constraints (Alves, Ramalho, and Damasceno 2007, 279; Marklund et al. 2019, 191).

In such a conflict-prone environment, team cohesion and interdisciplinary collaboration are paramount in the success of the development process: it has been argued that frequent and open knowledge sharing (Cohendet and Simon 2007; Llerena, Burger-Helmchen, and Cohendet 2009) and continuous informal dialogue (Tran and Biddle 2008) are more realistic strategies than planning (Cohendet and Simon 2007; Murphy-Hill, Zimmermann, and Nagappan 2014; Tran and Biddle 2008; Wang and Nordmark 2015).

However, there are many barriers to (indispensable) knowledge sharing. Given that knowledge evolves rapidly and is not widely codified and documented, VGDs have access to it through informal communication networks, as long as they are willing to share it. Ideally, they do so within the project team and their studio. In terms of personnel management, this means that the conditions of knowledge sharing must be clearly established.

Knowledge management can remain informal or be formal. A formal system could be a pool of knowledge to which employees are expected to contribute, post-mortem analyses of projects, or a logbook. Nevertheless, knowledge-management systems persistently face implementation challenges in which workers must be urged to contribute to management-controlled pools, particularly among the knowledge workers in the private sector (Legault 2008; Pemsel, Müller, and Söderlund 2016). Knowledge-pooling plans encourage employees who do not *a priori* feel an affinity for one another or for working together, who may feel they are working toward purposes that escape them, or who do not ensure any reciprocity in the exchange of knowledge (Robertson, Scarbrough, and Swan 2003; Robertson and O'Malley Hammersley 2000; Swan, Scarbrough, and Robertson 2002). Unlike employer-driven initiatives, communities of practice are peer-to-peer practices in which the group keeps control over the content as well as the spread of the exchanges; experts know to whom and to what extent they are disclosing vital information. Consequently, communities of practice have more success among practitioners subjected to competition in the job market.

Of course, VGDs commonly share knowledge within project teams and with peers throughout the course of their work, without keeping any written record or putting anything at managers' disposal. However, sharing is subjected to discretionary decision-making and workers' individual quirks. While some experienced developers claim that the industry's rigid IP regime produces "cultures of secrecy" among VGDs and prevents a collaborative and sharing-based work culture (O'Donnell 2014, 12–20), the importance of competition and of reputation are worth noting as well (Bulut 2020a, 166). A very specific and sophisticated body of knowledge is what makes a VGD valuable in the job market, in which their know-how and problem-solving skills confer upon them a position within the organization and constitute a significant tradable asset (Scarbrough 1999, 11–12). As the issue of know-how is crucial to mobile VGDs when bargaining over their wages, it is not surprising to see them protect their exclusive and (relatively) hermetic knowledge.

Indeed, the motivation to contribute to the employer's "knowledge bank" is far less than the motivation towards client satisfaction (Alvesson 2000, 1,109–11).

Work as a Privileged Training Venue

For VGDs, as in the cultural industry broadly, the benefits of exposure to diverse projects and production challenges are extremely valuable (Bellini et al. 2018, 3). This is the standard way of increasing one's knowledge, problem-solving capacity, experience, and overall reputational worth. When VGDs are looking for a new project, one of their selection criteria is often the extent of professional development involved. They tend to prefer an assignment that will serve their need to learn, not just make use of their acquired skills.

In principle, the HR department (if present) bears responsibility for the organization's long-term survival, while the producer focuses on a project's immediate success (Palm and Lindahl 2015). Yet these interests often clash, notably when producers face an emergency. Given the paramount importance of projects, producers often enjoy the upper hand. Many a producer will insist on retaining a developer for their current skills, regardless of the developmental opportunities that may arise. This introduces a professional development dilemma in which the interests of the developer and the producer diverge radically. Such barriers to advancement are a common motivation for VGDs to leave a job.

The process of project assignment becomes highly competitive and can give rise to confrontations and behaviours of zealous commitment. High stakes are reinforced because VGDs are part of the high-tech sector in which the risk of obsolescence is pervasive (Tarnoff 2018). Poor job assignments compound the risk of obsolescence. VGDs have "no choice" but to keep up with the "extremely exponential" changes in the industry or risk becoming "old fogeys" (M-12-16-04-M-W-10-10-13-13-19-15-JL):

> ▶ I think it's a tech-related field; there's a lot of importance being placed on being young, because being young is often associated with being innovative, so I think that may eventually become an issue. ... But I also know well-established people in the game industry, who are in their early to mid-forties, and they're very highly regarded and respected, so... (F-03-07-V-F-12-19-13-14-26-LT)

Ambitious VGDs do everything they can to get assigned to the most prestigious projects with the best opportunities for learning. This attitude reinforces the cycle of mobility in the industry:

> ▶ I think working on a bunch of different genres and types of games and different projects themselves is really important, and I think that working with a lot of different studios is really important as well, because the quicker you can get used to working with different types of people and different types of demands, I feel this ensures career longevity. (F-01-19-V-B-27-11-13-14-26-PB)

Developers are continually weighing the risks and rewards of signing on to or staying with certain projects:

> ▶ The other risk is, in this industry, if you're developing an expertise in one area, it means you could be pigeonholing yourself. So, if

you're working on social games, and you know a lot about that, it could be very difficult getting a job doing anything else. (M-05-07-V-M-26-11-13-14-26-PB)

> Sometimes, foreseeing the direction [technology] will change in means that if you misjudge that direction, you could be accepting a job or working on a project that is going to have no legs. Meaning, you're working on a project for a year, two years, and then by the time you're ready to ship or launch, the platform or the technology is obsolete, and the newest and the greatest thing that has come out is totally different. That's definitely a risk. (M-05-07-V-M-26-11-13-14-26-PB)

Employment insecurity and fear of obsolescence are compounded by aging. Though the industry's workforce is slowly aging, the stigma of age manifested itself among our interviewees. A large share of developers worried about their capability to succeed in the industry as an older worker:

> I'm an old person in this industry. And I don't know whether there's a stigma attached to an old person. So, I went to this one interview, and I completely breezed through the interview; it was the simplest questions. But the guy interviewing me was just out of college; he was twenty something. ... And I was thinking: I'm obviously going to get an offer, and I didn't. ... I'm guessing I wasn't considered because maybe I was too old or "have [an] attitude problem." I don't know. That's something you can do when you ask someone, "Would you want to work with this guy?" and he's, like, "No I don't think so." And you can't really get a way into that interview process. ... I'm wondering if this is going to be a problem for me because the games industry is very young. (M-14-15-V-N-21-10-14-14-26-AD)

An industry based on youthful activities, a high degree of socialization, and shared cultural touch points (Weststar 2015) can be hard to access for people who may be perceived as being unable to "fit in," due to their socio-demographic characteristics. Discretionary hiring processes exacerbate this risk (see Chapter 6). Another interviewee said that more experienced workers can demand higher pay than younger workers, and this may explain resistance to hiring them:

> You can't really be a programmer at fifty. I'm getting close to forty, and forty to fifty is, like... I have to move into management

or it's going to be really hard for me to find work. Because my rate will be really high and then it always boils down to what we could hire... You know... one other person who's just barely made senior and four juniors for your rate, so... You have to move into management. (M-19-20-T-M-22-05-14-05-13-JT)

In this way, the tendency in game studios to hire on demand can work for some senior and highly specialized developers who are picked up for specific tasks on specific projects. However, the higher price tag is often not worth it for management when faced with a large reserve of young, malleable labour, particularly for non-specialist roles. The industry's attitude toward age and aging still reflects a very young mindset. For some of our respondents, the reference point for "old" was just forty years, and, to them, it seemed a novelty that forty-year-olds could still do their jobs:

> ▸ I would like to work in this industry as long as I can. ... But this industry is so ... new that we don't have retirees—seniors, right? And so, by the time we're all forty, we might still be working—be relevant, right? ... The oldest people I've ever worked with were on the cusp of forty, and so ... in my head it's, like, "Oh God, when I hit forty..." ... There are certain people who are over forty who work in this industry and do their jobs perfectly. (F-07-04-T-X-27-05-14-04-11-JT)

Conclusion

In this chapter, we have challenged the portrait of the passionate developer who is not working so much as "playbouring" (Kücklich 2005) in a stimulating environment that is a flagship of the anti-bureaucratic movement. Though not always happy, VGDs are supposed to engage in projects as an entrepreneur might, rather than bearing the plight of adversarial relationships with exploitative employers. They exemplify what Neff (2012) has called "venture labour,"[3] with the VGI becoming a flagship of the "creativity dispositif" that has "bypassed normal work entitlements" (McRobbie 2018, 146; see also Larusso 2019, for discussion of the "entreprecariat").

But VGDs have many working problems. Based on the democratic aim of citizenship at work, the demographic structure in the VGI shows that

---

3. The term "venture labour" refers to the coined term "venture capital" and its inherent risk component. It also refers to the adoption of entrepreneurial values by non-entrepreneurs, telling the tale of workers in the New York internet industry during the 1990s and the beginning of the 21st century, who embraced the inherent risk of the trade as something as "cool" and "desirable" as an adventure.

women and members of racialized groups face obstacles that make them stand out as second-class citizens in the VGI. They are underrepresented, they lack critical mass, and they face overt discrimination, including harassment (see Chapter 10).

VGDs put up with "rampant crunch time due to bad management, the discourse of passion normalizing overwork and self-exploitation, lack of studio stability, large-scale contract employment, unpaid overtime, lack of comprehensive health care and poor crediting practices" (Arndt 2018). These features put them at risk of losing their job, their employability, and eventually their income.

Besides observing these problems, we noted that VGDs must cope with discretionary decision-making, a lack of equity and diversity, waiving their IP, health-related problems, and poor coverage when retirement comes.

Flexibility practices and the playful studio are often a guise through which neo-normative managerial control mechanisms impose self-regulation on game workers. This self-regulation, indeed, is not imposed from above, but is rather part of the project management professional ethos that VGDs claim to embody (Legault and Chasserio 2012). The requirement that they be highly mobile means they are considerably dependent on their network of immediate and future colleagues, clients, and managers to secure a position, get training to maintain current and future employability, and keep an eye on future job prospects to stay "on top" in the relentless placement process. In this they are individuals, and they lack protection. Their market value depends on their use value for clients and teams. They are forced to consent and commit to "given" conditions in their environment, while the real decision-maker remains out of reach in a financialized context.

What about citizenship at work in such a context? Do VGDs have access to any of the four key objects of industrial citizenship (see Table 1.1) to mitigate these risks or shape different alternatives? VGDs are very mobile—can they be citizens in any workplace? Could they be citizens in their industry or trade? These questions will be interrogated across Chapters 5 to 10, paying attention to the specific objects (that is, the risks and issues that are addressed), subjects (that is, the VGDs who have citizenship with respect to these risks), and domains (that is, which risks and issues are relevant to having a meaningful and participatory voice, which VGDs have access to that voice, and which territories facilitate that voice?).

PART THREE
Applied Analysis

CHAPTER 5

Are Game Developers Protected against Employment Risks?

In the previous chapter, we reviewed some important factors relating to the risk of losing employment income that are germane to VGDs. These help us to understand that project-based workers like VGDs face risks in a unique way when compared to employees in bureaucratic organizations. They have the same potential objects of citizenship in that they encounter similar events (firing or layoffs, occupational injury or illness, pregnancy, parenting, or retirement), but they do not face them at the same pace, nor in the same context. This means that these workers may cope with these risks in different ways and encounter different domains of citizenship (or not) regarding protection and recourse.

Historically, the share of risk individually assumed by workers has been limited by the establishment of permanent, full-time employment with a single employer and by the institutional developments of major legislative protection, collective bargaining, and a social safety net funded by income taxes and/or contributions by employers and workers. In this the responsibility for providing protection against the risk of lost income has been shared by employers, employees, and the state. Now, against the backdrop of the new corporate context described in this book, employers are looking for more "employment flexibility," that is, more "at-will employment," and hiring and firing according to business needs.

Centring on the first object of citizenship (see Table 1.1), this chapter examines how risk is distributed along the value chain in the project-based work environment of videogame development and evaluates the resources on which VGDs rely for protection against the various risks of lost income outlined in Chapter 4: physical and psychosocial risks, pregnancy and parenthood, aging, and unemployment.

A Theoretical Framework of Risk Transfer

Both the technological services sector and the game development sector experience a high level of commercial risk in a competitive international market characterized by constant innovation and capricious clients. Organizational forms have undergone a profound ideological change, from bureaucracy to the post-bureaucratic network organization wherein workers occupy a very different position in the employment relationship (see Chapter 1). Since the end of the twentieth century, young people have enthusiastically joined a new and risky start-up job market and see the risks they take as natural and nearly routine. New entrepreneurial subjects were born, fostering "a casual, even positive, attitude toward losing one's job" and "cultural messages about the attractiveness of risk"; risk was becoming "cool" (Neff 2012, 3; see also McRobbie 2016). This framing stems from the supposed need to staff new, risky businesses in a flexible way but is not devoid of consequences.

This chapter builds on the literature about how the contemporary economic environment, including the post-bureaucratic organizational landscape, has set up a "risk society" (Beck 1992, 1999; Giddens 1990, 1991; Lupton 1999; McCluskey 2002; Neff 2012; O'Malley 2004). We argue that the commercial risk in the VGI and the responsibility to mitigate the consequences of risk are being passed down the supply chain to VGDs. For workers, this manifests as the risk of losing one's employment income. With the help of financialization strategies, factors of risk avoidance have become features of the contemporary "fissured workplace" (see Chapter 3), with negative ramifications for workers and society (Weil 2014).

We use a previously published model of risk transfer through the deregulation of working time (Legault 2013). This was developed with respect to the technological services industry but applies to the VGI, since it combines the risk management strategy of networked firms with project management as an organization mode (see Chapter 2). In short, to deal with high commercial uncertainty, venture capital counts on two important conditions: easy international mobility according to state-based incentives and risk transfer down the value chain. Situated immediately down the chain, studios must deal with this risk. The three components of the contractual "iron triangle" (scope, budget, and schedule) constitute three strikes against planning and represent risks for the studio as an intermediate actor: neither the scope of the unique product nor the time required can be foreseen; however, they both will affect the amount of labour required, which is the main cost dominating the budget. Project management is an organizational approach to risk management. It is based on a system of flexible resource allocation and relies on the deregulation of working time as a risk management strategy with respect to the cost of human resources. In turn, studios transfer the risk to workers, who are the ones to bear the burden of on-demand hiring and firing, and unlimited and unpaid overtime. These act as a buffer against financial risk to the studio.

Project management is an efficient device to bring people into this environment, because of the professional ethos it carries (Legault and Chasserio 2012). In the VGI, if a game is a hit, developers will be able to share in it through bonuses, time off, and favourable future postings. Yet if it is a failure, they are the ones who bear all the costs of the risk through foregone earnings, adverse effects of being overworked, and lost employment (Burke and Fiskenbaum 2009; Legault and Belarbi-Basbous 2006).

Studios are disengaged from the protection of VGDs against risk of lost income and do not commit to their economic security. Without employer-based policies tailored to the workplace, the material security of unemployed workers in the project-based economy relies, at best, on government policies as a collective intermediary. However, these are often minimal and reserved only for salaried employees, and are not available to freelance or self-employed VGDs. Otherwise, VGDs must rely on individual savings or social support networks and hope for individually determined compensation such as severance packages. But these packages are often only available as a privilege (Quilgars and Abbott 2000; Taylor-Gooby 2004).

The lack of employer-based or private collective intermediary protection systems is part of a deficit in citizenship at work, as workers must rely on themselves without a commitment from their employer to their economic security. Consequent of the risk transfer practices among venture capital providers, individual workers tend to be more entrepreneurs of their own careers, even when they have the legal status of salaried employees (Beck 1992; Neff 2012).

Protection against the Risk of Losing Your Job

Faced with this employment insecurity, how are VGDs protected? How do the unemployed pay their bills? In this section, we will examine state and employer provisions, as well as the activities in which game developers engage to protect themselves.

Reliance on State or Employer Benefits

Social security systems and employment-related legal protection differ across countries; some workers in the global VGI have no access to state-based social security for unemployment (Social Security Association 2018a, 2018b, 2019a, 2019b).

In our interviews, 59 percent of respondents said that if they were not earning money, they would live on state-provided employment insurance (EI), and 51 percent of respondents said they would rely on their savings. Some of these respondents said that they did both because the maximum benefits under the Canadian EI scheme are much lower than their pay. Those who said they would not apply for EI gave various reasons, the likelihood of each closely related to their citizenship at work status and/or their political citizenship status. For instance, migrant workers who obtain work permits connected to a specific job are ineligible for EI in Canada. Some Canadian citizens or permanent residents do not have workplace citizenship rights to these universal programs. For example, freelancers and the self-employed are ineligible because the Canadian EI system is based on payroll deductions from both employers and employees to which the self-employed and freelancers do not typically contribute.[1] As well, part-time employees only become eligible if they have accumulated the required number of hours for their geographic region.

In many instances, our interviewees were able to obtain a severance package sufficient to tide them over until they found their next job. In this, they relied on the basic minimums for severance pay provided through common law and the employment standards regime, coupled with any individual bargaining power that they could bring to bear on their employer to gain a "top-up." The experience of a developer who faced two bouts of unemployment in one year is illustrative of the variability:

> ▶ [In] January 2011 I was laid off by [the studio]. They shut down the whole studio. Ended up getting a great severance payment, though, and basically sat around and enjoyed myself for a couple of months before looking for more work. And then roughly, let's say, nine months later, I was laid off again in December by the new company I was working for. ... [The severance payment was] enough to basically keep me going for the time that I was looking for new work. (M-16-05-V-E-24-09-13-10-23-JT)

The last and arguably most privileged group of our interviewees said that they were eligible for EI but did not apply for it because they counted on other resources: partners, families, investments, or savings.

As illustrated by the experience of a developer from Toronto, over the course of a career, VGDs may rely on a range of strategies, and some actively use a period of unemployment to recharge and retrain:

> ▶ Being a full-time employee, I do have employment insurance. My previous job was as a contract employee, so I really didn't. It was very risky. I did not enjoy being a contract employee. And my

---

1. As of 2011, self-employed persons in Canada may register for a program in which they pay EI premiums in exchange for access to select parts of the EI system.

> spouse is also a software engineer, so we have a fairly solid income and are both good at tucking away—because it is a sad truth in the industry that tomorrow [the studio] could shut down. ... we've had a lot of public layoffs, like 500 employees and 300 employees. We never know what's coming and also you're just, "Oh shit, John's gone!" So that's nerve-racking. But at the same time, the compensation that they give those employees that they layoff is [good], like, six-months-pay. ... You don't want to take the whole time, [but] you've got the income for it to kind of recharge, look at new technology, figure out what you want to do. So it's kind of nice. (F-18-07-T-Z-28-04-14-04-11-JT)

By carrying out these activities, these workers take advantage of what social citizenship rights they do have to state protection, but in the end, with a few exceptions, the employer is not involved in the process. Strategies to mitigate future employment insecurity and the outcomes of those strategies are individual.

Some were able to negotiate their terms of leaving above and beyond statutory benefits, but these remain "privileges" instead of the outcomes of policies. Interviewees spoke of their own successes and what they had heard others accomplish. These included obtaining computers and software programs to facilitate skill retention and retraining when out of work, promised bonuses related to the game's performance in part or in full, or company shares or dividends. However, these deals are made in secret. Many developers do not know that they have the right to negotiate or may not have the social capital to be successful. It amazed one of our interviewees when he learned what his friend once asked for—"You said that? ... Wow." And he attributed the ultimate success to his friend's unique skill and value: "He's good." (M-02-04-M-U-17-10-13-13-19-15-MSO)

To avoid any surprises, some VGDs can anticipate the financial hardships of their studios and plan their exits accordingly. By leaving a little earlier or staying a little longer, they can turn voluntary quitting into an economic layoff and enjoy any associated benefits. Such was the case of one veteran programmer who was ready to leave the industry because of concerns over work–life balance:

> ▸ Well, in my case it was planned. I was laid off in early February and my plan was to leave the company in mid-March, so I actually asked to be laid off when it happened. The company was working on a project for a publisher in Japan, and in late January, the publisher said that they were shutting down all the projects—all their foreign projects or anything not taking place in Japan, they were

shutting it down. And the next few days, it became pretty clear that the company wasn't doing very well. So, I talked to the project director and I said, "Look, there's going to be layoffs for sure and I'll be leaving the company anyway. So, if there're layoffs, I want to be part of that." (M-05-14-L-D-22-07-13-10-23-JT)

In some cases, studios have an incentive to retain workers. Thanks to the generous tax credits offered in each of the Canadian hubs (see Chapter 8), the labour costs of game developers are subsidized by the state, but in some instances, certain staffing rates must be maintained to receive the subsidies. This, and the associated costs of recruitment and selection, can act as an incentive for some large game studios to retain developers and assign them to other projects. If employers pay VGDs during undefined idle periods between two projects ("inter-project" or "being on the bench"), VGDs are saved frictional unemployment costs and employers avoid losing their trained developers. It also becomes an opportunity for employers to implement systems for professional development planning. They can document areas where training is needed in the industry and in their own workforce (often at the time of performance evaluations), prepare overviews of the matching of supply and demand, inquire about their employees' plans and desires, plan for the development and training of their employees, and take advantage of the available time between projects for training purposes. This results in more intentional reassignments, rather than hasty decisions made to keep workers busy. However, smaller and more dependent studios are less likely to enjoy the necessary conditions for such planning.

It's Up to You: Maintain a Good Reputation and Network!

We have seen that finding a new job is still considered by workers to be easy, but this sentiment comes with an important caveat that is often taken for granted: VGDs must have a strong network and a good reputation. For 60 percent of our interview respondents, networking was seen as the best way to look for a job and the surest protection against the risk of losing one's job (see Chapters 2 and 4).

In network building, workers are still on their own. VGDs commit considerable leisure time to formal and informal networking activities. These include evening meetups or talks at bars or restaurants sponsored by local gaming groups, fostering positive personal relationships with current and potential co-workers, attending conferences, and active participation in online and social media communities. Developers also frequent mailing lists, recruitment sites, and job boards to keep their eyes on the local market, as well as the national and international scenes. Such activity is deemed essential, and prospective VGDs become socialized to the culture of networking as part of the process of finding their first jobs. Within the playful ethos of the industry, networking over drinks can be seen as fun sociable time, but it is also critical work:

> ▸ I also did a lot of networking when I was at school, because it's hard to get into the industry. A lot, a lot of people want to get in. I said to myself, "I can't fool around. I've got to make contacts while I'm a student." I went on videogame career websites. I met some [locals] and we met up in real life as well. They were programmers studying [at university]. We worked on a common interuniversity project. After that, we stayed friends and we founded a videogame club at [university]. I cofounded the club. ... It's true that for getting in, a lot of it works through contacts. ... A lot of it works by referrals. ... But until you have a few years' experience, it's really very hard to get in. (F-18-02-16-M-W-01-10-13-19-15-JL)

Networking is more important for VGDs who plan to leave their steady jobs to go out on their own:

> ▸ I think one of the things that I do well that's been a big benefit to my career has been being well known. I do a lot of networking, I go to a lot of events, I spend a lot of time on Twitter and contributing to industry debate, I write for a lot of magazines, I talk at conferences. All of those things benefit me in terms of that motivating level of being there and hopefully being seen as someone who's a bit of a thought leader. (M-23-12-V-T-30-10-2013-14-26)

Unemployed developers also need to engage in personal "emotional labour" to keep up their own morale, self-confidence, and perseverance; they rely on their friends, families, and peers in this work as well. A developer from Vancouver explained how she did this work:

> ▸ [Layoffs are] a normal aspect of the industry, and I've kind of taken it upon myself to vocalize that to people. When they're feeling down about stuff, I feel like you have to be aware of that when you get into the industry because there are times when you're out of work more often than not and you're looking for something, networking sort of thing. It takes a special type of attitude to keep your momentum going, and it's just not for everybody. (F-01-19-V-B-27-11-13-14-26-PB)

In a time and space in which there is a lot of game development happening, an extended period of unemployment can look suspicious and can reduce employability. Relying on temporary placement agencies can be useful for quickly finding jobs in the event of layoffs, but VGDs must sacrifice a portion of their salary to the agency in exchange. There is an expectation that you should be working on games on your own even when unemployed; otherwise, you are clearly not committed. Developers told us that they were working on their portfolios all the time:

> ▸ It always seems like people are working on little Flash games or ... iPhone apps and things like that, so if you're laid off, then: "How come you're not working on a little indie game or something like that?" (M-17-13-V-U-25-09-13-10-23-JT)

But at the same time, one must take care not to be too deeply involved:

> ▸ I voluntarily chose to spend probably five months working on my own project. Just to take a shot and be entrepreneurial. But afterwards, I definitely had trouble finding a job—I think because I hadn't worked for a while. (M-02-01-T-S-08-06-14-05-13-JT)

Some developers had a strategy of freelancing across cognate industries such as film or visual effects so as not to put all their eggs in one basket. If worst came to worst, our respondents told us that they would lower their expectations and look for work down the occupational hierarchy—namely in game testing. After looking for a design job for three years, one Montreal developer devised a plan to offer himself as a one-stop QA shop for all the smaller studios in the area. Yet the strategy is risky, because, in his case, "when people start doing QA, they start to have a QA resumé and they're only hired for QA" (F-05-08-19-M-G-21-10-13-13-19-15-JL). For current and prospective game workers, testing and QA can be a trap that dangles the carrot of upward mobility and job stability, but rarely delivers (Bulut 2020a).

The myth of the indie studio, particularly among programmers, is that you can always go it alone or start a small studio. Some seem blissfully unaware of how difficult it can be to succeed on the indie scene. Others know that it might impede their ability to get another job, particularly if they lose contacts, lose touch with emerging technology, or have little to show for their time. Again, the availability of this option varies for developers depending on their occupation or discipline. One game designer told us about her own employment insecurity, which contrasts greatly with her subsequent story about her programmer friends:

> I feel less secure about [starting my own studio], because I don't really think I'll find another job easily in my field. I feel more secure [working at a company]. It's hard in game design. It's very much based on experience and you have to have worked on good projects. Otherwise, you have no credibility. I've got friends who've left really well-paid jobs to start up their own companies. ... They are getting a grant for one project, and after that project, I don't know what's going to happen. It will probably depend on how successful their project is. They're all programmers, to be honest, and I get the feeling they have the security of knowing they won't have any trouble finding another job. The jobs they're qualified for are really, really sought after, both in videogames and in other industries. (F-18-02-16-M-W-01-10-13-19-15-JL)

In the end, none of these "strategies" fully protect a game worker against the risk of pay instability. On the contrary, most of them introduce new risks. Most of all, all these strategies fall to VGDs themselves. If workers have not had the foresight or the opportunity to build a financial safety net, even with state unemployment benefits, job loss will mean a dramatic change in lifestyle. Respondents are often reduced to prayer and hope. A developer in Montreal rationalized that if she were ever laid off, her husband would "hopefully have a steady job by then," and maybe it would never happen in her company because "it's a company with a parent company that is pretty diversified ... they might not cut off everything all at once" (F-18-02-16-M-W-01-10-13-19-15-JL). Another developer just lived daily with the risk, knowing that he would be "in deep shit" if he ever lost his job, due to his student debt, which did not allow him the "luxury of being able to save money, build up a safety cushion or whatever" (M-07-22-M-E-20-10-13-13-19-15-JL).

The COVID-19 pandemic was accompanied by an employment crisis through 2020 to 2023 that did not spare the game development sector. Representatives from the labour rights group Game Workers Unite called for more protections:

> With tons of studios being forced to shut their doors for the time being, there are some industry workers left without work, and more importantly without pay. It's an issue the whole economic world is grappling with, as debate rages on over what sort of economic support workers should receive when the companies they work for close up shop during the COVID-19 shutdown. ... On one hand, some studios like EA and Rockstar have set up remote work solutions for their employees, allowing them to continue with

business as usual. On the other hand, GameStop was forcing employees to keep doors open amid COVID-19 concerns earlier this week, telling employees and law enforcement it was an "essential" business. Game Workers Unite is encouraging "everyone to use their voices to call out the companies and regions" that are not providing fair aid to their workers in an effort to help industry "workers cope with the devastating effects of COVID-19." (Smith 2020)

Protection in the Case of Pregnancy or Parental Leave

Our survey data from 2014 and 2019 suggest that 50 to 60 percent of VGDs are covered by some sort of program that protects their job, their income, or both if they become a parent (see Table 5.1). In most countries these programs are government-supported. Some workers, typically unionized ones, can negotiate an employer top-up of the government's financial minimum. We obtained low figures regarding the government programs because US workers are overrepresented in our sample and the United States is a glaring global exception in its lack of pregnancy and parental leave protection. Taken this way, we see a polarization across the industry and the emergence of some exemplary employers. Though less than half of the developers we surveyed received job or income protection from their employer, about 30 percent of them worked for studios that offered some form of paid leave, despite the absence of government programs. A full 35 to 40 percent simply did not know whether they had such protection—a finding reflective of the young workforce, but also its work-first culture.

In the absence of leave policies and supportive norms, some developers saw having children as impossible, while others were unprepared for the extra strain that a family brings. As the industry ages, a few of our interviewees noted that they were seeing a change with respect to family-friendly policies. Usually this was the result of the direct experiences of company owners or managers as they face the reality of having children themselves. However, ending up in such an enlightened studio is purely a matter of luck:

> ▶ [The studio]'s founder had a kid about six months ago and the ... co-owner had a kid about a year ago. ... I think only four or five of the thirty who worked there had children, but it would probably double, at least in the next few years, so [the studio] was intentionally figuring out what it could do to make that more reasonable. It was actually really cool, I think. ... other organizations maybe not so much. (M-15-01-V-K-02-10-13-14-26-LT)

Table 5.1
Distribution of answers (% of respondents) to the question: "Does your employer provide pregnancy and parental leave?" (2014 and 2019)

	Pregnancy leave		Parental leave	
	2014	2019	2014	2019
Don't know	40	32	41	35
Yes, paid by employer	26	31	23	28
Yes, combination of employer and government program	17	16	16	13
Yes, paid by government program*	—	13	—	13
Yes, unpaid by employer	7	4	8	4
No	10	6	13	8

Source: Original data from IGDA DSS 2014, 2019
* This option was not available in the 2014 DSS.

Protection against Health Risks

Burnout is one of the most significant health risks faced by VGDs. Due to its importance as an issue in the VGI, we devote an entire chapter to the regulation of working time (see Chapter 9). Suffice to say here that the most straightforward mechanism for protecting oneself against burnout is to reduce the hours of work. However, VGDs have no formal mechanisms to change the terms of the "iron triangle" enclosed in the project contract; they have no power to extend the deadlines, reduce the scope, or hire additional workers. Even if consulted at the very moment of planning the project, VGDs can hardly protect themselves by providing realistic or buffered estimates with respect to the duration of tasks. Drafted under market pressures, the project schedule is often doomed to fail right from the start. Consultation with developers inevitably results in an underestimate because of wishful thinking, image management, pressure to please the client, and a legitimate inability to accurately predict the duration of a new activity. Very few VGDs can refuse to work overtime.

After bouts of being overworked, VGDs rely on passive forms of citizenship to access regulatory minimum standards relating to vacation time and sick days. Yet even using what the law or the studio permits in a "bad moment" can be reproved by colleagues, so VGDs will often engage in presenteeism instead (see Chapter 4).

Across the IGDA surveys, we asked VGDs about the types of paid time off given by their studios. The majority (60 to 75 percent) reported that their employer offered a packaged policy for all forms of paid time off, while about one-third received separate allocations for sick leave, vacation, and, for some, personal days. Notably, contract workers were rarely entitled to such benefits. As one of our interviewees explained, the legal entitlements and employer good will can be used up in a hurry:

> ▸ I was off for two weeks due to a concussion. ... I was paid for that time, but I ran out of sick pay and I actually came back to work a lot sooner than my doctor recommended, because they said that they would stop paying me, and because I was on contract, I had no short-term disability or any sort of benefits. I don't qualify for any government programs. ... But I didn't have a choice, so I had to come back. ... I was told, when I received the e-mail saying that they were going to stop, that it had been sick pay and they used all my vacation days for the year too. ... It was a surprise to me, that it was my sick days and vacation days all used up at once. (F-03-07-V-F-12-19-13-14-26-LT)

As well, numerous developers spoke of open policies that allowed them to ostensibly "take what time they needed or desired." While seemingly very supportive, in practice such open policies give managers a considerable amount of arbitrary power in making decisions about whether and when a leave is granted. Unfortunately, sick leave and vacation time under these conditions can also slip away if the project needs the labour force. Some of our respondents explained the risks of being sick without adequate protection:

> ▸ There was an artist who was ... fired, because he was unresponsive or unreachable over a few days, a weekend, plus a Friday or a Monday, because he was sick. So, because he wasn't responding to email, wasn't at his laptop, on Skype, or otherwise reachable ... and due to that whole requirement for being online and available 24/7, he was dismissed. He was given two warnings as I understand it.
>
> *During that period of the weekend?*
>
> Yeah. He was sick. He was bedridden—you know, vomiting. (M-01-04-V-D-24-10-13-14-26-AD-JT)

Paid time off can only help protect workers from burnout and in the event of health problems or unexpected life events if it can be taken when needed, rather than when work allows it. Yet the pressure to sacrifice your needs for the sake of the project is widespread. In 2014, survey respondents took, on average, three sick days per year, and 10 percent reported that they took no vacation days (Weststar and Legault 2015, 34). In 2019, 50 percent of the survey respondents received one week or less of paid sick days (12 percent received none) and 25 percent received one week of vacation or less (9 percent had none). In addition, in 2014, 21 percent of developers reported that they had to cancel a vacation already scheduled and 22 percent said that they had been denied vacation time to which they were entitled (Weststar and Legault 2015, 35). The tendency to make sacrifices for a project is particularly prevalent among the self-employed. In 2019, 60 percent of survey respondents said that they had cancelled or rescheduled a vacation due to project demands.

What about Employer-Provided Health or Wellness Programs?

Some developers enjoyed protection against health risks in the form of employer-provided health or wellness programs. Across both the 2014 and 2019 surveys, about a third of respondents had a health care spending account (36 to 38 percent), received on-site medical services such as flu shots (31 to 33 percent), and/or had an employee assistance program (28 to 30 percent). A growing number reported wellness programs in 2019 (21 to 27 percent) and some had access to massages (18 to 21 percent). Indeed, some studios, generally the bigger ones, have very good health plans. As one respondent raved:

> ▸ We checked [our disability insurance] and it's the best on the market. [The only one better] is the government's. It's crazy what they have. I'm diabetic and all my prescriptions are paid for, travel insurance, dentist, dental care, private doctor [at the studio], who's there ten hours a day. ... You've got a massage therapist right there ... paid for by your insurance. Yeah, you've got it all: private room if you have an accident, two trips by ambulance per year. I broke my finger once, playing soccer, and [my co-worker] who was there said, "I'm calling an ambulance. [The studio] pays." (M-02-04-M-U-17-10-13-13-19-15-MSO)

Most VGDs also seem to have access to health insurance in the case of illness (see Table 5.2). However, these totals belie the great variation in the nature and scope of different plans and the fact that some developers can doubly benefit from combinations of providers (for example, a basic government plan plus an employer plan top-up).

Table 5.2
Distribution of answers (% of respondents) to the question: "Do you currently have health coverage?" (2014 and 2019)

	2014	2019
Yes, through my employer	62	54
Yes, through a government plan	22	29
Yes, individually through a private insurer/provider	10	10
Yes, through my partner/parent	6	9
Yes, through a group provider (i.e., union, professional association)	1	2
No, I don't have health coverage	10	10
Don't know	1	1

Source: Original data from IGDA DSS 2014, 2019
The categories for health coverage were not mutually exclusive; therefore, totals do not add up to 100%.

Protection against the Threat of Obsolescence

Scant Investment in Employee Training

Studios lack any incentive to "invest" in training mobile VGDs who will likely leave. Training is a risk if the returns can be recouped by competitors when employees move on (Long 2005). This is the case despite state-based incentives to provide training. Each of the three Canadian provinces where we conducted interviews offers grants in which the government shares the cost of training with employers (Ontario Ministry of Colleges and Universities, nd; WorkBC, nd). Quebec goes the farthest by imposing a training obligation of at least 1 percent of the total payroll, on employers with a payroll over $2 million.[2] If the employer fails to fulfill this obligation, it must pay into the province's Workforce Skills Development and Recognition Fund.

However, our interviews with Montreal developers revealed that some employers intentionally breach their legal obligations. One respondent had to sign an official document, at his manager's request, stating he had received training provided by the studio (and subsidized by the government labour tax credit program). However, the respondent had not received any training. Worse, he was even refused any form of financial support for training events:

> ▸ I have signed a work-related document that says I am receiving a set number of training hours per year. That is a lie. ... Part

2. Act to Promote Workforce Skills Development and Recognition, CQLR, c. D-8.3

Table 5.3
Distribution of answers (% of respondents) to the question: "Aside from a diploma or degree, have you completed any additional formal schooling/training related to the games industry?" (2014 and 2019)

	2014	2019
No additional formal training	49	54
Internship	17	14
Employer provided/sponsored training	15	15
College courses	12	10
University courses	12	10
Professional certifications/licenses	10	14
High school courses	8	4
Post-graduate courses	5	6
Don't know/decline to answer	3	2

Source: Original data from IGDA DSS 2014, 2019
The categories for training options were not mutually exclusive; therefore, totals do not add up to 100%.

of that corporate grant is that you will give your employees training, in return for corporate grants. [My studio] has not done that. I've never received paid training. I've requested it ... the Montreal International Game Summit, the Game Developers Conference, or minor micro-conferences like GameLoop in Boston. Never. Nothing. I tried to ask for part-time funds, I've tried to offer going to these events in exchange for some support and trying to bring back some information to share with my co-workers. I've never received any support for community activities ... such as organizing game jams or creating group outings or things like that. It's very hard to have access to funds and support internally. (M-14-02-M-G-07-02-14-16-02)

Rather than offering training, studios follow the hire-on-demand model in which they seek people who already possess the desired skills. Since there is no job security, employers do not assume the cost of outdated employees, because they can just as easily lay them off when their skills are no longer needed:

> ▶ I think that up until recently they were more keen to hire people with previous experience ... it's more like a peer-to-peer thing, training that is done between co-workers or on your own time sort

of thing. If they hire you, it means that you're already employable; they wouldn't otherwise, I guess. (F-01-08-V-I-28-11-13-14-26-MSO)

We surveyed VGDs about any formal training since earning their initial entry-level diploma or degree. Half had not sought any and only 15 percent had received training provided by their employer (see Table 5.3).

We also asked whether the employer or client paid for certain professional development initiatives. Across the survey years, the majority (54 to 61 percent) had no access to such programs and a good proportion (20 to 23 percent) did not know, which effectively means no access. In 2014, 16 percent did have professional development funds and this rose to 27 percent with the 2019 sample. About 10 percent of our interview respondents mentioned occasional in-house training or the provision of an annual allocation for courses or events (for example, $1,000). Yet these options were mostly available to employees in larger studios and not those in smaller shops:

▸ [My employer (a big studio)] have become experts at that, at training. They have huge classrooms, teachers who do that all day long.

How many have you taken in your 10 years?

[At that studio], I did maybe five or six. We're talking about very general training, like [a] video-editing program or virtual modelling for artists. (M-12-16-04-M-W-10-10-13-13-19-15-JL)

▸ [My employer (a big studio)] would send us to ... a Pixar workshop for three days, take a storytelling development kind of thing. (F-03-03-V-L-18-11-13-14-26)

▸ [My employer (a big studio)] actually does ... provide training to the employees ... once a year they give you a thousand dollars that you can spend on [courses] related to animation. (M-01-08-T-U-19-03-14-05-13-JT)

This is also the case regarding conference travel. The industry has some high-profile conferences that are very fruitful occasions for networking and that provide educational talks. In 2019, 50 percent of respondents said their employer provided conference travel, while 40 percent said they provided none and 10 percent did not know. This figure was driven heavily by the respondents who were permanent, full-time employees. It is also more typical for senior employees or those involved in business development and marketing to attend these conferences, as the primary purpose is to attract interest from venture capital and game players. One developer explained his range of experiences, including his viewpoint once he founded his own studio:

> ▸ At [one big studio], they don't want you to go to conferences, or do anything, they're like a super secretive company, right? [At another studio] they're more like: "If you *want* to go do that stuff, do it, but you're not associated with us! ... [Go] on your own vacation. We're not sending you to those things." At least as a developer or designer, that's usually how it goes. If you're an executive producer or something else, you've probably *got* to go to conferences, you're probably *going* to be doing interviews, on and on. Now I do a lot; I've gone to three conferences this year [through my own company]. ... I was invited to all of them, so they were all free and I didn't have to pay. (M-18-01-V-R-13-11-13-14-26-LT)

As this comment shows, the fear of leaking trade secrets can be a barrier to professional development for developers because it constrains their ability to share ideas and experiences. This is often formalized through non-disclosure agreements (see Chapter 6), though nothing prevents VGDs from signing up for events or activities as individuals. In the end, most VGDs pay for such events out of pocket and/or attend smaller-scale, local networking events. They cannot shoulder the cost and are not allowed the time away from work for larger events.

They are always able to ask to attend events, but managerial decisions about who gets to have training and professional development are shown to be quite arbitrary (see Chapter 6). VGDs are unaware of the criteria and sometimes perceive that funding is handed out as a privilege or quid pro quo, rather than in line with a rational needs identification policy.

Mixed Opportunities for Career Advancement

Given this context, the survey data about employer support for advancement is not surprising. In both 2009 and 2014, 45 percent of developers agreed that their current job gave them opportunities for promotion or a change of job responsibilities. Yet that left 30 percent who did not see many opportunities and the remainder who were unsure. In 2014 and 2019, we asked salaried developers to rate their company on its potential to provide promotion or career advancement. The responses were very mixed and became more negative in the 2019 sample (see Figure 5.1).

This does not come as a surprise, as creative careers are not organization-driven but rather sector- and trade-driven. However, this is part of

Figure 5.1
How would you rate the company on the potential for promotion or advancement in your career? (2014 and 2019)

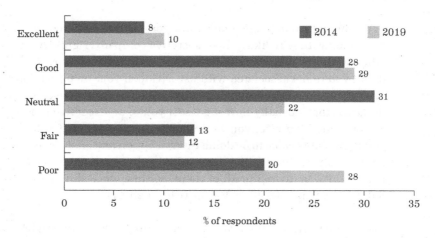

Source: Original data from IGDA DSS 2014, 2019

a larger trend toward liberalization that breaks down protection regimes based on collective citizenship and leaves workers responsible for their own career advancement.

Constant Career Curation as the Remedy

Getting assigned to coveted projects is an important challenge in project environments in general, and game projects in particular. Ambitious VGDs do everything they can to get assigned to the most prestigious projects with the best opportunities for learning. To protect against the risk of obsolescence, developers must curate their own careers to maintain their skills, portfolio, and reputation (and therefore their employability). In the absence of professional development policies, work assignments are often decided based on the producer's immediate needs rather than VGDs' professional development interests (see Chapter 4). It is left to individual workers to pursue the best opportunities. This means disappointing some producers and constantly networking.

Most VGDs assume the responsibility for updating their skills through informal or self-directed means. As noted by one Toronto animator, "I'm already levelling up my skills because every day I go [to work], I'm learning something new" (M-01-08-T-U-19-03-14-05-13-JT). Others say they go to IGDA meetings or other local networking events. Many rely on online resources such as podcasts, game post-mortems, game critic reviews, technical guides, sites for concept art, new product reviews and investor reports. Some find that specialized online courses, lectures, or master classes are well worth the fees and most tap into the rich knowledge shared in online communities and forums. And, of course, many still play a lot of games themselves or participate in game jams (an event in which a team creates a game from scratch over a short period like a weekend).

Among our interview respondents, 17 percent said the best way to stay up to date and improve their skills was to work on personal game projects. This is an inexpensive option that contributes to a portfolio, is an outlet for creative expression, and can act as a playground for trying new things:

> ▸ It's just more for my portfolio, which, I guess, could help me. If I do get fired, I have better stuff to show to other employers if I wanted to move on. (M-04-07-V-A-02-10-13-14-26-SM)

> ▸ So, one thing I've done recently, which I think has helped tremendously, is just program my own project and get a sense of the technical side of how things are done. (M-02-01-T-S-08-06-14-05-13-JT)

However, non-compete agreements can constrain what developers can do in their spare time (see Chapter 6), and training payback systems are a form of golden handcuffs used by employers to protect their return on investment (Long 2005).

Self-directed learning activities are normalized in the industry; however, many developers have little extra time to devote to such things, particularly outside of working hours. As one interviewee told us:

> ▸ When I leave work, I don't want to think about it anymore. I still love it, but it's just that ... I'd rather do it at work than outside of work; I'd rather do something else. It's just that I'm afraid that at some point you never get away from it. (M-06-15-M-W-20-11-14-13-15-19-MSO)

Another articulated the challenge of balancing the demanding day-to-day tasks with updating skills and knowledge:

> ▸ At first it was natural, because I was just out of school, and then I got here, and it was hard. ... You're at work, you're doing your

stuff, you're good, and then they tell you, "Read this article about the new way of using the mouse to model something." As time goes on, it gets harder, because the industry is moving at such a rate that you can [read articles] full time, ... but just on the side, it would take fifteen hours a day to do it. ... An average day, to be honest, we spend an hour or two a day reading or listening to talks. (M-02-04-M-U-17-10-13-13-19-15-MSO)

Nowhere more than in the domain of training can we note the relevance of Neff's (2012) concept of "venture labour." It captures "the investment of time, energy, and other personal resources that ordinary employees make in their employers' organizations" and the "explicit expression of entrepreneurial values by non-entrepreneurs." These workers "invest time, for example, in their off-hours as a way to support firms' goals and generate new demand," and "can invest their social capital in the companies where they work by tapping their personal connections for information and other resources that, in turn, often provide crucial support for their companies." Venture labourers "work to develop and maintain these ties through mechanisms such as after-hours networking," agree "to learn and update skills in their own time that could benefit their companies," and discuss "skill as a form of investment that an employee makes both in herself and in her company or industry." Yet, let us not forget that "skills are not costless to obtain, nor do they come without risk," and "the more specific the investment, the greater the cost and dislocation if that investment is left 'stranded' by economic change." (Neff 2012, 16–18). In a world of unfettered employment, VGDs run the risk of being driven out of the industry at any moment, whether for obsolescence or anything else, and assume this risk on their own. If they want to keep up to date, the combined job hunting and training activities can add up to twenty hours a week (Neff 2012, 25).

Protection of Income in Old Age

Developers have a keen sense of the amount of work required by their industry and how quickly wear and tear can take its toll. Perhaps their notion of forty years old as "old" is not so out of step after all. Like a professional athlete, career-savvy game developers protect themselves by thinking of their exit strategy almost as soon as they get into the industry:

> ▸ The average [time in the industry] is apparently nine years. Supposedly, after nine years, you usually crack; you can't do it anymore. I'm starting to see it. I was twenty-four when I started. I was

> young, enthusiastic, and full of energy. I'm twenty-eight, edging up on thirty. I'm starting to see that at thirty-seven, it's going to be hard doing what I do. ... A lot of people have turned to teaching; others go into management, which is generally less stressful and requires more experience. (M-02-04-M-U-17-10-13-13-19-15-MSO)

With their high mobility, many developers have little use for long-term employer-specific benefits such as pension plans, unless these are portable or universal. Yet they still need income protection in their old age.

Virtually all countries have some form of old age social security program (Social Security Association 2018a, 2018b, 2019a, 2019b). In most countries these benefits are modest and would not guarantee a comfortable retirement. As such, many government social security systems obliquely rely on their citizens having occupational pension plans or individual retirement savings to keep them out of poverty in old age. However, evidence from countries such as the United States suggests that retirement saving is in a state of crisis (Ghilarducci and James 2018). One report projected that 40 percent of older workers will experience downward mobility in retirement (Ghilarducci, Papadopoulos, and Webb 2018, 1).

In 2014 and 2019, we surveyed VGDs about their retirement savings (see Table 5.4). Our results first show that VGDs might lack an understanding about the retirement systems in place in their respective countries. Even though most countries do have some form of universal old age security, many respondents said they had no retirement savings at all and only a few said they had a government plan. More importantly, only 40 percent said that they had a plan through their employer and 22 to 25 percent had an individual savings plan. As these categories were not mutually exclusive, this data points to a significant shortfall in retirement savings for many VGDs.

Rather than offer their own pension plan, some studios will contribute to a worker's capital accumulation plan. These plans can be attractive because they are more portable, but they also face greater exposure to market risk. Also, company stocks can be included in the compensation package of VGDs; 23 percent had these in 2019. However, stocks are volatile in the boom-and-bust world of game development. One of our interviewees described his experience and said that these are not forms of savings to rely on:

> ▶ Well, what they have typically is RRSP matching. [The studio] had an employee share program or something like that. That was very good for me and my wife because I worked at [the studio] for four

Table 5.4
Distribution of answers (% of respondents) to the question: "Do you currently have a retirement or pension plan?" (2014 and 2019)

	2014	2019
Yes, provided by my employer	38	39
Yes, through an individual plan that I pay for myself (i.e., RRSP, IRA)	25	22
Yes, through a government plan	17	21
Yes, through a group provider (i.e., union or professional association)	2	2
Yes, through my partner	1	1
No, I don't have any retirement plan	25	28
Don't know	3	4

Source: Original data from IGDA DSS 2014, 2019

The categories for retirement options were not mutually exclusive; therefore, totals do not add up to 100%.

years and the company was sold twice in those four years, so we made some good money out of that. ... And, of course, they're more of a lottery ticket, right? If the company gets bought out, it can be very good for you, which is what happened to me at [my studio], but if the company doesn't get bought out, then it's just paper. [Another studio] used to have some share program, but then I left the company in 2008 so I lost everything I had. ... You just lose whatever shares were assigned to you. (M-05-14-L-D-22-07-13-10-23-JT)

Conclusion: A Risky Business

Three economic forces increased the level of economic risk that workers bore in the late twentieth and early twenty-first centuries: the increasing "financialization" of the economy, the rapidly changing market demand, and the widespread diffusion of flexible work practices (Neff 2012, 7). The VGI embodies all three. As Bulut (2020a, 144) critically observed, "entrepreneurialism, libertarianism and individualism are constitutive of the game industry. If one studio doesn't work out for a developer, [they] can either join another one or found [their] own."

In this chapter, we presented the combination of protections a developer has—from the state, from their employer, or mostly through their own means—to mitigate the risks of losing employment income. The available protection is insufficient because it displays great gaps in terms of the object, substance, and domain of citizenship. The existing EI benefits and pension plans are objects of citizenship, but they are poor ones. First, they may only exist as universal employment laws of the state and are therefore not well tailored to the risks that VGDs face. Second, they may exist at some workplaces and not at others. Employer-related protection of income, in the case of parenting, work-related injury, or illness, varies greatly and is more prevalent—though not guaranteed— among workers in large studios. As such, they are uneven objects of citizenship and produce subjects who are second-class citizens due to lack of access. When dissatisfied with the risks of their working conditions, VGDs must "make choices" and take what they can get to balance the different spheres of their life. Lastly, protection against obsolescence has never been an object of citizenship, being left to individual negotiation and discretionary decision-making, and devoid of any systematic protection by any collective intermediary.

On top of this, the few protections that come from social laws are therefore an object of *passive* citizenship (see Chapter 1). When protection mechanisms are not the object of active citizenship (collective participation, consultation, negotiation, and tailoring to the context of the trade), they can widen the gap between the "haves" and the "have nots." If limited to developers who can negotiate provisions, while others cannot, apparent subjects of citizenship are therefore not truly subjects of citizenship but merely successful individual achievers. This "successful" discourse is itself misleading, given the silence of those who do not reach the door of the realm. Due to both demographic and occupational characteristics, older workers, women and members of other equity-seeking groups, artists, testers, outsourced workers, and those working at small or capital-poor companies become second-class citizens and face additional challenges compared to the uniquely skilled, White cis-male programmer in a large, self-reliant AAA studio. Even members of that privileged group face considerable challenges.

CHAPTER 6

Do Game Developers Have Recourse against Arbitrary Treatment?

Human resource management (HRM) is an act of governance that deals with the issue of balancing property rights and labour rights; adopting a workplace governance mode is an ethical stance that embodies a particular notion of the human being (Budd 2004b, 66). To reconcile these two sets of rights with ideals of human dignity, we need to respect three core principles: efficiency, equity, and the ability to voice concerns (Budd 2004a, 6–8).

Voice is an important political feature of the republican democracy that is at the heart of the notion of citizenship. Therefore, one of the landmarks of citizenship at work is recourse against arbitrary decisions (at best) and ways to influence local decisions regarding work and working conditions (at a minimum) (see Chapter 1).

In this chapter, we examine decision-making processes regarding working conditions that are fraught with economic or professional consequences. The issue of assigning and compensating "crunch time" (overtime) is so important that we dedicate a specific chapter to it (Chapter 9).

Discretion in HRM Decision-Making

It is common knowledge that strategic organizational decision-making involves production, sales, and marketing, but HRM decision-making processes are ignored in this field of organizational study (Hodgkinson and Starbuck 2008). HR services are seen as simple providers to this core triad, and their decisions are considered simple, repetitive, and routine.

To bridge this gap, we turn to the philosophy of law for a robust definition of arbitrariness and discretion in decision-making, and to social psychology for studies about organizational justice and fairness, and a theoretical framework of discretionary decision-making in the context of HRM.

Within the philosophy of law, "arbitrariness" is defined as the nature of a decision that stems from individual motives instead of any publicly known and established order or set of rules (Lalande 1926). The individual motives behind an arbitrary decision can be based on whim. Thus, the term has acquired a mostly pejorative sense, particularly when set against the model of organizational bureaucracy. Bureaucracy typically refers to a detailed management ideal that promotes decision-making using rational and publicly known criteria through consistent procedures, rules, and regulations designed to maintain uniformity and avoid personal criteria such as beliefs, feelings, habits, or customs (DuGay 2005; Weber 1921).

"Discretion" is more formal. Discretionary power is defined as the power that is legally conferred, but not constrained by a legal framework, organizational policies, rules of behaviour, or political pressure. Discretionary decision-making has the same characteristics as arbitrary decision-making but does not have the same pejorative connotation. It can refer to the specific zone of power, free of scrutiny, that lies in the hands of an individual person.

Notion of Procedural Justice

An arbitrary or discretionary decision is not an inherently bad or unsatisfactory one; its recipient may be satisfied. However, there is an established relationship between the quality of the democratic process and the perception of fairness. It is widely held that workers evaluate their experience of work according to the outcomes they receive, but we now know that people evaluate processes as much as outcomes. They are usually preoccupied by how decisions are made about performance evaluation, allocation of resources, resolution of disputes, pay schemes, surveillance, attribution of sanctions, and so on. Moreover, if the process is perceived as fair, the outcome usually will be as well. Fair procedures lead to perceived fair distribution of rewards, or "distributive fairness" (Cropanzano and Ambrose 2015b; Greenberg and Colquitt 2005).

As such, a twofold notion of organizational justice accounts for fairness in decision-making. *Procedural justice* entails satisfaction with the decision-making process, while *distributive justice* entails satisfaction with the outcome (Greenberg and Colquitt 2005). We focus on procedural justice as a core element of citizenship at work (see Table 1.1). The perception of procedural justice affects attitudes and working behaviours such as satisfaction, motivation, cooperation, compliance, and trust in management. These can enhance performance, though other factors at stake make the relationship complex (Bobocel and Gosse 2015; Ko and Hur 2014; Shapiro and Brett 2005).

To perceive procedural justice, workers must be given an opportunity to express their point of view about their situation before, during, or after the process, thereby having a certain control over the process (that is, a voice or participation). They must have some knowledge of how information is gathered and used to assess its accuracy and potential for bias. They must know who is making the decision and understand the decision-making criteria. In this, workers prefer decision-makers to be familiar with the context at stake and face criteria that are transparent and consistent in their application. Following a decision, the worker must have the decision explained as a matter of respect of their stake in the issue. In the end, the worker must also have an opportunity to challenge or appeal the decision (Bobocel and Gosse 2015; Colquitt, Greenberg, and Zapata-Phelan 2005; Conlon, Meyer, and Nowakowsky 2005; Cropanzano and Ambrose 2015a; Van der Bos 2005).

Some authors argue that the process must also be representative (Konovsky 2000). This means that the decision must be taken in a way that takes into account the values, worries, and points of view of the affected groups. If a single person controls both process and decision, procedural justice is at risk and the decision-making process is discretionary. The possibility of appeal is an important factor, as it reduces the exercise of unilateral control over decisions. Even when it does not take the form of a formal appeal or cannot be guaranteed to change a decision, the possibility of having a say allows one to communicate a message to the decision-maker (Cropanzano and Ambrose 2015a). However, this condition is the least acceptable in the organizational context and often only appears in unionized environments.

Fair Procedure, Formal Procedure, and Citizenship

Most workplaces, especially non-unionized ones, do not achieve this ideal of a *fair* decision-making process. However, many workplaces, particularly unionized ones, do achieve a *formal* bureaucratic decision-making process.

The formal decision-making process is a legacy of the Weberian ideal of bureaucracy. In defining appropriate structural, procedural, and ethical conditions, the bureaucratic model embodied the ideal of organizational democracy. It was aimed at reducing the influence of emotional and self-interested considerations in decision-making and promoting rational and factual grounds, stemming from scientific knowledge, if possible. Discipline in the decision-making process was said to allow social groups "to position themselves advantageously within the structures of social and economic inequality" if they had rational arguments to support their point of view (Reed 2005). We can easily admit *a posteriori* the exaggerated optimism inherent in this model, as "the limitations of the approach have long been recognized by theorists from within, and outside, the paradigm" (S. Miller and Wilson 2006, 469).

Table 6.1
Comparison of arbitrary, formal, and fair decision-making processes

	General characteristics	*It consists of…*		*Typical environment*
Arbitrary/discretionary process	Can be based on individual motives, beliefs, feelings, habits, or customs	A decision-maker having much **leeway** and discretion in matters of procedure	An individual worker to which the decision applies, at the other end, or a group of workers **ignoring the grounds, procedure, or criteria of the decision**	No way or **recourse** to challenge it	Small, non-unionized private-sector business
Formal process	Based on procedural justice	**Constant** and **consistent procedures**, rules, and regulations designed to maintain uniformity in decision-making	Rational, bias-free, and publicly known criteria	A (top down) **feedback process** allowing for correction if stakeholders' input reveals some ethical issues	Established bureaucracies like public service, government agencies, utilities, or large private corporations
Fair process	Based on an exhaustive notion of procedural justice, allowing for a third-party evaluation of the process and **representativeness** (a participative concept)	**Constant** and **consistent procedures**, rules, and regulations; A **clearly identified person responsible** for the decision; Possibility of **voice** before, during, or after the process, and **explanation of** decisions	Rational, **bias-free**, and **publicly known criteria**; Guarantees of accurate information; Relevant **competence** of decision-makers	No **unilateral power**—allowance for **appeals** (**control over the decision**); Possibility of having a say on **information required** to make the decision (**control over the process**)	Unionized workplace with a grievance procedure

Source: Original comparative table

As summarized in Table 6.1, only fair process offers consistency of decisions over time and suppression of bias (equity) as well as representation of stakeholders in the process (voice) to properly balance efficiency in workplace governance. Thus, fair process alone can achieve citizenship at work.

Discretionary processes are faced more often by non-unionized workers. Their only recourse sits in universal social laws of the state, which provide remedies against certain (limited) managerial decisions. They usually cover the decisions with the most harmful consequences, such as firings or layoffs. Such laws can provide the right to make a claim before an administrative court and the support of a lawyer during the process. This is a form of passive citizenship in that employees make use of a regulation stipulating their rights and obligations as established by law, but they are not involved in defining the process in any way. Some employers value employees' input on a voluntary basis. This can be a managerial practice aimed at fostering a healthy working climate. However, a practice, unlike a policy, is usually informal and variable. Some groups or individuals may acquire some leverage in decision-making, arbitrary or not, but this does not make the environment fair overall. It merely shields the fortunate few.

HR Policies in Project-Based Environments

In bureaucracies, HR policies determine managers' actions. But in project-based organizations, managers have considerable discretion and leeway (Hobday 2000). Smaller organizations rarely have an HR department and, if they do, it is unobtrusive (Chasserio and Legault 2010; Legault 2005b). In a pervasive "culture of project management," HR policies and procedures are considered as avatars of bureaucracy and antithetical to efficiency. In the absence of policies and rules, project managers have autonomous power to decide who gets what (Legault and Chasserio 2012). Even when they have an HR department, project managers have discretionary authority to apply policies, which can result in uneven application and can lead to individualized working conditions (Chasserio and Legault 2010). In any case, it is hardly possible to challenge discretionary decisions because HRM policies do not have great coercive power over project imperatives. One Canadian respondent reveals that informal practices and favouritism are quite standard:

> ▸ It's a fairly flat hierarchy. ... I can go and talk to the VP of the company if I want, and say, "I've a got an idea, blah blah blah." Even the CEO has invited me into his office to talk. It's friendly that way, but as it's really informal, a lot of teams form. It becomes a kind

of informal influence, like, "He's so-and-so's friend," so he'll have more influence because of that. There are internal mechanisms to guard somewhat against favouritism, because it's really harmful in the industry. But there's still a lot of it. (F-18-02-16-M-W-01-10-13-19-15-JL)

In our surveys and interviews, we asked VGDs many questions about the decision-making process for many aspects of their working conditions. We discuss here the most often cited and most problematic.

Discipline and Dismissals: Not Much Formalism

Half of the interview respondents discussed the disciplinary procedure in their studios. Among these, 55 percent said their employer had a formal disciplinary procedure, and 45 percent had "just informal guidelines." Among those with a formal disciplinary procedure, 72 percent felt that the procedure was being followed and 28 percent said it was not. Many respondents worked in studios in which discipline was managed informally, irrespective of any formal policy:

> ▸ The discipline, generally, has come with a warning, and then they get let go. ... The times I've seen people let go, it's been without warning. I don't know if they had been warned, but they told us no.
>
> *What kind of things lead to this?*
>
> Not following the company's direction ... developing their ideas and getting things to go in a different direction from the way the project is heading. (F-18-01-M-E-21-11-13-16-02-PB)

A general legal principle called "progressive discipline" governs labour standards. The employer must impose different levels of disciplinary action depending on whether it is an employee's first or recurring offence. The intensity of the disciplinary action escalates from a simple reprimand or verbal warning to a written warning, fine, loss of certain privileges, suspension with or without pay, demotion, or dismissal. However, a serious type of misconduct, like theft, could be disciplined with a high-level penalty, even on the first occurrence. With progressive discipline, general principles of procedural fairness are applied whereby the points of view of all parties must be heard, employees must be given an opportunity to change their conduct and a reasonable time in which to do so, and they must be given an opportunity to understand how their conduct has adversely affected the workplace.

Among our respondents, 21 percent said that their employers respected the principle of progressive discipline. Most of these were working for big studios. A further 23 percent said that a first offence could lead to a dismissal:

> ▸ As far as I know, disciplinary action is giving you the boot. That's disciplinary action. I've never seen anything else. It's not unionized, so guess what? There are no grievances. You've done something the company doesn't like—on purely arbitrary grounds, of course. (M-19-10-M-I-17-7-13-13-10-12-MSO)

The remaining respondents (56 percent) were unaware of the legal framework governing them (9 percent bluntly said they did not know what would happen in the case of an assumed offense, and others provided vague answers). This constitutes a rather formidable share of employees with a lack of knowledge about matters as important as disciplinary procedure, their rights, and possible remedies. This ignorance does not necessarily mean that no disciplinary policy exists, but it does suggest that policies are not publicized or clearly enforced. Even team leads may not know whether the studio has a formal policy:

> ▸ Maybe this is important to note, but I'm not aware of, right now, what tools are allowed. I'm not aware of what my resources are at this very moment, inside and outside of the company, if I was to be fired. (M-14-02-M-G-07-02-14-16-02)

Even when principles of fairness for VGDs may be upheld, the case for managers can be harsh. At this level of responsibility, they are fired on their first offence:

> ▸ You don't get blamed once, twice, three times. It's "You're out, you've done enough damage." ... When you're a manager with a big job title, you can be kicked out from one day to the next, but for level designers, artists, programmers to be let go, they really have to have made some very serious mistakes or have been a really big disappointment. (M-13-01-03-M-U-30-10-13-13-15-19-MSO)

The practice in some studios of maintaining a "policy void" trivializes and makes invisible the arbitrary nature of decisions about dismissal and their consequences. Many respondents (52 percent) felt that the risk of being fired was part of the working conditions in the industry, the normal consequence of poor performance:

▶ It's hard to stand up for yourself and be resilient and force for some change because it can easily lead to getting laid off. And you know, and everybody knows, that it's because you opened your mouth. But it's very easy to find another [official] reason for the layoff. (M-01-02-M-E-28-09-13-13-19-15-MSO)

▶ If I was fired randomly? I would want to know why, obviously, but I feel like I've learned quite a bit and built a pretty nice profile for myself so that I could probably find a job anywhere else easily, so I wouldn't be too worried about it. (M-11-03-T-B-12-03-14-05-13-PB)

A closely related issue is the management of layoffs at the end of a project. There are often no policies or rules to guide this decision-making, either. VGDs perceive these layoffs as a convenient management practice to get rid of less satisfactory workers. Being laid off is considered a sanction, while retention is evidence of a positive performance evaluation:

▶ By way of thanks, I was one of the people who wasn't shown the door. That's the kind of atmosphere there was. "You worked hard; you're not one of the ones we're letting go." ... At the time, it was clearly company policy, or at least studio policy, that when a project was over, 10 percent of the team would be let go. (M-13-01-03-M-U-30-10-13-13-15-19-MSO)

▶ It's very uncomfortable. The [security guard] is going to be right there beside you: "Take your box, don't turn on your computer!" It happened to me once. ... It was a mass layoff—10 percent is pretty huge. They'd had a meeting. They'd asked all kinds of people to go to the main room and, at the same time, a producer came around to see those who hadn't been asked: "Leave your computers; pack up your stuff! We'll send you a letter." (M-12-16-13-M-B-24-10-13-13-19-15-JL)

Some companies only have "open-door policies," according to which managers spend some time answering questions and solving problems to do with working conditions (Legault and Weststar 2014, 2015b):

▶ We don't have HR, we don't have any sort of established process, and if somebody is having an issue or a concern there's nobody else to speak to, because it's just [the president]. (M-16-02-V-N-08-10-13-14-26-SM)

Disciplinary sanctions are also manifest in how workers are assigned to projects. In the VGI, reputation is as important as one's portfolio for vertical and horizontal mobility (Legault and Ouellet 2012). Getting assigned to coveted projects is a major issue; 11 percent of our Canadian respondents saw being reassigned to a less prestigious project as a disciplinary penalty equivalent to a demotion:

> ▸ What happens more often [than dismissal] is that someone is sidelined or put on another project or team. ... It may be a punishment. ... You're kind of put on the shelf. You've got nothing to do anymore. (F-18-02-16-M-W-01-10-13-19-15-JL)

This practice of "sidelining" has the advantage of pushing employees to leave "of their own free will" rather than be fired. It enables the employer to avoid the risk of a dispute and the cost of severance pay. In the most severe cases, it could be deemed constructive dismissal and illegal under labour law. However, these cases are hard to prove in court.

Without a consistent system in which the same causes always produce the same effects, respondents cannot connect disciplinary action with specific failings, nor anticipate and avoid repercussions:

> ▸ There was one guy—he got disciplined. He was promising things he could never deliver ... and when it came down to it, he wasn't doing his job. ... It took a while, but they finally managed to demote him; they didn't throw him out. ... Eventually he came back. ... He does easy jobs.
>
> *He was never let go?*
>
> No. But other people have been. ... And that's what's so weird. It's really case by case. (M-06-15-M-W-20-11-14-13-15-19-MSO)

This situation is common among knowledge workers. The case of a unionization campaign of the software firm Lanetix by NewsGuild-CWA (Communications Workers of America), provides an illustration of arbitrary disciplinary action as a trigger for unionization among software engineers:

> One issue that really motivated us ... is the role that managerial caprice plays within workplaces where there are no real defined rules. In tech ... the discipline isn't even acknowledged. A real turning point in the campaign came when the engineers recognized how much they had in common. ... As soon as they started

Table 6.2
Motives for firing, according to Canadian respondents (2014)

	% of respondents
A negative attitude or a personal conflict between a boss and an employee	39
Breaching a non-disclosure agreement (NDA)	19
Not doing enough overtime	18
Not working core hours, coming in late too often, underperforming	16
Making too many mistakes	15
Sexual harassment	11
Discriminatory behaviours (sexism, racism)	8
Insulting people	4
Refusing to work on projects	2
Surfing on the Internet	2
I don't know	8

Source: Original data from the Canadian interviews led by authors in 2013–14

to compare notes, they realized that each manager was just trying to *individualize* the complaints that everybody had [regarding management of time off]. For us, that was the major attraction of [unionizing]. We'd have a contract that would specify exactly how much time we got off, exactly when we would be on call, and so on. There couldn't be any more psychological gamesmanship between worker and manager. (Tarnoff 2018)

What was really at stake in this example, as in many disputes in the VGI, was the frustration of engaging repeatedly in highly personalized bargaining in the absence of set standards or clarity and transparency around rules. This leaves workers clueless when facing a manager who is acting inconsistently, or worse, capriciously, or vindictively.

Our interview respondents also revealed a range of events that are not always perceived as "professional misconduct," but that could be the subject of discipline or dismissal. The most frequent are presented in Table 6.2. The last seven (excluding "I don't know") are breaches that would be supported by Canadian case law, but two of the most common reasons would not necessarily pass the test of a labour court: "A negative attitude or a personal conflict between a boss and an employee" and "Not doing enough overtime."

A single instance might be tolerated, but refusing to work overtime too frequently is a definite risk. Some managers give warnings or make comments that are taken as warnings:

> ▸ There's no written warning, it's not a formal process, it's pretty casual. ... There's a technique that we use to apply pressure to an individual if they're not doing well, if they're slacking. ... If you let them know that "we're not able to rely on you" and "if this kind of thing continues, we might not have you on the project anymore," "I can't trust you on this anymore," stuff like this, it's kind of guilt driven. (M-11-03-T-B-12-03-14-05-13-PB)

Contesting managers' decisions is also frowned upon:

> ▸ I can't say for certain but anytime I speak out against the practices of a company or if I disagree with the direction of a game, and I give my reasons... I'm not just saying it's stupid, right? When I give reasons and I quantify it ... the management is looking at me and is, like, "Yeah, that's misconduct. He's not supporting our decisions outright." ... When it's things like people working all the time and not being compensated ... if I say that, I feel like as soon as I bring it up, in their head they're, like...
>
> *Well, is it your place?*
>
> Exactly. (M-03-19-T-B-15-05-14-05-13-JT)

At-will employment is the default condition in non-unionized workplaces; employers face few restrictions on how and when they hire and fire. This is even more the case in project-based environments (Rothfeld 2020). In principle, disciplinary firings are usually subject to labour laws that define rights and obligations. The duty to demonstrate a "just cause" for firing is the requirement for due process; however, it will only be examined if a fired worker files a complaint to some legal authority. A perceived "freedom to fire" fosters a threatening culture that endangers vulnerable workers, silences voices of dissent, and jeopardizes independent thought. Indeed, when "there is a surplus population that can easily replace the employed population, layoffs can be used as a threat, leading to overwork and superexploitation" (Bulut 2020a, 133).

VGDs considered to have a "bad attitude" (complaining, whining, blaming, being unavailable, or being unwilling to collaborate) may also be condemned by peers, which in turn influences managers' assessments and one's future reputation:

> Let's say we go for a beer—"Hey! A round for everyone!"—and there's someone who isn't doing his job, you just won't buy him one. ... It's an image, but that's the way it usually works. You'll get asked for your opinion less, you won't be the first to get the job... things like that. Why? You're punished for being a whiner, being a critic, not being a team player, not fitting in. (M-02-04-M-U-17-10-13-13-19-15-MSO)

Due to this peer pressure, VGDs practice self-discipline and this can reduce the need for overt managerial discipline.

Remedies in the Case of Disciplinary Action

To generate a perception of procedural justice, a formal disciplinary policy should include a procedure for appealing a decision. But in our interviews, 41 percent of respondents thought that they would have to go to an administrative court to contest a decision, in the absence of internal procedures:

> *If you were fired for unfair reasons would you contest it?*

Yeah, oh yeah.

How would you go about that?

... I haven't looked any of that up. I would go to the labour board first and get advice from them, and then I'd talk [to my boss] about it informally as a friend, but I don't really know what I would do after that.

But court would be an option after that?

Yeah. Which I think a lot of people in my industry wouldn't deal with. ... People just assume, "I lost my job and there's nothing I can do about it." But there *is* something you can do about it. (M-02-22-M-L-23-11-13-16-02-PB)

Yet, VGDs rarely consider contesting decisions because they fear it will damage their reputations. This was a common rationale among the 38 percent of respondents who said they would not consider contesting a disciplinary action or dismissal:

> *So if you were fired, would you contest it?*

Probably not, because it's a very small community. There are a lot of companies but word would get around fast, so if you are seen as a shit disturber, you wouldn't get hired anywhere else. You get blacklisted, which I think does happen. ... There was a point at which I knew a person at almost every single company in town. ...

So that good reputation really matters.

Yes, definitely. (M-17-13-V-U-25-09-13-10-23-JT)

A respondent who contested a dismissal would be more likely to negotiate conditions of departure and try to "leave on a good note," rather than seek a remedy. In fact, 32 percent of respondents suggested that contesting a dismissal would poison the workplace environment and seriously tarnish their reputations.

Enforcement of NCAs and NDAs

Non-compete agreements (NCAs) are common in the knowledge economy, in which "know-how" plays a leading role in a firm's competitive position. When key employees leave, the secrets they harbour becomes an issue that employers resolve by limiting their mobility in the sector. Under an NCA, "an employee agrees, for the term of employment and a certain period afterwards, not to work for a competitor of the employer and/or not to become involved in operating a competing organization ... within a specified geographic area" (Boiteau and Gauthier 2010, n.p.).

Non-disclosure agreements (NDAs) are also common in the VGI, in which business secrets are paramount; they protect confidential information by prohibiting any use or disclosure of a company's confidential information or those of its customers, suppliers, business partners, and employees, obtained in the course of work. VGDs work under a culture of secrecy dictated by strict intellectual property (IP) regimes (O'Donnell 2014, 12).

For a former employer to be entitled to sue for breaches of an NDA, secrets must be capable of providing an advantage to the next employer because of their decisive strategic value (Robinson and Jetté 2003). Leaked secrets can challenge a company's exclusive position in a market, its marketing strategy, and its sales.

Up to 97 percent of interview respondents had signed an NDA and 82 percent an NCA. Among them, 24 percent signed an all-encompassing NCA of the "everything that you produce belongs to the studio" type, depriving VGDs of the authorship of projects carried on outside of working hours and infringing on their IP rights. Moreover, these provisions can limit the job search (because VGDs cannot show or talk about some current projects), as well as fruitful exchanges with peers (O'Donnell 2014, 98). Such agreements can be arbitrarily enforced and are especially prejudicial to less qualified employees, like testers, who want to upgrade their status:

> ▸ There are some people at our studio who have their own game companies and make their own games for money, and they are apparently allowed to do that. I was given an opportunity to do something ... not testing, for another company on a freelance basis. I checked in with HR and they told me I couldn't. ... They just said it was a case-by-case basis. ... They sort of push this idea of wanting to keep everyone and wanting to bring them up ... If I can't improve my skills to move up within this company, then what am I supposed to do? ... It was just, "You can't do it." (F-07-13-T-U-10-05-14-04-11-JT)

On a case-by-case basis, using unknown criteria, and thus arbitrarily, managers control their expert labour by reserving their right to limit employees' opportunities for development, without justification, and while offering little internal development.

A Great Unknown: The Validity of the Agreed Provisions

Contractual clauses in agreed provisions can and do infringe on the law, but VGDs are generally unaware of the frail legal grounds of these agreements and take the document for granted. Unfortunately, though most VGDs' employment contracts include NCAs and NDAs, they are only subject to court scrutiny if an employee contests their provisions. When they are contested, the courts generally interpret these agreements in a narrow, restrictive manner and to the benefit of the worker. This is for three reasons (Béliveau 2008; Béliveau and Lebel 2011):

- First, these contractual agreements contravene an important principle in common law regarding universal duty of loyalty, which requires all employees, in any position or at any level, to act faithfully and honestly towards their employer. The courts require the agreement to have been entered into freely. There may have been a lack of consent if the employee was unable to negotiate, did not understand the meaning of the required commitment, or acted under the threat of a penalty or dismissal. The employer is often able to impose provisions on newly recruited employees deprived of bargaining power.
- Second, competition is only to be restricted if a higher interest must be protected, because the liberal economy is based on free-market principles.

- Third, restricting a former employee's freedom to work (and earn a living) conflicts with fundamental rights in a modern liberal society.

There is limited case law for the VGI, but based on the above and case law from other industries, agreements are often invalidated by the courts because they fail to satisfy the following three conditions of validity: 1) to set a reasonable duration on the prohibition of competition or disclosure, 2) to set reasonable geographic limits on the prohibition, and 3) to limit the prohibition only to activities that harm the former employer's legitimate interests (Legault 2015).

Regarding NCAs, NDAs, and pay, newly hired VGDs are seldom in a strong bargaining position. Inexperienced candidates crave jobs, engendering fierce competition for starting-level positions. Employee consent can be vitiated when the agreement is signed on the first day of work, when they have already left their previous jobs and are no longer able to negotiate or to refuse:

> ▸ In the case [of one big studio], I'd say that their hiring process is rigged slightly in their favour because they only give you the non-compete agreement to sign on your first day of work. So, you've already left your old job, you've signed a contract to go and work, you start to work, so the message is: "If you want to come back to work tomorrow, you better sign now." (M-13-01-03-M-U-30-10-13-13-15-19-MSO)

Regarding free consent, 26 percent of interview respondents had their agreement presented to them as non-negotiable, and 20 percent said that certain provisions were negotiable (including the duration of the restriction), while only 14 percent said that everything was negotiable:

> ▸ I don't think [I could] refuse to sign it. I've never tried, but I will point out certain things and say, "this time is too long." ... At one of the jobs I did, they have a non-compete thing for six months. I told them: "six months is too long, I only can do three months," and they changed it. (F-13-11-M-W-10-10-13-13-19-15-MSO)

At the time employees sign an agreement, they do not know whether it is valid according to the criteria of interpretation used by the courts:

> ▸ I wasn't happy about signing it! I was at school and the teachers were former industry people. Several of them who used to work

[at a big studio] told us about it ahead of time. They were honest with us. Those kinds of provisions are borderline illegal. There's virtually no other field where they can impose that on someone. We were told that unless we had a big reputation in the industry, no company was ever going to sue us for changing companies. But you still have doubts that leave you uneasy. (M-19-12-M-U-12-11-13-13-15-19-JL)

The remaining 40 percent of respondents knew enough to consider that the signed agreement was illegal, unenforceable, or wouldn't hold up in court. This could lead us to think that they are inconsequential and not worth being concerned about. Yet, such agreements still expose VGDs to the risk of legal proceedings:

> ▸ There are certain parts of the non-compete agreement that are non-enforceable, like you can't stop somebody from earning a living, so that part of the non-compete clause isn't enforceable. But taking intellectual property or designs to another studio, that is enforceable, because it's protected under the intellectual property laws. (M-20-22-V-A-12-19-13-14-26-PB)

> ▸ I sign an NDA for each project. ... They make you sign documents that are illegal. It's typically what they do ... and it's mostly a scare tactic. My understanding is that you can't tell someone to not work in the industry for three years when they leave their job, and that's pretty typical. ... But I've talked to lawyers, and they've told me that it's a non-valid contract that is not enforceable.

> *Have you ever refused to sign a non-compete or a non-disclosure?*

> No, I haven't. I always sign them. (M-19-20-T-M-22-05-14-05-13-JT)

Among those who believe contracts may be negotiated, 23 percent said their ability to negotiate the provisions was by virtue of their standing in the industry; they were "stars" with very impressive portfolios. The youngest recruits, who have no experience, hardly negotiate anything at all:

> ▸ It depends on how much the company wants you. If they really want you, they will change the contract. ... They get plenty of twenty-two/twenty-three-year-olds, recent grads who just want to work on games. And to these kids you can say: "You're going to

work for ten bucks an hour, but you'll be making games!" And a lot of them will just take the job. (M-05-14-L-D-22-07-13-10-23-JT)

▸ You'd have to be a big shot, someone who can say, "I made [a successful game]," one of the top-selling games in its category. A guy like that can go [to a big studio] and say, "I'm not having anything to do with your provisions." ... You can negotiate ... but generally, especially when you're just starting out, they give you a piece of paper, you say thank you and you sign. (M-02-04-M-U-17-10-13-13-19-15-MSO)

Besides the "star factor," we must add the "size factor." Big studios have more bargaining power and are not as flexible as small ones:

▸ Generally, [a big studio] is not flexible enough. Generally, the smaller the studio, the more flexible they are. Because the smaller the studio, the less talent they can attract, the more they want to keep hold of the ones they have, so are much more flexible. (M-01-02-M-E-28-09-13-13-19-15-MSO)

Is it possible to refuse to sign the provisions? Among the Canadian respondents, 13 percent of those who answered the question said they could refuse, 72 percent said that refusing meant giving up the job, and 15 percent said they simply did not know whether it was possible.

Selective Enforcement of NCAs and NDAs

Although 40 percent of respondents suspected that the signed agreements were illegal or unenforceable, half of those (45 percent) would not risk challenging them. Breaching an NDA can lead to disciplinary sanctions such as some discretionary reduction of a bonus:

▸ Like sharing NDA stuff: that's a serious case of misconduct. You can't do that. (F-07-04-T-X-27-05-14-04-11-JT)

▸ Giving away information, leaking information—that's the worst, in my view. Sometimes, you don't even know what you've just done. You are in the middle of a party and you meet some folks who work in another studio and ... it's a friend. ... You discuss things, but this friend will talk about this with someone else who will do the same with a higher-up ... who will brag about it, and first thing you know, here it's back to you. ... This kind of mistake is very harmful for the studio. It sucks, you've just lost 2 percent on your bonus. (M-12-16-04-M-W-10-10-13-13-19-15-JL)

Poaching staff is also taken seriously by management; breaches are subject to disciplinary action:

> ▶ If I went and spoke to a competitor about any of our numbers, that'd be a case of very strong professional misconduct. If I was attempting to poach staff internally for my own means or my own start-up, that would be considered professional misconduct. (M-23-12-V-T-30-10-2013-14-26)

Most of our interviewees said that the employer presents the agreements in a way that makes the restrictions seem acceptable. For instance, they may tell new VGDs that the provisions are never or almost never enforced, which is indeed a fact, just to get them to sign without negotiating:

> ▶ There's one clause in there that said that you could not work for a competitor for, like, a year after working [for a big studio]. Some people weren't even sure if that was legal. The company ... said: "Don't worry about that, that's fine, you can get a job somewhere else." That was something they put in there more for people who leave the studio and then form their own company using the technology and the stuff they learned from the studio—that's what they said it was primarily for. ... But it was worded in there like you couldn't get a job anywhere else. (M-14-13-T-G-18-02-14-04-11-DK)

Among themselves, VGDs play down the risk of enforcement, as well as the scope. The narrative is that they are reserved for key assets like star developers or senior managers.

> ▶ I went to a panel on the videogame industry and I asked the panelists about NDAs and NCAs, whether they ever had any practical effect, and they all said, "no don't worry about it." They said that the only way someone would pursue you ... is if they could legally prove that you took intellectual property or skills with you that were irreplaceable, and "you're not high level enough to worry about that," and almost nobody is. The guy said he knew of only two cases where someone successfully sued on the basis of a noncompete agreement. (F-10-22-07-M-G-22-11-13-16-02-PB)

> It seems like they only enforce it for the high-profile cases. So, if there's a very key person that they want to keep—like the creative director or the high-level manager—then I think that they would enforce that, if they find a threat. But for someone like me, then a lot of times they don't really do anything. (M-20-20-T-U-25-02-14-05-13-JT)

Nevertheless, all VGDs are exposed as soon as they sign:

> I tried to be as diplomatic as I could while still trying to get them to change it, but they told me: "Don't worry about it, [the studio (a big one)] never enforces those provisions anyhow. It's just an insurance policy in case someone tries to make off with the company's trade secrets or whatever." But you end up signing it anyway. I don't know what [the studio]'s official policy is going to be X years from now, so you're leaving yourself exposed. (M-13-01-03-M-U-30-10-13-13-15-19-MSO)

> I think it only happens for people like CEOs or something [*laughs*]. It's not for the bottom layer. They just want to be able to catch us if there's anything. ... The lawyers are very expensive. (F-13-11-M-W-10-10-13-13-19-15-MSO)

Therefore, these contracts are not innocuous. If an employer does decide to enforce them, this will compel employees to incur significant legal fees to fight them, and damage their own reputation. Even with a NCA, the power imbalance between an employer and a VGD would likely lead the latter to give up or conclude an out-of-court settlement. Since there is always the chance that they can be enforced, they are used as a threat in the event of any conflict. Employers remind their employees of this occasionally:

> When I handed in my resignation, they said: "You know that you signed an NCA, right?" ... I think those contracts won't really hold up in court. They're drawn up for the purpose of threatening or dissuading. (F-18-02-16-M-W-01-10-13-19-15-JL)

> It's a leash to keep you with the company for the longest time possible. ... "We won't call your non-compete agreement"—but I only have their word on it. They still own the power to prevent me from working. (M-14-02-M-G-07-02-14-16-02)

> I met with my HR representative conducting my exit interview, and then ... he mentioned that "your non-compete clause is not going to be imposed on you." [It was] this moment where somebody else could have decided my future employment. ... And that's the problem. (M-14-02-M-G-07-02-14-16-02)

In discussing IP rights for projects outside of company time, one respondent gave a telling example of the "grey area" of NCA provisions and their arbitrary enforcement:

> The HR person actually said something like, "manage your success," which is a very strange way of saying: "you can go ahead and keep working on your personal project, but if it gets too big [we] can just suddenly say 'oh, it's ours.'" ... It's probably another of those cases where they'd like you to be ignorant, and if you're not ignorant, then they'll take you to court about it and they know that you don't want to go to court over this stuff because you're just some peon who doesn't have a million bucks to go to court with. (M-11-02-M-U-16-12-13-16-02)

It is ironic that VGDs must comply with such a strict, unilateral, and depriving IP regime, while at the same time being invited to work with passion, devote the best of their whole selves, and become obsessed with the project. They are invited to buy into the post-bureaucratic workplace model (see Chapter 1) and then are alienated from it (Bulut 2020a, 24, 31). Indeed, "the moment they sign an employment contract, they waive any rights over their creative output due to intellectual property clauses" (Bulut 2020a, 34).

Crediting Policies Only Reasonably Satisfactory

The recognition of IP and the crediting of VGD contributions is also an object at stake for citizenship. In 2004, 44 percent of the VGDs surveyed felt they got the recognition they deserved. However, 34 percent added that management and publishers got too much credit in comparison with developers. Moreover, 24 percent said they would not be credited for the work they had done if they left before the end of a project.

In later years, the question was asked with a broader focus on the recognition of work done. Figure 6.1 shows that the situation remained satisfactory. Across the years, at least half of the respondents felt that their contributions were recognized.

Figure 6.1
Distribution of answers to the question: "My work is underappreciated and mostly goes unrecognized" (2009, 2014, 2019)

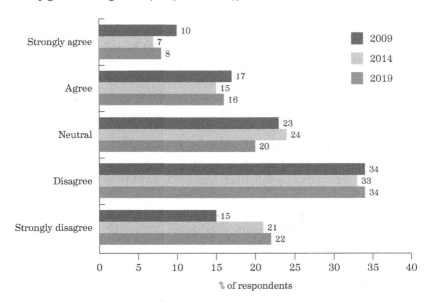

Source: Original data from DSS 2009, 2014, 2019

In game development, crediting is largely unregulated (Deuze, Chase Bowen, and Allen 2007) and crediting practices are in constant evolution. In our interviews, 66 percent of respondents said that their studio had adopted credit allocation policies and acknowledged their work; 34 percent did not know whether the studio would credit their work. Of those who were asked for their opinion of the crediting policy, 76 percent thought that credit was given accurately and 24 percent thought it was not.

Given the importance of their portfolio to their careers, accurate crediting would seem essential for a developer's claims of experience, yet there are mixed feelings among VGDs about crediting practices. Over one-third (37 percent) of interview respondents said that being credited at the end of a game is pointless (with mobile games, some studios now place a list of contributors on their website), and 33 percent said they preferred being acknowledged through merit bonuses or having permission to add the project to a portfolio (20 percent). Some saw crediting as a risk of exposure to irate fans over social media:

> If you get an official credit, you do get your name out there but at the same time you also have to deal with that clash from the gamer community. ... Some of our community managers got personal hate. ... If you're known to the community, then if something goes wrong, they'll give you a backlash. ... I'm not too worried about [crediting] in terms of future employment because I can just say on my resumé: here's what I did. (F-09-20-V-A-24-10-13-14-26-AD)

When present, some formal policies remain unsatisfactory. Our interview respondents raised several substantive issues:

1. Some studios do not attribute credit at all and/or the credit is only attributed to the studio or publisher brand. Smaller studios have no power to resist the demands of publishers, and VGDs have no say:

> It's unfortunate; there's no crediting anywhere. It's just this secret society of a little team or whatever. It's not even on the website, like, "Here's our team!" (M-13-10-T-B-20-01-14-04-11)

> When we're a partner in contracts I've done with [publisher X], our names aren't listed. [Publisher X] had that provision, which they call a "green flag." The big companies often do that. ... It'll be written: "Developed by [X studio]," but there are no names. (M-12-16-13-M-B-24-10-13-13-19-15-JL)

> It was a big client for us to work on for a tiny studio ... and the client didn't think that it needed credits in the game, so ... the company was just, like, "Okay!" and refused to fight them. (M-02-22-M-L-23-11-13-16-02-PB)

2. VGDs who leave a project before the end are rarely credited:

> They still have that attitude of, "if you leave the company, your name's not in the credits." And we had to fight for the people who left. ... I don't think the video game industry, in general, has a good crediting system. It's not like the film industry, where you can read a credit and know what that person did. ... I always have to explain from scratch what I did. (M-03-19-T-B-15-05-14-05-13-JT)

3. Allocation based on job titles is not always an accurate representation of a person's work. As reflected in the quote above, job titles vary greatly in the industry, do not signal a standard canon of work, and do not always

reflect the work or creativity that one considers that they have invested. In smaller studios, VGDs can hold many roles but only be credited for one, while in larger studios, VGDs on studio-wide support teams (for example, engineering tools or middleware) might not be adequately credited on any game. Van Roessel and Švlech (2021) have also raised specific challenges with crediting the work behind in-game monetization:

> ▸ They gave credit based on your job title. And at the time I was a quality assurance technician on the testing. And, because they asked me to ... work as a level designer on a game, I designed actually one-third of the levels that appeared in the game. When it came time to release the game, I was like, "Can I get credited as level designer because I did level design for a large portion of the game?" And I was told, "No. You can only get credited by your job titles." (M-10-03-T-D-15-05-14-04-11-JT)

> ▸ The original manager that we had when I started wouldn't let a person have more than one credit on a game. Which was a bummer because, back then, the team was only twelve people, so everybody had multiple jobs. ... I think it really just depends on who's editing the particular text file. (F-13-19-T-B-29-05-14-05-13-JT)

> ▸ I wasn't specifically working on [game X] or [game Y]. I was sort of on a tools team ... and basically when you're on one of those teams, you get a choice of which project you want to be credited on. ... And in that case, I asked to have a credit on [game X] and I never ended up on it. (M-16-05-V-E-24-09-13-10-23-JT)

4. There are no processes for contesting credits, and pushing back can harm your reputation and lead to further arbitrary treatment down the road:

> ▸ I kind of fought for [credit]. I had begrudgingly won. But from that point my employer didn't like me and actually made my job situation more uncomfortable. And I left not too long after that because ... they were like, "We're going to do it but ... we'll make your life miserable." (M-10-03-T-D-15-05-14-04-11-JT)

Overall, the process for putting together the list of credits can seem erratic. Producers play a major role in recognition practices that vary even within the same studio as there is room for discretion. Publishers sometimes play a role too.

Access to Training: An Arbitrary Decision

Access to training is a key issue when keeping one's knowledge up to date is essential. Training can be formal (in an institution) or informal (self-directed, through peer networks or virtual communities). We focus on access to formal training because it has a cost both financially and in absence from work.

Some companies incentivize training by paying for training sessions available on the market, covering expenses for taking part in events, or organizing them, but most VGDs do not have access to employer-supported training (see Chapter 5). Some cases are not so clear; employers allow VGDs to use internal resources to train during work hours or while between projects, or they pay conference registration fees as a reward:

> ▸ *Was there anything to help you stay up to date?*
>
> Yes, but they were all individually directed projects. One of my friends ... started internal training for new designers that ran for a while. They did roundtables once every two weeks. That was a personally directed project ... but that wasn't any kind of long-term skills development stuff; it was like, "You're going to be doing this next week; you need to know how to do it." And I got to go to the Austin GDC [Game Developers Conference] once, but I don't know if that was really training. That was because I won a game development contest. They did pay my ticket! (M-07-12-M-F-31-01-14-16-02-PB)

These situations highlight the discretion involved in these decisions and the lack of connection to any training plan or policy, besides a rudimentary support to the effect of rewarding "good" behaviour. When an employee asks for funding for their training, the decision-making process is quite murky. Even known policies can be bypassed under unknown conditions:

> ▸ They'll suggest [attending conferences] if they think it's appropriate for you, but you can also ask, and if they feel that you're a good fit for that type of conference, then they'll send you, if they have the budget for it. (M-05-07-V-M-26-11-13-14-26-PB)

> ▸ I don't know if they'd help me do it, but they definitely communicate events that are going on. Actually, sometimes they give us tickets. They do have the internal training program, which, again,

is on and off. It's not supposed to be available to people on contract but I've totally done stuff, so I don't know what that means. (F-07-13-T-U-10-05-14-04-11-JT)

Some studios are subject to laws or government policies that require companies to devote a certain percentage of their wage bill to training. However, some fail to meet their commitments or deliberately falsify their activities. Typically, if VGDs want to attend conferences, they must pay out of their own pockets:

> ▸ Definitely, I go to the occasional IGDA meeting for networking. I know of people at a lot of the other companies. I guess, just because it feels like a small industry here in that people move around a lot, [you need] a lot of networking. I read websites and articles. I haven't been ... to as many conferences as I'd like. Most of the time, they've been self-funded, and when I haven't been working. But I'd like to have employers who see the value in sending their employees to these kinds of conferences. (M-10-06-M-B-16-11-13-16-02-PB)

VGDs are largely on their own with respect to training, having to fund the process of updating their skills, which, in the end, benefits both themselves and their employer if they stay with the same studio.

Assignment to Projects

Placements are also a constant concern for VGDs because they evolve in a project environment. Being assigned to a specific project is an occasion for training and development, building a reputation and preparing for future employment. The issue of internal placement arises chiefly in medium to large studios with multiple projects and a deeper portfolio. The smaller the studio, the more VGDs will need to explore outside; small studios carry out only a few projects at any given time, frequently lay off employees, and are more apt to employ on contract.

Our interview respondents noted a range of policies for project assignment:

- 12 percent said there was a formal procedure (applications, interviews, etc.) (half of those respondents worked in big studios, the other half in smaller ones).
- 19 percent said there was a formal process, but you could bypass it through an informal procedure (two-thirds were employed in big studios, the other third in small ones).

- 48 percent said their studio did not follow a formal procedure, just an informal practice (one-third worked in big studios, two-thirds in small ones).
- The remaining 21 percent could not recall any policy.

There was no obvious link between the size of the studio and the formality of the assignment policy. In all, 88 percent of our interviewees were faced with informality and decision-making processes that *might* accommodate their development aspirations in some contexts:

> ▶ They started using a new engine I was really interested in, so I was just asking my friends and the lead on the project, and eventually I sneaked into their team. So, it's pretty much connections and hovering around. ... It's more like relationship than paper. (F-13-11-M-W-10-10-13-13-19-15-MSO)

Within projects, some tasks or roles are assigned informally. Workers can state their preferences and talk to the people in charge of the job they would like to do. Yet, asking for a specific assignment can prove challenging:

> ▶ Once you're in a silo [at a big studio], you're pretty much stuck in that silo. There are career paths that you can follow, but to jump between those is really hard. You have to know somebody, and they're going to fight for you. It's a very undocumented process. It doesn't happen very often, because there's a lot of friction associated with doing that. ... I contacted some of the studios that [the parent studio] had acquired. I emailed some of their CEOs and people in charge to find some contacts throughout the [parent studio's] wider global network to try to reach out, find mentors, and that kind of thing. I tried to build that up, with very little traction again. (F-11-11-V-R-26-11-13-14-26-JL)

A formal policy, however, does not eliminate arbitrariness, because most policies confer the ultimate authority over assignments to the producer. Our interviewees who were "in the know" recounted stories of how the formal system was bypassed in favour of direct networking:

> ▶ You have to go and talk to the right people. We have an HR person who says, when you're between projects, "What are you interested in?" ... Afterwards, she goes round and speaks on your behalf, to try and place you on a project. ... But most people I know—and

me, too—we get better results by taking steps ourselves. Let's say I know a guy who's working on a project: "Hey, do you need anyone?" ... Then, as a result of the chitchat, all of a sudden you've got an appointment with so-and-so. So, in the end, you're the one who tells the HR person: "I've managed to find something" [*laughs*]. (M-16-02-M-U-24-10-13-13-19-15-JL)

> When I think of what other people have had to do [to get an assignment], to get almost aggressive, literally an e-mail every week to HR! "Do you have any news for me? Have you heard anything? Any news?" It drives them crazy! The best way, I think, is to go and talk to the people working on the project, and afterwards send an e-mail to HR. (M-19-12-M-U-12-11-13-13-15-19-JL)

The support of a current producer can also facilitate the movement of VGDs across projects and tip the scales in formal processes:

> When the opening came up, the game hadn't been released yet and my boss as QA had always been so supportive! He said: "I want you guys to apply for it!" He found out that the studio had already started looking at other candidates. When he found out about it, he talked to the producers: "Hey! I've got QA people here who would probably do amazing!" A couple of us had interviews—four of us. (F-11-20-V-H-27-11-13-14-26-JL-MSO)

That said, a significant two-thirds of interview respondents said they were not consulted on assignments because these are managerial decisions:

> *If you applied for a job with your current employer to work on a different project, how is the decision made?*
>
> You could probably speak to someone about it, but generally, it's the needs of the business more. If there's flexibility to move between projects, then maybe they would, but generally ... they'll say you need to work on that project. (M-10-06-M-B-16-11-13-16-02-PB)

This comment leads us back to considerations raised in Chapter 3, about the conflicting interests at stake in the matter of assignments. When VGDs are looking for a new project, their own interest lies in potential professional development. Under a formal policy, they can also be supported by the HR policy in their quest to learn. On the other hand, the project manager will be inclined to retain the most experienced and efficient employees on their projects or those recommended by a trusted peer. It is common knowledge that producers can exert significant pressure over HR when they would like to keep employees in a certain role. That is the inherent limit of formal policies in a project environment (Turner, Huemann, and Keegan 2018).

Evaluation and Promotion

There is always an evaluation of employees in work environments, whether formal or informal. Though decisions are rarely groundless, the less formal the process, the more arbitrary decision-making can be. This is riskier for employees and farther from an ideal of citizenship. This is particularly the case in decision-making regarding performance evaluations, which is highly discretionary. Although it could be regarded as a conflict of interest for employees to have a role in determining the outcome of such decisions, their ability to participate in this process is appropriate within a citizenship-at-work framework.

Survey respondents were asked how frequently their employers conducted performance evaluations, a first indicator of a formal policy (see Table 6.3). Roughly half said they were evaluated once a year. However, the second most common response was, "my company does not conduct performance reviews." Given the importance of performance evaluations, it is surprising to note how many respondents did not know how frequently their performance was evaluated.

Among the interview respondents, 74 percent were subject to a formal performance review process, while 26 percent were subject to an informal one. Of those under a formal process, 70 percent said that the procedure was followed, 22 percent said that the studio did not follow the established procedure, and 8 percent did not comment. Many of our respondents (59 percent) described how the performance review was held (see Table 6.4).

The most common procedure essentially consisted of a meeting with one or more superiors, which, in the absence of any official policy, involved varying degrees of arbitrariness. The manager drew some conclusions about the employee's performance without any guidelines, known criteria, or consultation. In this procedure, VGDs were not given an opportunity to discuss the evaluation results or ask for more specifics, and had no means of contesting the evaluation:

> ▸ We have ... performance reviews, I guess, about once a year, but we don't get any feedback on that—we get given our feedback by

Table 6.3
Distribution of answers (% of respondents) to the question: "How often does your company conduct performance reviews of its employees?" (2014-19)

	2014	2019
Annually	52	43
My company does not conduct performance reviews	15	15
Every six months	12	14
Don't know	12	7
Quarterly	6	8
Ad-hoc/inconsistent	1	13
Other	1	—

Source: Original data from the IGDA DSS 2014, 2019

Table 6.4
Type of assessment procedure in my studio

	% of respondents who discussed it
Meeting with a manager	49
Meeting with a manager and evaluation through a questionnaire	17
Meeting with a manager and peer review	7
Meeting with a manager, peer review, and questionnaire	13
Evaluation via a questionnaire and peer review	4
Evaluation only via a questionnaire	4
Evaluation via software	2
Evaluation of teams only, no individual evaluation	2
Peer review only	2
Total	100

Source: Original data from the Canadian interviews led by authors in 2013-14

our director, but there's no recourse to say I disagree. ... It's on a scale of one to four, how well did you do? So, one is you completely failed to do anything, four is that you exceeded expectations. And it's very subjective, and it's very reliant on your director.

Is it fair?

No, I don't think so at all. (F-12-20-M-E-03-12-13-16-02)

In line with the survey respondents who said that performance reviews were conducted on an inconsistent or ad hoc basis, a few interview respondents said they were "evaluated" only when there was a problem. They thought that not being evaluated was good news—as if a performance review were part of the disciplinary process:

> ▸ *Do you have a formal evaluation process?*
>
> No. Essentially, in my experience with the management style that I'm in, it's "no news is good news." It's pretty much that I haven't been doing a bad job. (F-11-07-M-S-24-11-13-16-02-PB)

> ▸ I think if the product is not doing well, if we were not making our time, if I was forgetting about stuff, then I would be, "I'm not doing well." My boss is very quiet. If I don't hear from him it's a good thing. ... We only ever do full evaluations when people are having problems, which I guess is something I'd like to change. (F-13-13-V-I-15-11-13-14-26)

The VGI evolves rapidly with changes in technology. This affects the evaluation of new jobs: what's necessary to make a good evaluation? The following respondent served as an online community manager for a massively multiplayer online game (MMOG) when this type of game was just emerging. As is illustrated in their response, when there are no clearly established review criteria (see Dubois and Weststar 2021), there is room for arbitrariness:

> ▸ A really good example would be, when I'm trying to build up our Twitter following because they haven't been giving any sort of promotional budget, I would actually spend hours searching Twitter for specific hashtags that people are posting about and then engage with those users and, you know, try to build conversations and establish a rapport with them, in order for them to check out our profile and follow us back. And that takes a lot of time. (F-03-07-V-F-12-19-13-14-26-LT)

Some studios have very informal performance review policies, and managers may conduct evaluations in the manner they think appropriate, including speaking to a VGD about their own lives and career paths. According to some respondents, a formal review process would not be a good fit for a small studio:

> Occasionally ... the founder would check in with people, but it was not structured in a very formal [way]. ... It's a small organization so nothing like, "Here's our annual review thing!" I don't think it would be appropriate anyway. I just don't think it would jive with the people and the culture and all that. (M-15-01-V-K-02-10-13-14-26-LT)

> I think there might be [formal evaluations]. ... I think it was two times that we'd go and have coffee and have, like, a little review, "how things are going" type thing. ... I'm not really sure what formal would mean. (F-19-18-V-S-12-11-13-14-26-LT)

> I actually haven't had a formal evaluation but I'm going to have one on Monday, so after four years there's that. But, I don't know, I guess I do get feedback from my bosses as we go. ... They will thank me or tell me, "You've done a good job on this." So, there's that. I feel like there's a very direct feedback as far as seeing when I put something in, if it's successful or if it breaks. (M-01-19-T-D-28-11-13-05-13-JT)

Some respondents organize their own evaluations, soliciting their peers or superiors, to gain clarity on their performance or to agitate for better terms in a contract:

> No, I haven't had any sort of reviews. ... I make sure to sit down with people all the time and get, like, mini-reviews. When I'm setting up this new contract with the company, I'm like, "How are you guys regarding me? Am I doing a good job? ... Great, because your expectations have gone up, so here's a new contract to adjust for that." ... If the company's not *going* to have proper HR and process to review me, I will make sure that I get those reviews, and if there need to be adjustments. (M-18-01-V-R-13-11-13-14-26-LT)

Evaluation can trigger pay raise bargaining, and that may explain why some studios do not have an evaluation process, even if VGDs feel deprived of feedback and often initiate review meetings themselves:

> When I took the job, I asked, "Will I have a chance to be reviewed in my first year here?" And they said yes, but they never initiated any kind of review, so I had to raise the issue. And I said, "You know what? I'd like to have my salary looked at and I'd like your

feedback on my work." And they still didn't really give me formal feedback on my work, but they did do a salary review and they gave me cost of living, so... Okay, but I had to ask for it. ... And I still feel that I don't have enough feedback from management on the quality of my work. (F-19-09-T-S-17-01-14-05-13-JT)

Some VGDs do operate under a formal system, including built-in effects on the pay structure, but it is never explained or made visible to them. As a result, they cannot contest it and miss out on receiving feedback on their work. That said, many studios do have a comprehensive process, like a 360-degree review that combines personal, peer, subordinate, and supervisor reviews:

▶ We have a formal yearly evaluation. ... You do a self-evaluation. They have a relatively complex form that you have to fill out about your work ethic and the quality of your work, and they also give forms to three of your peers to evaluate you, and your lead evaluates you, and then you have a one-on-one evaluation meeting with your lead. ... And we get ranked in all of the things that we do: technical skill, artistic skill, work ethic. ... And higher-ups kind of take that evaluation and process to decide how big of a raise we should get every year, whether or not we should go from level one to level two, two to three, become a lead... (M-02-22-M-L-23-11-13-16-02-PB)

▶ So, what they did now is that everybody on your team evaluates everybody in an anonymous system with a one-to-five scale, five being the highest, perfect. ... If you get a five, you're exceeding all expectations beyond belief. Most people get three to four. On different standards you're being evaluated, with commentary, and this is all getting compiled, sorted with commentaries, and managed electronically, and this is being fed into a system. (M-14-02-M-G-07-02-14-16-02)

Yet even these systems have problems. Peer reviews are supposed to be anonymous, but can hardly remain so in many contexts:

▶ We do peer reviews, and peer reviews are people you worked directly with, [and you] answer questions about your work, leadership, communication, team working, and all those questions. Then, you review them with your manager, and they're all anonymous, and then you get reviewed by your direct manager, and then your product also has metrics, and the team, like the whole company itself, has metrics. ... I think it could be [a fair process], except right now, only three people reviewed me, so I knew—the comments that I got, I knew exactly who said them—and the same with the people who I reviewed. ... Afterwards, I was like, "Oh! I didn't know you felt that way about this." So I think it's kind of bad in that sense. I think it would be better if you got reviewed by more people. (M-20-22-V-A-12-19-13-14-26-PB)

This form of structured evaluation, which includes different types of assessment, helps to limit the arbitrary element in evaluations. But at the same time, it can generate conflicts or pressure to avoid them.

As well, managers can disregard the evaluation policy during crunch times when everyone is busy, which raises the issue of how important evaluations really are:

▸ We had a form of evaluation process that was basically ignored. It was ignored, especially towards the end, when everyone was in crunch. ... It's not super proactive development. There was a formally articulated process, but it was much more of a fiction than it was real. (M-01-18-V-E-18-10-13-14-26-JL)

Compensation: A Multi-Level System

Large game development studios have a three-layered compensation system. The first two parts are intertwined and appear to be one single operation. The first layer is a starting point, based on "market wages" for comparable jobs, which will end up being the pay level for many. The second layer is a supplement which can be individually negotiated based on one's market value, reputation, and achievements. These two constitute the individual base pay level. The third layer is performance based: the bonus. The latter two layers leave much room for discretionary decision-making.

The Individually Negotiated Pay Level

Our data show a general lack of formal pay policies based on rules and predetermined criteria or fixed pay scales that would standardize pay raises. When asked whether raises were part of their compensation, at least 65 percent of employee survey respondents said their raise was based partly or wholly on a discretionary estimate by one or more managers (see Table 6.4, rows 1 and 2). In 2019, respondents who were self-employed were asked if they provided raises to their staff. These represent indie/smaller studios and display an even greater use

Table 6.5
Distribution of answers (% of respondents) to the question: "Does your employer/do you provide raises as part of your compensation?" (2014–19)

	2014 (employees)	2019 (employees)	2019 (provision to employees)
1. Yes, based on a combination of merit, fixed percentage, and judgement of management	39	38	6
2. Yes, based on the judgement of management	16	18	25
3. Yes, based on merit	10	11	25
4. Yes, based on a fixed percentage	4	4	6
No	18	15	37
Don't know	13	13	—

Source: Original data from DSS 2014, 2019

of managerial discretion—that is, when raises are provided at all (see Table 6.5, column 3).

Pay levels can vary due to the perceived market value of any candidate and the incentive to hire or retain them. In the business of entertainment, acknowledging individual merit and translating its market value to pay levels is not contested as inequitable but is rather seen as necessary. The meritocratic pay and placement system is a source of pride that draws upon the post-bureaucratic movement of thought and the rejection of hierarchy-based authority.

Yet, in individual negotiations, most VGDs are in no position to make demands, and often take what they are given:

> ▶ I guess the problem is that I haven't renegotiated my salary at all, I just get raises, but I have to negotiate them, so I don't know [about others]. I feel like a few co-workers might have negotiated better salaries. ... Basically if you were doing something in crunch mode, though, and your product was successful, I think you'd expect to get a bigger bonus, and if you didn't, I feel like that you could probably be, like, "Can I get more money?" But it's not in my personality to actually bring it up, so I don't know. (F-09-20-V-A-24-10-13-14-26-AD)

Pay raises may be determined more formally in larger studios, but even so, the criteria for a raise and its proportions are still discretionary. Pay raises are negotiated individually and informally in small- to medium-sized studios:

> ▶ I managed to drag a minor pay increase [out of the CEO]. It required a lot of cajoling. ... It was just after [the game project] had shipped and I was, like, "Clearly, we did a lot of work on this game. I'm trying to figure out what my future is going to be like. I want to have some kind of financial security in my future!" ... And so there's a bit of back and forth, and then eventually I was able to drag, I think it was 7 percent or something like that. It's a small company. ... I mean it was kind of weird having to ask, but whatever, I don't imagine it would have happened in any other way. There's definitely no regularly structured reviews that would make my pay bigger. It's a small company, right? (M-15-01-V-K-02-10-13-14-26-LT)

The Arbitrary Bonus Level

If there is a bonus, it is also distributed according to discretionary criteria. Typically, bonuses come on top of any base salary as a share of the profits in the form of an overall sum to be distributed among the team. Both the decision to allow a budget dedicated to bonuses to be given to a project team and the amount of this budget depend entirely on the discretion of the client-funder, based on the commercial success of the game. This is regardless of the time invested in a project:

> ▶ I assume that for a smaller firm that gets a [publishing] contract, it's more or less the same process: you send your stuff [to the publisher] and they say whether they like it or not. ... If the game sells and gets back more than the initial cost, we get a bonus up to a certain percentage. So, bonuses can go up quite a lot. (M-19-12-M-U-12-11-13-13-15-19-JL)

If VGDs work hard on a game that is a commercial failure, their own dedication is not in question, but they cannot expect any pay for their overtime. In accordance with the "start-up" ideology present in the VGI, they are placed in a position to be wage earners but also partly entrepreneurs. Unlike the bureaucratic worker, they bear part of the risk of commercial failure because the bonus is only granted if they have fulfilled their obligation of results (see Chapter 2).

Bonuses for merit are calculated on the perceptions of producers. If a team bonus is shared, the distribution criteria are established by the management, who estimate each person's contribution to the success of the game:

> ▸ It's really arbitrary: your project manager has an amount and he decides how to divide it up. That's often the way it is. ... In any case, at [the studio], everybody working on the project was on contract, so everybody negotiated their own agreements. (M-19-10-M-I-17-7-13-13-10-12-MSO)

In creative environments, merit is highly valued, but the manner in which it is assessed lends itself to arbitrariness. "Contribution to success" comes down to the producer's perceptions—or worse, to poor proxies such as estimates of dedicated crunch time. In fact, "agreeing to work overtime sometimes becomes a condition of employment" (D. Harvey 2010, 275) and of reward (see Chapter 9). This way, assessment criteria are used as a leverage tool to generate desired behaviours like dedication to crunch time.

In terms of HRM, a performance-based rewards system is key to understanding the industry and its systems of self-discipline (Gaume 2006). Performance pay is a common practice in mass production or management jobs, where it is generally backed by precise metrics (for example, units produced, or quality level achieved) and a known output-to-pay correspondence scale. But in the VGI, there are none of these. Every element is discretionary: the publisher's decision to allow a bonus for a project team, the size of this bonus, the criteria on which to distribute this envelope among team members, the interpretation of these criteria, and the amounts offered.

Compensation for crunch time is also an arbitrary game (see Chapter 9). Often, there is no accounting for overtime work—work that, though pervasive, does not thereby officially exist. If counted, the estimation of time is mostly discretionary. VGDs can receive compensation to make up for unpaid overtime, but it is never guaranteed and never formal, and the calculation is arbitrary. As such, we cannot refer to this as overtime *pay*. It is more accurately a *reward*. Promises made regarding compensation while in crunch time often go unfulfilled (Legault and Weststar 2017). If granted some time off, VGDs are seldom able to choose the time when they can take it; that is also a discretionary decision.

Conclusion

We have outlined the discretionary character of the decision-making process on seven important topics of HRM and have drawn general conclusions about the three measures of citizenship at work (see Table 6.6).

Table 6.6
Discretionary decision-making in videogame development studios as object, subject, and domain of citizenship at work

	Object	*Subjects*	*Domain*
Dismissals and disciplinary action	No formal process	"Stars" can enjoy some leverage to negotiate	None
NCAs and NDAs	Quasi-formal process regarding uniformity and rational (if not legal) criteria; No feedback process for stakeholders' input, a "fictitious" formal process regarding the contractual freedom of independent agents; Fair process for those who contest this before the court; Decision to sue is arbitrary	"Stars" can enjoy some leverage to negotiate	Possible in independent, small-to-average studios
Crediting	Often, but: <ul><li>No feedback process;</li><li>Criteria often unclear;</li><li>Affordance for publishers and producers to opt out</li></ul>	Universal for those who still work in the studio, but absent for those who left	Nearly, but characteristics remain unknown
Access to training	No	Some VGDs in large studios, but policies are never coercive	Some rare large studios
Assignment to projects	No	Some VGDs in large studios, but policies are never coercive	None
Evaluation	Some large studios and some projects in small-to-medium studios have policies; No formal recourse; Criteria often unclear	Some VGDs in large studios and some projects in small-to-medium studios, but some projects can avoid this process	Some large and medium studios, still depending on projects
Compensation system	No	"Stars" can enjoy some leverage in individual negotiation	None

To sum up, there are few *objects* of citizenship, and these are not devoid of important shortcomings. Indeed, VGDs do not enjoy the representativeness that characterizes procedural justice or fair procedure, and we have not encountered any dispute resolution procedure for any of the objects at stake. Both process and decisions are controlled by management.

There can be no *subjects* of citizenship if there are few and imperfect objects. A few subjects may be found in studios that have formal policies or comply with laws. However, there can be discretion even within formal attribution processes. Some satisfied VGDs get what they wish for, since discretionary decision-making can lead to satisfying decisions. But, if some workers can enjoy certain leverage in individual negotiations and feel they are citizens of their workplace, such a granting of recourse based on the whims of management is in no way formal. Instead, it is arbitrariness manifested, as some can speak up while the majority do not. It reflects a hierarchy based on "market value" and is therefore bargaining power in the broader sense rather than citizenship.

In the end, such an obligation-free zone could hardly be a *domain* of citizenship in the absence of objects and subjects, and overall because of mobility. If VGDs enjoy formal processes where they exist but can also move to spaces where there are none, the situation they are facing is one of sporadic citizenship. If not framed by clear, disclosed rules that are uniformly applied, procedures remain a "black box" for VGDs.

Under the governance framework proposed in Chapter 1, VGDs are offered no more than HRM with an employer-initiated employee voice. This approach is inspired by liberal non-interventionism, which avoids standing in the way of "free" contractual employment relationships (Armbrüster 2005), while at times softening the edges. Both HRM departments and producers can be open to VGDs' input and voice, but in the absence of formal appeal systems, decision processes become strongly biased in favour of efficiency over equity or voice. At any time, an employer can unilaterally disband these mechanisms, particularly if profitability and efficiency are at stake (Budd and Colvin 2005). Studio managers cling to a notion of creating "special" workplaces, shielded from the flaws of bureaucracy and conflicts of interest between employers and employees. In a sort of "moral vacuum" (Osterman et al. 2001, 12), the random manager acts under the assumption that work contracts are concluded between "free agents" under the normal constraints of a tight product and job market. It is assumed that with "good management," employer and employee interests can be aligned.

CHAPTER 7

Do Game Developers Participate in the Local Regulation of Work?

The possibility for workers to voice their needs and wishes about their working conditions and have their say in the rules of the workplace was an important asset in the expansion to citizenship at work (see Chapter 1). Workers can attempt to gain a meaningful influence in the local regulation of work through a range of formal and informal means both as individuals and as groups (Wilkinson et al. 2014, 5). However, to *embody* citizenship, that is, to have a meaningful influence on the decisions that affect their work, workers must be part of the work regulation process. Among the different mechanisms available for employees to voice their concerns (Wilkinson et al. 2014), some allow workers to be citizens in their workplace, while others do not.

In the contemporary project-based environment (see Chapter 3), traditional forms of managerial oversight and control have been replaced with neo-normative control mechanisms (Alvesson 2000; Hodgson and Briand 2015; Huws 2011; Pérez-Zapata et al. 2016; Smith and McKinlay 2009; Thompson and Van den Broek 2010). These rely on the professional autonomy of creative workers and the reification of the project (Cicmil and Hodgson 2006). Ostensibly functioning through the personal choice of workers, these control mechanisms shift the responsibility and accountability for project success (and therefore individual, team, and organizational success) from management and onto project team workers (Legault 2013; Peticca-Harris, Weststar, and McKenna 2015). Casual observers to this environment might easily assume that project-based knowledge workers have great control and agency over their working conditions and are willing co-creators of the systems under which they work. However, project-based workers face a considerable deficit regarding their participation in the local regulation of their work (see Chapters 4, 6, and 10).

When a significant proportion of workers in a sector feel that their workplace problems are serious, it automatically raises the question of what action—individual or collective—they can take to solve them.

Hirschman's (1970) work on consumer action has been adopted as a framework in understanding the actions of disgruntled employees at work. An expanded model (Farrell 1983) sets out a typology of four approaches: exit (to leave the organization), voice (to speak out with the intent of change), loyalty (to hope and wait for conditions to improve), and neglect (to withdraw attention and effort). As captured in an expansive review of the topic (Wilkinson et al. 2014), employee voice has a long history prior to its treatment under this model (Kaufman 2014), and its diversity of form has been represented, interpreted, and reinterpreted across a range of scholarly disciplines.

The actions that workers choose to take, are forced to take, or are resigned to take (Donaghey et al. 2011) and the extent to which they gain individual or collective influence in the regulation of work depends on many different factors. These include the personal characteristics and strategic choices of individual workers and managers, formal and informal organizational structures, policies and practices of the workplace that can enable or stifle worker activity, the requirements and constraints of the legal environment, and the presence of formal representative bodies (like unions) that act on behalf of groups of workers. Like most things in labour relations, the success of these actions also hinges on the power held by the individual or the collective vis à vis that of the manager or employer. Taken together, different individuals and groups have different potentials and capacities for action or mobilization that are contextually specific (Kelly 1998).

Worker resistance and the struggle to gain voice, agency, or representation in the workplace occurs continually in large and small ways. Project-based knowledge workers are no different. This chapter presents an overview of the individual and collective actions taken by VGDs and assesses the degree to which these actions have enabled greater participation in the local regulation of work as an object of citizenship.

Individual Means to Participate

Employee Exit

Exit remains the top-of-mind action for workers who are unhappy with their work situation. "If you don't like it, leave," is a common refrain in the VGI. It is reinforced by the high mobility built into the project-based structure of game development and a hot job market. Many VGDs feel that exit is the only option. As one developer told us: "In a sense it may be easier to go and start up your own company and do contract work ... than it is to try to get a big company to change its ways" (F-05-20-U-25-06-08-01-07).

In the face of a dispute, another said that rather than suing the company or going to the "labour people," "it's probably more worthwhile and cheaper just to find another job in the industry. We get fired and get hired at another place all the time" (H-13-11-A-17-06-08-01-07).

Some VGDs convey a sense of toughness or machismo about "surviving" an epic crunch (an extended period of overtime), and these episodes become normalized in the lore of the industry ("I was there when..."). Those who complain or do not survive can be considered as those who cannot take it ("This industry is not for you"). Some take personal advantage of the high demand for labour in the industry, particularly in regional clusters where a lot of studios exist. Here, good VGDs can be head-hunted away from competitors and dissatisfied VGDs can look for greener pastures.

But the exit approach does not compel managers to fix any problems for the long term. When developers quit, studios have a large reserve of workers who are eager to take their place. Turnover is a concern for bureaucratic organizations because of the assumption of a reciprocal long-term relationship and the ensuing recruitment, selection, and training costs. Even then, in most organizations, turnover rarely produces structural change. In project-based organizations, mobility and labour turnover is part and parcel of the system and routinely practiced on both sides. Project-based organizations do not invest much in recruitment and selection processes or training. Most of their employees are hired or allocated "on-demand" and skills-ready through networks and by recommendation.

As well, exiting an organization is no guarantee of improved circumstances. Lucky VGDs might be able to find a "better" job in the industry, but most studios operate the same way. There is also the chance that the new studio could be worse, meaning for these VGDs it's out of the frying pan and into the fire. Some leave the industry altogether and seek more stable and less intense jobs in other industries (such as banks, programming, teaching, special effects, etc.), or they seek game making opportunities in studios with more favourable practices, but often less profile (such as making games for children's television shows or education, or making serious games).

Some "star" developers can negotiate favourable employment conditions or are head-hunted under favourable terms. This is highly advantageous on an individual basis, but it does not help anyone else and can create problematic systems of inequity that disadvantage VGDs who cannot provide the commitment deemed to be required. This also creates the conditions in which supporters of the status quo succeed and those with diverging opinions are chased out—this can lead to groupthink and stagnation because no one can see a different way of doing things. This is particularly challenging for underrepresented groups such as women.

Employee exit is therefore not an avenue to citizenship, and perpetual turnover is not an effective means to regulate work. So, what else can VGDs do?

Employee Neglect

Neglect is another worker response to work dissatisfaction. It encompasses a range of actions including putting in less effort, disengaging from work, absenteeism, or decreased attention to quality. Less pejoratively, recent studies have also examined the circumstances under which employees engage in silence, as the counterpart to having a voice (Donaghey et al. 2011). Activities of neglect are less commonly reported in the game industry. Visibility at work through logged hours is tied to performance evaluations and reputation is based on successes. The interdependency of the work and commitment to team success serve as normative constraints on reduced effort and disengagement. Ozimek (2019b) notes resistance in the form of neglect where game testers marked tasks as tested when they had not been.

One form of neglect that game developers have used is sabotage. In the VGI, one form of sabotage is leaking important or confidential information to competitors or the press. Novel IP and innovation is the lifeblood of the industry and companies hold information about their upcoming games or game technologies tight to their chests. The industry is rife with NDAs and NCAs. Therefore, this form of sabotage is very risky because the developers who engage in it can be sued or informally sanctioned, and it threatens their own reputation (see Chapter 6). This is not a common or very fruitful action for dissatisfied developers who want to remain in the industry.

A unique form of sabotage is to drop an "Easter egg" into a finished work. An Easter egg is a coded signature for the creator and is a means for individual workers or teams to gain credit for the work they produced. The first documented case of an Easter egg was at Atari, in response to the management's decision to stop crediting the contributions of individual programmers and only use the Atari brand (Yarwood 2016). In game development, crediting is largely unregulated (Deuze, Chase Bowen, and Allen 2007). Given the importance of a portfolio to a developer's career, accurate crediting is important for their claims of experience. Yet, most studios have no formal or transparent system for crediting, and the success of developers in negotiating crediting rights is highly dependent on their individual skills or their specific context (see Chapter 6).

Easter eggs have become ubiquitous in computer software and media (Yarwood 2016; Hester 2017). However, although Easter eggs were born out of protest of managerial dictate, the devaluation of individual developer contributions, and the reduction of developers' reputational power (Wolf and Perron 2003), this resistance was quickly co-opted by management. Employers soon saw the marketing benefit of having Easter eggs in their games, as players valued both the act of searching for an egg and the community status of finding one. Indeed, Easter eggs are now a mandated, budgeted, and resourced aspect of many games that are arguably leveraged against developers. The honour of doing the extra work to create the egg is a reward doled out to the most senior team members, and the threat of lack of budget or lack of time to include the eggs can be used to motivate the development team to work more (Hester 2017).

Individual Employee Voice

Employee voice refers to the "ways and means through which employees attempt to have a say and potentially influence organizational affairs relating to issues that affect their work" (Wilkinson et al. 2014, 5). Over the years we have gathered survey data regarding VGDs' opinions on voice mechanisms in their workplaces. Consistent across a ten-year time span, most VGDs felt that management seeks their (general) input and acts on it (see Table 7.1 in the Data Appendix). However, in each survey year, at least one-quarter of respondents were on the fence about whether they had a meaningful voice and 18 to 25 percent did not feel like they had one. The most common forms of expressing one's voice among the VGDs we interviewed were individual meetings with managers or speaking up at a team meeting. Some said that their studios had formal "open door" policies for managers to listen to employees (Legault and Weststar 2015b).

We also surveyed VGDs about the effectiveness of their companies' systems for resolving problems raised by individuals and for problems raised by groups of employees (see Table 7.2). Though the majority felt that company systems were at least somewhat effective, a large number were unsure. This was particularly the case regarding management's effectiveness in resolving problems that employees raised as a group.

The survey data also show that many VGDs would prefer not to speak up as an individual (Tô, Legault, and Weststar 2016, 24). In 2014, close to half of the respondents (48 percent) said that they would rather voice concerns through an employee organization than raise issues as an individual; 25 percent were undecided.

Overall, employee voice can be a fruitful mechanism to obtain a role in the regulation of work, but much depends on the motivations behind

Table 7.2
Distribution of answers (% of respondents) to the question: "How effective is your company's system for resolving problems individuals/groups have at work?" (2014)

	System for solving problems raised by individuals	System for solving problems raised by groups
Very effective	9	7
Somewhat effective	32	28
Not too effective	18	18
Not effective at all	14	11
Don't know	27	36

Source: Adapted from Tô, Legault, and Weststar 2016, 26–27

the establishment of voice mechanisms and their design. Our data support some of the known challenges of individual employee voice (Gollan, Kaufman, Taras, and Wilkinson 2014). First, approaches to employee voice that treat each employee concern as a separate issue as it comes, serve to individualize and make invisible problems that might be structural or collective. Managers employ discretionary decision-making that can result in arbitrary and inequitable outcomes across a group of workers. Much rests on the individual negotiating power and reputation of the developer who is speaking up.

Second, employee voice can be received poorly and invalidated if it is not seen as "constructive" or contributing to managerial directives (Morrison 2011), even when coming from committed and motivated employees. In an industry driven by portfolio and reputation, being labelled as a troublemaker, a whistleblower, or not a team player can be devastating. Non-union employee representation (NER) or employer-driven voice mechanisms have been criticized as forms of normative managerial control that can amplify voices deemed contributory and silence those deemed denunciatory (Donaghey et al. 2011).

Third, even in instances where the motivation of employers in establishing an employee voice mechanism is to achieve real mutual gains, research has concluded that they are not conducive to this end. They too often fail to confer any real agency and decision-making power to participating employees (Dobbins and Dundon 2014).

In terms of citizenship, these individual means of action do not offer a robust or consistent avenue to participation in the local regulation of work, as they are too often structured and mediated by management and are too often simply a feedback mechanism rather than a sharing of decision-making authority. They also require workers to go out on a limb and face the threat of reprisal.

Regulation through Collective Short-Term Mobilizations

"Job Actions" in Social Media

Pressuring an employer to change their behaviour through shaming mechanisms that jeopardize a studio's reputation in the public sphere is another form of action that has been increasingly taken up in the VGI. The affordances of the Internet and social media have amplified the impact of these approaches. Over the past twenty years, VGDs have engaged in activities to exert their voice that have become moments of short-term solidarity.

One example is the EA *Spouse* blog that was published online in November 2004 and started a trend of whistleblowing and public expressions of dissatisfaction about game studio practices. The blog came on the heels of the first IGDA *Quality of Life* report (IGDA 2004) and brought the issues of the report to life: burnout, depression, and broken social relationships due to long, uncompensated working hours. In the subsequent weeks and months, over 4,500 comments flooded the blog with similar accounts from beleaguered developers and sympathy from consumers. The story spread and rallied a movement against Electronic Arts (EA) (the focal studio) and overtime in general. Under this spotlight, EA reportedly banned work on Sundays and adopted a policy favouring five working days a week.

The event was a watershed moment for awareness about exploitative working conditions and is also an early example of the power of social media for sharing information, sparking change-oriented discourse, and building virtual communities of interest (Shirky 2008). The EA *Spouse* blog was followed by the Gamewatch.org website, created to monitor and report on studio management practices. It was turned into a wiki reserved for the Gamewatch community in 2012, after the community was hassled by trolls. The EA *Spouse* story also became part of the early academic discourse on digital game labour (Dyer-Witheford and de Peuter 2006; Peticca-Harris, Weststar, and McKenna 2015). Numerous acts of online whistleblowing have occurred since—first with more blogs posted by the wives of disgruntled developers (for example, *Rockstar Spouse* in 2010 and *38 Studios Spouse* in 2012) and later in a trend of investigative journalism into studio practices (i.e., D'Anastasio 2018; McMillen 2011, 2012; Schreier 2013a, 2013b, 2014b, 2015; see also Weststar and Legault 2019 and https://gameqol.org).

These largely focused on unlimited, unpaid overtime (UUO), but also included issues such as game crediting and layoffs. The past ten years have also seen a rise in discussions about the sexual harassment and discrimination experienced by women in the industry (see Chapter 10). Worker groups have mobilized at major studios such as Ubisoft and Activision Blizzard King (ABK) to pressure their employers through social media (such as @ABetterUbisoft and @ABetterABK on Twitter).

Direct Job Actions "On the Ground"

The withdrawal of labour is considered the strongest act that workers can take to pressure their employer to negotiate favourable terms; however, it is rare outside of a unionized environment because there are no legal protections for striking non-union workers. Despite this, VGDs seem to be increasingly inclined to engage in the direct job action of holding a strike or walk-out.

Roughly one hundred VGDs walked off the job at the Crytek UK studio in July 2014 to protest unpaid wages (Schreier 2014a). Though the walk-out focused attention on the issue, it did not improve the lot of Crytek workers, as the studio was closed within a month and its IP sold to another studio (Koch 2014). Many developers had already left the studio in the face of this uncertainty, but others followed the game IP (see Weststar and Legault 2019, and http://gameqol.org).

Developers at Riot Games in California also escalated their actions. Following journalist D'Anastasio's (2018) exposé about the culture of sexism at Riot, a class action lawsuit was filed. However, Riot attempted to thwart this legal avenue by holding up the company's forced arbitration policy. This required developers to forgo the right to sue their employer and settle disputes internally through a mechanism that many felt favoured the company. In May 2019, 150 VGDs at the studio walked off the job in protest over this policy (Grayson and D'Anastasio 2019). Amid other promises to change their sexist culture, Riot announced that it would allow *new* employees to waive the forced arbitration for sexual harassment disputes, but only after the current litigation was resolved. Walkouts also occurred at Activision Blizzard throughout 2021 as workers protested their employer's defiant response to a sexual harassment lawsuit (Anguiano 2021; Liao 2021).

In December 2021, quality assurance (QA) workers began a strike at Raven Software, a studio owned by Activision Blizzard (Carpenter 2021a). This followed the unexpected layoff of twelve QA contractors—30 percent of the QA team. Workers from other Activision Blizzard studios across the United States engaged in solidarity walkouts. Activision responded by saying that the layoffs were part of a broader restructuring that included converting five hundred temporary workers into full-time employees, and there was later speculation that the move was part of the acquisition deal with Microsoft (Francis 2022b). The strike had a surprise ending, when Raven QA workers announced that they had voted to unionize with the Communications Workers of America (CWA) under the name Game Workers Alliance (Carpenter 2022)

Lawsuits as a Collective Action

VGDs can also turn to labour and employment law to gain a role in the regulation of their work. It is not an uncommon avenue for dissatisfied non-unionized employees to sue their employers for violations of employment law, particularly in the United States.

US VGDs have had some success in challenging the overtime exemptions in their jurisdictions. Through 2004 to 2006, there were a few successful class action lawsuits against major game studios over unpaid overtime and the misclassification of developers as exempt from overtime laws. Two suits were filed against EA: one on behalf of game designers was settled for US$15.6 million, and one on behalf of programmers was settled for US$14.9 million (Surette 2006). There was also a suit against Sony Entertainment, which was settled for US$8.5 million, and similar suits filed against Vivendi and Activision. In the case of EA, the suit resulted in the reclassification of many developers so that they became eligible for overtime provisions under California law.

More recent wins were in the cases of Riot Games and Activision Blizzard, discussed above. In November 2018, women VGDs filed a class action lawsuit against Riot for violations of California's Equal Pay Act. The US$10 million settlement covered approximately one thousand women who had worked at Riot between 2014 and 2019. It also held the studio to a number of commitments: to improve reporting practices for sexual harassment and discrimination; to review all pay, promotion, and hiring practices; to hire a dedicated chief diversity officer; and to create employee groups empowered to track the company's progress (Dean 2019). Similarly, Activision Blizzard agreed to a US$18 million settlement in a sexual discrimination and harassment lawsuit filed by the US Equal Employment Opportunity Commission (K. Paul 2022). Related to the same events, it later agreed to a US$35 million settlement regarding charges brought by the US Securities and Exchange Commission for failing to properly handle employee complaints of workplace misconduct and violating whistleblower protection laws (Parvini 2023). Reportedly, Activision Blizzard enacted company-wide structural changes.

As these cases show, sometimes legal action can be more successful, less of a burden, and less individually risky when done collectively. Class actions can also bring redress to a larger group and are more likely to produce permanent changes to the system beyond the financial payout. This seems to be the case at Riot. Yet, the needle is continually moving. Although improvements to "crunch culture" were noted at EA (Paprocki 2018), an unforeseen side effect was that the studio relocated portions of its business to Florida and Canada, where overtime laws remained permissive (Legault and Weststar 2013).

As well, employers have many more resources than employees, and sometimes the law is not sufficient to support employee complaints. In addition, these recourses tend to be limited to the employees of large studios. VGDs may have a harder time collecting any settlement from a class-action lawsuit from a smaller studio, particularly if the company fails, and there may not even be sufficient employees to form such a suit.

This approach also requires that developers have some knowledge of their rights at work to determine if they have been violated in the first place. Data from the 2009 and 2014 surveys revealed that 64 to 75 percent of the respondents knew little to nothing about the labour/employment laws that governed their work (Tô, Legault, and Weststar 2016, 37). In line with this lack of knowledge, 42 percent of respondents to the 2014 DSS did not know if the labour/employment laws where they lived offered sufficient protection for them should a problem arise with their employer (Tô, Legault, and Weststar 2016, 37–38). One-third felt that the laws were sufficient and 27 percent said they were not.

In sum, VGDs have some ability to regulate the local conditions of their work through short-term collective actions. Due to the power of social media, online whistleblowing, investigative journalism, and event coverage by a sympathetic press, industry-wide discussion can be kindled. These media moments have heightened a desire for change and for a participative role in the regulation of work.

However, the actual impact of these actions on specific studio practices is harder to quantify and depends on the nature of the action itself. Some exposés seemed to exert sufficient pressure affecting a studio's reputation to provoke studio change. For instance, a change in practice was documented at Trendy Entertainment (Schreier 2013a, 2013b, 2013c; Schiller 2015), and Ubisoft responded when its culture of sexism was exposed (Glasner 2020). But in most cases studio change was not due to normative pressure, but to the developers escalating to a more direct form of short-term collective action or claiming access to universal labour laws. We see this is the case of EA, in which class actions led to changes, and in the more recent case of Riot Games, with class actions and developer walkouts.

Seeking a Lasting Collective: Professional Associations and Industry Groups

The 2014 survey data show that VGDs understand the limitations of individualized approaches to solving workplace problems and to approaches in which workers are not well supported by the law. When asked about the most effective means to ensure that VGDs had their say in their workplace and were treated fairly, almost half (49 percent) selected a collective option (see Table 7.3). All in all, respondents were split in three ways about the best way to have a say in the local regulation of their work: an individualized legal regime (25 percent), organizations or groups with legal decision-making powers that bargain with an employer (25 percent), and organizations or groups that discuss problems with an employer but have no legal authority or decision-making power (24 percent). The remaining 28 percent simply did not know.

Professional associations and similar entities like guilds are a means for VGDs to get together, and there has reportedly been a resurgence in these associations in high-tech sectors (Benner 2003). According to the founder of the HTML Writers Guild:

> The term "guild" was chosen to look back at the older, medieval-type guilds. What we liked from that model was the notion of sharing knowledge—that building web design was something of a craft. ... [The term "guild"] keeps in mind the main purpose ... sharing information to make everyone successful." (Benner 2003, 186)

As this quote shows, in high-tech, project-based labour markets with high mobility, limited employer investment in training and professional development, and a reliance on network-based hiring approaches, professional associations can play a role in improving their members' opportunities for finding employment within regional labour markets, helping them to improve their skills, and improving their individual negotiating positions. However, from a representational standpoint in the local regulation of work, these groups are at best of the type represented in Table 7.3 as "employee organizations that discuss problems"—the option selected least often by developers. They suffer from inherent constraints in scope in their mission and structure insofar as the representation of workers is concerned. As Bellini et al. (2018) stated:

Table 7.3
Distribution of answers (% of respondents) to the question: "There are a number of different ways to increase employees' say in workplace matters and make sure they are treated fairly. Which one of the following do you think is the most effective?" (2014)

	Overall	By legal authority	By individual or collective
Don't know	28	28	28
Laws that protect the rights of individual employees	25	25	25
Employee organizations that negotiate or bargain with management over issues	18	25	49
Joint employee and management committees that negotiate or bargain over issues	7		
Joint employee and management committees that discuss problems	17	24	
Employee organizations that discuss problems	7		

Source: Adapted from Tô, Legault, and Weststar 2016, 39

> These actors ... focus on the *professional* identity of the *industry* and have the goal to support its growth and promote its interests towards public authorities. Hence, they tend to cut across the traditional employer/employee divide, representing all industry members. ... Wages and working conditions are not on the agenda of these actors ... they are generally interpreted as a consequence of the development stage of the industry. (48)

The game industry has a relatively long-standing professional association in the form of the IGDA, as well as a host of other industry associations and issue-based groups. However, these bodies are not legal representative agents of a group of workers. They do not have the bargaining power of legal unions, nor do they have the presence in individual studios that is required to play much of a role in the local regulation of work. Unlike some stronger professional associations (for example, those of doctors, lawyers, and accountants), the IGDA does not have the ability to exercise a monopoly of control over access to skilled labour. It does not regulate and restrict entry into the industry through certification and exams, nor through the apprenticeship systems of many craft unions. It cannot enforce restrictions on production standards or bargain for working conditions on behalf of its members.

These groups may have some impact in the local regulation of work should participants bring new ideas and actions back to their studios, but their impact more typically shapes the participation of VGDs in the fourth object of citizenship: the broader social regulation of their work (Butler 2009) (see Chapter 8). Professional associations and trade associations simply do not have the mandate, the structural positioning, or the legal backing to be representative agents for workers in the struggle for a greater say in the local regulation of work. While groups like the IGDA, Women in Games groups (see Chapter 8), and other grassroots bodies can help foster important discussions about the challenges faced by VGDs, they do not have the structural capacity to follow though with concerted and meaningful collective action.

Collective Action through Unionization

In the original conception of industrial citizenship (Arthurs 1967), the local union was assumed to be the actor that would take up the fight in the local regulation of labour. In the North American context, unions are democratic bodies that are certified by the majority vote of an identified workforce. The union then becomes the sole bargaining agent for the workers of that bargaining unit, and collective bargaining takes place with the employer to negotiate the terms and conditions of work. These terms are set down in a collective agreement. In other jurisdictions such as Europe, this model can be a little different, with the allowance of multiple unions representing subsets of the same group of workers (that is, minority unionism) or tripartite negotiations among unions, employers, and governments at the sector level or other regional and country-specific variations (Eurofound 2018; ETUI n.d.). However, the basic idea of interceding in the local regulation of work through a legally protected representative collective of workers is the common theme in unionism.

In Europe, a non-union form of worker representation exists in works councils, a form that can be robust. Works councils are defined as institutionalized, mandatory, and representative firm-level bodies that represent the interests of all employees of a company to its management across a broad range of issues (Nienhüser 2014, 248). They can coexist with trade unions, often helping to tailor national labour agreements to local conditions. However, works councils vary considerably across European countries, particularly in their conferred rights (Nienhüser 2014). Some works councils hold only informational rights (for example, management must keep them informed), while others have co-determination rights over some social and economic issues. It is important to note, however, that even where strong codetermination models exist, works councils typically engage with the consequences of management's decisions rather than having control over the decision-making itself (Nienhüser 2014).

As well, employers sometimes try to bypass works councils for weaker "works council-like" models (such as non-mandatory/voluntary bodies, mere joint-consultative bodies, and committees restricted to a small scope of issues) (Nienhüser 2014, 254). For instance, even in Germany, where works councils are deeply embedded in the labour relations system, Teipen (2008, 330) has reported that management in game studios explicitly relied on "an informal interest representation in the style of communitarian culture" to avoid works councils that would afford greater participation rights. Examples of these weaker models are the "so-called Vertrauensteam ('trust team')" (Teipen 2008, 330) at EA Germany and the "Feelgood Team" at Germany's Goodgame Studios (Handrahan 2015; Goodgame Studios 2015).

With the decline of unionization across industrialized countries, some have speculated on their role and relevance in the contemporary economic, social, and political landscape (Amman, Carpenter, and Neff 2007; Frege and Kelly 2004; Heely et al. 2004). As well, knowledge workers have been somewhat overlooked as a population that might require support in their employment relationship (Hossfeld 1995; Hyman et al. 2004) and in some cases have been deemed unsuited to unionization (Hurd and Bunge 2004; for VGDs in particular, see Bellini et al. 2018, 49; Keune et al. 2018, 14–15).

However, our data show a representation gap in that many VGDs, even those in managerial roles, have a desire for unionization and through that a voice in the regulation of their work. Surveys conducted by the Game Developers Conference (GDC) show similar results (GDC 2021; GDC 2022).

Positive Views toward Unions

Recent activity in cognate sectors may have raised awareness about unionization among VGDs. Such was surely the case of the eleven-month SAG-AFTRA (Screen Actors Guild–American Federation of Television and Radio Artists) voice actor strike in 2016 to 2017 (Weststar and Legault 2019). About 25 percent of videogame voice actors in the United States are represented by SAG-AFTRA. There has also been a rise in worker activism and unionization among tech and new media workers (Amman 2002; Chu 2020; Coulter and Langley 2022; Fiorito and Gallagher 2013; Ghaffary 2019; Rodino-Colocino 2007; van Jaarsveld 2004), and unionization among digital knowledge workers such as online journalists (Cohen and de Peuter 2020; IWW 2019). Worker activists are experimenting with

Table 7.4
Voting propensity for enterprise and sectoral union (% of respondents) (developers: 2009, 2014, 2019)

	2009 Enterprise	2009 Sectoral	2014 Enterprise	2014 Sectoral	2019 Enterprise	2019 Sectoral
For	35	—	48	64	52	63
Against	33	—	25	14	9	8
No opinion or prefer not to say*	32	—	14	11	37	28
I would not vote at all	—	—	14	11	2	2

Source: Adapted from Tô, Legault, and Weststar 2016, 28, 36, with original data from IGDA DSS 2019

* The wording for this response option changed across the three surveys. Actual language pursuant to each survey was "no opinion or prefer not to say" (2009), "prefer not to say" (2014), "don't know or need more information" (2019).

alternative forms of representation, like worker centres, cooperatives, and collectives, sometimes as stepping stones to unionization (de Peuter 2020; Dreyer et al. 2020; Iantorno and Flanagan 2023; MacDonald and Kolhatkar 2021). VGDs are taking their place within this moment. Indeed, VGDs have been thinking about and engaging in actions to regulate their local conditions of work for quite some time.

Beginning in 2009, survey respondents were asked whether they would vote in favour of a union if a vote were held the next day. Opinions were canvassed for two different forms of union. First, respondents were asked about the enterprise or local union model that is dominant in North America. As noted above, in this case the union represents workers at a single workplace, and a collective agreement is negotiated between the employer and the workers at that workplace. Second, respondents were asked about sector-based or sectoral unionization. This is an alternative form of unionization that is better suited to project-based industries because it can maintain negotiated benefits across employers. Negotiated benefits that are specific to a collective agreement that is attached to a workplace or employer are lost when the worker leaves that space.

As shown in Table 7.4, the desire for unionization and propensity to vote in favour of a union has risen considerably across the survey data. As well, an increasing number of respondents seem to be "on the fence" rather than a "hard no" when it comes to joining a union. VGDs are also consistently in favour of a sectoral solution to their workplace challenges, as they well know the structure of their industry.

Though often linked to worker dissatisfaction and sparked by a collective sense of injustice (Kelly 1998), the perception of a need for representation cannot be reduced simply to poor relations between managers and VGDs. Indeed, a desire to have a voice can be related to a commitment to the work and the simple wish to make one's work and workplace better (Morrison 2011; Weststar and Legault 2017). In 2014, more than half of the survey respondents (57 percent) reported that they had a good or even excellent relationship with their immediate superiors.

In the VGI, and in other environments in which management by project is the norm, close supervisors such as team leads and producers are not essentially perceived as representing opposing interests, but rather as an employee of the same employer (in big studios), as well as a stakeholder subject to the inexorable forces of the market and the customer in an extremely competitive world. To this point, we see that managers and developers with managerial responsibilities also express an interest in unionization (see Table 7.5 in the Data Appendix).

Representation Gaps Exist, but They Are Closing

One of the first cases of unionization was the emergence of the anonymous virtual union Ubifree in December 1998. The group described the unfair working conditions at the Ubisoft headquarters in France and called for Ubisoft developers around the world to join the union. The small initiative harvested a wealth of supportive messages, many of them denouncing the working conditions of VGDs. After only a few months, Ubisoft France management announced some improvements, and the anonymous group disbanded the online union. One improvement was the addition of an employee representative in a few committees; however, this representative was never granted decision-making power. In 2010, the website Ubifree 2.0 appeared, seemingly as one person's account of the working conditions of Ubisoft Montréal. There is no evidence of its impact or uptake, but it was clearly created in direct homage to the original movement (Legault and Weststar 2014).

For the first time, the 2019 IGDA survey asked respondents whether they were currently union members. Among the developers who responded, 7 percent answered yes.

Sweden has had union representation for some VGDs since approximately 2004. Union organization in Sweden is based on the model of individual membership in a large national trade union. Therefore, in Sweden, it does not make sense to categorize studios as unionized or non-unionized; rather, we can situate them on a continuum reflecting the proportion of their employees who are union members. The national union may have direct collective agreements and local union representation at some studios, but not in others. As Teipen (2008) described:

> Although the vast majority of Swedish video game development companies are not unionized, both largest developers stand out as exceptions. At the time of the analysis, there was a branch of the Swedish union for white-collar employees, SiF, at Digital Illusions and approximately 50 percent of the employees were unionized. … The unionization rate at the Swedish developer Starbreeze is as high as 70–80 percent; in contrast to Digital Illusions, however, there are several unions, but there is no active union representation in the company. The company negotiates with an external union representative, who visits the company if required (329–30).

The Swedish Union of Clerical and Technical Employees in Industry (SiF) has since merged into Unionen, the largest union in Sweden and the largest white-collar union in the world. According to email correspondence with Unionen officials in 2018, the union had about two hundred workers from the videogame sector in its ranks. It has had a specific collective agreement with the EA subsidiary Digital Illusions Creative Entertainment (DICE) since 2004 and a few other larger studios. For context, DICE alone reportedly employed four hundred people in 2018 (M. Kim 2018). Game workers are also unionized through the Swedish Association of Graduate Engineers (Sveriges ingenjörer). In 2020, and in collaboration with Unionen, they negotiated a local collective agreement covering two hundred VGDs across the studios of Paradox Interactive (Carpenter 2020a).

In Finland, game workers can unionize with Game Makers of Finland, which sits within the Union of Professional Engineers. Bellini et al. (2018) reported the Danish case:

> Trade union density among Danish video game developers lies at around 50%, a level much lower than in other sectors of the Danish economy, but remarkably high in comparative perspective. Still, unionised workers are spread among different trade unions and this makes the representation of the specific interests of video game developers somewhat problematic. Indeed, Danish trade unions argue not to have specific strategies for organising the industry, also because of the limited number of workers it employs, and that these workers become members almost by chance (48–49).

In France, le Syndicat des Travailleurs et Travailleuses du Jeu Vidéo (STJV) formed in 2017 (Mosca 2018). Membership is open and includes VGDs (whatever their employment contract), students, the unemployed, and the retired. In France, unions can form without a majority at a specific workplace. With the goal to be a national union, the STJV is actively deploying regional organizers. Their members staged a high-profile strike from February to April 2018 at French game maker Eugen Systems, which resulted in mediated talks with their employer about insufficient occupational health coverage, low and arbitrarily determined salaries, and unpaid overtime (Turcev 2018). The French union Solidaires Informatique is also representing VGDs and has intervened in high-profile sexual harassment cases at Quantic Dream and Ubisoft (Batchelor 2020).

VGD unions also formed in South Korea in 2018 (Chung and Kwon 2020). The labour union Starting Point formed at Nexon, the largest developer and publisher in the country, and SG Guild formed at Smilegate, makers of the world's top online first-person shooter game (Ji-hye 2019). These unions each held demonstrations in September 2019 to protest job insecurity and lack of transparency in organizational restructuring (Ji-hye 2019; Valentine 2019). Starting Point has negotiated a collective agreement that included pay raises (Sinclair 2020).

Adding to the action, a group called Game Workers Unite (GWU) burst onto the scene at the 2018 GDC in San Francisco (Frank 2018; Ehrhardt 2018; Schreier 2018). Within days, GWU chapters were popping up all over the world. GWU has positioned itself as a facilitative organization with the goal of supporting unionization in any shape or form. There is a heavy focus on awareness-building, given the lack of knowledge among game developers about basic workplace rights and the role of trade unions. The international and many local chapters are highly visible at game-oriented conferences and meetups. GWU also placed an emphasis on union organizer training and quickly made ties with existing unions for resources and support. For instance, STJV became the French chapter of GWU, the UK GWU chapter became a legal trade union as a semi-autonomous branch of the existing Independent Workers' Union of Great Britain (IWGB) (Woodcock 2020), and the Irish chapter unionized with the Financial Services Union (FSU) (Moody and Kerr 2020). GWU Australia is now Game Workers Australia, under the banner of the existing union Professionals Australia.[1] They reported three hundred active members, many of them freelancers and contractors (Colwill 2021).

In the United States, the movement has been supportively recognized by the AFL–CIO (the US labour federation representing over twelve mil-

---

1. Game Workers Unite—Australia: www.gameworkers.com.au/join

lion workers) and key players in the Democratic Party (Minotti 2019; Shuler 2019). In January 2020, GWU announced a partnership with the CWA as part of CODE—the Campaign to Organize Digital Employees (Dean 2020). This campaign has a growing list of high-profile successes. It resulted in the formation of the Alphabet Workers Union at Google in 2021 (Schiffer 2021a) and the successful illegal strike that gained improved pay and transparency for contract scriptwriters of the visual novel series *Lovestruck* at Voltage Entertainment (Carpenter 2020b). In late 2021 this campaign resulted in the first certified game studio union in North America—Vodeo Workers United—at Vodeo Games. Vodeo management voluntarily recognized the union of employees and contracted workers (Carpenter 2021b), though the studio has since closed.. As noted above, the QA workers at Raven Software (a subsidiary of Activision Blizzard) have also unionized with the CWA, calling themselves the Game Workers Alliance. More QA workers are following their lead at other Activision studios and at Microsoft-owned ZeniMax Media (Scheiber and Browning 2022).

In 2020 the International Alliance of Theatrical Stage Employees (IATSE) also launched a campaign to unionize game workers, called Rights and Protections for Game Workers (RPG-IATSE). September 2023 marked a first success with certification at Workinman Interactive.

The first game-worker union was formed in Canada in when QA workers contracted to BioWare but employed by Keywords Studio in Edmonton certified in June 2022 (Francis 2022a). Notably these workers joined the United Food and Commercial Workers (UFCW) local 401, which is a powerhouse in the region.

Remaining Representational Challenges

Unions are an ideal mechanism for VGDs to gain participation in the local regulation of their work. VGDs are increasingly interested in unionization, and union campaigns are rising, but there remain many obstacles to changing the status quo.

In the press coverage of CODE-CWA, both the CWA and GWU spokespeople expressed a preference for an "industrial" union model over a "craft" model. Rather than organize workers by craft or trade (for example, actors' union, writers' union, stage employees' union), the North American industrial model involves a "wall-to-wall" approach and aims to unionize all workers within a workplace, regardless of occupational affiliation. In the case of VGDs, this would mean that all the game creators in a studio would belong to the same union, regardless of their job or role. Such an approach reduces the potential for inter-craft fracturing and builds the bargaining power of the unit.

However, most unionization in the industrial model is of the enterprise type. It is established on a workplace-by-workplace or employer-by-employer basis, with each workplace standing as an autonomous union local with its own collective agreement. In some ways this eases the path to unionization, as each certification drive is a discrete struggle and firms can be added one step at a time. However, this approach is not well suited to an environment of mobile capital and labour because union rights are not transferable across workplaces and employers. In a highly competitive environment, it also introduces the risk of altering the balance of competitive advantage across unionized and not-yet unionized firms.

The benefit of the contemporary craft approach is that it is sectoral. The same collective agreement applies across multiple employers in a similar sector, promoting worker mobility and the portability of rights and benefits. Employers are represented in the bargaining relationship through their own collective employers' association. This is the model favoured by VGDs. Yet this model may be harder to achieve because of its greater scope. It could be kickstarted through the great initial effort of forcing a few major players to the table and relying on their influence and competitive pressures to bring the rest of the industry into line. However, the more typical path is through statute—which would require a level of government regulation that is unlikely at this stage, given the pro-business stance that governments have taken to date (see Chapter 8).

The particulars of two of the successful unionization drives in the United States further highlight these representational challenges. According to a statement from Activision, the QA workers at Raven represent less than 1 percent of employees. Despite CODE-CWA aspirations, unionization efforts have not produced a "wall-to-wall" union of all developers at a single studio but rather a few small unions of only the QA workers. It is unclear whether future non-QA workers at Raven could organize to join the Game Workers Alliance because the US National Labor Relations Board determines bargaining unit composition based on a sufficient "community of interest" among the workers. Important differences in compensation structure, hours, and nature of work could result in fragmented unions based on craft. By extension, it is not clear whether QA workers at other Activision Blizzard studios could join the Raven Game Workers Alliance, leading to fragmented bargaining across studios even within the occupational type. And the larger question is whether individual game worker unions across studios could then ever amalgamate into a sectoral body. So far, all the QA unions in the United States are locals of the same parent union (the CWA). This could facilitate amalgamation or at least a system of pattern bargaining. However, the scene is complicated with IATSE's entry as there are now multiple unions with representational interests.

Taken internationally, game workers are negotiating their entry into a diverse range of established unions on various terms. Even within national contexts there is further potential for craft-based and sectoral fragmentation because some VGI workers can directly join well-established cognate unions. As noted above, videogame voice actors in the United States can be members of SAG-AFTRA. Similarly, US-based game writers can join the Writer's Guild of America. However, the process of integrating into an established structure and a pre-existing membership does not always flow easily. There can be existential issues of identity, and practical negotiations around autonomy and resource sharing. Sometimes specific activities can create internal tensions and alienate certain groups of workers. The Google Alphabet Workers Union had to deal with internal tensions in the early days of integration into the established body of the CWA (Schiffer 2021b). Two other examples involving game writers and the Writers Guild of America (WGA) are illustrative. The first concerns the perceived instrumentality of the WGA to videogame writers and the second is a controversy over the WGA videogame awards.

In the creative and cultural industries, important stakes like winning a high-profile award can influence the market success of a product and change the career path for a worker. Awards are a powerful means of regulation, as they serve to include and promote, but they can also exclude. Like all alleged "merit-based" adjudication processes, they can rarely remain neutral amidst intricate social relations. Moreover, the matter is made more complicated when members of a new group, such as game writers, join a pre-existing professional guild that serves an established membership. Guilds share the dual mission of professional organizations in general: they are hybrid organizations aiming both at protecting their working members and taking part in maintaining high standards of quality for the public. This can become tricky with a heterogeneous membership.

The WGA is a labour union representing thousands of members who write content for motion pictures, television, news, and digital media. Some game writers joined the WGA to gain protection against abuse. The WGA negotiates a standard contract with an organized group of employers that guarantees some decent working conditions. In return, writers must commit to deal only with "guild signatory companies." If they work for a non-signatory company, members face the consequences of violating the guild's working rules.[2]

---

2. WGA: www.wga.org/contracts/know-your-rights/writers-need-to-know

In our interviews, some game writers expressed dissatisfaction with this scenario. They felt that inclusion in the broader WGA was a greater gain for the union than it was for game writers themselves. Member game writers were now constrained to only work for "guild signatory companies," yet the WGA seemed keen to generally promote their "classical" writers by placing them in competition for game writing jobs, even when not experienced in that medium. As a result, some game writers did not feel welcome in the union nor appreciated at their fair value:

> ▸ WGA West has gone to companies and said you can't hire writers unless they're members of our writers guild. ... They convinced a whole bunch of companies that they had to do this [but] the Writers Guild of America was not very good at viewing video game writers as writers until 2009. They didn't even admit that video game writers existed, and so they're going around trying to sell these writers who are part of the guild as video game writers, when really they're screenplay writers, they're novelists, they're short story writers, saying, "but they're union so they're good." (F-12-20-M-E-03-12-13-16-02)

In this way, unions can disadvantage one group of workers in their efforts to protect another. Perceptions that the WGA is unable or unwilling to protect the interest of game writers detracts from further organizing efforts. Even with the creation of a Videogame Writers Caucus (now disbanded; see Kilkenny 2022), the game writer contingent remains small.

For this reason, the videogame writing category of the WGA Awards was suspended in 2020 until there was a "critical mass" of videogames represented among WGA members and therefore enough games to ensure a meaningful award selection process (Blake 2019). Though some were dismayed by the loss of the award, others intimated that the whole process was flawed and that the WGA Awards disadvantaged some game writers:

> For all the good and vital work that the WGA does for writers in the film and TV markets, they have *zero* presence in the games industry. Getting rid of this award at least does away with the charade that the WGA advocates for game writers in any capacity. (Shawn Kittelsen, writer of *Mortal Kombat 11*, as quoted in Blake 2019)

> ▸ [For] the WGA [game writing] Awards, every person who wrote the game has to have been a WGA member for the last year at least, and then you have to provide the full script of your game, which is

impossible because most of our stuff is not exportable. If you have a branching dialogue, how do you export that and give it to someone to read, and how do you show them the emotional impact that has if they're not willing to play your game? ... There was quite a big furor about it this year, where a bunch of people came out and said, "Are these really the best-written games of the year?" ... And so the WGA is building this reputation as having the best writers in the industry, because all of the people who win awards are part of the guild because they have to pay to be part of the guild to enter the competition. There is a problem here. (F-12-20-M-E-03-12-13-16-02)

These quotes unveil many objects at stake in inviting game writers to join broader organizations to make them citizens within a larger world. First, game writers produce written content that conflicts with the usual production of incumbent members, that is, linear scripts that read from front to back. A game script is built differently, has multiple story lines depending on what players decide, and is more like an algorithm than a linear document. The "script" hardly stands on its own, apart from the gameplay, given its essential character of having players "experience" the narrative. As long as the awarding system does not allow for conditions for proper assessment, the latter respondent above is doubtful about the benefit for game writers in taking part. The award is a poor incentive to join the WGA, since the process lets down a large pool of applicants who cannot meet the organization's standards. The result is that game writers do not join, making the WGA a poor representative for the group.

Such an experience with organizing leaves the issue of citizenship open for game writers and raises some questions for the other trades in game development. Would VGDs suffer the same type of exclusion in larger organizations if and when they exist? Do they need their own singular body, and if such would emerge, would the trades within game development succeed in speaking with a single voice?

We argue that project-based workers such as VGDs must find a new model from the old to suit their own needs and conditions. A union for all occupational categories of VGDs that operates with a single collective agreement across the entire sector would blend the most advantageous elements of the industrial and craft models. Such an approach could draw from the history of pattern bargaining and master agreements. A combination of the "wall-to-wall" solidarity of the industrial model coupled with the breadth of the sectoral craft model would produce the greatest domain of citizenship, to which every VGD would be an equivalent subject, but it is also the hardest to achieve. And even then, national-level industrial relations arrangements cannot account for the transnational mobility of capital and labour—an outstanding issue for many workers and for international solidarity movements (Greer, Ciupijus, and Lillie 2013; Hammar 2022; Legault and Weststar 2021; Lillie and Greer 2007).

Conclusion: A Quest for Change

Taking part in the local regulation of labour regarding critical issues is an important component of citizenship at work (see Chapter 1). HRM and state equity policies brought workers varying degrees of fairness, but taking part in shaping the workplace by bargaining a local collective agreement gave them a voice. No longer limited to passively *receiving* legal rights, employees became *active* citizens of a democracy. However, VGDs do not belong to such a territory.

This chapter has presented an account of how VGDs are attempting to gain a meaningful voice in the local regulation of their work. Project-based knowledge workers like VGDs continually engage in a range of activities—individual and collective, private and public, large and small (Weststar and Legault 2019). However, few of these actions have allowed them to become a legitimate and long-term participant in the work regulation process. Put simply, individual acts of employee voice, exit, and neglect; short-term collective mobilizations targeted to specific issues; works council–like joint consultative bodies; individual and collective legal action; and external professional or trade associations are, together and separately, insufficient in creating a long-term, institutional framework that accords workers a meaningful influence on the decisions that affect their work and working conditions. As such, they fail the citizenship test in that there are no constant objects, subjects, or domains of citizenship. We can only find occasional specimens. There are some objects "up for discussion," like discipline, crediting, training, and project assignment. There are some subjects in the form of workers with high bargaining power who could "feel" like citizens, or some emerging unionized groups of VGDs. There are some domains such as European nation states in which VGDs have made inroads in a sector-based form of defense of their interests, like France, the United Kingdom, and Sweden. Yet, all in all, an occasional but non-institutionalized mobilization does not involve any guarantee for VGDs to take part in the regulation of their environment.

As noted above, Arthurs (1967) saw the local union as the key to citizenship through the local regulation of labour. Despite dramatic changes in the nature of the employment relationship and a pattern of union decline across the industrialized world, we argue that this assumption remains valid. Unions remain the actor best positioned to bring in and enforce the conditions of citizenship at work.

In making this claim, we are not uncritical of unions, nor do we simply accept unions in their historical or even more contemporary forms. Without the space to venture into the deep literature on union typologies, forms, actions, and ideologies, and the many calls for union renewal on numerous fronts, we agree that unions have more work to do to reassert themselves and build relevancy and legitimacy with contemporary workers. With respect to the highly mobile, project-based knowledge worker of the VGI, the ideal form of union representation does not singularly exist. As such, VGDs, like many other workers, are engaged in active experimentation to find the form of collective action that will best address their circumstances.

CHAPTER 8

Do Game Developers Participate in the Social Regulation of Work?

In this chapter we outline participation in the broader social regulation of work as the fourth object of citizenship at work. What means do project-based workers have to exert any influence on what legislation is passed governing their specific working conditions or their industry at large, or on the amendment or application of existing laws or policies? What organizations represent them?

VGDs want a voice in the debate on the evolution of the industry and its ecosystem, but they remain disadvantaged in their efforts to influence the state. They face a highly organized landscape of employer and industry associations, while worker-based representational agents remain scarce and fledgling (see Chapter 7).

However, talking only about representation before state institutions would downplay the true scope and desire that VGDs have for participation in the social regulation of work. This narrow theoretical view is part of the folk tradition of labour institutions and is a disservice to informal, organic, and/or emergent forms of organizing, self-representation, and self-governance, as well as to loci of power based on the influence of one's position in the commercial market or social network:

> Digital games have historically been self-regulated while being subject to national and transnational contract, consumer, and trade laws. More recently, games have become subject to attention in relation to intellectual property, data, and privacy laws ... [and] in self- and co-regulatory age and content information systems. (Kerr 2017, 141)

There are new social stakeholders wanting to have a say in the regulation of work and, moreover, on the evolution of the industry. Action in this domain is as much before the state as in society. It is part of the discussion about the helps and harms of social media and IT; the representation of women and racialized minorities in arts and culture; and violence, gender-based violence, and misogyny. It is about whether games are art or entertainment, and the implications for such blanket categorizations. It is about ecologically, economically, and socially sustainable local and global development (Abraham 2022; Keogh 2021; Maxwell and Miller 2012; Whitson, Simon, and Parker 2018). It is in these domains that some VGDs act and want to act more.

Sotamaa and Švelch (2021, 8) argue that "public awareness about the production context of video games has arguably never been higher" and advocate for production studies research that critically reflects on the "economic, cultural and political structures that influence the final form of games." Production studies emphasize "specific sites and fabrics of media production as distinct interpretive communities, each with its own organizational structures, professional practices, and power dynamics" (M. J. Banks, Connor and Mayer 2016, x). In the game industry, "a range of institutional and organizational actors coexist with more bottom-up virtual and fluid ones" (Kerr 2017, 141).

Participation in the social regulation of work is therefore a domain ripe for objects and subjects of citizenship. We will discuss some of the main actors and stakeholders, acknowledging the limits of our data, our geographical and linguistic biases, and the quickly evolving landscape. We cannot do justice to the range of localized institutional, organizational, grassroots, and fluid bodies across the global VGI. Thankfully that research is emerging (e.g., Graber and Burri-Nenova 2010; Hjorth and Chan 2009; Huntemann and Aslinger 2013; Ito 2007; Jin 2010; Kerr 2017; Keogh 2023; Komulainen and Sotamaa 2020; Ruffino 2021; Sotamaa and Švelch 2021).

Lobbying and Direct State Involvement

Individual workers have a limited ability to lobby or influence the state. Such action requires a body, typically a union, that can craft and wield a collective voice. Though the union movement is expanding, VGDs do not yet have a collective policy voice. In contrast and as we will see below, videogame employers consolidate their interests and voice through industry, trade, and employer associations. Some have also managed to position themselves as regional economic actors of such importance that they have a direct line to local government officials. This leaves VGDs, for better or worse, as the recipients of decisions made without their representation.

Accounting for state lobbying by agents representing game employers is critical because institutional and state/regional factors are important to the growth and decline of creative and cultural industries. Though game industry policies are "difficult to study because the actors are often obfuscated by nondisclosure agreements, opaque licensing agreements written in legalese, and political posturing in civil debates that are sometimes funded by invisible donors" (Conway and deWinter 2016, 2), they are linked to the maturity of national game industries (Nieborg and de Kloet 2016).

There has been an intensification of state involvement over the past two decades (Kerr 2017, 139–41) and accompanying debate about its impact (Nieborg and de Kloet 2016; Sandqvist 2012). For instance:

> Canada is the poster child in the West in terms of institutional and public support for the game industry and this has attracted mobile multinational development companies from the United States and Europe and generated significant growth in employment ... France and the UK governments have introduced tax policies to protect certain types of game development after excessive lobbying from national and regional trade associations and national champions ... China has disrupted the dominance of Japan and South Korea through the introduction of state policies to support national game development and limit competition from imports. (Kerr 2017, 142–43; see Sotamaa, Jørgensen, and Sandqvist 2020, for a review of the Nordic region)

We will discuss as objects of citizenship two important areas of state intervention: tax credits and industry funding. Funding shapes the economic and geographic landscape of the industry, and workers have a stake in these decisions. Tax credits incentivize regional development and are therefore designed to secure employment in a particular territory so that workers (and their families) do not have to relocate to chase employment that has moved to more lucrative territories. These interests are localized and can create conflict among workers. Similarly, the parameters that dictate the conditions of industry funding can orient employer actions in ways that may conflict with workers' interests.

Tax Credit Regimes

Labour tax credit regimes are policies by which governments subsidize employers by reimbursing part of wages paid; they are an important object of citizenship in all major game development regions. Game studios can be found across Canada[1] but the scene is most robust where

---

1. Canadian Game Studios List: https://canadiangamedevs.com

Table 8.1
Tax Credit Regimes Across Canada: British Columbia, Quebec, and Ontario

Year	Credit amount and details
British Columbia: Interactive Digital Media Tax Credit	
2010–2023	• 17.5% of qualified BC labour spend • Cannot stack with federal SR&ED program
Quebec: Production of Multimedia Titles Tax Credit	
2015–present	• Category 1 (IP-generating products intended for commercialization): 30% (+7.5% if a French-language version) • Category 2 (all other products, e.g. vocational training): 26.25% • Can stack with federal SR&ED program
Post-June 4, 2014	• Category 1: 24% (+6% if a French-language version) • Category 2: 21%
2004–June 4, 2014	• Category 1: 30% (+7.5% if a French-language version) • Category 2: 26.25% of qualified labour
1996–2004	• Category 1: 40% (+10% if a French-language version) • Category 2: 35%
Ontario: Interactive Digital Media Tax Credit	
2009–present	• 35% of qualifying labour expenditures incurred by a qualifying or specialized digital game corporation for the development of eligible digital games • Cannot stack with federal SR&ED program
March 2008–March 2009	• In general, 25% for qualifying corporations • For small corporations, 25% for specified products and 30% for non-specified products
March 2006–March 2008	• In general, 20% for qualifying corporations • For small corporations, 20% for specified products and 30% for non-specified products
1998–March 2006	• 20% for qualifying small corporations for non-specified products

Sources: Boucher (2013); Brummond (n.d.); Canada Revenue Agency (2019); Finances Québec (2003); Government of British Columbia (n.d.); Ontario Creates (2020); Ontario *Tax Credits and Revenue Protection Act**; Quebec *Taxation Act***; Weaver (2014)

* Legislative Assembly of Ontario website: *Tax Credits and Revenue Protection Act, 1998*, https://www.ola.org/en/legislative-business/bills/parliament-36/session-2/bill-81

** LegisQuébec website: *Taxation Act, 1972*, http://legisquebec.gouv.qc.ca/en/showdoc/cs/I-3?langCont=en#ga:l_iii_1_1-h1

long-standing supportive tax regimes are found (Nieborg and de Kloet 2016). Indeed, a cottage industry of consultancy firms caters to game companies seeking to make the most out of tax credit programs (Benefact 2017; NorthBridge Consultants, n.d.). Table 8.1 summarizes the tax credit policies from the Canadian provinces that boast the largest game development clusters and most generous incentives (see Table 8.2 in the Data Appendix for policies across the remaining provinces).

The benefit of tax credits in Quebec is amplified because the system in that province allows a company to concurrently draw or "stack" tax credits from the provincial government and the federal Scientific Research and Experimental Development (SR&ED) tax incentive program for the same project. The SR&ED can consist of as much as 35 percent of eligible expenditures (Government of Canada 2021).

Though these tax credits are lauded as engines of economic growth, they can have negative consequences. Companies become sensitive to and dependent on the policy regime; reductions in tax credits and even a hint of political change can cause capital flight. This creates intense inter-state and international competition, and a "beggar thy neighbour" effect in which research and development gains to one region come at the expense of losses to neighbouring regions (Hui 2012; Hutchins 2012; McEwan 2019; Mudhar 2012; Wilson 2009).

The risk of capital flight contributes to labour mobility and employment insecurity. Industry protectionism often drives funding policy discussions (see Slattery 2021, regarding Ireland, and Sotamaa, Jørgensen and Sandqvist 2020, on Sweden). With this mentality, tax credit regimes can become an arms race and end in a stalemate, such that they are simply government subsidies. Research from the United States found that research and development (R&D) tax credits result in a zero-sum game among states operating at similar levels; when competing states make equiproportionate increases, there is no additional new capital formation in either state (Chirinko and Wilson 2008) and therefore no new incentivizing effect. However, the rhetoric of "promises" and "potential" is strong (Nieborg and de Kloet 2016; see IGEA 2021, for fanfare about a recent policy adoption in Australia).

We do not debate the economic and cultural value of state subsidies to the game industry. But when the state is subsidizing labour and/or total expenditure costs at levels of 20 percent and more, it becomes hard to treat the industry as a purely private enterprise. As funders, governments are implicated in the management decision-making of these studios and should be more concerned with whether their subsidies are creating quality jobs.

Though worker representative bodies might generally support industry association efforts to secure financing for the industry (see, for instance, GWU Australia 2021), some groups are pushing harder. The FSU, which now represents Irish game developers, "wants the Government to require employers to sign a written statement committing them to provide 'quality employment' before they can avail of the tax credit" (Curran 2021, para 6). This includes workers' right to collectively organize and negotiate working conditions. Such a demand expands the possible domain of citizenship on this issue. But as it stands, industry associations have direct lobbying pathways to governments, but workers do not have a consistent voice in decision-making over tax credits.

Funding and Industry Development

The state and state-affiliated bodies can also play a role in the development of a videogame cluster through investment in infrastructure and innovation (for example, business parks and incubators), training (for example, postsecondary educational programs), promotion and knowledge exchange (for example, regional and pan-regional conferences), commercialization, and trade (Nichols 2016; Nieborg and de Kloet 2016; Sotamaa, Jørgensen, and Sandqvist 2020). These are often long-term strategies for the development and retention of local talent and leveraging complementarities across cognate industries and actors. Sometimes states make direct cash injections in the form of loans (see Nichols 2016, for the cautionary tale of Rhode Island's disastrous $75 million loan to 38 Studios).

Game industry public policy can also manifest like arts funding and funding in support of cultural heritage. For instance, the genesis of Norwegian government policy was rooted in "the cultural importance of securing children's access to diverse [game] productions with high quality Norwegian language and content" (Sotamaa, Jørgensen, and Sandqvist 2020, 621). Funding can take the form of development and production grants as well as marketing dollars or trade-related travel. These are often targeted toward independent and/or emergent developers and studios, though large and commercially successful companies also submit to funding bodies.

Direct funding initiatives tend to be state supported but administered at arm's length by specific institutions. These bodies also tend to oversee funding across the cultural industries (for example, television and film). The Canada Media Fund (CMF) is one such entity. It is a nonprofit, public-private partnership between the Government of Canada and Canada's cable, satellite, and Internet protocol television (IPTV) distributors. It delivers roughly C$350 million in annual funding to producers of Canadian audiovisual media content (CMF 2021a, 88). In 2020 to 2021, 13.4 percent of that funding was directed to interactive digital media content, of which 75 percent was to fund game projects (CMF 2021a, 61, 89).

The game sector is also shaped by funding that is directed toward technology development. Such is the case in Finland, where a publicly owned R&D funding organization (Tekes) was important to the emergence and sustenance of the industry (Sotamaa, Jørgensen, and Sandqvist 2020). Tekes has contributed to the professionalization and internationalization of the Finnish industry through the leverage of capital via "collaborative relationships between the government organization, individual companies and private investors." (Sotamaa, Jørgensen, and Sandqvist 2020, 623)

In addition to determining which studios survive and which projects are made, funding models and the nature of direct investment can shape managerial decisions within companies. First, a differential emphasis on art versus commercial entertainment can direct the content that is made; the former would encourage more experimental work. There are regular discussions among industry leaders and policymakers about this balance and the proper purpose of funding bodies in supporting art versus rewarding commercialization. The successful case of the serious/applied games segment in the Netherlands has been attributed to intentional policy decisions and a high degree of direct and indirect state sponsorship (Nieborg and de Kloet 2016).

Second, funders establish the parameters by which studios and projects will be evaluated and, under the truism "what gets measured, gets managed," incentivize certain behaviours. For instance, how does the funder weigh past applications to the fund, past grants, the experience of the applicant, the longevity of the studio, or the commercial track record of past projects? The role of the scoring system comes to light in a case study of the CMF's recent attempts to increase the representation of women within CMF-funded projects. As reported by Perks and Whitson (2022), the new system awards three percentage points to applications in which the leadership team had "gender parity" (defined as at least 40 percent women). This initiative was intended to "help 'level the playing field' by incentivizing management to promote more women into project leadership positions"; "19 projects were successful due to the additional gender points, while a further 31 projects near the funding cut-off were refused because they did not meet gender parity" (Perks and Whitson 2022, 143–44). The policy was questioned, and many felt the system could be "gamed." However, the policy changes reportedly prompted hard discussions within regional game development communities, and this was seen to have led to awareness building and, perhaps, change (Perks and Whitson 2022, 148).

Last, the funding structure can dictate managerial decisions to hire and fire, to merge or relocate, and/or to expand or constrain a game's scope. The presence of state or quasi-state funding can shelter emergent local development from hard times and from acquisition and absorption by large incumbent players. Nieborg and de Kloet (2016) suggest that small European studios face difficulty in attracting venture capital and reaching a sustainable mass before being cannibalized by dominant entities from Asia and the United States. Acquisitions often trigger organizational restructuring that can result in layoffs, staff relocations, changes to or cancellations of games in progress, or studio closure (Bulut 2020b; Nieborg 2021). HRM decisions are also impacted because capital funding, whether state-based or from the private sector, is dispersed based on strict financial reporting time periods and tied to achievement milestones that require extensive documentation. These are often divorced from the actual cash flow or time horizon needs of the development companies, particularly those without other sources of capital. Funding models can therefore mimic and perpetuate the worst aspects of the financialized project-based environment (see Chapter 2 and 3).

Some of these funding bodies provide voice and representation opportunities for workers. The CMF claims "a deep history of industry consultations" (CMF 2021b, 2). In 2021 close to one thousand people participated in consultations as individual creators, through representative agents (regional trade associations, unions and professional guilds, major employers, or other funding or support agencies), and through industry stakeholders from three targeted groups: Indigenous, Black, and racialized communities; industry leaders; and emerging talent. Representative agents participated in by-invitation roundtables, while individuals participated through town hall forums (CMF 2021c; CMF 2021d).

Such consultations are to be lauded; however, they do not acknowledge the inherent power imbalances among the solicited contributors, nor in the structures set up to collect their points of view. Surely, it is undeniable that the collective voice of respected industry associations and employer representatives participating "by invitation only" would carry more weight in deliberations than interventions from individuals. And as we will see below, industry associations are dominated by employers. Surely also, the representatives of the "targeted groups" of BIPOC[2] stakeholders, industry leaders, and emerging talent were selected through some means subject to the idiosyncrasies of existing power dynamics and dominant social networks that likely bias studio founders, owners, executives, industry analysts, or the high-profile self-employed. We see

---

2. Black, Indigenous, and people of colour.

trade unions and professional guilds among the invited representational agents, but this point is moot for game workers (and other interactive media workers), since no such bodies yet exist in the Canadian context.[3] The subjects of citizenship are therefore up for debate.

As with tax credits, the point is not to suggest de facto negative outcomes for workers from government funding regimes. On the contrary, it has been well documented that these can be key supports. Rather, we highlight the failings of citizenship in the existing structures and processes. In showcasing the importance of institutional actors and their networks in shaping the game development ecosystem (that is, where, when, and how funding is allocated, and how its administration has upstream implications for where and how jobs are created and downstream implications for managerial decision-making within workplaces), we identify critical but often missed opportunities for democratic voice. Despite the importance of this social regulatory sphere, the voice of game workers is lacking, and we present this as a citizenship deficit.

Industry Associations Are a Strong Voice

As noted, state lobbying efforts by industry, trade, or professional associations are an important part of the social regulation of work, as it shapes the policy and regulatory landscapes of firms and industries within specific regions. The work of industry associations to raise the profile of their industry and advocate for facilitative conditions in areas such as fiscal policy, education and training, innovation, immigration, and trade can benefit workers and employers alike. However, from the perspective of citizenship at work, the most important element is the ability to have a participative role in the planning and/or execution of such efforts. This voice is more important even than the outcome. For instance, state lobbying that produces regulatory regimes that protect game content as free speech is a positive outcome for game industry workers and employers, but if workers were not involved in the process, it fails the citizenship test. The policy stage is dominated by industry and employer associations, with no seat at the table for worker representatives.

Numerous industry "trade" associations exist at the national and transnational level. Many of these are powerful bodies, yet relatively little is known about their inner workings (Kerr 2017). In general, they seek to promote industry interests through research, education, advocacy, and

---

3. We acknowledge that CWA Canada is beginning to represent game workers; however at the time of writing no bargaining units had been certified. As such, CWA Canada would have been most likely to participate in the CMF consultations on behalf of its Canada Media Guild film and television workers.

events "vis-à-vis the government and the rest of the economy and society, as well as abroad" (Keune et al. 2018, 13). However, an inspection of their representational foci reveals important tensions and power dynamics.

Kerr (2017, 145) identifies a divergence of interests within trade associations among companies that operate as game publishers versus development studios, and suggests that "at its crudest [the split] illustrates the different interests that multinational publishers have when compared to small- and medium-sized developer [studios]." Kerr notes generally that "a focus on development in the title of the association as compared to a focus on interactive software signals an ongoing tension as to whether games should be considered a software or a cultural product from a policy perspective." Small independent studios are often excluded from these trade associations or are drawn to associations that cater to the independent development milieu. The review by Keune et al. (2018, 13) of German, Dutch, Swedish, and UK associations also outlines representational differences and grey areas by size, region, and institutional mission.

Such categorizations of type and size are useful to understand the landscape of representational associations. But a more meaningful factor for our purpose is whether these bodies represent the interests of employers or workers. A review of association websites shows that most are employer focused. They offer membership by studio/company and not as individual memberships to game workers. For instance, the membership base of the transnational Interactive Software Federation of Europe (ISFE) is made up through the direct membership of seventeen major videogame publishers active in Europe and twelve national trade associations that are themselves comprised of game company representatives. According to their mission statement,[4] the ISFE represents the interests of the world's "most successful" game publishers and developers, engages actively with policymakers to contribute to the "development of smart regulations/policies," and is a "trusted provider of strategic data on the economics and demographics of the videogame ecosystem across Europe." Similarly, the Entertainment Software Association (ESA) in the United States offers company memberships and promises that:

> membership gives you a seat at the table. The ESA routinely convenes the US game industry to tackle our most pressing issues: potentially harmful or unfair legislation, overzealous regulation, conflicts over business models, concerns about game over use,

---

[4]. Interactive Software Federation of Europe: www.isfe.eu/about

[5]. Electronic Software Association: www.theesa.com/about-esa/#membership

First Amendment/content issues, and more. ESA *members protect their own interests by being part of the conversation.*[5] (emphasis ours)

As a further example, the Danish Producers' Association (Producentforeningen) offers membership to producers of film, television, and computer games. It identifies as both a trade association and an employer association because it seeks to "gain political influence and promote members' interests in relation to politicians, rights organizations, public institutions ... which have an influence on the production conditions" (translated from Danish) and negotiates collective agreements with relevant employee groups.[6]

A few associations are expansive and welcome publishers, developers, indie teams, individual workers, students, members of the eSports community, educational institutions, cogent industries, and general sponsors. As noted by Kerr (2017), these are more often the associations with "development" or "developer" in their title and are more likely to have smaller indie studios as members.[7] Even the US-based International Game Developers Association (IGDA), which pitches its membership and services to individual workers, allows companies to buy memberships through its Studio Affiliate Program. Along with the individual member benefits, Studio Affiliates receive free job postings on the IGDA Career Center and company features in IGDA publications, and are granted a presence at IGDA chapter events.

Associations that are open to both employers and employees have a complicated representational role (see more on the IGDA below). Perhaps in recognition of this, the South African Association of Game Makers—Make Games South Africa (MGSA)—engaged in discussions about the creation of a new body, Interactive Entertainment South Africa (IESA). This was proposed as a separate organization for a wider net of game-related companies to engage in lobbying and in policy and industry development (MGSA 2016), as opposed to the indie-maker community focus of MGSA.

Suffice to say that most trade associations act on behalf of companies and therefore employers. This is true even of associations that differentiate themselves from those representing large multinational publishers. According to their website, the European Game Development Federation

6. Producentforeningen: https://pro-f.dk/om-producentforeningen

7. For example, the Flemish Games Association (FLEGA) has a membership category for freelancers and offers a free membership, with no voting status, for students and enthusiasts. Pioneers of Game Development Austria (PGDA) seems unique in that it does not allow company memberships at all, but it still showcases company logos on its website and states that its "members are representing game companies in every region of Austria." https://pgda.at/members/

(EGDF) acts to "advance the political and economic interests of the European computer and video games industry," but there is no recognition that the political and economic interests of game *employers* often differ from those of game *workers*. Most public policy work is

> not concerned about the quality of jobs or workplace cultures and practices in the games industry. The industry and policy discourse seem to have converged on a narrow range of issues including locational competition and level playing fields, access to skills and creating a tax-friendly investment climate for corporations. (Kerr 2017, 149)

Some large developers and publishers enjoy a compounded influence because they are present in multiple representational spaces. Building on Kerr's (2017, 144) example of the developer/publisher Ubisoft, at the time of writing, we see that in Europe the company is a direct member of the trans-European ISFE due to its size and influence. But it is also a member of all twelve of the national associations who make up the ISFE. Of those twelve, a Ubisoft representative sits on the board of five and is the board CEO of one. Ubisoft is also well represented in the other trans-European association, EGDF, even though that association seems to attract smaller indie developers. Ubisoft is not a direct member, but it is a member of seven of the seventeen participating national associations. It is on the board of four of those associations, including as board CEO in the same case listed above. In North America, Ubisoft is a member of the ESA in both the United States and Canada. Within Canada, they have a representative on the board of Quebec's largest digital game trade association, La Guilde du jeu vidéo du Québec, and Ontario's interactive media trade association, Interactive Ontario, which are both members of the national association, Canadian Interactive Alliance/L'Alliance interactive canadienne (CIAIC). Ubisoft also has a representative on the board of the Quebec Employer's Council (Le Conseil du patronat du Québec) and the board of Montréal International, a public–private partnership tasked with attracting direct foreign investment, international organizations, entrepreneurs, talented workers, and international students to the region. The same case of multiple membership and compounded influence in powerful representational spaces could indubitably be made of many large multinational publisher-developers. As Kerr (2017, 144) observes regarding Ubisoft, this placement gives game companies significant economic, cultural, and social capital.

The game industry is also prominent in the advocacy efforts of broader associations that support the interactive media sector. Indeed, some may argue that the game industry increasingly dominates these policy discussions. For instance, in Canada, the website of the CIAIC, a national body comprised of eight provincial interactive digital media trade associations, is almost exclusively focused on game development, and their definition of "core interactive digital media" centres game creators (Nordicity 2013). DigiBC—the Creative Technology Association of British Columbia—is emblematic of the activities carried out by such bodies at the national and provincial level.[8]

Kerr (2017, 145) notes that sometimes publisher-associations and developer-associations "work toward the same goals and ends; at other times they act in opposition." Indeed, the state lobbying efforts of trade associations can often be of benefit to workers and employers, but in some situations, such as exemptions for overtime laws, interests are not in alignment. From a citizenship at work perspective, since interests cannot be assumed to align, and acknowledging inherent power imbalances in the employment relationship, the most important component is the ability to have a participative role—a voice—regardless of the outcome. As this review indicates, the policy stage is dominated by industry and employer associations, with no seat for workers or their representatives.

Who Governs Game Content?

Game content is also an important object of citizenship. VGDs are deeply concerned about their creative freedom and avoiding censorship. However, individual game makers, studio management, and the industry's representational bodies are also beholden to value systems that impact choices about game content. To the preference of most governments, the game industry remains largely self-regulated (Perks 2021); however, game content continues to be the object of regulatory discussions by state and non-state actors. Key topics are violence, sex, and sexualized violence, and, more recently, monetization strategies likened to gambling. Certain industry actors have mobilized in lobbying the state for free speech in game making. However, the voicing of workers as creators is less obvious, their power more diffuse and their interests perhaps less homogenous than corporations focused on capital accumulation.

Kerr (2006, 1–2) describes the censorship of cultural products as a "highly political, socially negotiated and nationally specific process," and the censorship of games as a "conflict between multinational cultural corporation(s) and local political, cultural and social actors." Similarly, Perks (2021, 219–21) calls for an examination of the regulatory spaces that shape

8. DigiBC: www.digibc.org/cpages/about-digibc

production and consumption in the game industry to better capture the complex system of interdependent actors, their disparate resources, and the disproportional impact of hard and soft regulation on these different actors. This fits with our broadened conception of the theoretical space for considering citizenship at work and the ability for workers to be subjects of citizenship within a broad domain of social regulation.

Industry associations have been prominent social actors in the long history of attempts to regulate access to videogames (Ivory and Holz Ivory 2016; Kocurek 2016; Perret 2016; Ruggill and McAllister 2016). The ESA and the Video Software Dealers Association[9] challenged regional laws and fought the issue at the US Supreme Court. The Court ruled that the potential negative effects of violent videogames were "insufficient to justify unique free speech limitations" (Ivory and Holz Ivory 2016, 146–48); however, the industry remains a target.

The Entertainment Software Rating Board (ESRB) was created in 1994 due to this scrutiny (see Chapter 3). In response to a US Congressional mandate to shield children from violent game content, the ESA[10] proposed the ESRB as a nongovernmental rating institution and system (Ruggill and McAllister 2016). Unlike a competing proposal, the ESA's plan maintained industry control over the governance of game content because, as an arm of the ESA, the ESRB is "organized by, but distinct from the industry" it oversees (Ruggill and McAllister 2016, 74). Similar systems have been established in other countries and regions.

Kerr (2006 13) uses the controversy over the "Hot Coffee" mod[11] found in *Grand Theft Auto: San Andreas* to show that "a range of stakeholders beyond the regulatory body may play a role in the censorship process." However, Ruggill and McAllister (2016, 75–76) raise questions about how a self-regulating system can meet the state mandate to protect public welfare. On the other hand, they also suggest that the ESRB has "intruded on creative expression, on the art and practice of game development itself" through its extensive review requirements. They note that the negative sales impact of receiving an "Adult Only" rating is a heavy constraint, since many stores will not sell such games and some countries ban them outright. Indeed, the creators of *Grand Theft Auto: San Andreas* are perceived to have engaged in deliberate subterfuge of the regulatory body to sidestep potential censorship (Kerr 2006). In this,

---

9. A representative agent of retail outlets that sold and/or rented console videogames; later subsumed within the Entertainment Merchants Association.

10. Then the Interactive Digital Software Association

11. "Hot Coffee" was the name given to a hidden code contained within *Grand Theft Auto: San Andreas* that, when enabled, allowed players to access a sexually explicit sequence within the game. "Modding" involves the modification of game code by players.

Ruggill and McAllister may be voicing the view of game workers as creators pushing back against new concessions made by the ESA to the state and the public following events like the "Hot Coffee" affair. These include increased reporting requirements to include inaccessible content (content that is ostensibly not intended to be seen by players). They may also be highlighting the tendency toward the bureaucratic entrenchment of regulatory bodies like the ESRB who seek their own legitimacy and dominance in contested social spaces.

In another example, the ESA, ESRB, and prominent game studios initially rejected public concerns about the introduction of gambling-like "loot boxes" as an in-game monetization strategy (Perks 2021). They attempted to shift blame and resorted to tactics of avoidance. Development studios and publishers were seen to "employ various discursive strategies in order to reframe the public discussion or divert attention away from these controversial monetization practices" (van Roessel and Švelch 2021, 198).

Within these controversies, the voices of game workers themselves are harder to locate and classify. A small study of Finnish game developers (Alha et al. 2014) showed negative views about aggressive in-game monetization strategies, including those that targeted children and those that compromised good game design. VGDs who were interviewed did not want to include these elements in their games. But VGDs also noted that the "freemium"[12] market had "come a long way" and felt that critiques or dismissals of the entire monetization model based on early and exploitative entrants were unfair. Similarly, Perks (2021, 225) documented how individual VGDs criticized the practice and how some independent development studios vowed to remove or not use loot boxes. Here, we perhaps see VGDs voicing a middle ground between extreme public outcry and dismissive corporate responses. Perhaps treading this line, the IGDA urged the industry to self-regulate to avoid the risk of intervention by the state (Perks 2021). Ultimately the ESA and the ESRB realized the need to act to reassert their regulatory legitimacy and announced a variety of alleviating self-regulatory measures (Alha et al. 2014; Perks 2021).

It could be that the issues of subject matter, censorship, game ratings, and ethical monetization are more general issues of free speech and societal morality, rather than an issue of citizenship at work. However, these elements, particularly monetization, can play a significant part in a game production process (van Roessel and Švelch 2021). We argue that it is important to consider an expanded lens of what counts within the

---

12. A business model that offers basic features of a product or service at no cost and charges a premium for additional or advanced features.

domain of social regulation of work. As it stands, the content of games is said to be "self-regulated" by the industry, but the "self" is rarely disaggregated. Upon cursory examination we see that it typically consists of hired bureaucrats who work for ratings boards or industry associations and who are overseen by a board of managerial-level representatives of major multinational game studios. It is harder to pinpoint the voice of smaller and/or more independent studio employers or workers, as individuals or collectives. The IGDA has maintained a long-standing special interest group (SIG) with the name Anti-Censorship and Social Issues, which supports the IGDA's education and policy efforts to, for instance, decouple violent videogame play from acts of real-world violence, and to ensure that games remain a protected form of free speech and are not unduly restricted in the market (Kocurek 2016). This SIG and the IGDA in general may represent a more bottom-up mechanism for establishing a voice. The IGDA has been an intervening voice on behalf of its members in policy debates and state hearings, particularly in the United States.

Ultimately, more systematic research is required, but the point here is that evidence of contestation exists and regulatory environments—whether social, cultural, or political, and whether binding or voluntary—shape the work of making games. Despite differences in localized sensibilities, dominant players can exert norms on others. While Mexico introduced their own game rating system in 2021, it is still in accordance with the ESRB because the ESA and its member companies lobbied the Mexican government to do so (Ruggill and McAllister 2016). Major game companies are directly involved in both the North American ESRB system and the Pan-European Game Information (PEGI) system.[13] That said, their power to regulate rating policy sits relative to that of respective states and local actors (see Kerr 2006; Perks 2021; Ruggill and McAllister 2016).

Overall, major multinational game companies and industry associations have clearly won the status of subjects of citizenship in the domain of game content. They have created and sustained various self-governing regulatory bodies and seem generally able to maintain a space free of censorship. However, debates about game content are fraught, with academics, players, and creators contesting the portrayal of gender, race, sex, and violence, and the ethical use of in-game monetization tools. It may be that there is a not a universal voice of game creators in this regard, but even if groups of workers were to articulate a position, there is no direct vehicle for it to be heard. Consequently, the processes that define and therefore shape creative freedom in game making might be driven

---

13. Run by the ISFE trade association

primarily by dominant market interests or by corporate value-systems. In this, they might not be the ones that VGDs wish for.

Events as a Showcase: Spaces of Social Dialogue

Game industry events and spaces of interaction for game workers are also domains of citizenship. They provide formal and informal opportunities to shape the larger social narrative about the values and image of the industry, to demark boundaries of what it is and what it is not, and to provide a space for those industry boundaries, norms, and values to be contested. Though game studios operate with extensive confidentiality and non-disclosure policies to protect their IP, the industry is porous. Information exchange and opportunities to showcase work are critical to the livelihoods of individual developers and to studio success. Media, marketing, and event planning are big business. As Ruffino (2018, 3) stated, "the video game industry is organized around a series of events that predict, explain and illustrate its own future." Understanding the networks of power behind the enactment of work-related events is critical to the theoretical expansion of the study of citizenship at work. Wherever the decision-making power over social organization is concentrated in the hands of a relatively small, interconnected elite group, VGDs fail to achieve the status of subjects of citizenship.

These spaces are exclusive and can therefore be exclusionary. First, they are expensive; most developers rely on their studio's support or funding from a trade association or industry development organization to attend. A perk of joining many associations is discounts to the top events (see, for example, O'Brien 2015). Second, events are often run and curated by a small, connected group of people or organizations. An examination of the ownership and governance structure of events and information outlets shows a concentration of power and influence over this social regulatory space. The companies running events are often connected to other representational branches of the game ecosystem. The Game Developers Conference (GDC) is illustrative of this.

The GDC is owned by a large marketing and business development conglomerate called Informa and managed under their InformaTech branch.[14] Informa also owns *Game Developer* (formerly *Gamasutra*; see Graft 2021), a leading outlet for industry information and commentary, and therefore an important curator of social dialogue. *Game Developer* hosts an online job board. This is not a neutral space, as studios can pay to be "Featured Employers" and *Game Developer* leverages their shared

---

14. Interestingly, this company also owns the Taylor and Francis publishing company.

ownership connection to list a "Who's Hiring @ GDC" section. Informa also owns the Game Career Guide as an extension of *Game Developer*. It lists schools that offer game programs and provides higher visibility to "Featured Schools" for a fee. *Game Developer* engages in marketing to sponsors and advertisers, and offers up the game community as an audience. In this way, sponsors and advertisers can push their content and brand through the *Game Developer* website and social media channels.

There is also a concentration of ownership and cross-pollination regarding conferences and award events. Award shows can fuel conference attendance, and conference attendance can be the prerequisite for award nominations. Two award shows sit under the GDC banner: the Independent Games Festival and the Game Developers Choice Awards. The judges and jury for these awards are typically editors of prominent game press and other high-profile industry members.

Connections can also be made between a conference's governing body and the resulting conference content. Conference governing bodies often have shared representation with studio employers, industry and trade associations, and other groups. An advisory board helps to build the GDC program each year.[15] At the time of writing, board members were a mix of representatives from prominent game studios (such as Ubisoft, Blizzard, Bungie, Microsoft), related tech companies (Facebook, Unity), representatives from nonprofit advocacy groups (Take This, Fair Play Alliance), representatives from co-owned organizations (*Game Developer*), and a handful of people listed as independents.

As we will discuss more below, Take This and Fair Play Alliance are what we might call formalized issue-based groups that promote their mission within the industry—in this case mental health and stopping negative game play behaviour, respectively. Representation on the GDC advisory board seems beneficial to exposure for such groups. GDC features an advocacy track that aims to "provide a forum for discussion and ultimately a place to effect change for the development community."[16] Unlike other sessions at the conference, this track is open to all attendees and is more financially accessible. The 2021 advocacy lineup included a nine-session Fair Play Alliance Summit and five sessions about mental health or featuring speakers from Take This. The IGDA also features prominently in the advocacy track through a long-standing partnership with the GDC. It was listed as the sponsor of nineteen sessions, and IGDA-affiliated speakers were listed in four additional sessions. These talks typically feature the work of IGDA SIGs. Past executive directors of the IGDA were also prominent in the program.

15. Game Developers Conference advisory board: https://gdconf.com/advisory-board
16. Game Developers Conference advocacy track. https://gdconf.com/advocacy

Operating under the auspices of the GDC, the advocacy track can be taken as a signal of accepted values and norms for the industry and can therefore be an influential space for the social regulation of work. The prevalence of "women in games" talks over the years has helped to mainstream that issue. There have also been talks about unions in recent years, including the infamous 2018 session that prompted the formation of Game Workers Unite (GWU).

In sum, game industry events and information outlets are sites where individuals and groups could be subjects of citizenship. They are spaces for information exchange and dialogue where opinions are shaped and from which actions may stem. However, the space of social regulation is not neutral. Information and events are curated, and the curators often hold influential and interconnected roles across formal and informal representational and governance spaces. The interests of event curators and individual game workers are not necessarily aligned. Nieborg and de Kloet (2016, 207) note that major industry events in Europe are "promoted and widely understood as 'European' events" and therefore act as mechanisms to harmonize individual game companies across diverse European countries under a pan-European cultural singularity. This suits the mission of trade associations, policymakers, and employers wishing to promote the European Union as a homogenous region of opportunity, but it may also divert time and resources from more regional, more organic, less mainstream, and perhaps more inclusive efforts. As Kerr (2017) also observes:

> Others have attempted to come up with alternative representational strategies. Virtual and networked communities at various scales coexist with the high technology circuits, and in the European context they find expression in a range of events and informal meetups that focus on games and play. ... These festivals provide temporary opportunities for face-to-face meetings and experimentation, but often lack the political power and capital of their high technology counterparts. (40)

We will discuss alternative representational groups and informal groups in more detail below.

Unions as Agents of Social Regulation

Unions act as representational agents of workers in policy discussions with government and quasi-government actors and influence the legislative environment by supporting workers in taking large-scale employment claims to the state.[17] Unions are also political and social actors; they can influence public opinion and values through education and awareness campaigns and direct action (for example, demonstrations and rallies). These campaigns have the potential to shape government policy-making and influence managerial decision-making outside of the local context of the legal industrial relations system. This makes the movement to unionize the game industry important for the achievement of several objects of citizenship at work.

As discussed in Chapter 7, VGDs are experimenting with old and new organizing modes. We argue that the activities of game worker organizers are blurring the boundaries between participation in the local regulation of work (that is, at the workplace) and participation in the social regulation of work (that is, in society at large). Much of the recent labour action being performed by game workers has been inherently broad-spectrum and rather dismissive of standard union operating protocols.

Case in point is the industry pressure group GWU, which has set out to organize the industry by whatever means necessary, seemingly without a care for homogeneity or centralization (see Chapter 7). It has thrown its support toward a range of existing unions without partisanship and advocates equally for better working conditions within studios (the local sphere) and improved conditions for quality of life (the social sphere). For instance, in March 2020, the GWU demanded "flexible working hours, health care for everyone, sick pay, rent freezes and a more sustainable way of making games" (Calvin 2020).

Existing unions are also acting outside their traditional scope and mandate regarding game workers and expanding the subjects of citizenship by supporting non-members. The GWU initiated a campaign on Coworker.org to fire Activision CEO Bobby Kotick.[18] In July 2021 the French union Solidaires Informatique announced a class action lawsuit against Ubisoft (see Chapter 8) in which the union would cover all legal costs associated with the suit, but not require claimants to be union members (Sinclair 2021). Though not a legal union itself, Game Workers Australia supports workers in individual employment claims to their employer and the state and directs game developers to join the Professionals Australia union for additional help and protection.

17. Over recent years in Canada, unions have made successful challenges under the Charter of Rights and Freedoms that have fundamentally shaped the interpretation of the freedom of association, the right to collective bargaining, and the right to strike (particularly in being acknowledged by Supreme Court decisions such as *Health Services and Support—Facilities Subsector Bargaining Assn. v. British Columbia*, 2007 SCC 27 [B.C. Health Services]; *Ontario (Attorney General) v. Fraser*, 2011 SCC 20 [Fraser]; and *Saskatchewan Federation of Labour v. Saskatchewan*, 2015 SCC 4.

18. Coworker.org: www.coworker.org/partnerships/game-workers-unite

The past few years have been a whirlwind of worker mobilization in the VGI that is unlikely to let up (D'Anastasio 2021b). With and without the help of established unions, workers are self-organizing into vocal and visible groups. These seem more robust than the ad hoc, short-term mobilizations described in Chapter 7. Exemplars are the Activision Blizzard King (ABK) Workers Alliance and A Better Ubisoft. These groups have leveraged the triggering events of sexual harassment scandals to harness worker frustration and consumer solidarity. This is channelled into stronger online and offline mobilizations that are successfully influencing the actions of VGI employers and shaping self-defining narratives of the industry.

These activist and solidarity groups can provide a logical stepping stone to unionization. Indeed, a unionization campaign by CODE-CWA is reportedly underway at Activision Blizzard,[19] and the ABK Workers Alliance created a strike fund to support worker efforts. This is what fuelled the QA strike at Raven Software and is represented in their successful unionization vote. However, there may be a drawback in worker collectives and solidarity groups if they do not move workers toward legal unionization. In the enterprise unionism context of North America, worker collectives that remain uncertified can deflect from full unionization drives, particularly if employers acknowledge their role in governance and are responsive to worker demands (Braley-Rattai 2014). Such a scenario has been postulated at Riot Games, which some felt would be an early candidate for unionization due to the worker activism in 2018 (D'Anastasio 2021b), and could be the situation with Google's Alphabet Workers Union. Ultimately, uncertified unions have weaker legal power, but they do have the potential to achieve very similar outcomes to certified unions with the political power delivered through member engagement (McAlevey 2020).

Other Actors in the Representation Role

International Game Developers Association (IGDA)

The IGDA engages in a variety of activities that influence the shape of the industry and provide a degree of participation and voice. These range from fostering networking and professional development, to lobbying governments against restrictive age ratings on games and moral panic about violent videogames, to advocacy regarding working conditions and

---

19. The successful certification of a second QA workers' union by the CWA (called the Game Workers Alliance Albany) at the Albany office of Activision Blizzard was announced in December 2022.

equity, diversity, and inclusion. In facilitating events and creating spaces for interactions, IGDA regional chapters have been described as "constellations of practice" in which communities of practice can develop, and as a "creative middle ground" between established game developers and companies, as well as emergent companies (Komulainen and Sotamaa 2020, 98).

Survey respondents see the IGDA primarily as a place for networking and building community, but also as a body that supports professional development and engages in some advocacy work (see Table 8.3 in the Data Appendix). The networking and community-building role was also reflected strongly across our interviews and has been reported in the IGDA chapters in Finland (Komulainen and Sotamaa 2020). Many noted the events held by the IGDA chapter in their cities:

> ▸ I feel like any benefits I derive from association from IGDA are ones that I would derive from going to their events. I've never experienced any effects of their involvement in my company as an employee, only as an individual. (F-10-22-07-M-G-22-11-13-16-02-PB)

> ▸ I think that they're an important movement. I think that there's value to having them here. ... They manage to get good speakers to come, and you have so many people from all different studios in this environment and everyone's friendly and it's cool, and it's not like the spirit of competition—it feels like it's a pretty close-knit industry. (M-10-06-M-B-16-11-13-16-02-PB)

Women and those who identified as transgender or nonbinary gender were more likely than men to report on the existence and benefits of the IGDA's networking, community, and professional development functions (see Table 8.4). This likely reflects the IGDA's institutional focus on building community among underrepresented groups and helping women developers in their careers. Some of our interviewees recognized the role that the IGDA has played—and can increasingly play—in promoting greater demographic diversity in the industry:

> ▸ I think that we have a real problem in games and that's an identity problem. ... Gender diversity, racial diversity, and to some degree age diversity as well is really poor. So you have a lot of White, middle-class men between the ages of twenty and forty, and there's very little outside of that. Maybe 10 to 15 percent. So, I'm very keen on groups expanding those groups. ... So the role that I see that IGDA can do is to bring about ways of improving that and improving the image that games has to people. (M-23-12-V-T-30-10-2013-14-26)

Table 8.4
Perceptions of the role of the IGDA by gender identity, 2015 (% of respondents)

	Networking and community	*Professional development*	*Advocacy*	*Outreach*	*Don't know*
Men	75	42	53	22	17
Women, transgender, and nonbinary gender	84	53	53	24	11

Source: Original Data IGDA DSS 2015
Note: Totals do not add to 100%, as this was a "check all that apply" question

One example of the IGDA's role in social regulation involved Intel, the world's largest semiconductor chip manufacturer, during Gamergate[20] (Weststar and Legault 2019). Those behind Gamergate successfully pressured Intel to pull its ads from the *Game Developer* website after *Game Developer* published a controversial article. Intel was criticized for kowtowing to and legitimizing the Gamergate movement, after which Intel reinstated its advertisements in a bid not to be seen as complicit. Intel also announced a US$300 million fund to improve the diversity of the company workforce and support efforts to bring more women into the game business (Wingfield 2015). What emerged was an example of political leverage and manoeuvring by the IGDA: a partnership with the IGDA Foundation to create the IGDA Foundation Intel Scholars program, which would provide mentoring and networking opportunities to women game developers (IGDA Foundation 2015).

In engaging in activities that promote the representation, inclusion, and belonging of women and other marginalized groups, the IGDA contributes to regulating some social aspects of work. It provides a space for participation and voice, directly and indirectly influences the activities of some organizations, and contributes to moving the needle regarding value systems and norms.

The work of the IGDA is driven largely through its Executive Director, SIGs, and local organizers of IGDA chapters. The SIGs are "global communities run by volunteer advocates."[21] The IGDA website lists thirty-four SIGs, grouped under three categories: advocacy (a focus on social

20. As summarized on Wikipedia, "Gamergate has been described as a culture war over cultural diversification, artistic recognition, feminism in video games, social criticism in video games, and the social identity of gamers." It manifested as a misogynistic harassment campaign against women, feminism, and progressivism in game culture and has been linked to the alt-right movement. See Blodgett 2020; Quinn 2017.

21. IGDA website, Special Interest Groups: https://igda.org/sigs

issues), discipline (a focus on elements of game development), and affinity (a focus on making space for developers with similar backgrounds to connect). The affinity SIGs include Women in Games, Black in Games, Devs with Kids, Latinx in Games, Chinese in Games, and Jewish Game Developers. A number of these SIGs, particularly in the advocacy category, seek to directly influence the regulatory environment and industry practice. An example is the Anti-Censorship and Social Issues SIG, noted earlier.

Some of our respondents also mentioned the work of the Developer Credits SIG, which promotes best practices for attributing game credits and tracks incidences of poor practice. As outlined in Chapter 6, crediting is important to the careers of VGDs. Our respondents noted the contribution recognition campaign by the IGDA:

> ▶ I guess, the credits, they've talked about that and making sure that everybody gets acknowledged for the contributions that they've made to the games. (F-18-01-M-E-21-11-13-16-02-PB)

This is another example of the exercise of developers' voice in the social regulation of work through a normative influence on organizational and industry practice. That said, the standards advocated by the IGDA are only put forward as "good practice," without any coercive power (Tô, Legault, and Weststar 2016). Van Roessel and Švelch (2021, 209) note the trend of "freemium" games, which eschew game credits altogether, and for some roles, such as monetization, to go under-recognized. Overall, our respondents were quite pragmatic in considering the power of the IGDA to make change in the industry on this issue and others:

> ▶ Well, the role that I liked it to be is, first of all, creating the meetups, being a community more or less—a forum for people in the industry, but also doing things like the crediting standards. Basically thinking in terms of a third party, making the industry into something that's a sane and humane industry where people are fairly compensated and treated fairly. ... One of the older elected heads of the association has said that in a lot of cases, he couldn't do very much and they can't really force companies to do anything. They can make these crediting standards and then hope that people follow them. (M-11-02-M-U-16-12-13-16-02)

The IGDA has also been active in the "quality of life" space since their first survey in 2004 (IGDA 2004; Weststar and Legault 2019). In partnership with us, the IGDA has since administered and reported on seven additional Quality of Life (QoL) and Developer Satisfaction Surveys (DSS)—resulting in the data behind much of this book. This data can be politically and normatively powerful because it can serve as a source for comparison for individual studios and developers, fuel the interest of the press, and promote dialogue on key issues. As well, and to varying degrees, when stories of poor working conditions make the press, the IGDA often issues statements urging better practices. Our interviews showed that developers are aware of and grateful for these efforts, but again there is doubt about the degree of real change:

> ▸ They're trying to address issues that exist by making recommendations that can't be enforced, unfortunately. (F-18-01-M-E-21-11-13-16-02-PB)

> ▸ I think they try to bring awareness to issues like crunch and quality of life, and all of those kinds of things. I'm not sure how much power they have in actually changing things, because they're not the same as a union, but their intentions are good, I guess. (M-10-06-M-B-16-11-13-16-02-PB)

In that regard, our quantitative and qualitative data about the effectiveness of the IGDA are mixed (see Figure 8.1 in the Data Appendix). Table 8.5 shows the 2015 survey data categorized by gender and into a racial binary of White/worker of colour. Men and workers of colour were slightly more likely than women and White workers to see the IGDA as being ineffective. It is likely that the more negative responses among workers of colour can be partially explained by the international makeup of the respondent sample relative to the incomplete global reach of the IGDA. A number of these developers were working in Asian, African, and Latin American countries, where the IGDA has a more limited presence. The more positive responses among women, and to a lesser extent workers of colour, can likely be attributed to direct activities by the IGDA. The contemporary IGDA is associated with ideological positions that support women and demographic diversity in the industry. The data suggest that developers from marginalized groups recognize this position and the efforts that the IGDA makes in this regard. On the contrary, developers and members of the game community who are threatened by the IGDA's stance on diversity feel that the association has strayed from its core principles, is a club for so-called insiders, and, at worst, is destroying the industry.

Turning to the heart of citizenship provision, some developers felt that the IGDA was ineffective in defending workers, that it could be doing

Table 8.5
"How would you rate the overall effectiveness of the IGDA?" Identity groups 2015 (% of respondents)

	Men	Women and nonbinary gender	White workers	Workers of colour
Extremely effective	4	6	4	5
Somewhat effective	26	31	26	25
Neutral	19	19	20	15
Somewhat ineffective	19	13	19	15
Extremely ineffective	14	13	12	25
Don't know	18	19	19	15

Source: Original Data IGDA DSS 2015

more, and that its existence has hindered the development of a more robust representational agent for workers, such as a union. This was certainly the view put forward by former board member Darius Kazemi (2013) in a public resignation (see also Sinclair 2013). Kazemi's views were referenced by some of our interviewees, who outlined the conflicts of interest experienced by the IGDA and a perceived cycle of inaction:

> ▶ I know that there were some issues recently, that some members left the IGDA over how they are told that they can't make changes when they're on the board. ... They're told ... basically, don't rock the boat; they get a lot of their money from their funding from games companies, so they're limited in how they can recommend things because those people will withdraw their funding because of that. (F-18-01-M-E-21-11-13-16-02-PB)

> ▶ The IGDA right now is not questioning current methods and how people are being treated. ... They're not a labour association. ... They don't take any risks, they don't question, because questioning current corporate sponsors and current relationships they have with big game development studios would, in fact, cut their funding and resources, and so it's a vicious cycle where they can't break the status quo, and I would like the IGDA to do more, question more. (M-14-02-M-G-07-02-14-16-02)

Some interviewees wished that the IGDA would provide more protection and more voice for workers:

> Maybe, being more active in terms of lobbying towards quality of life issues, and discouraging a lot of the major studios from thinking that it's a norm, and that it's expected in terms of crunch time, and more industry-wide. I feel like the big publishers and the studios, they tend to have all the power when it comes to the employer–employee relations, and the employee doesn't have much bargaining power. (M-10-06-M-B-16-11-13-16-02-PB)

But the mission of the IGDA is nothing akin to a union because a union must take a clear stance for workers' interests. The IGDA could not bring together both managers and employees, offer protection and services to both, and benefit financially from corporate sponsorships and partnerships. In fact, in calling for the IGDA to do more, VGDs might be misguided. In legal terms what many VGDs actually wish for is a union, and some are achieving that goal (Weststar and Legault 2017; see also Chapter 7).

The IGDA is held back by organizational capacity and the reliance on volunteers. The affiliations and interests of volunteers also greatly shape the nature of the SIGs and local chapters—who attends, what they do, and the connections to other groups or bodies (Komulainen and Sotamaa 2020):

> The studies that they've done and the recommendations that they've made, white papers that they've put out, I haven't seen many come out recently—I would like to see more recommendations made, more studies done. It's unfortunate that it's all volunteer driven, so, you can only do it as long as you've got the people who are willing to do it, which is hard in our industry with the crunch and everything. (F-18-01-M-E-21-11-13-16-02-PB)

> Sometimes I'm really impressed with it and sometimes I'm a little less impressed. I think that IGDA international as a whole, they're very organized at handling their different chapters and such, but having said that, each chapter has its own head, so depending on who the head of the chapter is, how organized they are, how they're handling... It's a volunteer position, obviously, they're not getting paid, so how they're able to handle it on a consistent basis can sometimes waver, and that's not a positive experience. (F-01-19-V-B-27-11-13-14-26-PB)

The capacity of the IGDA to be a social actor in employment relations and a consistent vehicle for developers to participate in the social regulation of their work is therefore hindered by the organization's mission and operational capacity, its corporate ties, and its institutional structure as a 401(k) charity rather than a certified sectoral labour union.[22]

Formalized Issue-Based Groups

Several other groups could be considered actors in shaping the game ecosystem and contributing to the social regulation of work through advocacy and education. We will briefly discuss four: Women in Games groups, BiG, Take This, and Fair Play Alliance.

Numerous groups work to promote women in the game industry, for example: the IGDA Women in Games SIG,[23] Women in Games International (WIGI),[24] and Women in Games (WIG).[25] They focus on awareness building, profiling women in the industry, and creating supportive spaces for dialogue, mentoring, and professional development. They host conferences, festivals, and awards shows, and maintain an active online and social media presence. They engage with educational institutions as well as corporate studios to spread their message. As such, these groups contribute to shaping expectations and norms for representation, participation, and equitable treatment. WIGI's website states that they work to "normalize women in the video game industry through increased representation."[26]

Our interviewees were quite favourable about these groups:

> ▶ I definitely believe in Women in Games, I think they need to have more of a voice, because I think one of the biggest problems is content. And it's not just content, it's like content who's making the games—it leads into everything. We need more women in games. (F-13-13-V-I-15-11-13-14-26)

> ▶ The Women in Games Group, yeah. That's helped a lot in terms of just having other women in games to talk to. ... That's been really

---

22. That said, at the time of writing, the IGDA was engaging more proactively with unions and the notion of unionism. At the 2023 GDC the IGDA sponsored two roundtable discussions on how to end crunch which were facilitated by the IGDA executive director and a union organizer from the CWA. Further joint initiatives to educate game workers about unions and their rights were also in the planning stages. Such activity supports worker participation in the local and social regulation of work.
23. IGDA Women in Games SIG: https://women.igda.org/about
24. Women in Games International: www.getwigi.com/about
25. Women in Games: www.womeningames.org/about-us
26. Women in Games International: www.getwigi.com/about

great having that networking event and having that group of support, because it can be tough sometimes. ... I think it's nice to have veteran game design women who can give you advice on how to progress in your career. Because you talk to a lot of men who are game developers, but not enough women. And this organization sort of brings them out a little bit more, the fact that you can see them more through that organization, which is great. (F-11-23-V-U-24-09-13-10-23 SM)

However, these groups also walk a fine line between responding to the workers in the industry and the employers. As they rely heavily on corporate sponsorship from game studios, these groups cannot afford to alienate studio management. Indeed, it is often a political game, and perhaps, more cynically, one of optics. Women and Games groups seek to partner with organizations that are "aligned and engaged" with their agenda.[27] Yet some studios seem to become aligned after they experience a corporate scandal. Such is the case with Intel, described above. Similarly, Activision Blizzard made a $1 million donation to WIGI (WIGI 2021) after their sexual harassment scandal. Ubisoft is a WIGI sponsor and a WIG Corporate Ambassador. Riot Games was recently celebrated as a WIG Corporate Ambassador (WIG 2021). The press release focused on the significant commitments that Riot was now making to equity, diversity, and inclusion, such as an annual Diversity and Inclusion progress report (Roseboro 2021).

In the same vein as Women in Games groups, BAME in Games (now called BiG) formed in 2016 (BAME stands for Black, Asian, and minority ethnic).[28] It is a grassroots advocacy group and professional network seeking to improve ethnic diversity in the game industry. The group is fledgling and has hosted some live and online meetups, launched a community Discord server, and initiated a Digital Mentorship Program in partnership with some UK game studios.

Take This is also a nonprofit seeking to influence the game industry, particularly to de-individualize mental health risks and challenges. The organization's mission is to "decrease the stigma, and increase the support for, mental health in the game enthusiast community and inside the game industry."[29] They provide resources, training, and support to individuals and game companies, and seek to address "underlying conditions that can create and perpetuate mental health challenges," including workplace cultures and work practices. Take This maintains a relatively

27. Women in Games: www.womeningames.org/ambassadors/corporate
28. BiG (BAME in Games): https://bameingames.org

large paid staff of clinical psychologists, social workers, and counsellors, and is overseen by a board of directors comprised largely of game industry representatives.

Fair Play Alliance is another example of groups participating in the social regulation of work. As stated on their website, Fair Play Alliance is "a global coalition of gaming professionals and companies committed to developing quality games."[30] By this they mean games that encourage healthy player communities and interactions, and a "world where games are free of harassment, discrimination, and abuse, and where players can express themselves through play." They claim membership from two hundred game companies, including publishers, distributors, platforms, and developers, and have an executive steering committee, though the names of those on the committee are not mentioned. The group has hosted webinars and summits, and produced reports, most notably the "Disruption and Harms in Online Gaming Framework" (Fair Play Alliance 2020), which is a resource to document and understand social and behavioural issues in game play. The goal is for game developers to self-regulate and apply this knowledge to create healthier player experiences and game communities.

Meetups and Informal Groups

Game developers also create informal spaces for support, participation, and self-promotion. Such spaces often take the form of recurring or ad hoc meetups at local establishments. Sometimes they are free-flowing social gatherings and sometimes there is formal programming, such as a speaker, a show-and-tell by a featured studio, or an open space to display works in progress. These groups come and go, as they are dependent on volunteers and the nature of the scene at a certain point in time. Examples in Canada include Dames Making Games and Torontaru in Toronto, the Mont Royal Gaming Society in Montreal (now defunct), and Full Indie in Vancouver. There are also groups for certain sub-disciplines or game tools. The Meetup website for users of the game development tool Unity, for instance, lists 488 groups and 264,131 members.

Many interviewees attended a variety of informal meetups in their regions. Though they enjoy the social side, the drive to attend is one of professional networking and learning:

> ▸ I find them all pretty relevant. I've been to Social Gaming, I've been to Vancouver Transmedia, I've been to WIGI, I've been to

29. Take This: www.takethis.org/about
30. Fair Play Alliance: https://fairplayalliance.org

Full Indie, and the Unity meetups. ... It's great that so many people come out on a monthly basis ... but there's also not really any kind of structure to what it is or who it is. ... I've met people who I can't figure out how they have anything to do with games at all, or it's become so big that you don't actually get to network and you don't hear the talks, and there's kind of growing pains, I think, when it comes to those meetups. I find WIGI really relevant because there are so few women in games, and it's great to have, like, fifty chicks in a room who are all related. That's really cool. The unity meetups are awesome because ... it's really relevant. ... You can really draw on each other's knowledge. (F-03-03-V-L-18-11-13-14-26)

▶ Yes, the Full Indie meetups, which takes place in town and is just independent developers getting together and chatting, and it provides a really good showcase for independent developers to just bring their games and stuff. The Unity meetup ... it's fantastic both to network and to see what other people are making and what tool is working for them. And even to get collaborators in your project. And Women in Games has been, again, it's good that they're starting to have a more clear agenda. ... It needs more of an agenda to actually get more data, help more women, do more seminars on how to interview, how to actually negotiate a salary, because that's something that is actively known we can't do. But yeah, it's good. (F-03-13-V-R-25-11-13-14-26)

Aside from the most obvious hurdle of maintaining a dedicated team of organizers, these groups also face challenges in finding the right balance, in terms of the size of the event, the focus of the event, and the composition of attendees. Students see incredible value in opportunities to rub shoulders with industry veterans, but too many students can ruin the atmosphere for experienced developers who want to talk deep shop, gossip, or just let off steam (see Komulainen and Sotamaa 2020). In this way, these spaces can be both inclusive and exclusive.

Some developers make their own groups that allow them to be creative outside of work, even under prohibitive industry regulations like NCAs. One developer who worked in mobile games felt that they were not allowed to work on other mobile games outside of work, so they worked on board games instead:

▶ I do something ... every two weeks where a bunch of people that are in this industry get together and we start throwing ideas at each other for board games and card games. Because we're all in the mobile game industry ... and we can't work on a new mobile game, but we can work on other types of games. ... Everybody does little things and then we test them up, we play them. That's basically all this group is about is trying out and also coming up with our own sort of games, and it's just for fun. (F-01-08-V-I-28-11-13-14-26-MSO)

Groups targeted at or created by indie developers seem to be more common than any specific groups for AAA developers. Indies are often small, sometimes a one-person shop, and work in a freer creative space (Ruffino 2021). These developers seek the interaction and sharing made possible by a meetup. But indies also face unique business challenges related to funding and discoverability, and can band together for informal and formal support. One of our interviewees described his group:

> ▸ We set up a very clear goal of putting together a mobile bundle, but the problem was that there were loads of technical issues around that. So, we ended up having meetings and talking about how we could benefit one another, so it would come down to things like, How do I deal with my tax? How do I do X, Y, Z? ... Another thing was a lot of the indies worked on their own, so we had social events where people could get together and people could be social like that. We'd have game jams where we'd actually release apps, we'd do issue awareness raising, we'd do cross promotion, there was even discussion of companies forming mergers or going out together to raise capital. So there were lots of functions they did but it was about developers together as a group, an advocate, working stronger than they could as individuals. (M-23-12-V-T-30-10-2013-14-26)

The list of activities undertaken by this group of self-organized developers shows the extent to which workers can be active participants in crafting their work and work environments, and therefore in both the local and the social regulation of work. In identifying common needs that flowed from gaps in the existing game industry ecosystem and working together to meet those needs, VGDs can subvert dominant industry forms and provide new avenues and alternatives. These workers are claiming citizenship for themselves. Such engagement takes extraordinary effort and collective commitment, but it can be invaluable to game workers (see also Browne and Schram 2021; Fisher and Harvey 2013; Keogh 2018; Parker, Whitson, and Simon 2018).

Some developers would like to see the mainstream industry give a little more support to these innovative spaces:

> I think it is really important for groups like IGDA, Full Indie, WIGI to exist, and I think a little support from the industry as a whole would be nice financially for them because I think that they do more good than I think a lot of people realize. ... All of the local independent game studios are offering to sponsor these groups. ... I think it would be nice if some of the bigger players were interested in that sort of stuff. (F-01-19-V-B-27-11-13-14-26-PB)

Keogh (2018, 15) expands the work of Young (2018) to discuss the importance of "everyday gamemakers" as "a broader spectrum of professional and amateur creators that are establishing their own cultural norms and practices to transform the professional infrastructure of the video game industry" (see also Keogh 2023). Browne and Schram (2021, 83–84) similarly argue that independent game developers are at the forefront of "ongoing reconfigurations of work and labour," and that they are supported in their efforts to survive and thrive by "cultural intermediaries" such as streamers, reviewers, commentators, people who produce and sustain exhibitions, game jams, meetups, support circles, and those who operate co-working spaces tailored to indie development. Directors of indie-focused co-working spaces have been credited with sustaining "centres for pedagogy, networking, outreach, knowledge dissemination and resource sharing" (Browne and Schram 2021, 92). Coupled with self-organizing hobbyists and amateur and professional game makers, these cultural intermediaries are also critical actors in the study of citizenship at work among creative, project-based workers because they are creating new domains and objects for citizenship and extending citizenship to a wider set of subjects than is allowed in the corporate game production ecosystem.

Conclusion

In this chapter, we turned to the last of the four objects of citizenship at work: the participation in the broader social regulation of work. Under the industrial citizenship model, this element was circumscribed to strictly work-related issues and gains consisted mostly in having legitimate representative unions lobbying the state in support of or in opposition to certain laws or regulatory regimes, carrying an industry or employment-based legal claim to the state or other relevant social authority, or forming professional bodies to address these topics. Looking at this with contemporary eyes, we note that the industrial citizenship framework implicated only the actors of the labour movement and constrained the regulatory context.

VGDs are early in their unionization project and most remain without a union. As such, they do not yet have a collective voice in the public policy debates surrounding work-related issues. However, like other contemporary workers, VGDs show great interest in taking part in a broader spectrum of issues that influence the social regulation of their work.

They wish to influence work-related issues and industrial and business policies, the planning activity of the development of an economic sector, and the regulation of the product. These influence a more widely defined working activity. Here workers' claims are not limited to well-being and compensation but also cover grounds like the blooming of creativity, self-actualization, social responsibility of game creators in portraying ethnic groups and genders, and the like. They are workers who have been told to commit to their creative work with their whole self, so it should not come as a surprise if they wish to be part of their industry as whole citizens.

We maintain that VGDs are yet disadvantaged as subjects of citizenship in traditional modes of the social regulation of work. They are hindered in efforts to influence the state through public awareness and lobbying campaigns, and they are also generally excluded from formal spaces of self-regulation regarding game content, events, and awards shows. They face a highly organized landscape of employer and trade associations while worker-based representational agents remain scarce and fledgling.

But we also argue that the activities of game worker organizers are blurring the boundaries between participation in the local regulation of work and participation in the social regulation of work. Much of the recent labour action being performed by game workers has been inherently broad-spectrum and deviates from standard union approaches. Actions led by both formal and informal groups in a sustained or an ad hoc fashion are working to shape the game ecosystem and contribute to the social regulation of work through advocacy and education. They spread their wings across studios and gather members across the industry. Consequently, there is a wealth of activity and a growing potential for it to coalesce into a meaningful voice. VGDs, everyday game makers, cultural intermediaries, emergent and existing unions, formal and informal industry collectives, workers in cognate industries, and the press are continually opening spaces for new dialogue and new participatory forms. These actors blur the boundaries between the local and social regulation of work, and their activities shape the actions of employers and regulators.

CHAPTER 9

The Regulation of Working Time Is a Citizenship-Free Zone

Labelled as "crunch," long working hours have become an inescapable feature of the VGI. "Crunch" refers to a period of long working hours typically leading up to a project deliverable or milestone. As these milestones are often tied to a funding contract, they represent "make it or break it" moments for the project; failure to meet a milestone could result in delayed or lost funding, the cancellation of the project, or missed marketing and sales opportunities. Crunch is synonymous with, though seemingly more innocuous than, the term "death march," which is used in other project-based work environments, particularly software development and software engineering. A death march signifies a project that participants feel is either destined to fail or requires an unsustainable period of being overworked, since its "'project parameters' exceed the norm by at least 50 percent" (Yourdon 2004, 1). Organizational working time regimes that are characterized by extra-long working hours, an expectation of constant availability, and an unpredictable, high-paced workflow, are salient in knowledge work. They are called "extreme working time regimes" in the context of the quest for work–life/family balance and sustainable work (Costas, Blagoev, and Kärreman 2016; Lee, McCann, and Messenger 2007; Perlow 2012; Pfeffer 2017).

The labour issue of working time stands out among others that besmirch the image of the VGI and has been the trigger issue for many individual and collective acts of resistance (Dyer-Witheford and de Peuter 2006; Peticca-Harris, Weststar, and McKenna 2015; Weststar and Legault 2019; see also the news archive at http://gameqol.org). The phenomenon raises important ethical issues because the work of crunch is rarely compensated and its true nature—as unlimited, unpaid overtime (UUO)—is obfuscated by the semantics of the term and enabling social norms. It represents a distinct encroachment on the private life of VGDs (Legault and Weststar 2017), and other salaried project-based workers (O'Carroll 2015). It has an impact on worker health, the quality of family life, productivity (through mistakes resulting from fatigue), income, and equity.

Building from Chapter 6, the regulation of working time is a striking example of arbitrary decision-making processes and lack of recourse. However, it is also an issue that can be interrogated across all four objects of citizenship (see Table 1.3). This chapter also takes up discussion of the protection against this employment risk and participation in the regulation of working time through procedures in the local workplace and through social laws. Are there domains of citizenship related to working time and are VGDs subjects to these domains? In answering this question we see that the issue of working time is an exemplar for the lack of citizenship across the board.

This chapter reviews the trends related to working time in the VGI, outlines the relevant legal frameworks for its regulation, and discusses the facts and perceptions related to the compensation of overtime work. We demonstrate that VGDs have limited citizenship in the regulation of working time by outlining how features of the project management regime inexorably dictate the working time regime.

Measuring the Regular Work Week

Using aggregate data since the IGDA's first QoL survey in 2004, we observe a decrease in the number of hours VGDs are working (both in workers' regular schedule and in crunch) and a decrease in the frequency and duration of crunch episodes. Yet, we ultimately conclude that UUO remains a problem among workers in the VGI.

Across the surveys, developers consistently reported that they worked more hours than they were contractually stipulated to work (Legault and Weststar 2015a). This tendency was also born out in our interviews; 64 percent worked longer hours on a regular basis. However, we do observe a general decrease in the extreme ranges of actual hours worked (see Figure 9.1). This means that there was an increase in the "standard hours" bracket of thirty-five to forty-four hours per week (Eurofound 2016) between 2004 and 2019, and a decrease in the longer duration categories.

There is a lower bound to ideal working time in a full-time employment schema. The rise in respondents reporting fewer than thirty-five hours per week could signal a rise in part-time, temporary, contract, or otherwise insufficient or precarious employment. In the DSS data, it could also reflect more students simultaneously engaged in part-time paid work or game commercialization projects.

Figure 9.1
Actual hours of work per week (2004-19)

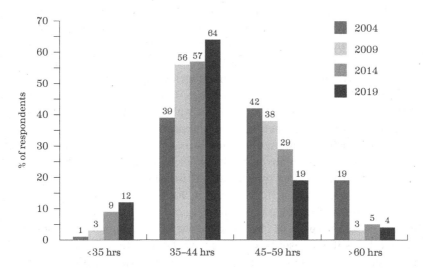

Source: Modified from Legault and Weststar 2015a, 11-12; original data from IGDA DSS 2019

Measuring the Dimensions of Crunch

Crunch is multifaceted. Its measurement requires an accounting of the frequency, intensity, and duration of a period of overtime. First, VGDs can face repeated episodes of crunch over the course of a particular period (such as number of times in crunch per year). Second, VGDs can face varying intensities of crunch that reflect how many additional hours they are required to commit (such as hours per week when in crunch). Third, VGDs can be required to sustain a period of crunch over varying durations depending on the scope of the perceived deficit of work (such as weeks in a row of crunch), which can be aggregated over a given period (such as weeks per year in crunch). Though the general practice of crunch is decreasing, it persists as an integral feature of game development.

With respect to frequency, we asked VGDs if their jobs involved crunch time. In 2019, the majority said "no" (58 percent), but that left 42 percent who said "yes." We subsequently asked those who said "no" whether their jobs involved long hours, or periods of extended hours or extended overtime, but that they would not term as "crunch." Of this group, 31 percent said "yes." Adding these figures brings the total of VGDs who felt that extended overtime was a part of their job to 73 percent.

We also asked respondents if they had experienced crunch time in the past two years (see Table 9.1 in the Data Appendix). More said "no" in 2019 than in 2014, and fewer reported "crunching" more than twice in the past year. However, this latter group was still more than 30 percent.

In measuring intensity, we see a trend towards fewer respondents working more than sixty hours a week while in crunch (see Figure 9.2 in the Data Appendix). Among our interview respondents, the average workweek during crunch was 63.5 hours. This is more than 150 percent of the normal working week. Extreme values ranged from forty-eight hours as a minimum to 112 hours as a maximum.

Our data for the duration of crunch is more varied. For 2009 and 2014 we compared the number of weeks spent in crunch (see Figure 9.3 in the Data Appendix). The number of VGDs who reported zero weeks in crunch was much higher in 2014 than in 2009, and overall, fewer weeks were reported in 2014. In 2009, 40 percent of respondents reported working ten or more weeks of crunch per year. This dropped to 22 percent in 2014, but still represents a large group. Despite the net progress, ten weeks of crunch amounts to 20 percent of the work year and can challenge workers' health and other aspects of life (Alfonso, Fonseca, and Pires 2017; Dembe 2009; Gibb, Fergusson, and Horwood 2012; Lee et al. 2017; O'Reilly and Rosato 2013; Sato, Kuroda, and Owan 2020; Virtanen, Ferrie et al. 2011; Virtanen, Heikkilä et al. 2012; Wong, Chan, and Ngan 2019; Yoon et al. 2018).

As an additional measure of duration, the 2004, 2009, and 2014 surveys asked how many weeks a period of crunch would last. Again, there seems to be a decreasing trend, but many VGDs still face harsh conditions (see Figure 9.4 in the Data Appendix). In 2004, 37 percent of respondents worked in crunch for five or more weeks in a row, compared to 30 percent in 2009 and 17 percent in 2014.

Despite the decrease of crunch as a general practice, the evidence is sufficient to suggest that long and unpredictable hours remain a persistent feature of game development. It is an employment risk that remains top of mind for many game developers, particularly when combined with the issue of payment for overtime (Côté and Harris 2020; Cross 2018; Glasner 2019; Milner 2018; Semuels 2019).

Compensation for Overtime

It is not only that VGDs are subject to working long hours, often without much notice and sometimes for extended periods. They are also inadequately paid for this extra time. Taken together, UUO is the biggest problem mentioned by the VGDs we consulted (Legault and Ouellet

2012; Legault and Weststar 2015a; Weststar and Legault 2012; Weststar, O'Meara, and Legault 2017) and a commonly discussed labour issue in the game press (Acton 2010; C. Campbell 2019; Handman 2005; J. Hyman 2008; Scott 2014; Sheffield 2009; I. Williams 2015). "Unlimited" overtime refers to the fact that there are no guidelines limiting the number of overtime hours a VGD can be expected to put in. As we have seen in previous chapters, it is their responsibility to work as much as necessary. "Unpaid" overtime means that the employee receives no wages, whether at the regular rate or at a premium rate, that match the overtime hours worked. It does not mean there will be no form of compensation:

> Unpaid overtime is a heterogeneous category, which can take varied forms. The fact that these varied forms are all categorised as "unpaid" does not mean that there is no compensation. ... Unpaid overtime can be associated with different types of compensation, ranging from retention of the goodwill of the employer (and therefore retention of the job) to more elaborate benefits such as a higher base salary and access to accelerated promotion and performance bonuses. (I. Campbell 2002b, 146)

Indeed, there are two forms of compensation for UUO typical in the VGI. However, both are post hoc to a project. They are subject to discretionary decisions, are never guaranteed, and come with no assurance that compensation will be proportional to the number of hours worked, since hours are rarely logged or tracked:

- Bonuses: At the end of a particular period, a financial amount can be allocated to the project team members based on the money made on the game. This is then divided among the VGDs, based on their contribution, as estimated by the team leads and the producers, and paid out (see Chapter 6).
- Time off: Leads or producers promise time off as compensation, and grant it at the end of the project, based on some criteria in each assessment round. Though sometimes explicit, these criteria are still discretionary and often not proportional to the overtime logged. Managers decide the amount of time off allowed and when developers will be permitted to take it.

We must acknowledge that some (small) studios limit, track, and pay overtime. But typically, they pay for overtime hours at the regular rate rather than at a premium (legal) rate.

Table 9.2
Distribution of answers (% of respondents) to the question: "Do you get extra compensation for working beyond normal office hours/stated hours for your job (i.e., crunch)?" (2004–19)

	2004	2009	2014	2019
No compensation	48	44	28	36
Perks during crunch (i.e., meals)	—	18	31	38
Time off	27	18	25	28
Lump sum bonuses	17	5	4	1
Time off and bonuses	—	7	3	6
Paid overtime (i.e., time and a half)	2	9	8	9
Company equity (i.e., shares)	—	—	1	1

Source: Original data IGDA QoL 2004, 2009; DSS 2014, 2019

Table 9.3
Modes of compensation for crunch time work, Canadian interviews, 2013–14

Modes of compensation	% of respondents
No compensation	9
Time off	34
Perks • Dinner during crunch • Occasional gifts (i.e., parties, sports, or show tickets)	30 28 2
Lump sum bonuses	15
Paid overtime (i.e., time and a half)	12
Time off and bonuses	7
Unclear future benefits/sanctions in the case of refusal	13

Source: Original data interviews with Canadian VGDs, 2013–14

Table 9.2 summarizes the forms of compensation for overtime work. The options are not mutually exclusive, as studios may compensate in several ways and respondents were instructed to select all applicable options. We see that a consistent and significant share of respondents across the fifteen-year period reported receiving no compensation of any form. The time off option has remained popular and stable across the years and perks (most often in the form of a free dinner) have risen. Reports of the bonus option have dropped steadily over the years and the number of respondents receiving true paid overtime has stagnated just shy of 10 percent.

These findings were echoed in our interviews. Respondents freely offered up a similar list of known forms of compensation (see Table 9.3), though paid overtime and lump sum bonuses were more frequently reported in this sample. Without any prompting, 13 percent of the respondents mentioned "compensation systems" that dangled the nebulous idea of unspecified future benefits as a reward for present-day commitment, or sanctions if the commitment did not make the bar. For instance, respondents discussed tales told by senior employees, or the lessons they had learned from observation about the impact of crunch time on employees' performance assessment, individual negotiation of pay raises, and career progress in the studio and in the trade.

It is common practice in project-based organizations to not pay overtime work at the regular rate, let alone the premium rate (I. Campbell 2002b, 2003; Hart and Ma 2008; Mizunoya 2002). The VGI is no exception. UUO is an unsatisfactory situation, despite some improvement in the practice of crunch over the past fifteen years.

Who Regulates Working Time and Its Compensation?

Taking UUO as an employment risk, we examine the broad regulatory role of the state and the project management regime that dictates industry and organizational practice and constrains the actions of both managerial and non-managerial developers.

Legal Regulatory Framework Permits Unlimited, Unpaid Overtime

At least in the North American context, the practice of UUO is supported by employment law and therefore sanctioned through the social regulation of work carried out by the state.

The term "crunch" may be purposefully used to avoid any association with the industrial and bureaucratic notion of overtime common among hourly wage earners. While legal frameworks in countries of the Northern/Western world usually oblige employers to pay salaried workers at a premium rate beyond the normal weekly hours, they often exclude some higher categories of workers. The definition of these categories varies, but they often include managers and executives, sometimes high technology workers, and sometimes professionals, most of them being paid on a yearly basis rather than by the hour.

For instance, the federal US Fair Labor Standards Act sets a yearly salary threshold over which private sector employees do not qualify for time-and-a-half pay if they work more than forty hours per week. That threshold was increased to US$35,568 per year in 2019, which amounts to US$684 per week. Many skilled computer professionals are exempt from overtime pay because they are paid above these rates and because they are listed as explicitly exempt due to the nature of their job description (US Department of Labor 2008). US states with high concentrations of high-tech workers tend to follow the federal precedent for exemption criteria (for example, New York and Texas). California has a more detailed set of laws dealing with computer workers, but they only serve to reinforce the exemption of VGDs from overtime laws.[1]

We see similar exclusions in the Canadian legal system. The province of British Columbia states in its Employment Standards Regulation that the hours of work provisions of the Act, including those governing meal breaks, split shifts, minimum daily pay, and hours free from work each week, as well as the overtime and statutory holiday provisions, do not apply to "high technology professionals" (including VGDs). Similarly, in the province of Ontario, information technology (IT) professionals are exempt from the hours of work rules of the Employment Standards Act and not entitled to overtime pay, nor other protections. Persons employed in the recorded visual and audiovisual entertainment production industry are covered by overtime pay legislation; however, the Act stipulates that "the industry of producing ... video games" is excluded from the definition of the recorded visual and audiovisual entertainment production industry.

In Quebec, the legislative provisions state that an employer who explicitly asks an employee to work overtime must pay for the overtime hours.[2] These provisions apply to non-managerial VGDs. As a result, the existence of overtime is covered up by the industry. Indeed, the cover-up starts with the use of the term "crunch time" rather than "overtime" and extends to the fact that developers are never actually compelled to put in overtime (it is often different for game testers, who are paid according to an hourly rate and are often compensated for overtime in Canada). Producers explain what needs to be done for the project, hint at the fast-coming deadline and the threat of unexpected problems, and, voila, the developers decide to stay at work, *on their own initiative*.

Sometimes managers mention the possible forms of future compensation, discussed above—bonuses and time off in lieu. Few studios keep records of overtime hours because any accounting of those hours would mean admitting that overtime exists. It could then be challenged as a

---

1. Section 515.5 of the California Labour Code and the Order for Professional, Technical, Clerical, Mechanical and Similar Occupations; Industrial Welfare Commission 2002; Division of Labor Standards Enforcement 2015.

2. ARLS, chapter N-1.1, sec. 52–55.

violation of the labour standards laws if it is not paid at a premium rate. According to past interviews, some studios go one step further and ask developers to sign formal time sheets declaring *normal* hours, regardless of the real number of hours worked (Legault and Ouellet 2012).

Beyond local differences in ways employers resist paying overtime, we must note a general trend in lobbying for a deregulation of working time that takes various forms throughout different countries and their different institutional labour regimes (see Chapter 1). For instance, at least three employers succeeded in contesting the application of overtime compensation in Quebec.[3] This created case law that rules out the claims to overtime pay by employees who, though not holding any management role, are hired under contracts providing yearly compensation rates. These decisions assert that an agreed hourly rate is required for an employee to claim overtime pay based on the Act.[4] The increased use of action led by employees (such as lawsuits), instead of labour institutions, represents an important shift towards a civil law approach that bears witness to the weakening of social laws and the provision of universal protection regimes.

In this case the state, through employment law, is the regulator of working time and overtime provision; however, policymakers are not acting in a vacuum. In the face of deindustrialization and a burgeoning low-wage service industry, it is well known that regional governments have jumped on the bandwagon of pursuing a "creative city" as a solution to low employment (Bodirsky 2012; Florida 2002; McRobbie 2016). Videogame studios promise relatively high paying jobs and employ young, educated, and skilled workers. As a result, studios and industry associations are a powerful lobby group and have negotiated permissive tax and labour regimes (see Chapter 8). Governments have a conflict of interest in this regard; they are not likely to institute regulatory policies that chase studios away after working so hard to attract them. As exemplified by a developer in British Columbia:

> ▶ Everyone, I mean we were all painfully aware that the industry lobby at the BC government changed tech law so they didn't have to pay overtime. (F-10-12-V-I-04-12-13-14-26-MSO)

---

3. Two recent decisions have dismissed the complaints of airline pilots (Québec (gouvernement du) (Service aérien gouvernemental) et Syndicat de la fonction publique et parapublique du Québec, 2014 QCCTA 241) and software designers (Commission des normes du travail c. Solutions Mindready inc., 2006 QCCQ 11439) to this effect, and there is a class action regarding this issue as well (Godin c. Aréna des Canadiens inc., 2019 QCCS 1678).

4. Of course, such jurisprudence could be reversed. The Court of Appeal has authorized the class action to follow its course.

As it stands, VGDs are denied citizenship on this issue, as they have no group, association, or union to act as a counterbalance to such an industry lobby.

The very fact that crunch is an option that is supported by labour laws in many jurisdictions brings about a certain laziness in management practice that perpetuates the practice of relying on crunch. Many developers do not condone the fact that it has become part of the business model in the industry:

> ▸ If you've built your game properly, and you're organizing your time properly from the beginning, then you shouldn't be running into crunch. It's the people, too—people are understanding, "we're not doing crunch." If in your head you say it's not even an option, then you'll start conforming your studio to not do crunch. But if it's already an option, we get lazy. (M-13-10-T-B-20-01-14-04-11)

Do any VGDs have any regulatory power or influence at this level, or is this a domain devoid of citizenship? One option that we have seen is for VGDs to leave their employment relationship and enter into labour agreements as an independent contractor. This status can allow for considerable bargaining leverage in a fee-for-service relationship, but only if the developer is in high demand. Given that independent contractors are also cut off from other protective employment standards, some studios even prefer this arrangement. It can save them money, despite being required to compensate for extra hours. All in all, most game developers are permanent or temporary employees and therefore subject to the exclusions in their applicable legislation.

We also must recall that perception of unfairness or injustice depends on prior information about the issues at stake. Our research suggests that VGDs have a limited knowledge of labour laws, and many may not realize that there is a different regulatory path to be had. In 2014, only 24 percent of survey respondents said they knew the labour laws where they lived; 57 percent said they had "a little" knowledge. This lack of awareness is not helped by the fact that this is a very mobile workforce, moving from one legislative territory to another.

Project Management Constraints Lead to Crunch

The practice of UUO is well known among developers and would-be developers. Many have been critical of the practice for a long time (IGDA 2004, 16–18). Though the legal regime has certainly upheld the desires of the industry, what local mechanisms make UUO so seemingly necessary and allow it to prevail?

The regime of project management is critical to unpacking this issue, as it controls and shapes all aspects of the experience of project work (Legault and Weststar 2017). As outlined in Chapter 3, there is a very high degree of uncertainty in the creation of an innovative product or service, juxtaposed against a strong requirement to deliver the project in a relatively specified way, by a specified time and for a specified cost. For more traditional or classic games, making sure the game is available in line with important buying seasons or industry events and conforming to the contract of internal or external publisher-clients remains paramount. For newer live-service and "freemium" games, public commitments made to the player community and their desires for fixes, modifications, and new content have taken precedent. The planning of working time is one of very few "free" or malleable variables available to producers. They use working time as the always available means to adjust to unexpected constraints. Very few project contracts have substantial amounts of resources or time, so crunch work is the magic link that guarantees the game will ship on time (Bulut 2020a, 119). It is a design feature in the politics of social relations in game development, what Bulut calls the "unequal *ludopolitical* regime" (Bulut 2020a, 10) "inherited from the media industries of earlier decades that has not made much progress in the context of digital labour" (Bulut 2020a, 121). Notions like "playbour" and "doing what you love" are powerful deceptive narratives (Bulut 2020a, x; Tokumitsu 2015).

Though the data suggest an overall decline in crunch work, the call to work more hours (for free) remains the preeminent solution for meeting scope, deadline, and budget constraints, and it has become deeply rooted in the rhythm and norms of game making. The 2009 and 2014 survey data allow us to compare the perceived studio practices related to crunch time (see Table 9.4). In 2014, if we combine the first two answers, 52 percent reported a company policy that seemed to actively avoid the practice, but the remainder reported regular engagement with crunch work. A portion of this group accepted or, as Côté and Harris (2020) describe, even valorized the practice. Furthermore, a large proportion of survey respondents felt that crunch work was expected at their workplace as a normal part of their job (see Table 9.5 in the Data Appendix).

In 2004, 82 percent of survey respondents expressed significant pressure to have the game ready to ship by a certain fixed date; only 8 percent said that their company policy was to ship when the game was ready, no matter how long it took. Of these same respondents, 88 percent were

Table 9.4
Distribution of answers (% of respondents) to the question: "How does your company manage crunch time?" (2009-14)

	2009	2014
Very rarely in extraordinary circumstances we have to crunch, but we do everything we can to avoid it.	37	44
We don't have crunch time; our schedules allow us to get things done without it.	7	8
Crunch is part of our regular schedule, and I don't agree that it should be.	22	24
We crunch often, but we view it as a failure in scheduling.	21	15
Crunch is a part of our regular schedule, and I don't mind.	4	6
What others call crunch, we call daily work schedules.	9	3

Source: Legault and Weststar 2015a, 15

very critical of the planning operations and estimates set in the pre-production phase. According to one review, unrealistic scheduling has been a long-time plague of game development (Politowski et al. 2016). The causes of crunch work identified in 2004—inadequate staffing, work organization problems, schedule planning, change in control policies for client orders (IGDA 2004, 18-20)—have not changed greatly over the years. In both 2014 and 2019, many VGDs linked crunch work to management problems (see Table 9.6 in the Data Appendix). Therefore, fewer VGDs perceive crunch work as inherent and unavoidable, as some would like to suggest. Having free overtime at hand is an easy solution that spares managers the critical examination of their management practices.

Most of the reasons for crunch work are completely out of the control of rank-and-file VGDs, who are not represented by a union and have no access to joint consultative or decision-making processes (see Chapter 6). They lie in the realm of managerial purview. Even then, within a project-based environment, frontline and middle managers can themselves feel trapped by the commitments and contracts that they have with their parent studio, central headquarters, external clients, and, increasingly, the customer base. Now that more than 90 percent of videogame consoles are connected to the Internet, game studios constantly update and refresh their existing games, in part through downloadable live content that players can access or purchase. With the emergent "games as a service" model, "gamers now expect and demand [regular release of downloadable live content], which studios can profit handsomely from—putting yet more pressure on workers for months or even years after a game's release date" (Semuels 2019, paragraph 8; Dubois and Weststar 2021; Weststar and Dubois 2022). The regulation of working time is deeply embedded in the existing power structure of the industry and its competitive strategies. Some few studios do escape the regular practice of crunch work, but they are less focussed on large market sales, and less prestigious as well (Semuels 2019).

Some challenges such as "feature creep" (the continual addition of new items to a game, beyond an initially agreed upon scope) or creative changes driven by external stakeholders can be managed in certain circumstances. The hardest for a team to deal with are those tied to elements of a contract or to the ultimate viability of a game. External and internal stakeholders can cancel a game if they do not like the direction it is taking or if it is not meeting expectations. The same can be said in the more contemporary live environment for games that are not meeting the desires of the players or for which the subscription base is not growing sufficiently.

Anecdotally, this was an issue that came up in the comments to the *Rockstar Spouse* blog posted on the *Gamasutra* (now *Game Developer*) website about the poor working conditions at Rockstar San Diego in 2010. A former Rockstar employee wrote:

> It goes down to really bad upper management (NY guys) with too much money to spend and little idea of what a game development cycle is and no backbone on the studio managers, who understand that their employees are being abused like hell but don't have the balls to stand up against NY. (comment posted by "Game Developer," January 15, 2010, *Rockstar Spouse* 2010)

In the 2004 survey, developers reported how their company controlled changes to game design during the production phase (see Table 9.7). Adding features was seen as a big problem for 35 percent of respondents and 51 percent engaged in the practice routinely. Some studios implement a strict change-control policy, or at least try to protect projects from such situations by adding restrictive contract language that can buffer the cost of these changes. But, in a context of high competition, these restrictive demands can be given up on. Only 13 percent of respondents said that there were policies in place to protect them against changes that would have a direct influence on their working time.

An interview excerpt sheds light on the whimsical nature of changes to scope during a project. A team lead described his experience as a powerless go-between with his development team and multiple managers with frequently changing views, likely prompted by meetings with the client:

Table 9.7
Distribution of answers (% of respondents) to the question: "How does your company control changes to the game design during production?" (2004)

	2004
We often add features when someone on the team comes up with a good idea or sees something great in a competing product, but we're careful not to impact the schedule too much.	51
Feature creep is a big problem for us, and it messes up our schedules big time.	35
We have a formal change control policy that minimizes changes.	13
We never change anything to the game once production begins.	1

Source: Original data from IGDA QoL 2004

> ▸ I've been caught in a situation in which I was leading a team, I was responsible for quality and deadline, I really had to urge my team for them to [deliver]. But I had no control at all over quality or deadline! That is, the deadline was set by some manager above, my boss actually, who could decide that what was due in three months now was due in one month because that's it, that's all. ... But besides this, regarding quality, there were directors on a parallel hierarchy, sort of "content directors" who just have to monitor quality. They have a veto, they can accept or refuse regardless of the timeline. Thus there I was, in an impossible trap because I was responsible for something I had no control over, and that is one of the reasons why I was looking for another project to work on. I was no longer interested to stay there. ... It was a bureaucratic nightmare wherein different people have promised this and that [to the client] and felt tied by [those promises], shovelling problems down to me, who was caught with the problems. (translated from French) (M-13-01-03-M-U-30-10-13-13-15-19-MSO)

Aside from some exceptions, most of our interview respondents were aware and accepting of the fact that uncertainty is inherent to any creative project. However, they were critical of the general system that makes studios negotiate unrealistic contracts with publishers only to immediately transfer the burden of such a risk to VGDs, who will necessarily have to work crunch time to keep the cost and the timeline constant. What they attribute to mismanagement is the planned part of crunch, the part that can be predicted from the outset because it is based on the conditions of the contract. Acknowledging the highly competitive international market to produce profitable games, respondents described the pressure on studios to settle very demanding contracts for very sophisticated products. To preserve profitability they rely on understaffed teams, whom they overwork. The constraints and risks are transferred to VGDs (Legault 2013).

Crunch Becomes Pervasive

Passion for the work is often put forward as a factor in fostering the game industry's culture of crunch (Côté and Harris 2020). As seen in Table 9.6 in the Data Appendix, it is even a reason put forward by developers themselves. However, the alleged "self-driven" propensity to work crunch time can be motivated not by altruism and love of the work, but by the reputational system of career advancement that is enforced in studios across the industry (see Chapter 4).

The VGI is not alone. Consenting to extreme work for fear of marginalization or negative career consequences is a plague in the realm of knowledge work (Blagoev and Schreyögg 2017; Alvesson 2000; Perlow, Mazmanian, and Hansen 2017; Reid 2015). Neither purely voluntary and freely agreed to nor completely required and forced, overtime falls under the broad category of "voluntary but expected" working hours (I. Campbell 2002b). As UUO becomes more institutionalized, it becomes harder to contest:

> When unpaid overtime becomes widespread in individual workplaces, occupations or industries, another layer of difficulty is laid down. Unpaid overtime can easily appear as just a condition or aspect of the job, as part of an implicit contract of employment that employees accept when they enter the job. It can be a condition that is simply tolerated or perhaps even welcomed as a sign of the high status of the job. In such cases, unpaid overtime appears institutionalised, as part of a new definition of what is normal or expected in the job. Reluctance to undertake unpaid overtime can appear as a reprehensible personal fault—as a breach of a contract with supervisors and colleagues (I. Campbell 2002b, 128).

Our interviewees often spoke about this pervasive and yet unofficial and often invisible system of regulating working time. Many described circumstances in which hours were not logged at all, while others described a complicated mix of official and unofficial policies for determining whether overtime hours were mandatory, enforced, validated for payment, actually paid, and logged. One noted that even when hours were not counted officially, it was widely known, unofficially, that the record of the turnstile that granted access to the building was monitored. VGDs discussed the threat of firing or another form of reprisal, all of which reinforces the "professional" ethos of the autonomous creative worker, or the "honour code" of the trade (see Chapter 4). VGDs who accept or condone the existence of UUO often use the rhetoric of "duty to the project" as a powerful device to justify the needed "flexibility." They appeal to the "sovereign needs" of the project that wipe out the need for any direct managerial control or authority. They obey an injunction to make the project succeed instead of obeying a boss. VGDs are part of a new category of "entrepreneurial professions." Fatalistic discourse about working time is construed around a post-bureaucratic model of "passion" for work and on the liberalist rhetoric of free choice: "It's something you accept when you go into it; that's the kind of choice you're making," "most game developers wouldn't put up with the long hours unless they really, really love what they're doing," "I knew what I was signing up for," and "one can learn how to take crunch times in stride" (Bulut 2020a, 119–21). This is not much of a domain for citizenship at work.

In understanding the practice of free overtime in the industry, the question of crunch time is closely linked to the question of performance assessment. If putting in extra hours entails a good assessment, in a world of reputations and individual bargaining over working conditions, this could help explain the practice (see Chapter 4). Across 2009 to 2019, 15 to 22 percent of respondents felt that they were judged more by the hours they put in than by the quality of their work, and a further 18 to 22 percent were unsure (see Table 9.8 in the Data Appendix). Across the same period, 21 to 31 percent of respondents also agreed that the time they spend with family lessened their chances of promotion or advancement (see Table 9.9 in the Data Appendix). This jumps to almost half when the neutral responses are included.

Among our interviewees, two-thirds said they were evaluated according to the quality of their work, but more than half said that hours worked could be a criterion:

> ▸ I totally agree [that we are assessed on hours of work], because I was already given a bad rating in an evaluation [at a big studio] because I hadn't willingly agreed to do overtime. The dude who did my review said, "Yeah, but you know, you're never keen on doing overtime." I said, "Are you fucking kidding?" ... Who the fuck cares whether I'm keen or not? At the end of the day, was your fucking game tested? Yes. Was it debugged? Yes. Did my maps screw up?

No. ... They're definitely going to look at your hours, at your timekeeping. (M-19-10-M-I-17-7-13-13-10-12-MSO)

▶ There have been a few times where if I haven't come in on several weekends in a row, I'll be given a talking-to basically. Not like anything formal, just: "Hey, you haven't come in on this amount of weekends. You should come in." ... It's a very small passive-aggressive kind of intimidation. Just demanding more of your time when it shouldn't exactly be expected of you, and that's kind of the Catch-22. ... I shouldn't also feel pressured or obligated to do so. (M-07-19-T-B-24-03-14-04-11-JT)

Willingness to do overtime is still a huge factor when it comes to the evaluation of an employee's contribution to a project, but there is no rigorous form of timekeeping in any studio that we know of. It depends on the producer's perception, memory, and skills in persuasion when discussed in the evaluation committee:

▶ So, your evaluation [can give you] a pay raise that is [biased by the] fact that you helped the people in your team by doing overtime. So that's how they compensate you. It really varies from person to person: [you could have] someone who's really gone all out, who put in two hundred hours of overtime, but because his boss is lousy [at arguing his case], he's only going to get fifteen hours of vacation. Plus, in his evaluation, he'll get told, "Yeah, well, you always put on a song and dance about doing overtime, so you really need to work on that. You got average on your review." So, it's pretty well: "Fuck you." Don't expect to be compensated one for one. (M-02-04-M-U-17-10-13-13-19-15-MSO)

We argue that the working time regime is partially regulated by the pressures of the industry's career system. Within that system, the "passion for games" argument is a powerful mobilizing force (Consalvo 2008; Bulut 2020a), yet we suggest that management uses it to their advantage as a normative tool and a veil covering a more complex system of rewards and punishments (see Chapter 4). In this environment, the need for hard regulatory oversight and direct coercive action by management diminishes (Burawoy and Wright 1990; Weststar and Dubois 2022). Even if more workers become dissatisfied, this can make the practice harder to contest because workers cannot readily identify its source—or they are implicated in it (Peticca-Harris, Weststar, and McKenna 2015). VGDs are phantom citizens in this case—they feel as though they have some say or control, but it is largely an illusion.

Peers as Powerful Actors of Regulation

As much as managers prompt extra work, VGDs are also subjected to group norms and symbolic meanings of time that "act as a guide of appropriate behaviours" and do not allow for "free choice" (Rose 2016, 18). Managers do not ignore the existence of peer pressure—far from it. But arrangements of work time are presented as each individual worker's decision, which allows for punishment of those who do not cooperate in the team effort as well as for skirting the law. Refusing to work overtime when the rest of the team does is not a negligible fact in game studios or project-based organizations in general (Chapter 4). The peer group is a key link in the employment network that is essential to a developer's internal and external mobility.

Although the regulation of time by unions seems to be lessening, labour laws provide an array of individual rights. Formally, work time "is exchanged by the employee for wages" and "constitutes subordinate time," during which the employees must make themselves "available to the needs and will of the employer, in contrast with the employees' free time" (Rose 2016, 21). Yet, labour laws are powerless in the face of informal collective norms and the law does not acknowledge the blurring of work and non-work time. Moreover, the ensuing links between pay and normal time worked, and between pay and overtime work (with a premium) are disappearing, along with the frontier separating workspace and personal space (Rubery et al. 2005; Supiot 2001):

> This has become increasingly so in recent decades as the demise of collective bargaining, and union power in general, has reduced the last vestiges of collective work time—typically that undertaken during standard work hours, with extra compensation given for work outside of those hours. (Rose 2016, 19)

The collective peer pressure over individual decisions regarding working time confers a social dimension that is critical in a context of teamwork. The setting of informal group norms among workers can be an act of resistance and give a sense of agency over a particular dimension of work, but in this case, they act in alignment with managerial design and against the rights of the worker. Consistently, there is a growing desire and need for predictability of work schedules (Perlow 2012; Rose 2016,

21), but there are limited citizenship mechanisms available with which to exert that change.

Managerial Discretion Regarding Compensation

As in other creative trades, VGDs have a multilayered compensation system, with some components being universal and minimal (wages), while others are variable and meritocratic (bonuses, negotiated fees or royalties), and dependent on a discretionary process. Developers receive a share of the added value generated by their intellectual contribution, in alleged proportion to their market value. This system has nothing to do with seniority or with any accounting of working time; it generates uneven benefits based on arbitrary determinations of merit (Legault and D'Amours 2011; D'Amours and Legault 2013). However, it is very difficult to assess individual merit given the large and highly interdependent teams used in game development. As well, in the VGI, the commercial success of a game is easier to measure than actual performance at work and this becomes an important consideration for merit-based bonuses and royalties. Yet, VGDs can put hours of work into a high-quality game that turns out to be a commercial flop. Their performance may have nothing to do with the failure, but they still will not be paid for the overtime hours they put in.

The very existence of any compensation for overtime is part of a discretionary decision process (see Chapter 6) that is never guaranteed, nor based on any formal policy or criteria. The regulatory environment here is loose and arbitrary (see also Chasserio and Legault 2009, 2010, regarding the similar technological services industry). For most VGDs we interviewed, the fact of no compensation was an unwritten rule, and any variation was ad hoc. It remains unequivocally more of a reward or privilege than a form of payment. The vast majority seemed assured of at least receiving a free meal and others had become accustomed to something more if the crunch was particularly bad—a party or tickets to a sports game or a movie. At one interviewee's studio, the reward for crunch and other extraordinary effort was the chance to win a quarterly prize—in this case a trip to Las Vegas.

Some interviewees said that it was formally written into their contracts that they would not get paid for overtime and this was explained up front in job interviews. Those who opposed such a policy presumably did not get the job.

Other interviewees did describe formal overtime policies, but it was not the norm in our data. These involved elements such as an approval-granting process for overtime pay, a process for logging and validating hours, and/or a clear articulation of when overtime kicked in and which rates were being used. Some reported policies whereby studios paid overtime at the legal premium rate of 150 percent, but only if the weekly hours rose past the legal threshold of forty-four hours, even though the normal workweek might be much less (such as 37.5 or 40 hours). The result is that developers must work more hours at the regular rate just to reach eligibility for overtime, and for many this is not worth it.

Studios generally do have a clear policy for their hourly staff (such as quality assurance testers). Hourly workers are not exempt from overtime legislation and therefore log their hours and receive the premium wage rate for overtime.

Beyond the arbitrariness in allocation, promised compensation often never materializes (32 percent of respondents said this), often for obscure reasons. And VGDs do not usually act to reclaim the promised benefits. A few will go to the HR department, but often unsuccessfully. In some cases related to small or independent studios, the failure to live up to these promises is blamed on the constraints typical of start-ups (such as forgoing wages at the start for the promise of a pay-off when the company makes it big). But we heard just as many cases of established studios making the same broken promises. Companies can easily claim that a game did not make enough money, that tax credits were delayed or not forthcoming, or that the studio was just too busy to grant extra time.

As well, many developers are laid off at the end of a project and therefore lose access to any previous entitlements:

> ▸ They just decided to cut all of the existing employees out of the deal and they actually owe us back pay, they owe us vacation time. When we were let go, we were given no severance or anything like that. They just pull the rug out from under everybody. (F-03-07-V-F-12-19-13-14-26-LT)

Given that there are no formal policies or written rules regarding compensation and no sanctions for broken promises, it is easy for management to mention future benefits as a way to motivate VGDs to put in more hours in the present.

Policies for Compensatory Time Off

Though the survey data above indicated a rise in the use of compensatory time off, some interviewees felt that time off was only used in serious cases. As one described it, time off was only granted when "people who have been doing overtime are seriously burnt out. Like, if they seem like they're on the verge of a nervous breakdown, then they get days off" (F-13-19-T-B-29-05-14-05-13-JT). As well, when crunch time is compensated in time off in lieu, workers report the days off are arbitrarily granted by managers and there is no tracking system of hours.

Time off in the context of project management is a very complicated notion. When promised or agreed on as a form of compensation, it is usually assumed that it will be granted at a less busy time, after a milestone or a closing deadline, or between two projects. It would seem quite easy to tuck a couple of days in after a milestone is completed. However, it is a greater hassle to accommodate many weeks of time off if a crunch period has lasted a long time, and in practice there are very few times in studios when things are "calmer." Rather, the studio schedules and work processes are so tight that instead of being granted allowances to make up for being overworked, VGDs are restricted in their time off. For instance, some have felt pressure to cancel vacations, been denied vacation time, or been asked to cancel vacations already scheduled (see Table 9.10 in the Data Appendix).

It may also be the case that what was promised at one time may have been made on the whim of the employer or as an allowance of the moment and not in accordance with a set policy:

> ▶ There were some instances that I was actually very happy with what I got. I put in two/three months of crazy amount of hours at [a former studio] but then I ended up getting three weeks of paid vacation that was really awesome. ... But then there's been other cases where I've done the exact same thing but I've only got two days of vacation and obviously you're not happy when that happens. (M-14-19-T-G-08-01-14-05-13-JT)

Refusal to Crunch

It is difficult to actively refuse something that has not been asked of you. Whether or not they are actively responding to a legal framework, either general labour standards (in Canada) or potential class actions (in the United States), during conversations with VGDs employers often prefer to refer implicitly to the needs of the project, the problems in the schedule, or the additional work that needs to be done. Or a manager will just start taking dinner orders. These approaches place the onus on the employee, and leave room for what may seem like a decision on their part to wilfully stay at work. One team lead we interviewed was frank:

> *Did you have to ask your employees specifically to come in on the weekends?*

Yes.

Was that just a normal thing to do?

Eventually.

Did they ever push back or protest?

"I have kids! I never see them! Why are you taking my family time away?" "I can't work. I have a lot of things to do outside of this job!" "I am not happy! My marriage is falling apart!" That kind of stuff.

How would you deal with this?

Well, you listen and you make concessions. You can't force anyone to do anything. Eventually, you say: "Look, I'm not coming to your house, I'm not picking you up in a car and bringing you here. I need you here. This project needs you to do stuff." You find the best story you can, that respects the most people, and try to be objective. (M-01-18-V-E-18-10-13-14-26-JL)

However, once the potential for crunch has become clear, VGDs have identified several means by which to refuse it. First, if you are in very high demand, then you can set conditions. Second, if you are willing to accept the consequences, you can make your refusal to work overtime clear when negotiating your contract. In doing this, VGDs are aware that they will not be promoted as quickly as those who consent to crunch. Those who do not consent will eventually be sidetracked—be it a poor evaluation, not being considered for promotions or not selected for the most interesting projects, being fired or laid off in the case of downsizing, or taking the blame of peers for delaying the project or "slacking off." As a result of their decisions not to crunch, VGDs usually end up having to limit their career ambitions:

> ▸ There is definitely an impact in your advancement within the company. Definitely. ... Because you're not seen as being the most productive employee. So, I was a senior programmer, I did not want to be a lead and... But I had my preferences in terms of what I wanted to work on, and I saw, in the last two years that I was with the company, I saw that my preferences were not really respected that much anymore, so ... I never really felt any pressure,

but I did see my career stagnating. ... So the pressure came more from within because even though I made the conscious decision to let my career stagnate a little bit, it weighed on me. It wasn't easy. It was definitely not easy because I wanted to do more. I wanted to participate more but I also knew that I couldn't spend the energy. (M-05-14-L-D-22-07-13-10-23-JT)

Third, if you are older and have experience in the industry you are better able to evaluate your options and select opportunities that fit your needs. There is a generation gap when it comes to willingness to do overtime. While experienced VGDs have acquired a critical take on how studios manage overtime, novices are just starting to build their portfolios and reputations, and so are willing to work long hours. Refusal is more widespread among experienced VGDs and those who have children. These VGDs will tend to negotiate up front or to look for studios that have a "no crunch" policy. Some have opted for taking on a contractor/freelancer status, so they can save some control over their hours.

Advice shared by a developer on the popular *Game Developer* website shows that negotiating for fair working time is an individual game in which developers put in the hard work upfront and hope for reciprocal outcomes:

> I've been blessed to find an employer who creates a work environment conducive to getting some great games made while holding family values high. But with that said, in the past whenever my work environment did constantly clash with my personal life, *I simply had to choose the right strategic moments* to be firm and go home for the night. That can *only be done successfully* (that is, without getting fired) if you maintain your work at a high-quality level. It's hard to argue with high quality work combined with a teamwork attitude displayed in *good and bad times*. Choose your battles wisely, then your employer *will most likely* listen and respect your management of your own time. Unfortunately, *we don't live in an ideal* world, so if the quality of your work is high, you've shown that you are a team player, but the respect is still not there, then continue to do your job to the best of your ability while searching for another position (Scott 2014; emphasis ours).

All in all, one-quarter of our interview respondents felt they could refuse to work in crunch time. They either worked in studios that made use of crunch but they independently refused, or that had the option to refuse from time to time with a good reason, or they worked in studios that had a no-crunch policy. But in general, things are less clear, and respondents did not precisely know the formal or informal rules. Instead, they built on what they saw around them and provided anecdotal examples of the tolerance or retaliation they encountered in studios to justify their own positions. The variety in these examples across the interviews can help explain the diverse positions held by VGDs on whether crunch time can be refused, and points to a Wild West approach to regulating the time regime.

Conclusion

Despite some improvements over the past two decades (Legault and Weststar 2015a), the long and unpredictable working hours of crunch are still seen as "a normal part of doing business." This can generally suit the male workforce in the industry (and in project-managed environments), which is generally imbued with a "play hard, work hard" culture (see Chapter 2).

In this chapter, we have used working time as an exemplification of the lack of citizenship for VGDs. We illustrated how VGDs face risks without protection and discretionary decision-making processes without any say in their regulation. We demonstrated a marked tendency of employers in the VGI to manage their operations, including HR, through informal practices or policies. This tendency is built on a certain distrust of any formal structures that could lead them into the kind of bureaucratic system that they associate with reduced efficiency (that is, flexibility) and stunted creativity. In these non-regulated, project-based environments, producers have full discretionary power over working time and the compensation of overtime.

Consequently, working time is not an object of citizenship because: 1) VGDs do not have a say in its attribution or in the application of policies (when they exist), 2) they can hardly refuse to cooperate in the team effort, and 3) most of all, because policies can be bypassed when necessary. Peers can exert pressure as much as managers, yet this should not lead us to forget the overarching conditions, which are set forward by publishers and on which every actor depends (see Chapters 2 and 3). Policies are protective barriers that could shield VGDs, but their discretionary application can prevent this protection. VGDs are not subjects of citizenship, even if some studios offer more formal processes, some producers care not to impose crunch time, or some privileged workers can enjoy some leeway. In the end, as we said in Chapter 6, such an obligation-free zone could hardly be a domain of citizenship in the absence of objects and subjects, and because of the mobility that makes VGDs face sporadic citizenship. On top of this, there can be no domain of citizenship where the legal regulatory regime exempts VGDs (among tech professionals) from paid overtime at the outset.

Historically, working time has been regulated and hours curtailed for health, security, and ethical reasons. Long hours of work are not sustainable. Yet the VGI has been successful in lobbying for the inclusion of VGDs in the list of those workers exempt from overtime laws. Governments find themselves overseeing an uncomfortable contradiction, ruling out overtime work through legislation on the one hand, and subsidizing the VGI through tax credits or other indirect means on the other (see Chapter 8). In this quest for hosting high-tech industries, governments are led to condone the very practices that they try to eradicate.

These workers have an uphill battle in terms of their struggle to gain a say in both the local (that is, at the workplace) and the social (that is, through the legal regime) regulation of their working time and compensation.

CHAPTER 10

Second-Class Citizens in the VGI

In previous chapters, we have discussed the objects and domain of citizenship as defined in the four important gains that allow the exercise of citizenship at work (see Table 1.3). Until now, we have only generally highlighted some conditions that favour groups of workers in making them subjects of some aspects citizenship but that keep others from accessing these same aspects. Given that three-quarters of VGDs are White men under thirty-five without children, it can be argued that "white masculinity is the elephant in the room for the industry's dominant demographics" (Bulut 2020a, 45). In the contemporary context, this issue of subjects is paramount. In Chapter 4, we assessed the socio-demographic characteristics like gender and ethnicity that can influence the conferral of citizenship status. In this we continue on, and frame the lack of diversity, inclusion, and belonging in the industry as another exemplary case of a lack of citizenship.

Theoretical work on the issue of gender in the VGI took time to emerge, notably through the work of Cassell and Jenkins (1998):

> Work on gender and video game play is relatively scarce before the publication of Justine Cassell and Henry Jenkins's (1998) edited collection *From Barbie to Mortal Kombat*. Prior to that, most of the research ... had been confined to ... the technological dimension of games, situating computer games as part of the larger domain of "gender and technology" studies. ... Cassell and Jenkins theorized, and others have since (AAUW 2000), that perhaps one entry point for girls and women into the world of computing might be generated ... through the development of skill and interest in playing video games. (Jenson and de Castell 2010a, 55)

Besides this interest in women's access to science and technology careers, investors also wanted to develop untapped markets:

> what this concern materially and theoretically produced were accounts of gender and gameplay in terms of attitudes toward and

preferences for certain types of games, as well as documentation of who was playing games and how often. (Jenson and de Castell 2010a, 55)

While the industry has been able to dodge and delegitimize individualized experiences as anecdotes, three high-profile events plus a growing list of industry scandals are harder to brush off. The first event occurred in 2012, when feminist media critic Anita Sarkeesian announced a Kickstarter campaign to fund a video series critically examining the common tropes used in the depiction of women in videogames (Sarkeesian 2013). The initiative gained considerable attention, both positive and negative. While it raised over twenty-five times the original funding request, Sarkeesian became the target of a vicious and prolonged misogynistic campaign of online abuse. She is now a key spokesperson on sexism and misogyny in games and the game community, as well as online harassment.

The second event occurred on Twitter in late 2012. Game designer Luke Crane tweeted, "Why are there so few lady game creators?" and mostly women VGDs replied with a deluge of accounts of sexist and inequitable treatment under the hashtag #1ReasonWhy. In response, prominent women VGDs began using the hashtag #1ReasonToBe to celebrate the positive reasons why they worked in games. The 2013 Game Developers Conference (GDC) held a high-profile and well-attended session on the topic. #1ReasonToBe has become a standing session in the Advocacy Track of the GDC and has expanded beyond the topic of gender. In 2017, the session spotlighted the importance of geographical diversity and featured six speakers from emerging regions:

> ▸ I feel like you look at some of the Game Developers Conferences and where what used to be the special interest group panel, you know, on 8 am on the Friday, had some people talking about it. Now it's centre stage and it's really being talked about a lot more. There is an interesting microtalk at this year's GDC. A fellow had gone up and said: "Okay, at GDC this year, here are the five different people in game development I've been mistaken for, and a waiter"—just on the basis that they all had particular ethnic traits in common. ... [But] I don't have a lot more to go on other than just seeing the conversation evolving over the last few years. (M-04-07-T-U-22-04-14-05-13-JT)

However, after this same 2013 GDC, Darius Kazemi (then an elected member of the IGDA board) and influential game developer Brenda

Romero (then co-chair of the IGDA's Women in Games SIG) left their positions. They were disheartened in the wake of a sexism controversy following the IGDA co-sponsored YetiZen party that featured women dancers in skimpy attire and topless models (Chalk 2013). Reports suggest a slight improvement at GDC conferences since the organization took actions and adopted a code of conduct.[1]

The third event was Gamergate. In 2014 developer Zoë Quinn was negatively portrayed in a blog post. Quinn immediately became the target of online abuse and harassment, and was accused of entering into a relationship with a journalist to garner favourable reviews for their videogame (Quinn 2017). Quinn's accusers coalesced under the moniker "Gamergate" and professed a desire for higher journalistic standards and ethics in videogame media. However, Gamergate was quickly associated with sexism and misogyny in the game community due to the nature of abuse and harassment directed at Quinn and other prominent women and nonbinary VGDs, journalists, and media critics (including Sarkeesian). Vitriolic hate speech and threats became a defining feature of Gamergate and the locus from which emerged a subsequent debate about gender equality and inclusion in the industry and in game content:

> The response to such criticism has been extreme at times—a phenomenon Consalvo (2012) refers to as "toxic gamer culture." In particular, feminist video game critics have faced massive backlash in the course of the recent "#GamerGate" debate. ... At the heart of this conflict is the alleged divide between a White, young, male community of hard-core gamers and the criticism of the gamer community by perceived feminist interlopers. (Paaßen, Morgenroth, and Stratemeyer 2017, 421–22)

With respect to industry scandals, Riot Games faced legal action in 2019 for alleged sexual harassment and discrimination, which the studio settled with a US$10 million out-of-court agreement (Dean 2019). In 2020, the major publisher Ubisoft faced allegations of sexual misconduct and discrimination that led to the removal of senior men and a complaint of institutional harassment filed in a French court (Gach 2021). In 2021 Activision Blizzard, another major publisher, was sued for the same by the State of California Department of Fair Employment and Housing (D'Anastasio 2021a) and the US Equal Employment Opportunity Commission (K. Paul 2022), which led to a suit by shareholders through the

---

1. GDC Diversity and Inclusion: https://gdconf.com/diversity-inclusion; GDC Code of Conduct: https://gdconf.com/code-of-conduct.

US Securities Exchange Commission for improper handling of issues of workplace misconduct (Parvini 2023; see also Chapter 7). Now in this fourth wave of feminism, where does the industry stand with respect to diversity,[2] equity, and inclusion in the workplace?

Attempts to deal with the issue of ethnic diversity are not as well organized. Gamers wishing for games to echo their reality and culture are somewhat organized, but groups or associations of would-be developers from the targeted audience are fledgling, with limited lobbying for their claims to be heard (see Chapter 8). Despite some inroads, many people are excluded from subject status within a mostly White and male territory.

We have collected rich survey and interview material on diversity that covers a broad scope, from experiences to causes and solutions. We are unable to do justice to this wealth of material and fully map the multiple issues within the scope of this chapter. However, we have attempted to extract the key points from our data and synthesize them using a handy operational framework of diversity, inclusivity, and belonging (DIB) aimed precisely at understanding and attaining diversity in the videogame development environment.

A Framework of Diversity, Inclusivity, and Belonging

To help synthesize our data in the categories of DIB—a challenging process—we have adopted a framework from Westecott et al. (2019) (see Figure 10.1). They accounted for the existing literature and produced a model for analyzing the game development environment. It is a practical instrument favouring comparative work. DIB is an evolving concept that can account for individual experience as well as group or social experience (Westecott et al. 2019, 7). Note that we employ this as an organizing framework for our wealth of data rather than as a theoretical framework. Even so, we do not present this as the singular, or only, framework from which to investigate diversity and equity. There is now a deep literature on this theme generally and in the VGI particularly that informs and underlies our interpretations in this chapter, but which we do not have the space to review. Our preference here has been to foreground our data and the narratives of VGDs on this subject.

DIB focuses on visible actions with a long-term perspective. *Diversity* is the objective or outcome of DIB; it is a state of things in a studio in which the social groups of the wider environment are represented. We can

---

2. As much as possible we will adopt a broad perspective on diversity, not limited to gender but considering additional sources of "otherness," such as ethnicity, disability, sexual identity, and occupational status. However, the effect of many socio-demographic characteristics on participation in the workforce is far less statistically documented than that of gender, and often the numbers in our industry surveys are too small to generalize.

Figure 10.1
Mapping Diversity, Inclusivity, and Belonging (DIB) in the Game Industry

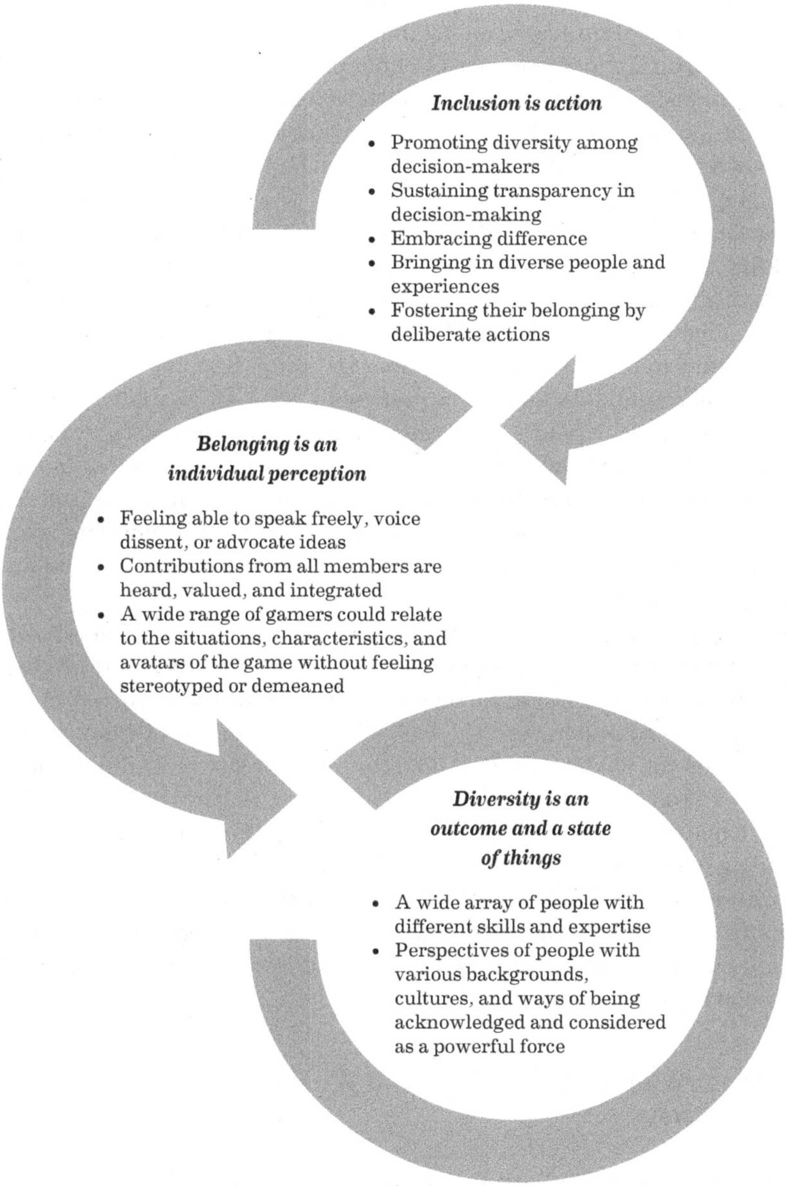

Inclusion is action
- Promoting diversity among decision-makers
- Sustaining transparency in decision-making
- Embracing difference
- Bringing in diverse people and experiences
- Fostering their belonging by deliberate actions

Belonging is an individual perception
- Feeling able to speak freely, voice dissent, or advocate ideas
- Contributions from all members are heard, valued, and integrated
- A wide range of gamers could relate to the situations, characteristics, and avatars of the game without feeling stereotyped or demeaned

Diversity is an outcome and a state of things
- A wide array of people with different skills and expertise
- Perspectives of people with various backgrounds, cultures, and ways of being acknowledged and considered as a powerful force

Source: Adapted from Westecott et al. 2019, 6–8

measure diversity by statistics and figures, comparisons over time and space, and surveys on perceptions.

Inclusion is an endeavour to reach diversity that we can measure by actions aimed at attracting and retaining a diverse workforce. Indeed, once a diverse group has been established, it cannot stand on its own without nurturing and care. Sustainable processes are required to provide an inclusive environment, establish welcoming structures and policies, and monitor cultural practices and behaviours. Inclusive practices boil down to action, leading to diversity as an end result and hopefully to belonging.

Belonging is a perception of diversity, the experience and outcome of well-functioning inclusive practices. When people feel as though they belong, they are secure, feel loyal, and take care of their organization's health. You can have belonging without diversity in a uniform group; this is easier to maintain than in a diverse group. Keeping statistics on diversity is essential to support a process to diversify the labour force, and can be used to document any relevant legal compliance. Yet without cultural shifts and changes in mindset, people do not experience belonging. The outcome is mere differentiation that results in the ghettoization of groups into specific roles (Westecott et al. 2019, 8–14). Belonging is an experience that we can only measure by surveys on perception and accounts of experiences (Westecott et al. 2019, 7–8).

In Chapter 4, we made the case that there is very limited diversity in the contemporary VGI. On these grounds alone, we would argue that many workers in the VGI are not subjects of citizenship and are second-class citizens. To understand the lack of diversity in the VGI better, we will position the challenges identified through our survey and interview respondents using the DIB framework (see Figure 10.1) to determine what is being poorly done or not done at all in terms of inclusion, and what is not being felt in terms of belonging. Much occurs at the level of the workplace and therefore implicates recourses against arbitrary treatment and participation in the local regulation of work as objects of citizenship at work. Some elements of DIB are broader and implicate social laws and the social regulation of work.

Inclusion: What Is Poorly Done and What Is Not Done That Could Be Done

"What Do the Bosses Do?" HR *Policies and Programs*

Local workplace policies and programs that support diverse recruitment, neutrality in processes, and so on, are a common way to facilitate a more diverse workforce and equitable environments. Yet for these to operate, they must be public, enforced, and supported by management.

In 2015, over one-fifth of our survey respondents did not know whether there was any internal policy to reduce discrimination in their workplace (see Table 10.1 in the Data Appendix) and one-third had no knowledge of whether their company offered any program to encourage more diverse job applicants (see Table 10.2 in the Data Appendix). This ignorance was only slightly lower among the 2019 respondents. In each year, about one-tenth of the sample said that their company did not have any diversity-related policies and over one-third reported that their company did not have any diversity programs. The most common policies were those regarding non-discrimination (70 percent), anti-sexual harassment (62 percent), and equal opportunity hiring (59 percent). These policies are proliferating under the enforcement of fundamental human rights in the application of labour laws and offer a form of passive citizenship.

In some countries, like Canada, organizations of a certain size are required to implement such policies, and this can influence our results. However, specific, targeted, enforced, and publicized programs to address problems in the industry were sparse. For instance, we saw little evidence of programs supporting flextime and telework, early childcare, equal pay, and pay transparency; measures to address gender stereotyping; or initiatives to recruit, attract, and retain diverse talent. In general, compensation policies put a premium on full-time work and physical presence, if not formally then informally (Ciminelli, Schwellnus, and Stadler 2021, 8), though issues regarding flextime and telework may have benefitted from measures taken during the COVID-19 pandemic. In fact, even more than full-time work, the VGI is the land of crunch time, which we will address in the next section as an example of the lack of inclusive policies.

Regarding harassment, some of our respondents appreciated big studios with a large HR department because they offered procedures, recourse, and ways to solve claims regarding sexism and harassment:

> ▶ With a larger studio, I found that people could be disciplined and spoken to and kind of taken in hand. I felt at one point I had a personal issue. The gentleman who I was working with on my very first project, he was mentoring me, but in a manner like... he had a daughter at home, and I felt that I was constantly being talked down to as though I was a toddler. It was a weird, quirky kind of problem, and it was frustrating after about a month of that. And I couldn't resolve it on my own without perhaps getting too aggressive in the situation, so I spoke to one of my supervisors, we discussed it, I

voiced my concerns, and he brought it to his attention, in a nice, mature, mediated fashion. A lot of the time, as a female, in these settings, I feel like I have to be very careful about what I do say, for fear of appearing too emotional, or unsocial. You're either the bitch who can't take a joke, or you're the overemotional, "here's a tissue, maybe you're not really ready to work here" kind of thing. It's a balance and I'd prefer not to be perceived as either. I'd rather let it be, let the small stuff go, if I can let it go, and otherwise, let's just discuss this and get it handled. I'd say the biggest pro to working at a bigger studio is knowing that there is an HR that can be consulted if something was a huge issue. (F-11-07-M-S-24-11-13-16-02-PB)

HR departments can deal with individual situations, but in the VGI these cases seem to radically challenge HR offices. In the context of the sexism and discrimination being denounced in their Toronto and Montreal studios, Ubisoft's HR system was "compared to a wall against which abuse allegations have been crashing for years" and a system that "allegedly perpetuated toxic behaviours" (Dealessandri 2020; Gach 2021). Workers raised problems with the company's workplace harassment code of conduct, and the global head of HR resigned amidst the scandal (Blain 2020). The head of HR also stepped down at Activision Blizzard following accusations of protecting workplace aggressors and discounting victims (Ballestrasse 2021; Farokhmanesh 2021). There were also issues with the dispute resolution approach at Riot Games, where management pushed for individual arbitration to get around the class action lawsuit on gender discrimination (Dealessandri 2021). Activision Blizzard also used to include mandatory arbitration clauses in all employee contracts, but these have been contested as "intimidation and coercive tactics" intended to bypass open discussions about pay discrepancy on a collective scale (Parrish 2021a). The California Department of Fair Employment and Housing alleged pervasive gender discrimination at the publisher in a July 2021 lawsuit (Sinclair 2022). Mounting turmoil in the press led Activision Blizzard to retreat and implement "a zero-tolerance" harassment policy and waive forced arbitration in sexual harassment and discrimination claims (Parrish 2021b).

Even though some HR policies might address some structural inequalities, other policies can exacerbate problems. Such is the case of pay-for-performance compensation practices among senior executives. As revealed at Activision Blizzard, these practices incentivized the CEO to focus on the company's (skyrocketing) market capitalization, often to the detriment of the job security, compensation, and well being of rank-and-file developers (Yin-Poole 2021). In the face of multiple sexual harassment and discrimination lawsuits, the board of directors imposed a significant pay cut on the CEO (who had a billion dollar net worth) "until ... certain diversity, equity, and inclusion goals are met" (Parrish 2021b). Yet, many market-based incentives remain (Yin-Poole 2021).

Moreover, policies or programs that are not clearly enforced are merely wishful thinking leading to poor outcomes. We have attempted to learn more by surveying respondents about their perceptions.

Do Policies Work? Perceptions and Facts

Adopting formal policies is one thing, but making them known and useful to targeted groups is better. Studios have struggled to change the perception of equal treatment, equal opportunity, and equity (see Table 10.3). In 2015, many respondents felt that their studio "pursues diverse candidates" and "supports diversity," but they also felt that hiring diverse candidates was challenging. Respondents felt that their studio looked first and foremost for "qualified applicants," with the resulting demographic distribution we have seen in Chapter 4. This was different in 2019, when fewer respondents thought that the focus was on "qualified applicants" without regard for diversity.

In 2019, a growing share of respondents believed that the industry was more diverse than two years previously (56 percent; see Table 10.3). However, only a small minority were convinced that there was equal opportunity and treatment for all in the VGI (19 percent; see Table 10.3). The progress is very slow.

Deeper analysis revealed differences by gender and ethnicity. In 2015, 69 percent of women reported that there was not equal treatment and opportunity. This was 23 percentage points higher than among men. Many White workers agreed that "obtaining diverse applicants is challenging" (51 percent), while fewer workers of colour agreed (35 percent).

In 2019, 77 percent of women reported that there was not equal treatment and opportunity—19 percentage points higher than among men. However, women were more likely (62 percent) than men (57 percent) to believe that the industry was more diverse than it was before. Workers of colour were also likely to state that the industry was more diverse (60 percent), while White workers were slightly less in agreement (56 percent). Still, more White workers (52 percent) than workers of colour (32 percent) agreed that "obtaining diverse applicants is challenging." Interestingly, women (62 percent) and workers of colour (57 percent) were more likely to think that their studio pursued diverse candidates.

The conviction that affirmative action in employment policy acts as a countervailing force to meritocracy and the "search for excellence"

Table 10.3
VGDs' agreement with statements about diversity (% of respondents), 2015-19

Agree/strongly agree	2015	2019
My company/studio pursues diverse candidates.	51	54
My company/studio supports diversity initiatives.	45	57
Obtaining diverse applicants is challenging.	46	51
My company/studio does not consider diversity; they only look for qualified applicants.	53	35
The industry is more diverse than two years ago.	37	56
There is equal treatment and opportunity for all in the game industry.	31	19

Source: Original data from the IGDA DSS 2015, 2019

has waned, become muddied, and lost political force since the 1970s and 1980s. Indeed, a common present-day understanding of affirmative action policies in hiring tends to overlook the very important fact that these policies recommend hiring a member of a minority group when "at equal competence" or "if the qualifications of candidates are equal," until a pre-set target proportion of employees is reached. While many of our respondents believed in the asserted neutrality of the recruitment and selection process, a better understanding of systemic discrimination in the ongoing process seems to be making inroads.

One important area of increased awareness is pay inequity. We have collected respondents' perceptions and we can also review the facts about compensation according to gender and ethnicity. Employers' HRM policies reveal intentions about equity, but their actions disclose even more. It is unfortunate that data on game development salaries remain scarce, as this does not facilitate the ability of VGDs to negotiate a fair deal for themselves. Some data are collected piecemeal by various industry or advocacy groups or collated on career websites from voluntarily contributed salary data. *Gamasutra* (now *Game Developer*) used to produce a salary survey, which was a key reference in the trade. In recent years, the Skillsearch survey has addressed this gap.

According to Skillsearch (2021), the average mid-career salary was US$61,092 across Europe, the United States, and Canada (converted from the British pound using January 31, 2021, rates). It was highest in the United States (US$81,043) and lowest in Eastern Europe (US$33,784). However, a gender analysis revealed discrepancies. Considering all career levels, the average salary for men across these regions was close to the mean average salary (US$61,674), while for women it was US$56,192.

In the United States, men's average salary was US$110,397, while women's was US$97,684. The gender pay gap is reportedly widening in the UK game industry (H. Taylor 2019). Already alarming, these average figures can conceal large gaps between trades segregated by gender (see Chapter 4).

Controlling for job tenure and occupational role, our data also show gender discrepancies. These emerge at the lowest and highest income brackets (see Figures 10.2 and 10.3 in the Data Appendix), where women were markedly absent. Women tended to cluster around the middle-income brackets. Women VGDs are aware of these gaps and expressed their desire for change:

▶ *What about the industry would make you feel compelled to leave?*

... If I was still experiencing a huge wage gap against my male counterparts everywhere, that would be enough to do it. (F-11-07-M-S-24-11-13-16-02-PB)

In this, the VGI fits with broader trends. According to a trans-European OECD study (Ciminelli, Schwellnus, and Stadler 2021, 20), there remains an average gap of around 15 percent in hourly earnings between similarly qualified men and women of all sectors across twenty-five countries and despite changes in social norms and policies.[3]

We also observed a wage discrepancy according to ethnicity (see Figures 10.4 and 10.5 in the Data Appendix). In both 2015 and 2019, workers of colour were disproportionately represented at the lowest income levels relative to White respondents. The compensation for both groups was more evenly matched in the mid-range earning brackets, but more White workers reported earning over US$75,000 than workers of colour.

Systemic pay gaps are closely related to the issue of citizenship at work. Equity is one of the three core principles in the reconciliation of property and labour rights, alongside efficiency and voice (see Chapter 1). In the VGI, pay level is an object of HRM discretionary decision-making (see Chapter 6), not subjected to any compulsory internal norm, nor to

---

3. On average across countries, approximately 40 percent of the gender wage gap precedes the birth of a first child and is therefore independent of this factor. It is rather bluntly imputable to social norms regarding the value of work according to gender and is called the "sticky floor" phenomenon. The remaining 60 percent occurs around the date of childbirth and is called the "motherhood penalty": the gender wage gap (or compensating differential) due to childbirth, pay interruption due to absence from work, lowered pay, and slower advancement due to part-time work and slowed skill accumulation (Ciminelli, Schwellnus, and Stadler 2021, 3; Ferrant, Pesando, and Nowacka 2014). Both could in fact be said to constitute a barrier to women's upward advancement, often referred to as the "glass ceiling."

any employee scrutiny. This is important because pay equity policies achieve far greater success and satisfaction in large bureaucratic organizations and/or unionized workplaces than in those in which the operation is management-led. This is due to the importance of employee participation and appropriation of data and process (Chicha 2006). A discretionary process relies on a unilateral job evaluation that is piecemeal, personal, and subject to ambient cultural biases of the dominant population, which is White and masculine, as well as to project constraints. Unobtrusive HRM policies are a very poor buffer against discrimination and an unsatisfactory guarantee of fair procedure.

Simply sharing pay data and having to make decisions in an open, multilateral process leads to more and bigger pay adjustments, but through our framework of citizenship at work, any management-led pay equity operation is still equity without voice in the local regulation of work. Yet, equitable treatment (equity) and employee participation (voice) can reinforce efficiency in "reducing turnover, increasing commitment and harnessing workers' ideas for improving productivity and quality" (see Chapter 1). Despite the short-term cost of instituting and balancing equity, efficiency, and voice, workplace governance absent any of these three elements could be a time bomb. This is because knowledge workers are increasingly demanding democracy at work and the right to participate and consult for the sake of dignity, respect, justice, and fairness. So far, pay equity operations remain the "blind spot" of project-based environments. However, there lie the grounds for perceptions of unfair evaluation and compensation among some groups.

For instance, communication is part and parcel of project-based labour. In the necessary daily interactions of teamwork within a rapidly changing and often contested creative environment, VGDs draw upon their relational and social skills (see Chapter 2), as well as their technical abilities. This is frequently a matter of sharing knowledge and responsibility rather than of exerting power. Woodfield (2002) showed that managers perceive that these "soft skills" are indispensable to manage projects well and that women are generally more effective than men in this regard. However, skills related to interacting with others—communication, listening, negotiating, and resolving conflicts or teamwork—remain ill-defined in job evaluation terms (Grugulis and Vincent 2009).

Given the range of ways these skills can be expressed, their evaluation is embryonic, which hinders their recognition and compensation (Buckle and Thomas 2003; Thomas and Buckle-Henning 2007). Such skills are underestimated even within the standardized "body of knowledge" on project management (the *PMBoK Guide*), which confers more importance on the technical factor. Moreover, Woodfield (2002) showed how such skills then become seen as "innate" or "natural" qualities and are not recognized as competencies but, rather, associated with "nature" (see also Alksnis, Desmarais, and Curtis 2008; Lemière 2006; Wajcman 1991). Indeed, qualities that do not stem from professional skills acquired in training are less likely to be remunerated, because remuneration policies compensate for the investment necessary to qualify for a job (Buckle and Thomas 2003). While these "natural" attributes do influence recruitment, selection, assessment, and compensation, they are not valued or appreciated, and this leads to exclusion.

Across the surveys from 2009 to 2019, about half of the respondents agreed that they were compensated fairly for their experience and the responsibility of their job title. Around one-third consistently disagreed. However, we again see differences across identity groups. In all years except 2015, women and workers of colour were two to six percentage points more likely to report unfair compensation than men and White workers, respectively (Weststar, O'Meara, Gosse, and Legault 2017, 22–23).

Open-ended comments from the 2015 survey illustrate the sense of dissatisfaction with pay inequity among women and members of racialized groups:

> ▶ I was hired at a significantly lower salary than my male predecessor—8.5 percent less. When another man was brought on-board just three months later into the same position with the same level of experience as myself, he was hired at the same pay level as my predecessor. (F.T.02740.2015)

> ▶ I learned that a male co-worker of mine, while doing the majority of content design work on our main project, was the lowest paid designer at the company in spite of having the most seniority. He was Black. I don't know for sure that was why, but I do know that they took him for granted and treated him poorly. Women in QA at that same company were paid significantly less than their male coworkers. (F.D.02730.2015)

Throughout our project, our aim was to broadly canvass VGD's working conditions, and therefore our data is not up to the task of systematic pay inequity analysis. Yet, our data highlight the impact of pay equity on feelings of inclusion. It is hard to feel included when one's work is unrecognized and devalued. It is our hope that researchers will collect longitudinal data to study the comparative career paths that could explain large, gendered gaps in average yearly earnings (Skillsearch 2021).

Crunch Time Practice: A Black Hole for Mothers

In previous chapters, we saw how the practice of crunch time makes working time both long and unpredictable. Our data suggest that women and workers of colour are engaged in similar working time practices as men and White workers. Indeed, in the 2019 DSS, women and workers of colour reported the highest incidences of crunch time (42 percent in each group had worked in crunch more than two times in the previous two years). This ethos does not welcome members of all demographic groups. In particular, the pressure to work long and unpredictable hours drives women away from a career in the VGI (Consalvo 2008; Fullerton et al. 2008, 164). The hurdles faced by fathers are not negligible, but they are also not as dire as those of mothers because reproductive labour remains highly gendered (Cerrato and Cifre 2018; Moyser and Burlock 2018; Workplace Gender Equality Agency 2016).

Complaints about long hours and inadequate policies regarding work-life balance tend to increase with years of experience in the trade, and complaints about lack of promotion tend to rise with weekly hours of work, as if hours of work were expected to pay off in that way (Prescott and Bogg 2011b). What Hochschild and Machung (1989) called "the second shift" has not disappeared:

> ▸ We're, by society, expected to be kind of like the caretakers of the home, and then in this industry—fifty to eighty hours a week—and then you want me to come home and make sure there's groceries and stuff like that. It's just... It's a total killer. It just gets you. (F-18-07-T-Z-28-04-14-04-11-JT)

Another female developer speculated about how male colleagues coped with the arrival of children and contemplated her own need to leave the industry or turn to less demanding, less prestigious projects:

> ▸ I feel like with the amount of time I spend working, how can you manage a family? It's kind of beyond me. ... I figure they've probably also got *really helpful* partners. Actually, I feel like I may start thinking about [leaving the industry] when I'm ready to start a family. ... I'm not necessarily closing the door on it. Actually, I've thought about maybe changing industries or moving into less demanding games. ... The teams aren't big, about thirty people, but

they don't do much crunch time. So, people really covet those projects, even though there's less glory. They're less blockbusters. To combine family life and work, that's the kind of project that might be more tempting. (F-18-02-16-M-W-01-10-13-19-15-JL)

Bulut (2020a) noted that essential domestic contributions made by the spouses of male VGDs allowed men to keep up with their jobs. Many developers take only the minimum paternity leave offered by their studios and hurry back to work while their wives claim the full government-provided leave. Yet, many others do not have the benefit of a "stay-at-home mom" that is so often the secret behind men's heroic crunch hours. Those with greater domestic responsibilities such as childcare or elder care find it harder to sustain the normative standard without additional support. In this mostly masculine workforce, the burden of domestic work devolves upon their female partners. The culture of overworking is "in fact rendered tolerable thanks to the mobilization of women's emotional capacities at home" (Reay 2004). Bluntly put, if partners refused this burden, it could challenge the industry's future. In Marxist terms, partners produce "surplus value for the studio by reducing the potential reproduction investments to be undertaken by [the studio]" (Bulut 2020a, 108).

To deal with the conflict between a very demanding organization of work and dependents needing care, studio management still relies on an outdated solution, separating breadwinners and caretakers according to gender (Bailyn 1993, 77). As long as the issue of sharing domestic work remains unsolved and the organization of work relies on archaic family structures, adding more women to the workforce will not change the overall situation of institutional or systemic sexism (Consalvo 2008). This issue of citizenship extends to the sphere of the social regulation of work and, indeed, society.

There are still options for mothers in the VGI if they do not strive for high-profile projects. But we must account for a bare fact: more women than men remain nulliparous in game development, while more men have young children (see Table 10.4 in the Data Appendix).

Our survey data show the toll of the game development environment on work–life balance (see Table 10.5). Over half of the respondents said they needed more time for themselves and were too tired after work to do some of the things they would like to do. Almost half felt constantly behind at home and at work, and emotionally drained by the effort to keep up. These data suggest a problematic work–life balance that is not improving.

The issue of crunch time impairs women more than men, but policies regarding work–life balance could surely help all developers with

Table 10.5
Perceptions of work–life balance (2014–19) (% of respondents who agree or strongly agree)

	2014	2019
I have a hard time dragging myself away from work to go home.	31	35
I am more organized because of all the demands on my time.	42	44
There is enough time in my day to accomplish everything I need to do.	24	26
I feel that I am constantly behind at work and at home, and never have enough time for either.	42	44
The tension of trying to balance my work and home life leaves me feeling emotionally drained.	41	45
Because my work is so demanding, I am often irritable at home/outside of work.	30	29
I need more time to myself.	57	60
After work I am too tired to do some of the things I'd like to do.	55	59

Source: Weststar and Legault 2014, 54; original data from DSS 2019

caregiving responsibilities and those with aspirations outside of work. Inclusive workplaces take action to ensure that all members can thrive in their environments and receive support to overcome the barriers they face.

We observed that about one-quarter of DSS respondents consistently did not know if their studio provided pregnancy or parental benefits and very few reported studio-provided or subsidized daycare. As well, women and workers of colour more frequently reported that having a family diminished or would diminish their chances for advancement (31 percent and 27 percent, respectively), particularly when compared to White men (22 percent). In Westecott et al.'s (2019) DIB model, work expectations that are not attainable or sustainable are in fact exclusionary, by sending the message to women that they "can't cut it" and therefore do not belong.

From this viewpoint, mothers, would-be mothers, and single parents are prime candidates for second-class citizenship. The widespread "passion-driven" discourse about the ideal dedicated project worker who deserves a place in the business of games (Consalvo 2008; Reid 2015) fosters a fierce resistance to the practice of part-time work, as well as to any alternative practice in project management around the organization of work (Gill 2002). In the actual social division of domestic work, such an organization of work gives an edge to men over women who are parents (Simpson 1998, 45). While the industry is overdue for a re-examination of this aspect of work culture (Bailyn 1993, xii), as long as studios have a mostly male workforce, there will be no significant improvement to work–life balance. Thanks to supportive partners, studios do not have to account for the diverse needs of the women they employ.

Belonging: What Is Felt and Not Felt

Chapter 4 detailed observable facts regarding the distribution of sociodemographic groups in the VGI workforce. We will now turn to another area, the contours of which are less obvious. Belonging is a perception of diversity that is experienced by workers when they also feel a sense of inclusion. We argue that while members of the socio-demographic majority of White men feel a sense of belonging, this is not as easily achieved for minority groups. From a citizenship standpoint, one cannot be a true subject of citizenship in a workplace without feeling a sense of belonging. As such, belonging (or not) has important consequences in a work environment in terms of commitment and the health of an organization.

VGDs' Experience of Inequity

We have documented the personal experiences that VGDs have had with inequity, either with it affecting themselves or others. In 2015 and 2019, the most frequent inequities involved microaggressions and social/interpersonal actions (see Table 10.6). Microaggressions are verbal, behavioural, and environmental indignities, comments, or gestures that subtly and often unconsciously or unintentionally express a prejudiced attitude toward someone as a member of a marginalized group, such as a racial minority (Nadal et al. 2016). We define social/interpersonal actions as exclusion from a social or peer group or different treatment in a group or by the employer. These are critically related to the culture of a workplace. They can be widespread and tolerated, if not promoted, by the majority.

We argue that these inequities amount to harassment in the form of bullying and, because of their often public character, sometimes of mobbing. The US Workplace Bullying Institute (quoted in Levchak 2018, 107) defines workplace bullying as "repeated, health-harming mistreatment of one or more persons (the targets) by one or more perpetrators" and as abusive conduct that interferes with work and is verbally offensive, "threatening, humiliating, or intimidating." We note that the rates of bullying for VGDs are close to or surpass those for the general US population.[4]

Bullying is characterized by three conditions: a hostile intent, building on strength or advantage in a context of imbalanced power, and which is reasserted over time to maintain the imbalance (Burger et al. 2015). It is reinforced (and made highly predictable) when most of the influential leader(s) of the majority group approve or condone the bullying behaviour (Steinfeldt et al. 2012). Mobbing consists of the collective dimension of a similar phenomenon, used when people in social gatherings like sport teams, schools, or workplaces gang up to target certain people by disrespecting them, spreading innuendos and rumours, or discrediting them publicly, ultimately to force them out of that space (Davenport et al. 2005).

Our respondents reported witnessing inequity towards others at greater rates than they experienced it themselves (see Table 10.6). Compared to 2015, respondents in 2019 reported higher rates of inequities targeting both themselves and others, with a notable increase in reported perceived inequality towards others in the context of promotions.

We have also analyzed the 2019 data according to gender and ethnicity (see Table 10.7). White workers (mainly men) and men (mainly White) were the least likely to report personally experiencing any form of inequity, compared with women and workers of colour. The most frequent indignities encountered by all identity groups were microaggressions and social/interpersonal exclusions, aimed both toward themselves and toward others, except for men who declared experiencing inequity primarily in their own recruitment or hiring process. Women consistently reported experiencing the highest rates of inequity across most response options, and the rates at which they experienced social inequity (55 percent) and/or some form of microaggression (52 percent) are alarming. Men and women only reported comparable rates in the areas of "working conditions" and "workload."

There were important quantitative differences between men and women in other types of inequity that they experienced. For instance, in 2019, 30 percent of women reported experiencing inequity in compensation, compared to 9 percent of men. This is consistent with the above-

---

4. "According to the [US Workplace Bullying] Institute (2017), '27% of Americans have suffered abusive conduct at work; 21% have witnessed it; and 72% are aware that workplace bullying happens.' With respect to gender, women are targets in 60% of the cases. ... Fox and Stallworth (2005, 439) ... found that Asians, African Americans, and Latino employees report being targets of racial/ethnic bullying at rates higher than White employees (2005, 448). ... In a recent survey, half of Black respondents and one-third of Latino respondents reported being the victim of racial discrimination in the workplace" (Levchak 2018, 107).

Table 10.6
Experiences with inequity (% of respondents) 2015–19

	Perceived inequity on the basis of gender, age, ethnicity, ability, or sexual orientation			
	Toward yourself		*Toward others*	
	2015	*2019*	*2015*	*2019*
Microaggressions	19	23	26	38
Social/interpersonal	20	23	27	38
Hiring process	11	18	15	27
Disciplines/roles	—	13	—	27
Promotion	9	14	13	26
Monetary/salary/bonuses	10	14	14	26
Recruitment	10	17	13	24
Workload	7	17	8	17
Working conditions	5	8	8	17
None of the above	63	51	57	36

Source: Weststar and Legault 2015, 14; original data from the IGDA DSS 2019
Note: Columns do not total 100% due to multiple response allowances

noted data about persistent wage gaps. Women also reported more experiences of inequity than men based on job roles/tasks (28 percent versus 9 percent) and promotions (30 percent versus 10 percent). As noted above and in Chapter 4, women are clustered more in mid-level managerial and artistic roles, and the "soft skills" in these jobs often go unvalued. Some respondents reported being assigned additional, unwelcome tasks or tasks unrelated to their actual job role:

> ▶ I once worked with a woman who was an absolute genius sound designer. In fact, she taught me many of the fundamentals that I still use and build upon to this day. Our boss at the time, while acknowledging her as an important asset to the team, still would have her do tasks that were "typically a woman's," like some secretarial duties, bookkeeping, etc., which ate into the time she could have been using to create more sound design. I need to stress this: she was *the* talent in that studio. I was an intern at the time, and there were four other people working with us, all sharp individuals more than able to file things away, take down notes, and create spreadsheets. Everyone could have taken turns, but the boss always made

Table 10.7
Experience of inequity, by identity group, 2019 (% of respondents)

	Inequity towards yourself				Inequity toward others			
	Women	Men	Workers of colour	White workers	Women	Men	Workers of colour	White workers
Social/interpersonal	55	12	28	23	66	32	41	42
Microaggressions	52	12	28	23	65	31	43	40
Promotions	30	10	21	13	43	21	27	28
Monetary/salary/bonuses	30	9	17	14	40	21	26	28
Discipline/role	28	9	19	12	47	22	31	29
Recruitment	27	15	24	16	37	20	31	23
Hiring process	25	17	25	17	40	24	31	28
Workload	22	7	13	10	31	13	22	17
Working conditions	16	5	10	8	30	14	20	17
None of the above	21	68	43	59	18	47	33	40

Source: Original data from the IGDA DSS 2019
Note: Columns do not total 100% due to multiple response allowances

the woman do it. She took it in stride, but it still seemed pretty bullshit to me. (N.D.02922.2015)

This raises questions regarding potential informal workplace hierarchies that may favour certain male-dominated roles over those that include more women, or inversely, that marginalize and undervalue women who work in male-dominated positions. Men seem to enjoy greater citizenship status regarding these objects.

In Figure 10.6, we have represented significant gender gaps in perceived structural inequities from Table 10.7—otherwise known as systemic discrimination (see Chapter 1)—to highlight the general trend of discrepancy. These differences also existed for workers of colour, but to a lesser degree (see Figure 10.7).

Undoubtedly, VGDs experience inequities in their everyday lives that manifest through both daily workplace behaviour and HRM processes and decisions. The first type is that which is most often denounced: verbal, behavioural, and environmental indignities; exclusion from a social group or peer group; and differential treatment, which are all very much related to the culture of the workplace. Still, HRM decisions in terms of

Figure 10.6
Structural inequalities experienced by developers, by type and gender, 2019

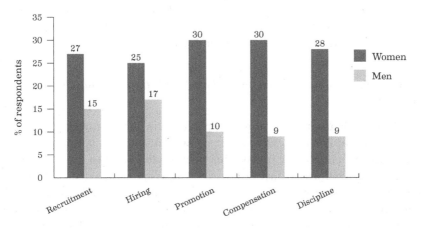

Source: Original data from DSS 2019
* Compensation here is a short version of "Monetary/salary/bonuses"
Note: Columns do not total 100% due to multiple response allowances

Figure 10.7
Structural inequalities experienced by developers, by type and ethnic group, 2019

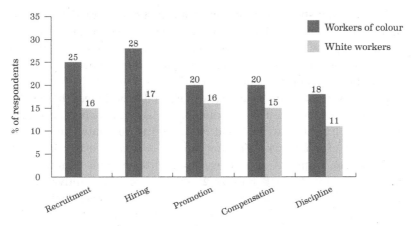

Source: Original data from the IGDA DSS 2019
Note: Columns do not total 100% due to multiple response allowances

273

hiring, job roles, promotion, compensation, and recruitment also give rise to a poor experience in an inequitable workplace culture. As inequity across gender and ethnicity is perpetuated through workplace culture and everyday communicative practice, it amounts to a deep-rooted denial of belonging and therefore a situation of second-class citizenship.

Exclusionary Effect of Rampant Sexism: "Yeah, the Company Culture Wasn't Awesome"

Sexism and harassment in the workplace was a commonly cited barrier to diversity in our surveys and interviews. Indeed, we do not have the space in this chapter, or indeed this book to do justice to the hundreds of stories shared with us over the years. Our respondents depicted a pernicious "bro culture" comprised of common attitudes and beliefs built on immature and informal "frat boy" relationships, inherited from the "garage hacker" culture typical of the emergence of game development, but which is inhospitable to women and members of other marginalized groups:

> ▸ Brogrammer culture, a culture that involves a lot of alcohol, an overall unwelcoming culture that wants people to prove they're hardcore/experienced/whatever enough. The perception that games are only for fifteen to thirty-five-year-old males and therefore might as well be made by them. (F.M.00945.2014)

While the industry tries to cultivate an image of a creative industry that maintains links to its anarchic/hacker origins, academics have underlined the culture of "militarized masculinity" that gave birth to this and to the "militainment" that continues (Blackburn 2018; Kline, Dyer-Witheford, and de Peuter 2003). The concept of "technomasculinity" (Johnson 2018) distils an array of shared experiences that lead to the stereotyped (and essentialist) belief of the boy/man being "naturally" gifted for technical matters: "good command of computer knowledge, machinic manipulation, passion for games ... ordinary use of language that bears the imprints of gendered imaginations and assumptions" (Dovey and Kennedy 2006; Selwyn 2007) that are "often cultivated during childhood" (Bulut 2020a, 63). This framework "shapes their ethos" regarding who "has it" and who does not. It is an effective gatekeeping device providing the grounds for inclusion and exclusion (Bulut 2020a, 64; Bulut 2020b; on the same among IT workers, see Chasserio and Legault 2010).

In the face of the public allegations against Ubisoft and Activision, our women respondents reported what now seem like common experiences of harassment or intimidation on the job:

> Women get into the industry and many are frightened away by harassment. The industry is so small that reporting these issues will very likely result in retaliation in the future, if not be a career destroyer. Unless aggressors are blacklisted from influential positions, the best option for those being harassed is to seek another job. Limited jobs means they are more likely to accept a position outside of games due to wanting to escape a situation and end up staying there. (F.N.00935.2014)

> Some co-workers at a contract gig made comments evocative of rape at a company whose workforce was one-third women. (F.M.02583.2015)

> An inebriated recruiter kissed me on the ear at a recruitment dinner. No action taken. (F.D.00869.2014)

Not only are these advances condoned, but the women who are "hit on" can get the unwelcomed "sack":

> This [executive producer] said, "I may need to let [a female developer] go because all of the guys are hitting on her and it's slowing the work down. We need to get the E3 build on time." My response: "If you do that, I will personally escort her to report your ass to the Labour Department." He looked startled and then realized what he had said was off-the-charts inappropriate, and then mumbled: "What did you come out here for?" Never apologized or even said "just kidding" to back off from the statement. After that our relationship was contentious, and this was not an isolated incident with him. I left the company at my first opportunity. (F.M.02580.2015)

Respondents also voiced concerns regarding sexism and sexual harassment at conferences or networking events:

> I was sexually harassed (physically and verbally) during the Game Developers Conference a few years ago by a game designer. Although it was reported at the time, those I reported it to did not

follow through and did not escalate the issue. These people are part of the problem. They enable sexual harassment to continue by not taking reports seriously. They harbour sexual harassers, and their inaction permits it to happen again. This situation makes me feel unwelcome in my own industry. I'm glad that GDC has better policies now and a clear escalation procedure, as well as enforcement procedures. (F.S.01031.2014)

▶ We have like these little parties every month and when one of my female co-workers started, this guy said to her, "I'm a producer"—he's not a producer—"I'm a producer and if you don't dance with me, I'll fire you." (F-07-13-T-U-10-05-14-04-11-JT)

These experiences are particularly damaging to one's sense of belonging in the industry; colleagues should represent your "tribe," and the workplace is an important place of professional development and advancement.

Women frequently reported experiences of everyday sexism in the form of inappropriate jokes:

▶ I've seen a male employee cover a female employee's ears so she couldn't hear the joke he was telling because it was too inappropriate. (F.D.00986.2014)

▶ I had plans to get out of there; I was not happy there at all. It was very much a boys' club. ... It's very much a male-dominated place, so it can be very sexist. I've had horrible things said to me, like, men judge my looks, told me I was hired because I was cute. I've been in board rooms with all men and they're talking about the size of their genitalia, and making really derogatory sexist jokes, not really seeing my other female comrades because they put them in one position. They act like little boys; they really do. The game industry is very much like that. It's highly dominated by men. (F-13-13-V-I-15-11-13-14-26)

▶ I once had a phone conference with several men working for my publisher. One casually asked me how I was, and I told him I was fine given the circumstances—it was high summer in an un-ACed office. A few of my phone call partners started moaning, "Oh, it's so hot!" It was meant as a joke but given that they were my clients and hierarchically far over me, I found it quite intimidating. (F.M.02593.2015)

Discrimination can be gross or obvious, but it can also be systemic, and thus more subtle. For instance, in this very competitive industry, women feel they have more pressure to perform, stand out, and get promoted:

> ▶ For instance, none of the women in the department were ever officially promoted, even if someone was doing the work. You'd be kept out of conversations. ... It just was a culture thing, too, I think. Yeah, the company culture wasn't awesome. (F-13-13-T-U-05-05-14-04-11-JT)

> ▶ Some people who think they're helping, singling you out and treating you like a dancing bear ... instead of treating you like an equal. (F.M.02576.2015)

This connects the issue of legitimacy with belonging. Who defines what is "valuable creative work" (Bulut 2020a, 65)? When this kind of work is made to seem like a "male" form of creative work, we observe some women adopting a more androgynous gender identity or identifying more strongly with their profession than with their gender to avoid displaying the stereotyped image of women as VGDs. This is true of women in technological fields in general (see Chapter 1).

Overwhelmingly, respondents are silenced when their harassers hold a position of authority:

> ▶ Because he occupies a position of power within the company, we have not yet worked out an effective way to deal with this issue. For a specific example, he recently told the team: "With all the fuss that feminists make about games online I feel that I need to make extra sexist jokes to balance things out." I personally find this attitude shocking and repugnant. (T.D.02191.2014)

> ▶ Co-workers and the boss making slighting remarks about women (for example, blaming a client's indecisiveness on her gender, telling male squabbling co-workers to "stop being such women"). The boss is less "pal-y" with me than with male co-workers (for example, all male co-workers get nicknames; I do not). (F.D.00830.2014)

> ▶ When I was leaving a company I used to work at, the CEO made an extremely offensive (and untrue) gendered remark about why I was leaving. At the time I was too shocked to stand up for myself and I regret it every day. (F.D.00879.2014)

When such interactions are commonplace in a work environment, and not acted on, employers who claim to be "gender-neutral" in their policies, programs, or decisions are in fact simply gender-blind and part of the problem (Prescott and Bogg 2011a, 208; Valenduc et al. 2004). Some women attempt to raise awareness in a comical and less threatening way:

> ▸ I've been in offices where they've had swear jars. Somebody says something profane, and [they have to put money in the jar]. They [a small studio] have a sexism jar. It's ... when the guys are particularly abrasive, and the one female developer feels that they've gone too far, they can put a buck in the sexism jar. (F-11-07-M-S-24-11-13-16-02-PB)

Meanwhile, normative stereotypes tend to fossilize into internalized bias and "outdated attitudes" based on gender, race, or other attributes that are not challenged. Men can feel like they legitimately belong and tend to "support the existing industry norms as credible and legitimate, while relegating other types of participation, including that by women and other marginalized creators, to subordinate positions within hierarchies of production" (A. Harvey and Shepherd 2017, 492). Using the example of a Women in Games initiative in Montreal as a case study, Harvey and Shepherd (2017) indicated how these norms act with a constraining and enabling force to perpetuate a long-standing delegitimization of women's creativity and technical abilities. One woman respondent referred to unconscious bias, prejudice, and assumptions about the kind of person who plays videogames, which excludes everyone outside of that norm:

> ▸ People's subconscious biases—we all make judgements without realizing it, and we often penalize people who don't fit the "norm," which is a very narrow definition. These judgements can lead to both overt sexism and microaggressions. (F.D.00962.2014)

"They Just Don't Apply!": Stereotyped Profiling

Many VGDs and observers strongly believe that the statistical underrepresentation of women is rooted in a gendered profile of gamers—girls and boys showing different skills and preferences early in childhood—and of a subsequent gendered occupational profile based on a similar "essential, authentic or inner truth of gender" (Jenson, Fisher, and de Castell 2011, 151).

A lack of resources or access to computers and games are barriers to entry for children from underprivileged backgrounds. These barriers stem from general socio-economic factors, outside of the game industry, that can influence access to games jobs. A crowded field of candidates wish to make it into this job market and rise up the competitive ranks. Many are ready to make personal investments to make inroads into the trade as proficient gamers, before even reaching the first steps of a game studio. They play a wide array of games with the appropriate, updated equipment; attend gatherings, clubs, and associations; take part in competitions; start up an initial project or business; enrol in specialized schools; and put up with low wages in entry-level positions. These things remain out of reach in poorly funded school districts, where access to technology-based programs is more limited. Survey respondents attest to this discrepancy in early access and resources:

> ▸ There is a background of knowledge that economically disadvantaged students lack, which leads to further distancing and of course is tied to race. (F.M.02580.2015)

> ▸ Entry into the game industry requires either taking an entry-level position with a very low wage (in relation to candidates' alternatives) or accomplishing something in one's own free time. In both cases there is a challenging financial cost, which can be an obstacle to candidates from less affluent backgrounds. (M.M.01448. 2014)

It is much easier to maintain a regular practice of high-level gaming and to weather the constant risk during the first steps toward the game industry when one's social class allows for a well-provided school, a well-stocked technological environment, and a family's financial assistance to attend events and support unpaid internships. Furthermore, this situation contributes to a racializing of the workforce. The career path in games is like that of the movie industry:

> The film industry is notorious for its high risk–high return profile, requiring years of networking, investment in skills and, most important, access to work opportunities in order to build a career. While educational training may provide an initial entrée, for example as a lowly production assistant, it is the ability to self-finance one's career for a number of years, along with luck and the right connections, that construct the road to success. Studies of students in media programmes and their career paths note that even the ability to get a foot on the career ladder depends on continued parental financial support for a series of "internships" beyond

graduation. Students without affluent parents and carrying significant educational debt cannot afford this route. (Christopherson 2009, 87–88)

However, according to a current belief in a non-biased meritocratic selection process, the White and male demography of games only confirms the belief in White men's "natural gift" for gaming and game development.

Open-ended survey questions provided a fair share of comments referring to an essentialist belief that women just do not *enjoy* the technical trades like programming, with some of them heavily invested in fighting against it:

> ▶ Women will *never, ever* want to go into STEM fields [science, technology, engineering, and mathematics] in the same capacity as men! and when they do [come to game development], isn't it odd that the vast majority of women go into the arts? I personally work at [a studio] together with only female artists, never a female programmer. The same went for the women whom I worked under for thirty weeks during my last internship! By "diversifying" the industry, you maggots, you forcibly place women into positions they are not good enough at instead of treating each individual based on their own skillset and professionalism! This is not only discriminatory towards men who are now discriminated against, this is also causing people in the workplace to go, "well, she only got hired cuz of diversity," instead of just trusting their employers to choose the right people! You stupid IGDA twats, when are you just going to close down your pathetic little clubhouse, because absolutely nobody needs you! Get the fuck out of my industry … and *do not* come back! (M.N.01419.2015)

The highly emotional and fuming tone of this comment echoes the "unique affective character of gendered labour in games culture" (A. Harvey and Shepherd 2017, 493; Hirshfield 2010; Lees 2016). Men perpetuate a notion of what constitutes legitimate, credible, and authentic participation in games that feeds both the notion of the "core gamer" and the good developer (Fullerton et al. 2008; Consalvo and Paul 2019). As they constitute a majority, these notions spread out in the sector. Men subscribe more easily than women to the profile of the "good" or "real" developer who "loves" his trade so much that he is ready to sacrifice private and leisure time for the sake of the project (Legault and Chasserio 2012). This current of thought is akin to the post-bureaucratic organizational model (see Chapter 1), which attests that when you have the privilege to hold a creative job in the realm of "passionate and affective labour," the work itself can be fuelled by passion instead of being a burden to endure (Ashkanasy and Humphrey 2011; Consalvo 2008; de Peuter 2011; A. Harvey and Fisher 2013). Such a "privilege" usually means that employees fully commit themselves to doing what they love without counting the time they devote to it. "Passion" can then become a label used to (re)entrench exclusionary discourses and practices against those who are not ready to put in the hours needed. Set out this way, some jobs become earmarked as "men's jobs." These affects are powerful instruments to "naturalize" the marginalization of women, demarcate boundaries, and normalize exclusion in games production and culture (A. Harvey and Shepherd 2017).

Some researchers challenge this preconceived idea of an "essential, authentic or inner truth of gender" that manifests in "girls" tastes and preferences in gaming, as does research on occupational segregation (L. Miller et al. 2004). For instance, Jenson, Fisher, and de Castell (2011, 151) contest this gender-based dichotomy as a social stereotype sustained by careless research design. Indeed, there remains much to unpack in gender studies of gaming to challenge the running stereotypes about women VGDs.

First, "boys' play" generally acts as the reference for gameplay to which "girls' play" is compared. There is no such thing as a "neutral standard." Studies have examined the criteria defining the "true gamer" and "real games," and distinguishing the casual from the hard-core gamer. These include time investment; self-identification to the gamer community; genre; and design elements and content, including high difficulty and non-interruptibility; as well as skill, gaming knowledge and attitudes, playing habits, buying habits, and game-related social identity enacted in out-of-game spaces (Paaßen, Morgenroth, and Stratemeyer 2017, 423–26). These criteria of core gaming are directly retrieved from the masculine repertoire and therefore constitute and perpetuate the "male gamer stereotype," even when claims to gender differences are unwarranted or disputable (Paaßen, Morgenroth, and Stratemeyer 2017). To sum up, gendered tastes in games are more inferred than demonstrated.

Second, and more importantly, the level of access to and therefore experience in gaming (novice versus seasoned) seems to be a more important factor than gender in explaining gameplay behaviour. Gendered equivalencies in skill level emerge with a level playing field of access, which also suggests similarity (or difference) in play patterns, pleasures, and preferences (Jenson, Fisher, and de Castell 2011, 149–50). The things that have traditionally been characterized in the research as the "characteristics of girls" are, in fact, the characteristics of novices, due to overlooked features of the gameplay context.

That said, the conditions favouring a level playing field and young girls' access to games are not widespread at home or school, because institutions reflect the power relations within society. They must be intentionally implemented and monitored. In practice, this rarely occurs and girls are often marginalized and dismissed in contexts of mixed gender gameplay (Jenson and de Castell 2018). This contributes to the enduring stereotype of the male gamer, while confusing the cause and the effect.

We have previously critiqued the normative "pipeline" to a career in game development in which women are disadvantaged in spaces of early access/exposure and in formal schooling environments (Weststar and Legault 2018; discussed more below). As has been further detailed here, this lack of inclusion and belonging carries on into the workplace. Referring to controversial practices of gender discrimination at Riot Games (D'Anastasio 2018; Ramos 2018), Bulut (2020a, 44) concluded that the so-called meritocracy in some studios is in fact a disguise to hide systemic or institutional sexism. Instead of a "meritocratic utopia," there is inequity (Bulut 2020a, ix).

For instance, many of our VGD respondents (mostly men) explain away the uniform workforce by claiming there is a "lack of diverse applicants," thus justifying the status quo as being grounded in nature. However, this viewpoint conveniently and cruelly ignores the paramount importance of networking for placement and job hunting, and how hiring managers tend to reach out to candidates and canvass with their usual approaches, in places they know, and make their selections according to criteria well-established for the dominant group and existing collective norms:

> ▸ The people doing the hiring—in my experience they are more often concerned about preserving the status quo and their own positions rather than expanding into diversity. (F.D.01058.2014)

> ▸ The people hiring the staff—some (but not all) are just unwilling to look beyond the "typical game developer" image, which seems to be male, young, and having to live, eat, and breathe video games. (M.D.01517.2014)

The hire-on-demand environment of project-based work exacerbates this, since managers look for immediately available and "proven-to-deliver" candidates and are risk averse. The situation is akin to the film industry, as studied by Handy and Rowlands (2016). They argued that the unrelenting emergency in hiring onto a project team (see Chapters 2 and 3) creates anxieties among managers that result in hirings that are safe and that uphold the status quo, and "consequently, discriminatory hiring practices ... become collectively accepted as rational responses to organizational problems" (Handy and Rowlands 2016, 312). VGDs see this first-hand:

> ▶ It seems to be very difficult to find diverse talent, but I'm sure our hiring process does not help. Because we're such a small company, and we can't afford to take many chances, we almost always hire people we already know—our friends or people we've worked with before. Somehow this has resulted in a team of twelve people with no women, no homosexuals (that I know of), and only one non-White employee. I find this highly regrettable, but at present we are not in a position to change it. (M.M.02005.2014)

> ▶ It's easier to hire someone who on paper has all the right experience and skills, which keeps the pool of people small. There is a lot of risk aversion in the hiring process. (F.M.01083.2014)

This very conceptualization of women and others as "risky candidates" stands in the way of inclusion and belonging, since diversification is an unwelcome threat. This sentiment was at the heart of the Gamergate rhetoric. Those expressing their own fear of change, often imploring critics to "leave game-makers alone and let them create what they wish," can be quite prejudicial:

> ▶ Triple A studios have an obvious unwillingness to change. They think they can keep making money the way they made money fifteen years ago. Too much is changing around them and they try to hold it back. ... Keeping people out, and trying to reach only one target demographic (White males) because it's what they think worked in the past. Fear leads to anger, anger leads to hate, etc. (F.M.00933.2014)

> ▶ My friend was openly told by a recruiter that their company was made up of all men and they weren't sure that she would be comfortable in that environment. (F.N.02545.2015)

Though more than half of our respondents reported equal opportunity hiring policies in their studios (see Table 10.1), open-ended comments revealed ignorance about how the lack of a critical mass of a minority population within a workforce can be a risk factor for harassment (see Chapter 1). When in a minority position, it does not take much to feel like you do not belong. As one woman told us:

▸ It doesn't feel quite as good as when there was at least one other. They don't really make any bad jokes or anything, but... It just doesn't feel good. (F-19-18-V-S-12-11-13-14-26-LT)

Worse, when the environment is gender segregated, men and women have less interaction, and gendered stereotypes become perpetuated. Gender-based occupational segregation also keeps women in roles that are lower in the occupational hierarchy and more precarious. This also perpetuates inequities and precludes a sense of belonging:

▸ Through some combination of lack of candidates and unconscious discrimination, out of a studio of roughly twenty, only two hires were women: the community manager and producer. These were apparently considered "non-essential" roles, and they were the first jobs cut, over a month before any other layoffs. Management swears up and down it wasn't gender-based, but it seemed pretty easily arguable that the reason that they were considered "non-essential" was that they were not allowed to "become" essential during the time they were here (for example, frequently ignoring the producer's recommendations for process improvements). (M.D.02300.2015)

A critical and well-distributed mass of members of a minority group is needed for them to lead a comfortable life. As a result, as long as members of a minority group do not have a critical mass, they are doomed to feel like they are "earmarked," like they do not belong, and, in fact, are not subjects of citizenship.

Feeling Able to Speak Freely, Being Heard and Valued

A sense of belonging also manifests in feeling able to speak freely in teamwork, voice dissent, or advocate fresh ideas. Women respondents expressed much embarrassment on that front:

▸ You just had to suck it up because you didn't want to be seen as a prude. It was hard to be myself. You had to be one of the boys, [or else] you're very much a girlfriend or a mother. That's how they see you. (F-13-13-V-I-15-11-13-14-26)

▸ Bar humour and being crude is great and fun after hours, but upsetting when (in my case) it comes from someone older and in a position of helping/hindering my career, and I've made it clear that I'm speaking to them for career reasons. (F.N.02484.2015)

Some women feel they are not heard or considered, even though they work as hard as their colleagues:

> I've had the QA director smirk at me and tell me to talk to the "producer in charge of editing," when I *am* the producer in charge of editing! I told him it was me, and I still got the dismissive smirk and brush off. (F.M.02617.2015)

> Well, it goes without saying, but being a woman in games you encounter a lot of random bullshit. ... I should make it clear it's not everybody, but there're some people who will value your opinion less because you're a girl. (F-03-07-V-F-12-19-13-14-26-LT)

Many women shared professional experiences of being overlooked based on their gender. For example, one of them explained:

> Business partners often refer to my co-founders for decision-making or assume they are the leads, I believe, because they are male and I am female, despite the fact that I am much more experienced. I quickly corrected their error and moved on with the meeting. Similarly, journalists or consumers will sometimes assume I am the marketer or PR person when I represent the game at conferences and conventions, and ask to speak to a developer on the team, or to speak to the game designer. I correct their error and try to continue the conversation. (F.D.02712.2015)

> He was dismissive towards any input I gave and assumed I was an artist (rather than a programmer, which is what I actually was) for a full month. (F.N.00867.2014)

Women feel the not-so-subtle internal hierarchy of occupational roles in which the male-dominated role of programming is valued above other roles, and women are not deemed true developers:

> Other incidents include having men in the community insinuate I am not a real developer due to not being a programmer, and yet my male colleagues who are artists or writers have never had their developer status questioned. (F.M.00876.2014)

Taken together, women face being silenced, overlooked, cancelled, and caricatured on a daily basis, and when they do speak up, their ideas, their dissent, or their advocacy are dismissed. The same can be said of women gamers, who are often rebuffed, insulted, and harassed when playing (Tison 2019; Zampolini 2018a, 2018b).

Feeling Able to Relate to the Game Content

When they enter the game industry workforce, would-be developers have usually come a long way as gamers. Their experiences as game players will have nourished the feeling that they belong—or do not belong—in the game community broadly and in the workplace (Weststar and Legault 2018). Belonging manifests in an ability to relate to the situations, characteristics, and avatars of game content without feeling stereotyped or demeaned (see Figure 10.1). Game content has significant social effects through offering to consumers a representation of society and its distribution of roles. Entertainment devices are important symbolic objects that contribute to the modelling of social identity and perceptions of social reality, from social justice and power imbalances to stereotype formation (Daviault and Schott 2015). For instance, groups who appear more often in the media enjoy more status and power in daily life (D. Williams et al. 2009, 816–18).

Games provide much in terms of affordable contemporary "identity tourism" and escapism (Bulut 2020a, 45–46). Yet whose tourism is it? The definition of what is considered "fun" is largely influenced by White men who give us questionable and problematic game content with respect to gender (Burgess, Stermer, and Burgess 2007; Chess 2015; Dunlop 2007) and ethnic origin (Srauy 2019). When pointed out, problematic content is trivialized as "just a game" or "what the consumer wants" (Bulut 2020a, 35–37). However, VGDs produce entertainment that is no more innocent than any other:

> [VGDs] code values and ideologies into games, but they are either not aware of it or deny it. ... Foregrounding how racialized and gendered practices and imaginations inform the desire behind the global game industry is crucial, especially in the aftermath of Gamergate and the rise of authoritarianism. (Bulut 2020b)

If there is any doubt regarding the influence of games in shaping youngsters' minds, it may be enlightening to have a look at the portion they represent in the media diet of young people, according to aggregated survey results from France, Germany, India, Italy, Japan, Singapore, South Korea, the United Kingdom, and the United States:

> Video gamers spend an average of 7.11 hours each week playing games. This is an increase of 19.3% in the last year. 34% play more than 7 hours each week, with 19.6% playing more than 12 hours a week. ... Men play almost eight hours per week. This is an average of one hour 37 minutes longer than women, who play 6.28 hours. 23.0 percent of men play for twelve hours or more, compared to just 15.9 percent of women. (Limelight Networks 2020)

While initial studies of game content concentrated on the sensitive topics of violence and sexuality (Alloway and Gilbert 1998), since the 2000s, studies have focussed on the representation of identity groups. A large-scale content analysis of characters in videogames (D. Williams et al. 2009) studied representations of gender, race, and age in comparison to the US population in 150 games across nine platforms over the course of a year. The results were weighted according to game sales. Through this ambitious analysis, researchers found a systematic over-representation of men and of White characters (particularly adults), and a systematic underrepresentation of women, Hispanics, Indigenous peoples, children, and the elderly (D. Williams et al. 2009, 817). Other studies have also found scant representation of racialized people, and people living with a disability or alternative body types (Downs and Smith 2010; Ivory 2006; Martins et al. 2009; L. Miller and Summers 2007). The representation of gender in games is often very stereotyped, hyper-feminized, and hyper-masculinized, and women lament the fact that they continue to be overrepresented as non-player characters.

The way in which games are made contains a feedback loop that helps to explain the uniform workforce (Weststar and Legault 2018). The type of games available "panders towards the presumed preferences of a young, male, heterosexual audience" (Paaßen, Morgenroth, and Stratemeyer 2017, 421), who then develop a passion for the medium, pursue careers in the industry, and ultimately make games that fit the established model. These then appeal to the same audience. In this way, a vicious cycle linking game content and risk aversion among decision-makers and gamer culture is perpetuated. Women and members of other minoritized groups can feel disenfranchised from the product that they are making.

That said, scholars take care to disclaim any risky theoretical pretention that women would know how to make games that would please women (often referred to as "pinkwashing"), and that the same could be said of VGDs of colour or members of other social identity groups. Attributing tastes, skills, aptitudes, and leanings to members of a demographic group as if this very group were a uniform whole would fly in the face of common sense, as well as current research outcomes (Carr 2005; Jenson and de Castell 2005, 2010a; Krotoski 2004; Yee 2008).

Conclusion

We have used Westecott et al.'s model (2019) as an organizing framework that presents diversity as both a goal and an outcome of inclusion measures that favour belonging. Diversity is attained in an environment in which diverse people are represented, acknowledged, and considered as a powerful force and are not singled out, excluded, or preferred based on the characteristics of their group. As a result, they feel like they belong. This framing is well suited to a study of citizenship at work in which one must be included as a subject of citizenship.

In Chapter 4, we assessed the lack of diversity in game development via demographic statistics. In this chapter, we carried on with surveys on perception. We showed what is being poorly done and what is not being done but could be done in terms of inclusion measures, and what is felt and not felt in terms of belonging.

According to our data, some initiatives exist towards obtaining differentiation in the workforce, but we cannot assert the existence of a diverse workforce. First, many early obstacles continue to hinder the ability of girls (N. Taylor, Jenson, and Castell 2009; Weststar and Legault 2018) and less privileged children (Tokumitsu 2015) to get acquainted with and develop high skills in gaming.

Second, if they nevertheless make it to a job in game development, informal social rules within the industry establish unequal power relations between the majority who belong and some minority groups who do not. Arbitrary processes and discretionary decision-making in management support these power relations. Discretionary decisions based on personal criteria leave room for personal preferences, social networks that gather together similar people, and exclusionary practices, and thus discrimination. As game development studios are an iconic offspring of the anti-bureaucratic movement (see Chapter 1), they are the home of youthful, able-bodied, White cis men who are free of caring responsibilities and free to dedicate much of their time to their projects (Hester 2018). Unchallenged normative stereotypes and "outdated attitudes" foster assumptions about the targeted group members' game knowledge and competence. Members of minoritized groups have a harder time making discretionary mechanisms work for them and therefore have fewer recourses available to them. They do not have the needed "social capital" that "star" developers hold, nor the trump cards that are acquired through the embedded socialization of inner circles.

Third, while social laws guarantee a formal "equality of rights," members of marginalized groups who make it through to the workplace will be reluctant to take any recourse because of the importance of maintaining one's reputation in an environment of relentless job hunting. A path to passive citizenship may appear to exist, but it is a hard road in practice.

Our citizenship framework (see Chapter 1) also raises additional ethical considerations. There is a growing demand for democracy at work and the right to participate and be consulted. This allows workers to mobilize both their labour power and a richer set of human ideas, inputs, and positions about the management of the workplace and about justice and fairness (Budd 2004a). Yet this demand cannot be universally met if some demographic groups are not subjects of citizenship in the same environment. In this re-enchanted post-bureaucratic workplace, we wonder as does Bulut: Who is free to "enjoy" (2020a, 23–29) working in it? If it is a dream job, whose dream is it? In an environment in which the participation of minority group members is reduced or exploited, stereotyped assumptions and normative behaviours are free to take hold, denying these workers citizenship and relegating them to second-class citizen status. Hammar (2022) makes this point in using the concept of labour aristocracy to illustrate how the privileges of game workers at the "core" are built on the exploitation of those in the "periphery."[5] The case of equity, diversity and inclusion is exemplary of the lack of citizenship in the VGI.

In canvassing our data from the last fifteen years, we note that responses to diversity-related questions became more polarized and less neutral after Gamergate. With subsequent industry scandals and broader social movements like #MeToo, #BlackLivesMatter, and decolonization, views on these issues have become increasingly definitive. An increased assertiveness in respondents' answers regarding diversity, both positive and negative, could result in a beneficial long-term outcome for the industry, insofar as it propels a diversity agenda and/or compels individuals or companies toward positive action. This requires continued monitoring. We must recall that only 19 percent of respondents in 2019 felt that there was "equal treatment and opportunity for all in the game industry," even though many felt that diversity had increased over the years.

5. Hammar's focus is primarily on the internationalization of the game industry and the super-exploitation of workers in the Global South by imperialist companies in the Global North; however, his discussion also includes the disadvantaged position of migrant and immigrant workers and racialized workers within domestic contexts.

As it stands, there is limited evidence that employers are setting forward efficient policies and programs to bring about a more diverse workforce and more equitable environments. At the very least, the data presented in this chapter suggest that there is both an opportunity and an imperative to act on rampant sexism, and to bring in certain policies and formal changes to workplace culture, including:

- policies to favour more widespread access to gaming for girls and less privileged children;
- incentives for greater diversity in game content;
- measures for employers to seek and foster diverse applicant pools;
- efficient equal opportunity hiring policies that aim toward achieving and maintaining a critical mass of members of a minority group, without occupational segregation;
- efficient and extensive anti-harassment and anti-discrimination policies, including effective recourse, designed to ensure a safe and equitable working environment; and
- work–life balance policies and changes in the organization of work consistent with a real balance.

We have documented the point of view of VGDs, and yet this study remains limited for not having delved deeper into HR decision-making process. It is challenging to gain access to organizational data, but such empirical studies are useful to see how particular discretionary decisions vary regarding gender or ethnicity, in order to conduct deeper analysis of occupational hierarchies or examine additional demographic categories such as sexual orientation or disability. Such research endeavours are sorely needed, though burdened with many practical obstacles.

CONCLUSION

As we stated in the Introduction, we started this research project to dig into the state of citizenship at work in the private creative sector, which has adopted the practice of project management. We studied the VGI as a case, aiming to assess citizenship at work in this sector and the importance of the project-based organizational context to the contemporary redesign of work and the resulting state of working conditions. This builds on the previous research by Legault and colleagues into by-design IT services to businesses, which drew our attention to the importance of project management in the contemporary redesign of the organization of work.

We conclude this book with reflections about the state of citizenship at work among VGDs and the deficits faced by workers in private sector project-based knowledge work, who participate very little in the regulation of their working conditions and work environment. We call for new or renewed systems and institutions to close the citizenship gaps in the contemporary employment landscape. Yet, even as we acknowledge these deficits, we also argue for the need to revise the theoretical construct of citizenship to account for a fuller range of participatory activities, participating actors, and regulatory spaces. In this we join a larger call to identify and promote greater mechanisms for democracy at work and, indeed, humanity in work. Increasing worker citizenship at the local and social level is a contributory means to achieve the greater goals of economic bicameralism, democratization, decommodification, and environmental remediation called for by Ferraras and colleagues (Ferraras 2017; Ferraras, Battilana, and Méda 2022).

The Four Components of Citizenship at Work

In practice, citizenship at work requires a degree of organizational democracy such that the governance mode of HRM can reconcile between property rights and labour rights by balancing three core principles:

efficiency (in operations), equity (fairness in treatment and procedure), and voice (meaningful employee input). Having a voice turns workers into actors in the regulation of their work. From the viewpoint of the welfare state, citizenship at work refers to the exercise of state power to enforce laws, institutions, and practices that shape and regulate markets and communities—including workplaces—to achieve this balance. Historically, researchers in the mid-twentieth century concluded that society had progressed on the road of what was then called "industrial democracy" in observing four important gains of the labour movement (see Table 1.1):

- policies and programs to protect against economic insecurity and the risks of lost income,
- recourses against arbitrary decisions and ways to influence local decisions regarding work and working conditions,
- participation in the local regulation of labour regarding critical issues, and
- participation in the broader social regulation of work, industry, or sector.

However, the nature of work has changed considerably from the Fordist era. In this book we have used the case of VGDs to argue that industrial democracy has been eroded and that citizenship at work is elusive for many workers, particularly those in project-based environments in the private sector. Borrowing from the conceptual terms of Bosniak (2000, 2003), this is because they are not recognized as citizens in the environment (subjects), they have no say regarding certain important issues (objects), or there is no space or territory within which they can exercise a voice (domains).

Three economic forces increased the level of economic risk workers bore in the late twentieth and early twenty-first centuries: the increasing "financialization" of the economy, rapidly changing market demand, and the widespread diffusion of flexible work practices (Neff 2012, 7). The VGI embodies all three. Consequently, VGDs face important citizenship challenges with respect to the risk of losing their employment income, whether because of firing, layoffs, illness, injury, the birth of a child, or so on.

Even when hired as employees, VGDs are supposed to engage in projects in the same manner as do entrepreneurs, bearing the plight of economic or market variations. In many senses they are "entrepreneurial workers," that is, entrepreneurs of their own career and employability, in a context that favours those who are better equipped to manage risk. This has a knock-on effect on the workforce's (lack of) diversity.

However, these workers are clearly not entrepreneurs as far as profits are concerned. The VGI offers many temporary, intermittent, and precarious jobs, as well as high levels of mobility due to project management practices. Constant underlying job insecurity makes VGDs dependent on immediate and future colleagues, clients, and managers. If they fail to maintain a reputation and a network, get training, and maintain employability, they are at risk of being sidetracked.

Project management means long hours and bulimic patterns of working. Some VGDs enjoy employment stability in some large studios, but generally there is poor coverage when health problems or retirement come. VGDs are generally not unionized, and existing associative bodies tend to serve the business interests of the industry. Therefore, VGDs have little opportunity to play an active public policy role—for instance, in commissioning independent health risk research that would be a prerequisite to establishing protection and compensation. The lack of specific research and advocacy considerably constrains progress on protection. When dissatisfied with the health risks of their working conditions, VGDs face poor options. They can turn to a less prestigious project at a smaller company; turn to part-time, temporary or contract work; accept the minimum employment standards; or leave the industry altogether. The few protections that are shared by most VGDs have come from social laws and as such are an object of passive rather than active citizenship.

Passive citizenship through state laws is a start, but it is inferior to actively negotiated mechanisms that can be tailored to suit all workers in a particular environment. In the VGI, state-based protection systems are not adaptable to the specific context of game development and many workers fall through the cracks. In some cases, the cracks have been explicitly created. In many jurisdictions, employers have used their representational power to exempt VGDs from the prevailing standard. VGDs have no counterpart. Some highly rated workers and "star" developers can negotiate working conditions beyond minimum standards. But these systems and practices only widen the gap between "the haves and the have-nots," increasing arbitrariness, reducing universal citizenship, and contributing to inequity and the individualization of risk.

The individualization of risk constitutes the basis of the major change that project management represents, because the pervasive financial risk in the games market is ultimately transferred to workers through the "iron triangle" of projects (see Chapter 2) in which working time is used as an "adjustment variable," while budgets, deadlines, and deliverables are fixed. In this context, VGDs face risks without protection. Working time management is a discretionary decision-making process and VGDs do not have a say in its regulation (see Chapter 9). This privatization of risk is part of a deficit in workplace citizenship.

At minimum, a democratic workplace would set forward voicing mechanisms for workers. More so, it would include means for workers to influence local decisions regarding their working conditions. Instead, we have uncovered a host of instances in which VGDs must cope with discretionary decision-making processes that advantage some and disadvantage others and in which an ability to negotiate is based on "market value." We have documented citizenship gaps regarding NCAs and NDAs, IP and game crediting systems, performance evaluation policies, compensation systems, working time, access to training, internal assignment to projects, and any recourse to discipline and discharge (see Chapters 6 and 9). In general, VGDs are forced to consent and commit to "given" conditions in their environment and they have limited access to the real players who shape the context of their work. Due to financialization, project funders hold the strings, but are not accessible to workers as legal employers (Legault and Weststar 2021).

In addition to disadvantaging individual workers, such gaps in citizenship leave room for exclusion and preference based on arbitrary criteria that work against diversification in the industry (see Chapter 10). The VGI labour force still mostly consists of youthful, able-bodied, White cis men, without child or elder care responsibilities. Even in countries where laws guarantee a formal "equality of rights," members of marginalized groups who make it through to the workplace will be reluctant to exert any legal recourse (even if they are provided for free) because of the importance of worker reputation in an environment of relentless job hunting.

VGDs have engaged in a range of voicing and resistance activities (see Chapter 7). However, few of these actions have allowed game workers to become legitimate and long-term participants in the work regulation process. To date, the means they use are insufficient for creating an institutional framework that accords workers a meaningful influence over the decisions that affect their work and working conditions. Industry majors maintain their hold over the social regulation of work, and they are the ones consulted in public policy debates. VGDs are early in their unionization project and most of them are not protected by a union. As such, they do not yet have a robust collective voice in the local or public policy debates surrounding work-related issues. They remain in a passive, or at best reactive, role as opposed to participatory actors in the regulation of the workplace (Budd 2004a, 2004c; Kaufman 2004).

We conclude that VGDs experience significant gaps across the four components that characterize citizenship at work. VGDs are not subjects of citizenship as defined by Arthurs (1967) because they are not unionized. Nor are they citizens as defined by Marshall (1964), since they are denied the protection of some "universal" labour laws such as the regulation of working time. Some VGDs who have high market power can negotiate over certain objects, and some individuals or groups of VGDs can sometimes enjoy some rights in some places or over some objects (such as when they undertake collective actions against a particular employer, when they run successful social media campaigns, when they threaten a particular employer with leaving, or when they can negotiate an advantageous salary or a bonus or reprieve from crunch time). In this, they can enjoy a locus of citizenship here and there, but none of these are guaranteed or formal. This does not make these workers subjects within a citizenship domain; rather, they are merely successful individual achievers in a certain time and place. On top of that, due to both demographic and occupational characteristics, older workers, women, and members of other equity-deserving groups, artists and testers, outsourced workers, and those working at small or capital-poor companies become second-class citizens and face additional challenges when compared to the uniquely skilled White cis male programmer in a large, self-reliant AAA studio. Moreover, if VGDs enjoy formal processes where they exist in one studio but can also move to a studio where there are none, their situation is one of sporadic citizenship and an incomplete domain across the industry.

Citizenship at Work Requires Organizational Democracy

Within the VGI is applied a new form of management and organization of work that challenges the labour institutions and the traditional HRM designed for bureaucracies or mass production. In this, VGDs do not enjoy the representation that characterizes fair procedure: processes are one-sided, VGDs' points of view are not considered, and there is no feedback process that leaves room for correction. Non-unionized workers are left with an approach inspired by liberal non-intervention (Armbrüster 2005)—a system of individual representation that amounts to little more than "free market" bargaining power. If parties are free to contract as they wish, the law of supply and demand supposedly provides for automatic adjustments, balance in the job market, and optimal outcomes. Unfortunately, there is no such symmetry between the parties, and workers have only minimum standard labour laws to protect them (Fudge 2005). In the meantime, employers can lobby governments to change laws (or leave them as they are) (for example, in the case of overtime exemptions) (Legault and Weststar 2017) or hire experts to represent them before the courts—all of which can keep working conditions poor (Budd 2004c). If sought-after VGDs have more leverage, this just illustrates the primacy of the market principle.

Is such "market citizenship" the only form of citizenship foreseeable in a reorganized, globalized labour market (Kaufman 2004, 607–8)? Notwithstanding a love for their work, the risk, arbitrariness, and absence of voice experienced by VGDs has become a critical matter of work regulation that we argue is inherent to a project management environment.

VGDs and workers like them are denied access to a procedural justice framework (see Chapter 6). We observe a general absence of constant and consistent policies based on known criteria and an absence of the ability for stakeholders to voice their concerns and receive an explanation regarding decisions. We note the opportunity, seemingly random, to voice concerns on an individual basis that is sometimes formally planned and at other times dependent on the initiative of individual workers, the style and approach of producers and managers, or circumstances such as friendship or happenstance. To overcome these deficits and achieve true sustainability and humanity at work, we call for new or renewed systems and institutions to better deliver citizenship in the contemporary employment landscape.

The application of co-determination models and systems of procedural justice could be expanded, strengthened, and mandated through employment legislation. We noted that joint committees do exist in some places, but employee participation is more likely to be found in decision-making related to organizational performance (such as about production processes or content) than in issues of governance or HRM. We have not encountered any dispute resolution procedure for any of the objects at stake. Both process and decision are controlled by management. It is true that both HRM departments and producers can be open to VGDs' input and voice. Voluntary non-union workplace procedures allow for some voicing mechanisms, typically as "open door policies" under the employer's control. But in the absence of formal appeal systems, decision processes are strongly biased in favour of efficiency over equity or voice. At any time, an employer can unilaterally disband these mechanisms, particularly if profitability and efficiency are at stake (Budd and Colvin 2005). This does not mean that all HRM procedures are used underhandedly to undermine employees' rights. Rather, the fairness of the decision-making process largely depends on managerial goodwill and can thus vary considerably.

Public policies and state social laws must also be reformed to close the loopholes of existing exemptions (such as for overtime pay) and to better protect equity and the ability for individual workers to contest decisions (such as in cases of wrongful dismissal or discriminatory pay). The complaints-based procedure is flawed, since precarious workers reliant on maintaining a strong reputation are unlikely to complain, not to mention their inability to purchase equivalent legal expertise to that of their employers (Vosko and Closing the Enforcement Gap Research Group 2020). VGDs face mobility costs that are in no way symmetrical with those of employers. Also, universal laws are not customized for project-based environments and offer no protection for internal decisions such as assignment to projects, access to training, discipline, evaluation, compensation, or crediting.

Above and beyond these possible solutions, collective bargaining through unionization remains an important mechanism to promote organizational democracy. It is increasingly seen as a place of citizenship for VGDs, although VGDs do not easily find their place in the "old" unions. The nature of the employment relationship has changed since the original conception of industrial citizenship (Arthurs 1967) and the role of the local union. The creative modes of action taken by VGDs are just one among many indicators for union renewal that is necessary to build relevancy and legitimacy with contemporary workers. With respect to the highly mobile, project-based knowledge worker of the VGI, the ideal form of union representation does not singularly exist. As such, game developers, like many other workers, are actively experimenting to find the form of collective action that will address their circumstances.

The contemporary practice of citizenship at work requires conditions for alternative or expanded modes of workplace regulation to better protect VGDs that would also apply to other knowledge workers in project-based settings. First, funders must be recognized as important actors of the bargaining system. Second, new regulatory forms must acknowledge that very important stakes transcend the borders of individual workplaces, individual employers, and, increasingly, nation states. These include communities of interest, portable rights, unstable employment, a porous boundary between work and private life, holding down several precarious jobs simultaneously, and mobility across studios and between the status of salaried employee and self-employed worker. Third, labour and representational institutions must tackle the public policies and sector-wide issues that are major concerns for workers.

On these points, as workers are increasingly called upon to harness their creativity and autonomy to the corporate yoke, there is a growing demand for democracy at work and the right to participate and consult. VGDs are proud of committing to their creative work with their whole self, so there is no surprise in their wish to voice their concerns about their immediate working conditions and the industry.

Indeed, VGDs show great interest in taking part in a broader spectrum of issues that influence the social regulation of their work (see Chapter 8). These include overtime regulation, tax credit policies (and their important consequences on local employment and employment stability), and the granting process of state funding and support policies (and the conditions that could be attached regarding the quality of jobs created, equitable representation of demographic groups, and ethical stances in HRM). They wish to influence work-related issues and industrial and business policies, the planning around the development of the economic sector, and the regulation of the products of the industry. They are concerned with policies that influence a more widely defined working activity and cover grounds like the blooming of creativity, self-actualization, the social responsibility of game creators in portraying ethnic groups and genders, and the like. As Keogh (2023, 102) argues, a "nascent collective politics of gamework" is beginning to emerge which could challenge and redetermine the structure and nature of the videogame filed even outside of the formalized commercial "industry."

In this, VGDs are part of a larger group of workers in the high-tech, white-collar work environment who seem more readily provoked by strategic issues that relate to customers, vendors, suppliers, the community, or the world at large. These include social justice issues such as transparency, accountability, fairness, equity, diversity and inclusion, climate change, and the ethical implications of technology in society (Ferraras, Battilana, and Méda 2022; Marculewicz, Model, and Thompson 2021; Philipupillai 2021). The precarity of creative and high-tech labour is also a prominent issue.

There are illustrative cases of this activism. Google workers protested the firing of members of the ethical artificial intelligence team (Nieva 2021) and over contracts with the US military (Shane and Wakabayashi 2018). The website of the Alphabet Workers Union at Google reads: "Our union ... strives to protect Alphabet workers, our global society, and our world. We promote solidarity, democracy, and social and economic justice."[1] The website of CODE-CWA reads: "We use our collective strength to improve conditions for temp, vendor and contractor workers; to fight against the unethical use of our labour; to end hiring, wage, and retention discrimination; and to ensure that our work is a benefit to our society, not a burden."[2] A trigger in the wave of organizing among digital journalists was maintaining editorial independence from corporate conglomerates and protecting the provision of local news (Cohen and de Peuter 2020). Tech, professional, and other workers increasingly focus on gaining access to their company's executive leadership, board of directors, and other stakeholders to address key social justice issues. For instance, across the labour movement we see growing activism directed

---

1. Alphabet Workers Union: https://alphabetworkersunion.org
2. CODE-CWA: www.code-cwa.org

toward pension plan governance and exposing the operation and influence of private equity firms (Appelbaum and Batt 2015; Baker, Corser, and Vitulli 2019; Coleman-Lochner and Ronalds-Hannon 2021; Skerrett et al. 2018).

Emergence of New Subjects, Objects, and Territories of Citizenship

While we call for changes that will bring "industrial" citizenship to contemporary workers, our analysis of the case of VGDs has made it clear to us that the conceptual model of citizenship at work also needs an overhaul.

The unionized subjects of industrial citizenship existed only as members of a collective subject: the trade union. They acquired their power by entrusting a collective stakeholder with the authority to represent the collective interest. In gaining the right to negotiate they gave up their individual power to do so. Unions generally lay claim to a set of identical rights for all the workers they represent, as they aim to achieve equal rights in opposition to the employer's arbitrariness.

VGDs are a different kind of citizen, wanting to be both collective and individual subjects. VGDs have a common collective interest, but an individual one as well. They have adopted modes of representation that are both individual and collective, although in different proportions. Individually, they hold market citizenship, due to their strategic position. This power can be very strong for some objects, at certain times, but very weak for others. Collectively, they participate to some extent in the local regulation of their work, with respect to certain objects. But their participation is ad hoc; they do not participate as a matter of course. Since they are not protected against discretionary decision-making, not always protected against risks, and never protected against the transfer of business risk, we would conclude that they are, at best, a stakeholder without guarantees and that they do not take part in the substance of traditional citizenship.

However, knowledge workers want a new substance. For instance, they want individual merit to be reflected in pay and certain benefits. They want a share of the added value created by their intellectual contribution, through reputation or merit, prorated to their market value. Like performing artists, they favour a multilevel compensation structure in which the first level is universal and minimal, and the second is variable and merit based. A system of this kind will generate unequal benefits but is preferred for that very reason. In these environments, the substance of citizenship at work is a blend of different types of logic, giving certain basic rights to all, while demanding other market-based benefits for some. This is a key distinction between the substance of citizenship at work in contemporary creative communities and that of the old model of industrial citizenship. It could be described as a form of hybrid citizenship: industrial in terms of the negotiation of minimum conditions to limit arbitrariness, market-based in terms of individual merit-based negotiation, and social democratic in terms of its aim to follow workers from one contract to the next, in both time and place.

The citizenship at work model also needs to transcend the limits of the liberal concept of industrial citizenship, acknowledge the existence of inequity among workers and workers-to-be, and make the subjects of citizenship part of the analysis instead of assuming that where there is citizenship, every worker enjoys its benefits. It needs to address the problem in which some workers can be second-class citizens within an ostensibly protective system at the regional, national, and international level. To ensure diversity in the VGI—that is, a state of things in which the social groups of the wider environment are represented and feel like they belong—inclusive actions aimed at attracting and retaining a diverse workforce are needed. An effective and extensive anti-harassment policy, including effective recourse, is imperative to ensure a safe and equitable working environment. Besides banning and punishing harassment, it is important to prevent it by setting out the conditions to avoid it. These include increasing the general representation of groups and spreading their presence throughout the workplace, avoiding gender segregation in teams and projects, ensuring easy interaction between groups by maintaining a critical mass of members of a minority, which allows them to blend into the crowd, and ensuring that workers feel like they belong. In the present state of things, it is far easier for able-bodied, White cis men who do not have caring responsibilities to feel as though they belong. Other groups experience more differentiation than diversity, being concentrated in specific roles.

This study of VGDs also reveals that debates over policies, funding and regulations, game content, game industry events, and spaces of interaction are domains of citizenship in which participation in the social regulation of the industry is called for. However, VGDs fail to achieve the status of citizenship in those spaces because the decision-making power is concentrated in the hands of a relatively small, interconnected, and elite group of employers. Taking part in the networks of power that lie behind the enactment of policies and events is critical to the expansion of citizenship at work and may involve a broader range of social actors than just trade unions (see Chapter 8).

The union is the hallmark of industrial citizenship. It generally establishes a set of working conditions that apply locally, with a single employer or at a single worksite. VGDs need a new territory for citizenship at work. Benefits tied to an employer or to a specific jurisdiction have little relevance to project-based work settings where knowledge workers are highly mobile. The priority must be one of nationally and internationally portable rights. This starts with the model of a sector-based system of certification for highly mobile workers, such as that enjoyed by performing artists or building trades workers, but that continues to push past the limits of any national territory.

Nieborg and de Kloet (2016) applied Mosco's (2009, 158) concept of spatialization—"the institutional extension of corporate power in the communication industry"—to examine the European game industry, arguing that a full understanding requires close examination of regional, national, and international political economies and macro-economic contexts. We would add that such analysis is also critical in broadening the theoretical lens of citizenship at work, particularly the scope for participation in the social regulation of labour. For the labour organizing of VGDs, it appears that the distinction between participation in the *local* regulation of work and participation in the *social* regulation of work is less theoretically relevant, and thus VGDs must find a form of labour action that is different from standard union operating protocols. VGDs' formal and informal industry collectives, and connections across cognate industries, blur the boundaries between the local and social regulation of work. Actions led by both formal and informal groups in a sustained or ad hoc fashion are shaping the game ecosystem and contributing to the social regulation of work. We hope that our lens of citizenship at work can complement existing historical and contemporary investigations into game production studies (M. J. Banks, Connor, and Mayer 2016; Keogh 2023; Kerr 2017; Sotamaa and Švelch 2021), regulatory spaces (Perks 2021), and cultural intermediaries (Browne and Schram 2021; Parker, Whitson, and Simon 2018) to better ascertain the complex interplay of voices that shape the game industry and to spur more work in this area.

Can Studying Videogame Developers Shed Light on Other Knowledge Workers?

We have presented important features of project-based work in the private creative sector of the knowledge economy (see Chapter 2) to make our case that our conclusions on citizenship at work among VGDs will be highly applicable to other workplaces, at least in the relevant geographical area. Indeed, the conditions described in Chapter 2 are common to this larger sector of employment and have become prominent features of the future of work spreading out across the economy. The employment practices shared by workers in the private creative sector situate them in an indefinite zone on the verge of entrepreneurship, with all the ensuing risks. As the product is original, there is always uncertainty about the production process and its outcome, and thus a risk of failure. Project management forces the constraints of the "iron triangle" and the use of unlimited working time as a buffer against the unexpected. Workers are assessed based on results instead of conformity to norms, even when success or failure does not lie with them. Constantly scouting for jobs, they must maintain a good reputation in the eyes of peers, clients, and managers to remain employable. While teamwork and reputation building require many behavioural skills, these skills are poorly considered in assessment and pay. Parents of young children, and mostly mothers, often withdraw from these sectors. All these common features make a good case for generalization.

However, some features of the VGI (see Chapter 3) keep us from hastily generalizing our conclusions to the private creative sector as a whole (for example, the very high risk of commercial failure, the persistence of uncertainty until a very late stage of development, the blend of technology and art in the daily work, and the resulting importance of IP and restrictive NCAs and NDAs). Moreover, the financialization process of games is an attempt to counterbalance the high risk by setting up a top-to-bottom chain of risk transfer: first from funders to employers through a system of the "closed budget envelope," tightly linked to periodic progress and results, and second from employers to workers via pressure for unlimited and unpaid overtime. Workers, who are often compensated poorly, carry on for "future returns." In this, the discourse of "working out of passion" helps to seal workers' attachment to the work and to the identity of the creative labourer; and an attitude and mindset that is a blend of bohemianism and entrepreneurialism contributes to the rejection of any labour institution protection.

This is not to undermine the generalizing power of the framework we have developed, but to remain cautious and invite more research in other sectors that we have not investigated. Indeed, many workers could likely share in the concerns of VGDs. An industry-specific pension plan is one of the demands of VGDs and in this they join many groups fighting for pensions and other benefits: music video dancers, adjunct professors on college campuses, fast-food workers trying to unionize, and New York jazz musicians pressuring non-union nightclubs (Neyfakh 2014). We also see other workers experimenting with alternative representational forms. In 2014, a group of US dancers got a multi-employer, industry-wide contract that covered all music videos produced by major record labels, even though they all worked for subcontractors, as opposed to being direct employees of the record labels bankrolling the videos. In the fashion industry, the Model Alliance serves as a support centre for models—most of whom are classified as independent contractors—and asserts public pressure to help protect them from inhumane working hours, malnourishment, and sexual harassment. Significant victories include a 2013 New York law extending child labour protections to underage models and the recently passed New York Fashion Workers Act, which regulates management agencies and provides labour protection for models and other behind-the-scenes creatives (Phelps 2022). The National Guestworker Alliance, founded by Saket Soni, has leveraged workplace activism, media, and consumer, legal, and political pressure to fight for immigration reform. It also seeks to force companies that are higher in a value chain to the bargaining table, in addition to immediate employers (Eidelson 2013). Soni has more recently founded Resilience Force to support and defend the rights of often migrant labourers who follow climate disasters for work.

These workers might seem like they have nothing particular in common. But behind their disparate organizing efforts is a profound economic shift. More and more working people, at all levels of income, are operating in a gray area in terms of their employment status and are mobilizing for public policies. Research on work in the private creative sector highlights a number of relatively stable risk factors shared by VGDs: a preponderance of temporary, intermittent, and precarious jobs; long hours and bulimic patterns of working; the collapse or erasure of the boundaries between work and play; poor pay; high levels of mobility; informal work environments and distinctive forms of sociality; and profound experiences of insecurity and anxiety about finding work, earning enough money, and "keeping up" in rapidly changing fields (Banks 2007; Banks et al. 2000; Batt, Christopherson, and Rightor 1999; Caves 2000; Christopherson 2002; Christopherson and van Jaarsveld 2005; Gill 2002, 2007; Gill and Pratt 2008; Jarvis and Pratt 2006; Kotamraju 2002; McRobbie 2002, 2003; Neff, Wissinger, and Zukin 2005; Perrons 2007; Taylor and Littleton 2008; Ross 2003; Kennedy 2008).

From this point of view, there is a need for researchers to survey the situation of citizenship at work in other project-based sectors of production, to broaden the scope of our conclusions, if appropriate, and to adjust the concept itself to the new claims of citizens in project-based organizations.

Where formal unionization seems out of the question for millions of workers, the labour movement has begun to experiment with new possibilities for how workers might negotiate for better conditions. These ways harness collective action without the official bargaining rights that made unions powerful in the past. Such developments, actors, and institutions need to be incorporated into the logic of any new citizenship model.

Theorists of the network organization cannot easily disregard the constant tension between liberal HRM practices, with or without employee voice, and the persistent grounds of a "labour problem" (Reed 2005). Stakeholders can show enough disruptive power to convince businesses that they cannot be ignored, and they can appeal to broad social values that attract political support (Heckscher et al. 2003b). A perception among workers of procedural unfairness leads to dissatisfaction, a lack of motivation and cooperation, noncompliance, conflicts, and distrust in management (Bobocel and Gosse 2015; Ko and Hur 2014; Shapiro and Brett 2005). Unfair procedures may carry the seeds of an organization's destruction, leading workers to rise up or to subvert a decision that was forced on them (Conlon, Meyer, and Nowakowsky 2005).

Conversely, real commitment, knowledge sharing, teamwork, and responsiveness to clients need more than the "instrumental compliance" generated in a climate of threat, fear, and individualism (Heckscher et al. 2003a; Ko and Hur 2014). Should performance metrics be needed, a review of 183 empirical studies of organizational justice suggests that a perception of fairness and distributive and procedural justice is a strong predictor of outcomes such as job satisfaction, commitment, an acceptance of authority, a reduction of withdrawal behaviours, and performance (Colquitt et al. 2001). All forms of participation can build trust between employees and employers. Furthermore, direct participation can enhance performance through increased job satisfaction and motivation due to fulfilled individual needs for personal growth and development (Kaufman and Levine 2000).

Limits of Our Research

Before closing the process of reflection that guided this book, we must acknowledge some limits to our data and scope. Because we recruited respondents on a voluntary basis, we do not pretend to have statistical representation of the international population of VGDs. First, though they are evenly distributed among publisher-owned AAA studios, third-party studios, and indie studios of various sizes, our study of citizenship at work assumes the existence of an organizational context, an employment status, and a minimal hierarchy of authority and decision-making. As a result, the portrait that we draw is one of workers in medium and large studios and will not precisely reflect the situation of small and very small indie developers or the self-employed VGD. The situation of self-employed or independent developers remains to be examined thoroughly, as they are important actors in the industry and not inherently separate from employed developers (see Keogh and Abraham 2022; Keogh 2023). The frontiers are blurred between these worlds, and actors can navigate in and out of both. We are just adding our contribution to the larger enterprise of grasping the political economy of the industry. As we noted previously (see Chapter 3), large studios producing AAA games will not necessarily represent the business model of the future; platform games and games-as-a-service are on the rise and have a different production process. Moreso, some gamemakers are "carving new paths to game creation and distribution" which could disrupt or subvert dominant models (Anthropy 2012, 18; Keogh 2023).

Second, we cannot pretend to report the full reality of many countries that are nonetheless very active in the VGI, like Scandinavian countries, Japan, and South Korea. Though there are no reliable population statistics for the industry, we are quite sure that the distribution of respondents to our online surveys does not represent their weight in the total global employment, nor does it ensure an even geographic coverage. As explained in the Introduction, our analysis of citizenship at work among VGDs is most applicable to the VGI of Canada and the United States, with reasonable expectations of generalization for the United Kingdom, Australia, and New Zealand, and with greater caveat to Europe.

Third, we collected enough information to assert that the VGI is an unevenly distributed domain of citizenship, not a uniform one. But we cannot establish the precise portrait of where we can find citizenship and where we cannot. Part of the VGI is an obligation-free zone, but we need more research to define its contours. The significant mobility of VGDs combined with an uneven distribution of conditions means they will alternate between periods of citizenship and its absence.

Last, our review in this book has been far ranging, but it is not complete. The picture we have taken reflects the dominant scene of console games that are based on an *editorial logic* (Kerr 2017, 16), that is, funded by publishers who own IP. This world is moving towards a *platform logic*, producing games that start as free-to-play or are built as games-as-a-service (Dubois and Weststar 2021; Weststar and Dubois 2022). The production process is different, games are more customizable, an important part of the work consists of maintaining a close relationship with an online community of players, and the funding sources include more crowdfunding. This new scene must be constantly studied to keep tabs on the state of citizenship at work—not to mention, VGDs' own efforts to claim citizenship are developing and evolving every day in a zone of active experimentation with representational forms.

REFERENCES

Abraham, Benjamin. 2022. *Digital Games after Climate Change*. New York: Springer

Acton, Mike. 2010. "It Doesn't Have to Suck #gamedev." Reposted with permission on *Gamasutra* by Brenda Brathwaite, December 25. https://www.game developer.com/game-platforms/mike-acton-s-quot-it-doesn-t-have-to-suck-gamedev-quot-.

Alfonso, Pedro, M. Fonseca, and J. F. Pires. 2017. "Impact of Working Hours on Sleep and Mental Health." *Occupational Medicine*, 67, no. 5: 377–82. https://doi.org/10.1093/occmed/kqx054.

Alha, Kati, Elina Koskinen, Janne Paavilainen, Juho Hamari, and Jani Kinnunen. 2014. "Free-to-Play Games: Professionals' Perspectives." *DiGRA Nordic '14: Proceedings of the 2014 International DiGRA Nordic Conference*, 11. http://www.digra.org/wp-content/uploads/digital-library/nordicdigra2014_submission_8.pdf.

Alksnis, Christine, Serge Desmarais, and James Curtis. 2008. "Workforce Segregation and the Gender Wage Gap: Is 'Women's' Work Valued as Highly as 'Men's'?" *Journal of Applied Social Psychology* 38, no. 6: 1,416–41. https://doi.org/10.1111/j.1559-1816.2008.00354.x.

Alloway, Nola, and Pam Gilbert. 1998. "Video Game Culture: Playing with Masculinity, Violence and Pleasure." In *Wired Up: Young People and the Electronic Media*, edited by Sue Howard, 95–114. London: Routledge.

Alves, Carina, Geber Ramalho, and Alexandre Damasceno. 2007. "Challenges in Requirements Engineering for Mobile Games Development: The Meantime Case Study." *Proceedings-15th IEEE international requirements engineering conference, RE 2007*: 275–280. https://doi.org/10.1109/RE.2007.53.

Alvesson, Mats. 1995. *Management of Knowledge-Intensive Companies*. Berlin: Walter de Gruyter.

—. 2000. "Social Identity and the Problem of Loyalty in Knowledge-Intensive Companies." *Journal of Management Studies* 37, no. 8: 1,101–24. https://doi.org/10.1111/1467-6486.00218.

Amar, Jacques. 2007. "Travailler plus pour gagner... quoi au juste?" *Controverses* 6: 180–2. https://core.ac.uk/reader/6464940.

Amman, John. 2002. "Unions and the New Economy." *WorkingUSA* 6, no. 2: 111–31. https://doi.org/10.1163/17434580-00602007.

Amman, John, Tris Carpenter, and Gina Neff. 2007. *Surviving the New Economy*. Boulder: Paradigm Publishers.

Anderson-Gough, Fiona, Christopher Grey, and Keith Robson. 2000. "In the Name of Client: The Service Ethic in Two Professional Services Firms." *Human Relations* 53, no. 9: 1,151–74. https://doi.org/10.1177/0018726700539003.

Anguiano, Dani. 2021. "Activision Blizzard Employees Walk Out over Harassment and 'Frat Boy' Culture Allegations." *Guardian*, July 28.

Anonymous. 2020. "'The Cost of Free Shipping:' A Review." *Stansbury Forum*, November 26. https://stansburyforum.com/2020/11/23/free-shipping-a-review.

Anthropy, Anna. 2012. *Rise of the Videogame Zinesters*. New York: Seven Stories.

Appelbaum, Eileen, and Rosemary Batt. 2015. "Private Equity at Work: When Wall Street Manages Main Street." *Socio-Economic Review* 13, no. 4: 813–20. https://doi.org/10.1093/ser/mwv026.

Armbrüster, Thomas. 2005. " Bureaucracy and the Controversy between Liberal Interventionism and Non-interventionism." In *The Values of Bureaucracy*, edited by Paul DuGay, 63–87. Oxford: Oxford University Press.

Arndt, Dan. 2018. "Nerf Bosses: An Interview with Game Workers Unite." *The Fandomentals*, September 10. https://thefandomentals.com/nerf-bosses-an-interview-with-game-workers-unite.

Arthur, Michael B., and Denise M. Rousseau. 1996. *The Boundaryless Career: A New Employment Principle for a New Organizational Era*. Oxford: Oxford University Press.

Arthurs, Harry W. 1967. "Developing Industrial Citizenship: A Challenge for Canada's Second Century." *Canadian Bar Review* 45, no. 4: 786–830. https://www.jstor.org/stable/23077679.

—. 1999. "The New Economy and the New Legality: Industrial Citizenship and the Future of Labour Arbitration." *Canadian Labour and Employment Law Journal/Revue canadienne de droit du travail et de l'emploi* (CLELJ) 7: 45–63. https://heinonline.org/HOL/LandingPage?handle=hein.journals/canlemj7&div=4&id=&page=.

—. 2000. "Private Ordering and Workers' Rights in the Global Economy: Corporate Codes of Conduct as a Regime of Labour Market Regulation." In *Labour Law in an Era of Globalization: Transformative Practices and Possibilities*, edited by Joanne Conaghan, Richard Michael Fischl, and Karl Klare, 471–87. Oxford: Oxford University Press.

—. 2010. "La nouvelle économie et le déclin de la citoyenneté au travail." In *Travail et citoyenneté: Quel avenir?*, edited by Michel Coutu and Gregor Murray, 43–70. Quebec: Presses de l'Université Laval.

Ashcraft, Catherine, Brad McLain, and Elisabeth Eger. 2016. *Women in TECH: The Facts*. National Center for Women and Information Technology (NCWIT). https://www.ncwit.org/sites/default/files/resources/ncwit_women-in-it_2016-full-report_final-web06012016.pdf.

Ashkanasy, Neal M., and Ronald H. Humphrey. 2011. "Current Emotion Research in Organizational Behavior." *Emotion Review* 3, no. 2: 214–24. https://doi.org/10.1177/1754073910391684.

Auvray, Tristan, Thomas Dallery, and Sandra Rigot. 2016. "Domestiquer la finance: Le rôle des investisseurs publics de long terme." In *La Caisse de dépôt et placement du Québec à l'épreuve de la financiarisation*, edited by Frederic Hanin, 3–22. Quebec: Presses de l'Université Laval.

Avery, Jodoin, and Laurie Cornell. 2016. *Manitoba Interactive Digital Media Tax Credit (MIDMTC) Program Guidelines*. Manitoba Jobs and the Economy, Science Innovation and Business Development Division, Government of Manitoba. Accessed January 18, 2023. https://www.gov.mb.ca/jec/busdev/financial/midmtc/pdfs/midmtc_guidelines.pdf.

Bailyn, Lotte. 1993. *Breaking the Mold: Women, Men and Time in the New Corporate World*. New York: Free Press.

Baker, Jim, Maggie Corser, and Eli Vitulli. 2019. *Pirate Equity: How Wall Street Firms are Pillaging American Retail.* United for Respect. https://united4respect.org/pirateequity.

Ballestrasse, Michelle. 2021. "Activision Blizzard Employees Detail 'Broken' HR Department, HR Head Leaves." *Screenrant,* August 3. https://screenrant.com/activision-blizzard-employees-lawsuit-hr-department.

Banks, Mark. 2007. *The Politics of Cultural Work.* Basingstoke, UK: Palgrave Macmillan.

Banks, Mark, Andy Lovatt, Justin O'Connor, and Carlo Raffo. 2000. "Risk and Trust in the Cultural Industries." *Geoforum* 31, no. 4: 453–64. https://doi.org/10.1016/S0016-7185(00)00008-7.

Banks, Miranda J., Bridget Connor, and Vicki Mayer, eds. 2016. *Production Studies, the Sequel!: Cultural Studies of Global Media Industries.* New York: Routledge.

Barbour, Neil. 2021. "Global Video Game Content Revenue on Course to Cross $200B in 2022." *S&P Global Market Intelligence Blog.* https://www.spglobal.com/marketintelligence/en/news-insights/blog/global-video-game-content-revenue-on-course-to-cross-200b-in-2022.

Barley, Stephen R., and Gideon Kunda. 2004. *Gurus, Hired Guns, and Warm Bodies: Itinerant Experts in a Knowledge Economy.* Princeton: Princeton University Press.

Baruch, Yehuda. 1998. "The Rise and Fall of Organizational Commitment." *Human Systems Management* 17, no. 2: 135–43.

Batchelor, James. 2020. "French Union Preparing Collective Lawsuit against Ubisoft amid Abuse Allegations." *Gamesindustry.biz,* July 22. https://www.gamesindustry.biz/articles/2020-07-22-french-union-preparing-collective-lawsuit-against-ubisoft-amid-abuse-allegations.

Batt, Rosemary, Susan Christopherson, and Ned Rightor. 1999. *Net-Working: Working Life in a Project Based Industry—A Collaborative Study of People Working in New Media in New York.* Working paper. Ithaca: Cornell University Press.

Beck, Ulrich. 1992. *Risk Society: Towards a New Modernity.* London: Sage.

—. 1999. *World Risk Society.* Malden, Massachusetts: Polity Press.

Béliveau, Nathalie-Anne. 2008. "Les conditions de validité des clauses de non-concurrence dans les contrats d'emploi: Synthèse." In *Développements récents sur la non-concurrence,* Service de la formation continue du Barreau du Québec, vol. 289, 336. Cowansville: Éditions Yvon Blais.

Béliveau, Nathalie-Anne, and Sébastien Lebel. 2011. "Les clauses de non concurrence en matière d'emploi et en matière de vente d'entreprise: du pareil au même?" In *Développements récents en droit de la non-concurrence,* Service de la formation continue du Barreau du Québec, vol. 338, 113–92. Cowansville: Éditions Yvon Blais.

Bellini, Andrea, Luigi Burroni, Lisa Dorigatti, Alberto Gherardini, and Cecilia Manzo. 2018. *"Industrial Relations and Creative Workers: Overall Report,"* commissioned by the European Commission. https://flore.unifi.it/retrieve/handle/2158/1134948/351188/WPA2_Overall%20report.pdf.

Benefact. 2017. *SR&ED Tax Credits for Gaming Companies.* https://www.benefact.ca/sred-tax-credits-gaming-companies.

Benner, Chris. 2003. "Computers in the Wild: Guilds and Next-Generation Unionism in the Information Revolution." *International Review of Social History* 48, no. 11: 181–204. https://doi.org/10.1017/S0020859003001317.

Bernstein, Stéphanie. 2010. "Travail et citoyenneté: Redéfinir les communautés, éliminer les frontières." In *Travail et citoyenneté: Quel avenir?*, edited by Michel Coutu and Gregor Murray, 371–96. Quebec: Presses de l'Université Laval.

Blackburn, Gregory. 2018. "Army Men: Military Masculinity in *Call of Duty*." In *Masculinities in Play*, edited by Nicholas Taylor and Gerald Voorhees, 249–62. Cham, Switzerland: Palgrave Macmillan. https://doi.org/10.1007/978-3-319-90581-5_14.

Blagoev, Blagoy, and Georg Schreyögg. 2017. "Locked-In Working Time Regimes: Exploring Barriers to Change in a Management Consulting Firm." *Academy of Management Proceedings*, no. 1. https://doi.org/10.5465/ambpp.2015.17160 abstract.

Blagoev, Blagoy, Sara Louise Muhr, Renate Ortlieb, and Georg Schreyögg. 2018. "Organizational Working Time Regimes: Drivers, Consequences and Attempts to Change Patterns of Excessive Working Hours." *German Journal of Human Resource Management* 32, nos. 3–4: 155–67. https://doi.org/10.1177/2397002218791408.

Blain, Robert. 2020. "HR Director Quits amid Sex Scandal at Ubisoft." *Human Resources Online*, July 17. https://www.humanresourcesonline.net/hr-director-quits-amid-sex-scandal-at-ubisoft.

Blake, Vikki. 2019. "Writers Guild of America (WGA) Drops Video Game Writing Category for 2020 Awards." *MCV/Develop*, October 8. https://www.mcvuk.com/business-news/the-writers-guild-of-america-wga-drops-video-game-writing-category-for-2020-awards.

Blodgett, Bridget M. 2020. "Media in the Post #GamerGate Era: Coverage of Reactionary Fan Anger and the Terrorism of the Privileged." *Television and New Media* 21, no. 2: 184–200. https://doi.org/10.1177/1527476419879918.

Bloom, Peter. 2017. *The Ethics of Neoliberalism: The Business of Making Capitalism Moral*. New York: Routledge.

Bobocel, Ramona, and Leanne Gosse. 2015. "Procedural Justice: A Historical Review and Critical Analysis." In *Oxford Handbook of Justice in the Workplace*, edited by Russell S. Cropanzano and Maureen L. Ambrose, 51–88. Oxford: Oxford University Press.

Bodirsky, Katharina. 2012. "Culture for Competitiveness: Valuing Diversity in EU-Europe and the 'Creative City' of Berlin." *International Journal of Cultural Policy* 18, no. 4: 455–73. https://doi.org/10.1080/10286632.2011.598517.

Boiteau, Lucie, and Alepin Gauthier. 2010. "Le contrat d'emploi: Les clauses de non-concurrence, est-ce légal?" Réseau juridique du Québec. http://www.avocat.qc.ca/affaires/iinconcurrence.htm.

Bosniak, Linda. 2000. "Critical Reflections on Citizenship as a Progressive Aspiration." In *Labour Law in an Era of Globalization: Transformative Practices and Possibilities*, edited by Joanne Conaghan, Richard Michael Fischl, and Karl Klare, 339–49. Oxford: Oxford University Press.

———. 2003. "Citizenship." In *Oxford Handbook of Legal Studies*, edited by Peter Crane and Mark Tushnet, 183–201. Oxford: Oxford University Press.

Boucher, Paul. 2013. "Ontario Interactive Digital Media Tax Credit (OIDMTC)." PowerPoint presentation. Accessed March 25, 2003. https://www.nwoinnovation.ca/upload/documents/bdo-oidmtc-services.pptx.

Braley-Rattai, Alison. 2014. "Harnessing the Possibilities of Minority Unionism in Canada." *Labor Studies Journal* 38, no. 4: 321–40. https://doi.org/10.1177/0160449X14530706.

Bresnen, Mike, Linda Edelman, Sue Newell, Harry Scarbrough, and Jacky Swan. 2003. "Social Practices and the Management of Knowledge in Project Environments." *International Journal of Project Management* 21: 157–66. https://doi.org/10.1016/S0263-7863(02)00090-X.

Britannica Online Encyclopedia. n.d. "Welfare State." https://www.britannica.com/topic/welfare-state.

Briziarelli, Marco. 2016. "Invisible Play and Invisible Game: Video Game Testers or the Unsung Heroes of Knowledge Working." *TripleC* 14, no. 1: 249–59.

Browne, Pierson, and Brian R Schram. 2021. "Intermediating the Everday: Indie Game Development and the Labour of Co-working Spaces." In *Game Production Studies*, edited by Olli Sotamaa and Jan Švelch, 83–100. Amsterdam: Amsterdam University Press. https://library.oapen.org/bitstream/handle/20.500.12657/47043/9789048551736.pdf?sequence=1#page=84.

Brummond, Kari. n.d. "Receiving Tax Credit for Production of Multimedia Titles in Québec." https://quickbooks.intuit.com/ca/resources/pro-accounting/tax-credit-production-multimedia-Québec.

Brunelle, Christian. 2010. "Le droit à la dignité: Un vecteur de la citoyenneté au travail." In *Travail et citoyenneté: Quel avenir?* edited by Michel Coutu and Gregor Murray, 273–306. Quebec: Presses de l'Université Laval.

Bryant, J. Alison, Anna Akerman, and Jordana Drell. 2010. "Diminutive Subjects, Design Strategy, and Driving Sales: Preschoolers and the Nintendo DS." *Game Studies: International Journal of Computer Game Research* 10, no. 1. http://gamestudies.org/1001/articles/bryant_akerman_drell.

Buckle, Pamela, and Janice Thomas. 2003. "Deconstructing Project Management: A Gender Analysis of Project Management Guidelines." *International Journal of Project Management* 21, no. 6: 433–41. https://doi.org/10.1016/S0263-7863(02)00114-X.

Budd, John W. 2004a. "Introduction." In *Employment with a Human Face: Balancing Efficiency, Equity and Voice*, edited by John W. Budd, 1–12. Ithaca: Cornell University Press.

—. 2004b. "Balancing Outcomes Revisited: The Ethics of the Employment Relationship." In *Employment with a Human Face: Balancing Efficiency, Equity and Voice*, edited by John W. Budd, 66–81. Ithaca: Cornell University Press.

—. 2004c. "The Balancing Alternatives: Workplace Governance." In *Employment with a Human Face: Balancing Efficiency, Equity and Voice*, edited by John W. Budd, 82–100. Ithaca: Cornell University Press.

—. 2004d. "The New Deal Industrial Relations System." In *Employment with a Human Face: Balancing Efficiency, Equity and Voice*, edited by John W. Budd, 101–17. Ithaca: Cornell University Press.

Budd, John W., and Alexander J. S. Colvin. 2005. *Balancing Efficiency, Equity, and Voice in Workplace Dispute Resolution Procedures*. Working paper. https://www.researchgate.net/publication/5100577_Balancing_Efficiency_Equity_and_Voice_in_Workplace_Resolution_Procedures.

Bulut, Ergin. 2015. "Glamor Above, Precarity Below: Immaterial Labor in the Video Game Industry." *Critical Studies in Media Communication* 32, no. 3: 193–207. https://doi.org/10.1080/15295036.2015.1047880.

—. 2020a. *A Precarious Game: The Illusion of Dream Jobs in the Video Game Industry*. Ithaca: Cornell University Press.

—. 2020b. "White Masculinity, Creative Desires and Production Ideology in Video Game Development." *Games and Culture* 16, no. 3: 329–41. https://doi.org/10.1177/1555412020939873.

Burawoy, Michael, and Erik Olin Wright. 1990. "Coercion and Consent in Contested Exchange." *Politics and Society* 18, no. 2: 251–66. https://doi.org/10.1177/003232929001800206.

Bureau of Labor Statistics. 2020. "Table 3: Employment Status of the Civilian Noninstitutional Population by Age, Sex, and Race." *Current Population Survey*, quoted in Catalyst website. https://www.catalyst.org/what-we-do.

Burger, Christoph, Dagmar Strohmeier, Nina Spröber, Sheri Bauman, and Ken Rigby. 2015. "How Teachers Respond to School Bullying: An Examination of Self-Reported Intervention Strategy Use, Moderator Effects, and Concurrent Use of Multiple Strategies." *Teaching and Teacher Education* 51: 191–202, https://doi.org/10.1016/j.tate.2015.07.004.

Burgess, Melinda C. R., Steven P. Stermer, and Stephen R. Burgess. 2007. "Sex, Lies and Video Games: The Portrayal of Male and Female Characters on Video Game Covers." *Sex Roles* 57: 419–33. https://doi.org/10.1007/s11199-007-9250-0.

Burke, Ronald J. 2009. "Working to Live or Living to Work: Should Individuals and Organizations Care?" *Journal of Business Ethics* 84: 167–72. https://link.springer.com/article/10.1007/s10551-008-9703-6.

Burke, Ronald J., and Lisa Fiksenbaum. 2009. "Work Motivations, Work Outcomes, and Health: Passion versus Addiction." *Journal of Business Ethics* 84: 257–63. https://link.springer.com/article/10.1007/s10551-008-9697-0.

Burns, Tom, and George MacPherson Stalker. 1961. *Management of Innovation*. London: Tavistock.

Butler, Peter. 2009. "Non-union Employee Representation: Exploring the Riddle of Managerial Strategy." *Industrial Relations Journal* 40, no. 3: 198–214. https://doi.org/10.1111/j.1468-2338.2009.00521.x.

Canada Media Fund (CMF). 2021a. *Annual Report 2020–2021*, Canada Media Fund. https://cmf-fmc.ca/document/annual-report-2020-2021.

———. 2021b. *2021 CMF Virtual Industry Consultations Spark Courage Discussion Paper*, Canada Media Fund. March 11. https://cmf-fmc.ca/document/2021-consultation-discussion-paper.

———. 2021c. *Spark Courage What We Heard: 2021 Consultations Summary Report*, Canada Media Fund, June 17. https://cmf-fmc.ca/document/2021-consultations-summary-report.

———. 2021d. *Spark Courage CMF's 2021 virtual consultations*, Canada Media Fund. https://cmf-fmc.ca/document/2021-consultations-roundtable.

Calvin, Alex. 2020. "Game Workers Unite Says Staff Deserve Greater Security." *PCGamesInsider*, March 23. https://www.pcgamesinsider.biz/news/70753/game-workers-unite-says-staff-deserve-greater-security.

Campbell, Colin. 2019. "How Fortnite's Success Led to Months of Intense Crunch at Epic Games." *Polygon*, April 23. https://www.polygon.com/2019/4/23/18507750/fortnite-work-crunch-epic-games.

Campbell, Iain. 2002a. "Extended Working Hours in Australia." *Labour and Industry* 13, no. 1: 91–110. https://doi.org/10.1080/10301763.2002.10669258.

———. 2002b. "Snatching at the Wind? Unpaid Overtime and Trade Unions in Australia." *International Journal of Employment Studies* 10, no. 2: 109–56. https://search.informit.org/doi/abs/10.3316/informit.297847452775492.

———. 2003. "Puzzles of Unpaid Overtime." In *Flexible Work Arrangements: Conceptualizations and International Experiences*, edited by Isik Urla Zeytinoglu, 25–43. The Hague: Kluwer Law International.

Canada Revenue Agency (CRA). 2019. Government of Canada. Accessed April 2, 2003. https://www.canada.ca/en/revenue-agency/services/tax/businesses/topics/corporations/provincial-territorial-corporation-tax.html.

Cappelli, Peter. 1999. *The New Deal at Work*. Boston: Harvard Business School Press.

Carpenter, Nicole. 2020a. "Paradox Interactive to Sign Collective Bargaining Agreement with 200 Members." *Polygon*, June 3. https://www.polygon.com/2020/6/3/21279427/paradox-interaction-unionizes-collective-bargaining-worker-rights-sweden.

———. 2020b. "These Game Workers Made History by Going on Strike—and Winning." *Polygon*, August 11. https://www.polygon.com/2020/8/11/21363817/lovestruck-voltage-entertainment-writers-strike-video-game-industry-unionization.

———. 2021a. "Call of Duty: Warzone QA Workers Continue Walkout in Protest of Layoffs." *Polygon*, December 6. https://www.polygon.com/22820273/raven-software-layoffs-walk-out-protest-activision.

———. 2021b. "North America Has Its First Video Game Union at Vodeo Games." *Polygon*, December 15. https://www.polygon.com/22834924/vodeo-games-first-video-game-union-north-america-code-cwa.

———. 2022. "Raven Software QA Workers Unionize within Activision Blizzard." *Polygon*, January 21. https://www.polygon.com/22894041/call-of-duty-warzone-raven-software-union-activision-blizzard.

Carr, Diane. 2005. "Contexts, Gaming Pleasures, and Gendered Preferences." *Simulation and Gaming* 36, no. 4: 464–82. https://doi.org/10.1177/1046878105282160.

Carré, Françoise. 2010. "Quelles politiques publiques pour la citoyenneté au travail?" In *Travail et citoyenneté: Quel avenir?*, edited by Michel Coutu and Gregor Murray, 397–420. Quebec: Presses de l'Université Laval.

Carter, Bob, Andy Danford, Debra Howcroft, Helen Richardson, Andrew Smith, and Phil Taylor. 2013. "'Stressed Out of My Box': Employee Experience of Lean Working and Occupational Ill-Health in Clerical Work in the UK Public Sector." *Work, Employment and Society* 27, no. 5: 747–67. https://doi.org/10.1177/0950017012469064.

Cassell, Justine, and Henry Jenkins, eds. 1998. *From Barbie to Mortal Kombat: Gender and Computer Games*. Cambridge: MIT Press.

Castells, Manuel. 2000. *The Rise of the Network Society*, 2nd ed. Oxford: Basil Blackwell.

Caves, Richard E. 2000. *Creative Industries: Contracts between Art and Commerce*. Harvard: Harvard University Press.

Cerrato, Javier, and Eva Cifre. 2018. "Gender Inequality in Household Chores and Work-Family Conflict." *Frontiers in Psychology* 9: 1,330. https://doi.org/10.3389/fpsyg.2018.01330.

Chalk, Andy. 2013. "Brenda Romero Resigns IGDA Post over GDC Party." *Escapist*, March 28. https://v1.escapistmagazine.com/news/view/122967-Brenda-Romero-Resigns-IGDA-Post-Over-GDC-Party-UPDATED.

———. 2022. "Here's Everything That's Happened since Microsoft Acquired Activision Blizzard." *PC Gamer*, January 24. https://www.pcgamer.com/heres-everything-thats-happened-since-microsoft-acquired-activision-blizzard.

Charmaz, K. 2000. "Grounded Theory: Objectivist and Constructivist Methods." In *Handbook of Qualitative Research*, 2nd ed., edited by Norman K. Denzin and Yvonna S. Lincoln, 509–35. Thousand Oaks, California: Sage.

Chasserio, Stéphanie, and Marie-Josée Legault. 2005. "Dans la nouvelle économie, la conciliation entre la vie privée et la vie professionnelle passe par... l'augmentation des heures de travail!" *Recherches sociographiques* 46, no. 1: 119–42. http://r-libre.teluq.ca/174.

———. 2009. "Strategic Human Resources Management Is Irrelevant When It Comes to Highly Skilled Professionals in the Canadian New Economy!" *International Journal of Human Resource Management* 20, no. 5: 1,113–31. http://www.informaworld.com/smpp/title~db=all~content=g911806569.

———. 2010. "Discretionary Power of Project Managers in Knowledge Intensive Firms and Gender Issues." *Revue canadienne des sciences administratives/Canadian Journal of Administrative Sciences* 27, no. 3: 236–48. http://onlinelibrary.wiley.com/doi/10.1002/cjas.147/pdf.

Chebotareva, Veronika. 2019. "Why Ukrainian CG Market Is One of the Driving Forces behind the Success of Games Industry." *Gamasutra*, April 4. https://www.gamedeveloper.com/business/why-ukrainian-cg-market-is-one-of-the-driving-forces-behind-the-success-of-games-industry.

Chess, Shira. 2015. "Youthful White Male Industry Seeks 'Fun' Loving Middle-Aged Women for Video Games—No Strings Attached." In *Routledge Companion to Media and Gender*, edited by Cynthia Carter, Linda Steiner, and Lisa McLaughlin, 168–79. New York: Routledge.

Chicha, Marie-Thérèse. 2006. *A Comparative Analysis of Promoting Pay Equity: Models and Impacts*, working paper 49. Geneva: International Labour Office (ILO). https://www.ilo.org/wcmsp5/groups/public/@ed_norm/@declaration/documents/publication/wcms_decl_wp_27_en.pdf.

Chirinko, Robert S., and Daniel J. Wilson. 2008. "State Investment Tax Incentives: A Zero-Sum Game?" *Journal of Public Economics* 92: 2,362–84. https://doi.org/10.1016/j.jpubeco.2008.07.005.

Christopherson, Susan. 2002. "Project Work in Context: Regulatory Change and the New Geography of Media." *Environment and Planning A* 34, no. 11: 2,003–15. https://doi.org/10.1068/a34182.

———. 2009. "Working in the Creative Economy: Risk, Adaptation, and the Persistence of Exclusionary Networks." In *Creative Labour: Working in the Creative Industries*, edited by Alan McKinlay and Chris Smith, 72–90. Houndmills: Palgrave MacMillan.

Christopherson, Susan, and Danielle van Jaarsveld. 2005. "New Media after the dot.com Bust: The Persistent Influence of Political Institutions on Work in the Cultural Industries." *International Journal of Cultural Policy* 11, no. 1: 77–94. https://doi.org/10.1080/10286630500067846.

Chu, Haidee. 2020. "2019 Was the Year Tech Workers Organized." *Mashable*, January 20. https://portside.org/2020-01-20/2019-was-year-tech-workers-organized.

Chung, Sun Wook, and Hyunji Kwon. 2020. "Tackling the Crunch Mode: The Rise of an Enterprise Union in South Korea's Game Industry." *Employee Relations: The International Journal* 42, no. 6: 1,327–52. https://doi.org/10.1108/ER-10-2019-0382.

Cicmil, Svetlana, and Damian Hodgson. 2006. "Introduction." In *Making Projects Critical*, edited by Damian Hodgson and Svetlana Cicmil, 1–25. London: Palgrave.

Ciminelli, Gabriele, Cyrille Schwellnus, and Balazs Stadler. 2021. "Sticky Floors or Glass Ceilings? The Role of Human Capital, Working Time Flexibility and

Discrimination in the Gender Wage Gap." *OECD Economics Department Working Papers*, no. 1668. https://dx.doi.org/10.1787/02ef3235-en.

Clement, J. 2019. "Distribution of Game Developers Worldwide as of March 2019, by Region." *Statista*. https://www.statista.com/statistics/453785/game-developer-region-distribution-worldwide.

Cohen, Nicole S., and Greig de Peuter. 2020. *New Media Unions: Organizing Digital Journalists*. London: Routledge.

Cohendet, Patrick, and Laurent Simon. 2007. "Playing across the Playground: Paradoxes of Knowledge Creation in the Videogame Firm." *Journal of Organizational Behavior* 28, no. 5: 587–605. https://doi.org/10.1002/job.460.

Coleman-Lochner, Lauren, and Eliza Ronalds-Hannon. 2021. "PetSmart Investors Prodded by Labor Group over Worker Safety." *Bloomberg*, September 30. https://www.bloomberg.com/news/articles/2021-09-30/worker-group-seeks-investor-ears-over-petsmart-safety-concerns.

Collins, Hugh. 2000. "Is There a Third Way in Labour Law?" In *Labour Law in an Era of Globalization: Transformative Practices and Possibilities*, edited by Joanne Conaghan, Richard Michael Fischl, and Karl Klare, 449–70. Oxford: Oxford University Press.

Colquitt, Jason A., Donald E. Conlon, Michael J. Wesson, Christopher O. L. H. Porter, and K. Yee Ng. 2001. "Justice at the Millennium: A Meta-Analytic Review of 25 Years of Organizational Justice Research." *Journal of Applied Psychology* 86, no. 3: 425–45. https://doi.org/10.1037/0021-9010.86.3.425.

Colquitt, Jason A., Jerald Greenberg, and Cindy P. Zapata-Phelan. 2005. "What Is Organizational Justice?: A Historical Overview." In *Handbook of Organizational Justice*, edited by Jerald Greenberg and Jason A. Colquitt, 3–58. Mahwah, New Jersey: Lawrence Erlbaum Associates.

Colwill, Tim. 2021. "Game Workers Unite Australia." Presented at Labour Unions and the Future of Work in the Game Industry, online symposium, April 28. https://stream.liv.ac.uk/66ckjczj.

Conaghan, Joanne, Richard Michael Fischl, and Karl Klare, eds. 2000. *Labour Law in an Era of Globalization: Transformative Practices and Possibilities*. Oxford: Oxford University Press.

Condon, Mary, and Lisa Philipps. 2004. *Connecting Economy, Gender and Citizenship*. Ottawa: Law Commission of Canada.

Conlon, Donald E., Christopher J. Meyer, and Jaclyn M. Nowakowsky. 2005. "How Does Organizational Justice Affect Performance, Withdrawal and Counterproductive Behavior?" In *Handbook of Organizational Justice*, edited by Jerald Greenberg and Jason A. Colquitt, 301–28. Mahwah, New Jersey: Lawrence Erlbaum Associates.

Consalvo, Mia. 2008. "Crunched by Passion: Women Game Developers and Workplace Challenges." In *Beyond Barbie and Mortal Kombat: New Perspectives on Gender and Gaming*, edited by Yasmin B. Kafai, Carrie Heeter, Jill Denner, and Jennifer Y. Sun, 177–92. Cambridge: MIT Press.

Consalvo, Mia, and Christopher A. Paul. 2019. *Real Games: What's Legitimate and What's Not in Contemporary Videogames*. Cambridge: MIT Press.

Conway, Steven, and Jennifer deWinter. 2016. *Video Game Policy: Production, Distribution, and Consumption*. London: Routledge Press.

Cooper, M. 2008. "The Inequality of Security: Winners and Losers in the Risk Society." *Human Relations* 6, no. 9: 1,229–58. https://doi.org/10.1177/0018726708094911.

Costas, Jana, Blagoy V. Blagoev, and Dan Kärreman. 2016. "The Arena of the Professional Body: Sport, Autonomy and Ambition in Professional Service Firms." *Scandinavian Journal of Management* 32, no. 1: 10–19. https://doi.org/10.1016/j.scaman.2015.10.003.

Côté, Amanda C., and Brandon C. Harris. 2020. "'Weekends Became Something Other People Did': Understanding and Intervening in the Habitus of Videogame Crunch." *Convergence: International Journal of Research into New Media Technologies* 27, no. 1: 161–76. https://doi.org/10.1177/1354856520913865.

Coulter, Martin, and Hugh Langley. 2022. "Google's Union Kickstarted a Landmark Year for Silicon Valley Activism. We Asked Insiders about the Highs, Lows and What to Expect for Tech Organizing in 2022." *Business Insider*, January 4. https://www.businessinsider.com/google-union-alphabet-workers-tech-activism-labor-in-2021-2022-1.

Courpasson, David. 2000. *L'action contrainte: Organisations libérales et domination*. Paris: PUF.

Coutu, Michel. 2004. "Industrial Citizenship, Human Rights and the Transformation of Labour Law: A Critical Assessment of Harry Arthurs' Legalization Thesis." *Canadian Journal of Law and Society/Revue canadienne Droit et Société* 19, no. 2: 73–92. https://doi.org/10.1017/S0829320100008140.

Coutu, Michel, and Gregor Murray, eds. 2010a. *Travail et citoyenneté: Quel avenir?* Quebec: Presses de l'Université Laval.

———. 2010b. "Travail et citoyenneté: Rétrospective et perspectives." In *Travail et citoyenneté: Quel avenir?*, edited by Michel Coutu and Gregor Murray, 5–39. Quebec: Presses de l'Université Laval.

Cropanzano, Russell S., and Maureen L. Ambrose. 2015a. "Organizational Justice: Where We Have Been and Where We Are Going." In *Oxford Handbook of Justice in the Workplace*, edited by Russell S. Cropanzano and Maureen L. Ambrose, 3–14. Oxford: Oxford University Press.

Cropanzano, Russell S., and Maureen L. Ambrose, eds. 2015b. *Oxford Handbook of Justice in the Workplace*. Oxford: Oxford University Press.

Cross, Katherine. 2018. "What Will Be Left of the People Who Make Our Games? Our Games Are Getting Bigger, but the Cost Is Way Too High." *Polygon*, October 17. https://www.polygon.com/2018/10/17/17986562/game-development-crunch-red-dead-redemption-2-rockstar.

Crotty, James R. 2005. "The Neoliberal Paradox: The Impact of Destructive Product Market Competition and 'Modern' Financial Markets on Nonfinancial Corporate Performance in the Neoliberal Era." In *Financialization and the World Economy*, edited by Gerald A. Epstein, 77–110. Northampton, UK: Edward Elgar Publishing.

Crouch, Colin. 1998. "The Globalized Economy: An End to the Age of Industrial Citizenship?" In *Advancing Theory in Labor Law and Industrial Relations in a Global Context*, edited by Ton Wilthagen, 151–64. Amsterdam: North-Holland. http://hdl.handle.net/11858/00-001M-0000-0012-58FE-7.

———. 2011. *The Strange Non-Death of Neo-Liberalism*. Cambridge: Polity Press.

Curran, Ian. 2021. "Ireland's Digital Game Workers Say New Industry Tax Break Should Be Tied to 'Quality' Pay and Conditions." *Journal*, May 14. https://www.thejournal.ie/game-industry-tax-credit-5436230-May2021.

D'Amours, Martine. 2009. *Les travailleurs indépendants face au risqué: Vulnérables, inégaux et responsabilisés*. Rapport de recherche, Département des relations industrielles, Université Laval. http://www.cms.fss.ulaval.ca/upload/rlt/fichiers/protectionsocialetirapportcomplet.pdf.

D'Amours, Martine, and Marie-Josée Legault. 2013. "Highly Skilled Workers and Employment Risks: Role of Institutions." *Labour Studies Journal* 38, no. 2: 89–109. https://doi.org/10.1177/0160449X13495920.

D'Anastasio, Cecilia. 2018. "Inside the Culture of Sexism at Riot Games." *Kotaku*, August 7. https://kotaku.com/inside-the-culture-of-sexism-at-riot-games-1828165483

—. 2021a. "The Activision Harassment Suit Feels Painfully Familiar." *Wired*, July 7. https://www.wired.com/story/activision-blizzard-harassment-complaint.

—. 2021b. "Why 2021 Was the Biggest Year for the Labor Movement in Games." *Wired*, December 28. https://www.wired.com/story/2021-biggest-year-labor-movement-video-games.

Daneva, Maya. 2014. "How Practitioners Approach Gameplay Requirements?: An Exploration into the Context of Massive Multiplayer Online Role-Playing Game." In *2014 IEEE 22nd international requirements engineering conference, RE 2014-Proceedings*: 3–12. https://doi.org/10.1109/RE.2014.6912242.

D'Antona, Massimo. 2000. "Labour Law at the Century's End: An Identity Crisis?" In *Labour Law in an Era of Globalization: Transformative Practices and Possibilities*, edited by Joanne Conaghan, Richard Michael Fischl, and Karl Klare, 31–49. Oxford: Oxford University Press.

Davenport, Noa Z., Ruth Distler Schwartz, and Gail Pursell Elliott. 2005. *Mobbing, Emotional Abuse in the American Workplace*, 3rd ed.. Ames, Iowa: Civil Society Publishing.

Daviault, Christine, and Gareth Schott. 2015. "Looking beyond Representation: Situating the Significance of Gender Portrayal within Gameplay." In *Routledge Companion to Media and Gender*, edited by Cynthia Carter, Linda Steiner, and Lisa McLaughlin, 440–50. New York: Routledge.

Deakin, Simon. 2000. "The Many Futures of the Contract of Employment." In *Labour Law in an Era of Globalization: Transformative Practices and Possibilities*, edited by Joanne Conaghan, Richard Michael Fischl, and Karl Klare, 177–98. Oxford: Oxford University Press.

Dealessandri, Marie. 2020. "Toxic Culture at Ubisoft Connected to Dysfunction in HR Department." *Gamesindustry.biz*, July 14. https://www.gamesindustry.biz/articles/2020-07-14-toxic-culture-at-ubisoft-connected-to-dysfunction-in-hr-department.

—. 2021. "Toxic Culture at Ubisoft Connected to Dysfunction in HR Department." *Gamesindustry.biz*, February 14. https://www.gamesindustry.biz/articles/2021-01-29-riot-games-seeks-arbitration-in-gender-discrimination-lawsuit.

Dean, Sam. 2019. "Riot Games Will Pay $10 Million to Settle Gender Discrimination Suit." *Los Angeles Times*, December 2.

—. 2020. "Major Union Launches Campaign to Organize Video Game and Tech Workers." *Los Angeles Times*, January 7.

Deeming, Christopher. 2017. "The Lost and the New 'Liberal World' of Welfare Capitalism: A Critical Assessment of Gøsta Esping-Andersen's *The Three Worlds of Welfare Capitalism* a Quarter Century Later." *Social Policy and Society* 16, no. 3: 405–22. https://doi.org/10.1017/S1474746415000676.

Dejours, Christophe. 2000. *De la psychopathologie à la psychodynamique du travail*, 3rd ed. Paris: Bayard.

Dembe, Allard E. 2009. "Ethical Issues Relating to the Health Effects of Long Working Hours." *Journal of Business Ethics* 84: 195–208. https://link.springer.com/article/10.1007/s10551-008-9700-9.

de Peuter, Greig. 2011. "Creative Economy and Labor Precarity: A Contested Convergence." *Journal of Communication Inquiry* 35, no. 4: 417–25. https://doi.org/10.1177/0196859911416362.

—. 2012. "Level Up: Video Game Production in Canada." In *Cultural Industries.ca: Making Sense of Canadian Media in the Digital Age*, edited by Ira Wagman and Peter Urquhart, 78–94. Toronto: Lorimer.

—. 2020. "Organizing Dark Matter: W.A.G.E. as Alternative Worker Organization." *Cultural Workers Organize*, April 2. https://culturalworkersorganize.org/organizing-dark-matter.

de Peuter, Greig, and Nick Dyer-Witheford. 2005. "A Playful Multitude?: Mobilising and Counter-Mobilising Immaterial Game Labour." *Fibreculture Journal*, 5. http://five.fibreculturejournal.org/fcj-024-a-playful-multitude-mobilising-and-counter-mobilising-immaterial-game-labour.

Derks, Belle, Naomi Ellemers, Colette van Laar, and Kim de Groot. 2011. "Do Sexist Organizational Cultures Create the Queen Bee?" *British Journal of Social Psychology* 50, 519–35. https://core.ac.uk/download/pdf/34626612.pdf.

Deuze, Mark. 2007a. "Game Design and Development." In *Media Work*, edited by Mark Deuze, 201–32. Cambridge: Polity Press.

—. 2007b. *Media Work*. Cambridge: Polity Press.

Deuze, Mark, Martin Chase Bowen, and Christian Allen. 2007. "The Professional Identity of Gameworkers." *Convergence: The International Journal of Research into New Media Technologies* 13, no. 4: 335–53. https://doi.org/10.1177/1354856507081947.

Division of Labor Standards Enforcement. 2015. *History of Rate of Pay for Exemption of Computer Software Employee (California Labor Code Section 515.5, no. a) (3))*. https://www.dir.ca.gov/dlse/LC515-5.pdf.

Dobbins, Tony, and Tony Dundon. 2014. "Non-Union Employee Representation." In *Handbook of Research on Employee Voice*, edited by Adrian Wilkinson, Jimmy Donaghey, Tony Dundon, and Richard Freeman, 342–62. Cheltenham, UK: Edward Elgar Publishing.

Donaghey, Jimmy, Niall Cullinane, Tony Dundon, and Adrian Wilkinson. 2011. "Reconceptualising Employee Silence: Problems and Prognosis." *Work, Employment and Society* 25, no. 1: 51–67. https://doi.org/10.1177/0950017010389239.

Dovey, Jon, and Hellen W. Kennedy. 2006. *Games Cultures: Computer Games as New Media*. Berkshire: Open University Press.

Downs, Edward, and Stacy L. Smith. 2010. "Keeping Abreast of Hypersexuality: A Videogame Character Content Analysis." *Sex Roles* 62, nos. 11–12: 721–33. https://doi.org/10.1007/s11199-009-9637-1.

Dreyer, Biance, Greig de Peuter, Marisol Sandoval, and Aleksandra Szaflarska. 2020. "The Co-operative Alternative and the Creative Industries: A Technical Report on a Survey of Co-operatives in the Cultural and Technology Sectors in Canada, the United Kingdom and the United States." *Cultural Workers Organize*. https://culturalworkersorganize.org/wp-content/uploads/2020/12/The-Cooperative-Alternative-Technical-Report-Web.pdf.

Dryden, Joel. 2019. "Alberta's Video Game Industry Assess Future after Tax Credit Axed." *CBC News*, October 31. https://www.cbc.ca/news/canada/calgary/gaming-keith-warner-new-world-interactive-reboot-develop-1.5343885.

Dubois, Louis-Etienne, and Johanna Weststar. 2021. "Games-as-a-Service: Conflicted Identities on the New Front Line of Video Game Development." *New Media and Society* 24, no. 10: 2,332–53. https://doi.org/10.1177/1461444821995815.

DuGay, Paul. 2005. "The Values of Bureaucracy: An Introduction." In *The Values of Bureaucracy*, edited by Paul DuGay, 1–13. Oxford: Oxford University Press.

Dumenil, Gerard, and Dominique Levy. 2005. "Costs and Benefits of Neoliberalism: A Class Analysis." In *Financialization and the World Economy*, edited by Gerald A. Epstein, 17–45. London: Edward Elgar Publishing.

Dunlop, Janet C. 2007. "The U.S. Video Game Industry: Analyzing Representation of Gender and Race." *International Journal of Technology and Human Interaction* 3, no. 2: 96–109. https://doi.org/10.4018/jthi.2007040106.

Durand, Cedric. 2017. *Fictitious Capital: How Finance Is Appropriating Our Future*. New York: Verso.

Duruflé, Gilles. 2009. *L'économie canadienne et le capital de risqué: L'importance du capital de risque pour l'économie canadienne*, Association canadienne du capital de risque et d'investissement/Canada's Venture Capital and private equity Association (ACCR-CVCA). http://fr.ebdata.com/wp-content/uploads/2012/04/CVCA_Impact_Study_FRENCH_March_2009.pdf.

Dyer-Witheford, Nick. 1999. "The Work in Digital Play: Video Gaming's Transnational and Gendered Division of Labor." *Journal of International Communication* 5, no. 1: 69–93. https://doi.org/10.1080/13216597.1999.9751883.

Dyer-Witheford, Nick, and Greig de Peuter. 2006. "'EA Spouse' and the Crisis of Video Game Labour: Enjoyment, Exclusion, Exploitation, Exodus." *Canadian Journal of Communication* 31, no. 3: 599–617. https://doi.org/10.22230/cjc.2006v31n3a1771.

—. 2009. *Games of Empire: Global Capitalism and Video Games*. Minneapolis: University of Minnesota Press.

Dyer-Witheford, Nick, and Zena Sharman. 2005. "The Political Economy of Canada's Video and Computer Game Industry." *Canadian Journal of Communication* 30: 187–210.

ETUI. n.d. National Industrial Relations. Webpage of the European Trade Union Institute (ETUI). https://www.worker-participation.eu/National-Industrial-Relations.

Edmiston, Daniel, Ruth Patrick, and Kayleigh Garthwaite. 2017. "Introduction: Austerity, Welfare and Social Citizenship." *Social Policy and Society* 16, no. 2: 253–59.

Eidelson, Josh. 2013. "Guest Workers as Bellwether." *Dissent* (spring). https://www.dissentmagazine.org/article/guest-workers-as-bellwether.

Ehrhardt, Michelle. 2018. "IGDA, Union-Busting and GDC 2018." *Unwinnable Monthly*, March 22. https://unwinnable.com/2018/03/22/igda-union-busting-and-gdc-2018.

Ekstedt, Eskil, Rolf A. Lundin, Anders Soderholm, and Hans Wirdenius. 1999. *Neo-Industrial Organising: Renewal by Action and Knowledge in a Project-intensive Economy*. London: Routledge.

Employment Standards Act. 2000. Ontario Regulation 285/01, s. 8, no. 1). Exemptions, Special Rules and Establishment of Minimum Wage. Government of Ontario. Accessed March 15, 2021. https://www.ontario.ca/laws/regulation/010285#BK11.

Engström, Henrik. 2020. *Game Development Research*. Skövde, Sweden: University of Skövde.

Entertainment Software Association of Canada (ESAC). 2013. *Canada's Video Game Industry in 2013: Final Report*. https://policycommons.net/artifacts/1972317/canadas-video-game-industry-in-2013/2724082.

—. 2017. "Essential Facts about the Canadian Video Game Industry." http://theesa.ca/wp-content/uploads/2017/10/ESAC2017_Booklet_13_Digital.pdf.

Esping-Andersen, Gosta. 1999. *The Social Foundations of Postindustrial Economies*. Oxford: Oxford University Press.

Eurofound. 2016. *Working Time Developments in the 21st Century: Work Duration and Its Regulation in the EU*. Luxembourg: Publications Office of the European Union. https://www.eurofound.europa.eu/sites/default/files/ef_publication/field_ef_document/ef1573en.pdf.

—. 2018. *Measuring Varieties of Industrial Relations in Europe: A Quantitative Analysis*. Luxembourg: Publications Office of the European Union. https://www.eurofound.europa.eu/sites/default/files/ef_publication/field_ef_document/ef18033en.pdf.

Everingham, Christine. 2002. "Engendered Time: Gender Equity and Discourses of Workplace Flexibility." *Time and Society* 11, no. 2/3: 335–51. https://doi.org/10.1177/0961463X02011002009.

Fair Play Alliance. 2020. "Disruption and Harms in Online Gaming Framework." Fair Play Alliance and ADL Center for Technology and Society, December. https://fairplayalliance.org/framework.

Farokhmanesh, Megan. 2021. "Activision Blizzard Employees Say HR Department Failed Them." *Axios*, August 3. https://www.axios.com/activision-blizzard-harassment-lawsuit-hr-da4f678a-510c-4975-9d64-f5d744aa5c02.html.

Farrell, Dan. 1983. "Exit, Voice, Loyalty, and Neglect as Responses to Job Dissatisfaction: A Multidimensional Scaling Study." *Academy of Management Journal* 26, no. 4: 596–607. https://www.jstor.org/stable/255909.

Favereau, Olivier. 2016. "L'impact de la financiarisation de l'économie sur les entreprises et plus particulièrement sur les relations de travail." Bureau International du travail. http://researchgate.net/publication/310801543.

Feldman, Daniel C. 2003. "The Impacts of Layoffs on Family, Friendship and Community Networks." In *Resizing the Organization: Managing Layoffs, Divestitures and Closings*, edited by Kenneth P. DeMeuse and Mitchell Lee Marks, 188–219. Professional Practice Series, Society for Industrial and Organizational Psychology. San Francisco: Jossey-Bass.

Ferrant, Gaëlle, Luca Maria Pesando, and Keiko Nowacka. 2014. *Unpaid Care Work: The Missing Link in the Analysis of Gender Gaps in Labour Outcomes*. OECD Development Centre. https://www.oecd.org/dev/development-gender/Unpaid_care_work.pdf.

Ferraras, Isabelle. 2017. *Firms as Political Entities: Saving Democracy through Economic Bicameralism*, New York: Cambridge University Press.

Ferraras, Isabelle, Julie Battilana, and Dominique Méda. 2022. *Democratize Work: The Case for Reorganizing the Economy*. Chicago: University of Chicago Press. https://democratizingwork.org.

Finances Québec. 2003. *Additional Information on the Fiscal Measures*. Accessed June 2023. http://www.budget.finances.gouv.qc.ca/budget/2003-2004a/en/pdf/AdditionalInfoMeasures.pdf.

Fine, Cordelia. 2010. *Delusion of Gender: How Our Minds, Society and Neurosexism Create Difference*. New York: Norton and Company.

Fiorito, Jack, and Daniel G. Gallagher. 2013. "Distrust of Employers, Collectivism, and Union Efficacy." *International Journal of E-Politics* 4, no. 4: 13–26. https://doi.org/10.4018/ijep.2013100102.

Fisher, Stephanie, and Alison Harvey. 2013. "Intervention for Inclusivity: Gender Politics and Indie Game Development." *Loading...: Journal of the Canadian Game Studies Association* 7, no. 11: 25–40. https://loading.journals.public knowledgeproject.org/loading/index.php/loading/article/view/118.

Flew, Terry, and Richard Smith. 2011. "Games: Technology, Industry, Culture." In *New Media: An Introduction*, edited by Terry Flew and Sal Humphreys, 122–40. Melbourne: Oxford University Press.

Flores, Andrew R., Jody L. Herman, Gary J. Gates, and Taylor N. T. Brown. 2016. *How Many Adults Identify as Transgender in the United States?* UCLA Williams Institute and School of Law. https://williamsinstitute.law.ucla.edu/publications/trans-adults-united-states.

Florida, Richard. 2002. *The Rise of the Creative Class*. New York: Basic Books.

Fournier, Valerie, and Chris Grey. 2000. "At the Critical Moment: Conditions and Prospects for Critical Management Studies." *Human Relations* 53, no. 1: 7–32. https://doi.org/10.1177/0018726700531002.

Francis, Bryant. 2022a. "Keywords Studios Contractors at BioWare Have Successfully Unionized." *Game Developer*, June 6. https://www.gamedeveloper.com/culture/keywords-studios-contractors-at-bioware-have-successfully-unionized.

———. 2022b. "Raven Software QA's Strike Has Ended." *Game Developer*, January 24. https://www.gamedeveloper.com/culture/raven-software-qa-s-strike-has-ended.

Frank, Allegra. 2018. "Pro-union Voices Speak Out at Heated GDC Roundtable. An Open Dialogue Turns Contentious." *Polygon*, March 22. https://www.polygon.com/2018/3/22/17149822/gdc-2018-igda-roundtable-game-industry-union.

Frege, Carola M., and John Kelly. 2004. *Varieties of Unionism: Strategies for Union Revitalization in a Globalizing Economy*. Oxford: Oxford University Press.

Fullerton, Tracy, Janine Fron, Celia Pearce, and Jacki Morie. 2008. "Getting Girls into the Game: Towards a 'Virtuous Cycle.'" In *Beyond Barbie and Mortal Kombat: New Perspectives on Gender and Gaming*, edited by Yasmin B. Kafai, Carrie Heeter, Jill Denner, and Jennifer Y. Sun, 161–76. Cambridge: MIT Press. http://www.lcc.gatech.edu/~cpearce3/PearcePubs/LudicaBBMK.pdf.

Fudge, Judy. 2005. "After Industrial Citizenship: Market Citizenship or Citizenship at Work?" *Relations industrielles/Industrial Relations* 60, no. 4: 631–56. https://doi.org/10.7202/012338ar.

———. 2010. "Au-delà de la citoyenneté industrielle: La citoyenneté marchande ou du travail?" In *Travail et citoyenneté: Quel avenir?*, edited by Michel Coutu and Gregor Murray, 421–51. Quebec: Presses de l'Université Laval.

Fullerton, Tracy, Janine Fron, Celia Pearce, and Jacki Morie. 2008. "Getting Girls into the Game: Towards a 'Virtuous Cycle.'" In *Beyond Barbie and Mortal Kombat: New Perspectives on Gender and Gaming*, edited by Yasmin B. Kafai, Carrie Heeter, Jill Denner, and Jennifer Y. Sun, 161–76. Cambridge: MIT Press. http://www.lcc.gatech.edu/~cpearce3/PearcePubs/LudicaBBMK.pdf.

Game Developers Conference (GDC). 2020. "State of the Game Industry 2020," Game Developers Conference, InformaTech. https://reg.gdconf.com/gdc-state-of-game-industry-2020.

———. 2021. "State of the Game Industry 2021," Game Developers Conference, InformaTech. https://reg.gdconf.com/state-of-game-industry-2021.

———. 2022. "State of the Game Industry 2022," Game Developers Conference, InformaTech. https://reg.gdconf.com/state-of-game-industry-2022?BLG_GDC&_mc=blog_x_gdcsfr_un_x_gdcsf_x_x-13.

GWU Australia. 2021. "GWU Australia Welcomes 30% Tax Rebate News." Press release, Game Workers Unite Australia, May 6. https://www.gameworkers.com.au/statement-on-digital-games-tax-offset.

Gach, Ethan. 2021. "Ubisoft CEO and Others Blamed for 'Institutional Harassment.'" *Kotaku*, July 16. https://kotaku.com/ubisoft-ceo-and-others-blamed-for-institutional-harassm-1847306435.

Gaume, Nicolas. 2006. "Nicolas Gaume's Views on the Video Games Sector." *European Management Journal* 24, no. 4: 299–309.

Gemünden, Hans G., Patrick Lehner, and Alexander Kock. 2018. "The Project-Oriented Organization and Its Contribution to Innovation." *International Journal of Project Management* 36: 147–60. https://doi.org/10.1016/j.ijproman.2017.07.009.

Ghaffary, Shirin. 2019. "Tech Workers Have Been Reluctant to Unionize, but Google Contractors Just Changed That." *Vox*, September 25. https://portside.org/2019-09-25/tech-workers-have-been-reluctant-unionize-google-contractors-just-changed.

Ghilarducci, Teresa, and Hamilton E. James. 2018. *Rescuing Retirement: A Plan to Guarantee Retirement Security for All Americans*. Chichester, New York: Columbia University Press.

Ghilarducci, Teresa, Michael Papadopoulos, and Anthony Webb. 2018. *The Impact of Guaranteed Retirement Accounts on the Retirement Crisis*. Schwartz Centre for Economic Policy Analysis and Department of Economics. The New School for Social Research Policy Note Series. https://www.economicpolicyresearch.org/images/GRA_Impact_Policy_Note.pdf.

Gibb, Sheree J., David M. Fergusson, and L. John Horwood. 2012. "Working Hours and Alcohol Problems in Early Adulthood." *Addiction* 107, no. 1: 81–88. https://doi.org/10.1111/j.1360-0443.2011.03543.x.

Giddens, Anthony. 1990. *The Consequences of Modernity*. Stanford: Stanford University Press.

———. 1991. *Modernity and Self-Identity: Self and Society in the Late Modern Age*. Stanford: Stanford University Press.

Gill, Rosalind. 2002. "Cool, Creative and Egalitarian?: Exploring Gender in Project-Based New Media Work in Europe." *Information, Communication and Society* 5, no. 1: 70–89. https://doi.org/10.1080/13691180110117668.

———. 2007. *Technobohemians or the New Cybertariat?: New Media Work in Amsterdam a Decade after the Web*. Network Notebooks. Amsterdam: Institute of Network Cultures. https://www.networkcultures.org/_uploads/17.pdf.

Gill, Rosalind, and Andy C. Pratt. 2008. "In the Social Factory?: Immaterial Labour, Precariousness and Cultural Work." *Theory, Culture and Society* 25, nos. 7–8: 1–30. https://journals.sagepub.com/doi/abs/10.1177/0263276408097794.

Glasner, Eli. 2019. "'I Just Broke Down Crying': Canadian Video Game Creators Face Gruelling 'Crunch' Hours." *CBC News*, April 26. https://www.cbc.ca/news/entertainment/burnout-crunch-canada-1.5109599.

———. 2020. "Pushback against Sexual Harassment in the Gaming Industry Grows with High-Profile Resignations." *CBC News*, July 22. https://www.cbc.ca/news/entertainment/gaming-ubisoft-metoo-harassment-1.5657963.

Gollan, Paul J., Bruce E. Kaufman, Daphne Taras, and Adrian Wilkinson, eds. 2014. *Voice and Involvement at Work: Experience with Non-union Representation.* New York: Routledge.

Gompers, Paul, and Josh Lerner. 2001. "The Venture Capital Revolution." *Journal of Economic Perspectives* 15, no. 2: 145–68. https://www.aeaweb.org/articles?id =10.1257/jep.15.2.145.

—. 2004. *The Venture Capital Cycle*, 2nd ed. Cambridge: MIT Press.

Gonzalez-Mulé, Erik, and Bethany Cockburn. 2017. "Worked to Death: The Relationships of Job Demands and Job Control with Mortality." *Personnel Psychology* 70: 73–112. https://doi.org/10.1111/peps.12206.

Goodgame Studios. 2015. "Statement on Layoffs and Works Council." Goodgame Studios, December 18. https://www.goodgamestudios.com/blog/statement-on -layoffs/2015/12/18.

Gourdin, Adam. 2005. *Game Developers Demographics: An Exploration of Workforce Diversity.* International Game Developers Association (IGDA). https://gamesindustryskills.files.wordpress.com/2009/11/igda_developer demographics_oct05.pdf.

Government of British Columbia. n.d. "Interactive Digital Media Tax Credit." https://www2.gov.bc.ca/gov/content/taxes/income-taxes/corporate/credits/ interactive-digital-media.

Government of Canada. 2021. "Guidelines on the Eligibility of Work for Scientific Research and Experimental Development (SR&ED) Tax Incentives." October 6. https://www.canada.ca/en/revenue-agency/services/scientific-research -experimental-development-tax-incentive-program/policies-procedures -guidelines/guidelines-eligibility-work-sred-tax-incentives.html.

Government of Prince Edward Island. n.d. "Apply for a Labour Rebate." https://www.princeedwardisland.ca/en/service/apply-labour-rebate.

Graber, Christopher Beat, and Mira Burri-Nenova, eds. 2010. *Governance of Digital Game Environments and Cultural Diversity: Transdisciplinary Enquiries.* Cheltenham, UK: Edward Elgar Publishing.

Graft, Kris. 2021. "*Gamasutra* Is Becoming *Game Developer.*" *Game Developer*, August 23. https://www.gamedeveloper.com/culture/gamasutra-is-becoming -game-developer.

Gray, Kishonna L., Gerald Voorhees, and Emma Vossen. 2018. *Feminism in Play.* London: Palgrave Macmillan.

Grayson, Nathan, and Cecilia D'Anastasio. 2019. "Over 150 Riot Employees Walk Out to Protect Forced Arbitration and Sexist Culture." *Kotaku*, May 6. https://kotaku.com/over-150-riot-employees-walk-out-to-protest-forced-arbi -1834566198.

Greenberg, Jerald, and Jason A. Colquitt. 2005. *Handbook of Organizational Justice.* Mahwah, New Jersey: Lawrence Erlbaum Associates.

Greer, Ian, Zinovijus Ciupijus, and Nathan Lillie. 2013. "The European Migrant Workers Union and the Barriers to Transnational Industrial Citizenship." *European Journal of Industrial Relations* 19, no. 1: 5–20. https://doi.org/10.1177/ 0959680112474748.

Grugulis, Irena, and Steven Vincent. 2009. "Whose Skill Is It Anyway?: 'Soft' Skills and Polarization." *Work, Employment and Society* 23, no. 4: 597–615. https://doi.org/10.1177/0950017009344862.

Grunberg, Leon, Richard Anderson-Connolly, and Edward S. Greenberg. 2000. "Surviving Layoffs: The Effects on Organizational Commitment and Job

Performance." *Work and Occupations* 27, no. 1: 7–31. https://doi.org/10.1177/0730888400027001002.

Guida, Victoria. 2019. "Income Inequality Is Highest on Record, Boosting Democrats' Message." *Politico*, September 26. http://politico.com/news/2019/09/26/income-inequality-is-highest-on-record-boosting-democrats-message-003706.

Hagen, Ulf. 2012. *Lodestars for Player Experience: Ideation in Videogame Design*. Stockholm: Stockholm University. https://www.diva-portal.org/smash/record.jsf?pid=diva2%3A530460&dswid=7713.

Haines, Lizzie. 2004. "Why Are There So Few Women in Games?" Research for Media Training North West. https://fr.slideshare.net/IGDA_London/why-are-there-so-few-women-in-games.

Hammar, Emil. 2022. "International Solidarity between Game Workers in the Global North and Global South: Reflections on the Challenges Posed by Labor Aristocracy." *Gamenvironments* 17: 141–82. https://journals.suub.uni-bremen.de/index.php/gamevironments/article/view/195/174.

Handman, Daniel H. 2005. "Electronic Arts Settles a Class Action Overtime Lawsuit for $15.6 Million: Red Flags and Practical Lessons for the Entertainment Software Industry." *Entertainment Law Reporter* 27, no. 6: 4–22. http://elr.carolon.net/BI/v27n06.pdf.

Handrahan, Matthew. 2015. "Goodgame Studios Denies Allegations of Unfair Dismissals." *Gamesindustry.biz*, December 4. https://www.gamesindustry.biz/articles/2015-12-14-goodgame-denies-allegations-of-unfair-dismissal.

Handy, Jocelyn, and Lorraine Rowlands. 2016. "The Systems Psychodynamics of Gendered Hiring: Personal Anxieties and Defensive Organizational Practices within the New Zealand Film Industry." *Human Relations* 70, no. 3: 312–38. https://doi.org/10.1177/0018726716651690.

Hart, Robert A., and Yue Ma. 2008. "Wage-Hours Contracts, Overtime Working and Premium Pay." *Labour Economics* 17, no. 1: 170–79. https://doi.org/10.1016/j.labeco.2009.04.002.

Harvey, Alison, and Stephanie Fisher. 2013. "Making a Name in Games." *Information, Communication and Society* 16, no. 30: 362–80. https://doi.org/10.1080/1369118X.2012.756048.

Harvey, Alison, and Tamara Shepherd. 2017. "When Passion Isn't Enough: Gender, Affect and Credibility in Digital Games Design." *International Journal of Cultural Studies* 20, no. 5: 492–508. https://doi.org/10.1177/1367877916636140.

Harvey, David. 2010. *A Companion to Marx's Capital*. London: Verso.

Heckscher, Charles, and Lynda M. Applegate. 1994. "Introduction." In *The Post-Bureaucratic Organization*, edited by Charles Heckscher and Anne Donnellon, 1–13. Thousand Oaks, California: Sage.

Heckscher, Charles, Michael Maccoby, Rafael Ramirez, and Pierre-Eric Tixier. 2003a. "The Current Impasse." In *Agents of Change: Crossing the Post-Industrial Divide*, edited by Charles Heckscher, Michael Maccoby, Rafael Ramirez, and Pierre-Eric Tixier, 180–98. New York: Oxford University Press.

———. 2003b. "Towards Post-Industrial Relations." In *Agents of Change: Crossing the Post-Industrial Divide*, edited by Charles Heckscher, Michael Maccoby, Rafael Ramirez, and Pierre-Eric Tixier, 199–212. New York: Oxford University Press.

Heely, Geraldine, Edmund Heery, Phil Taylor, and William Brown. 2004. *The Future of Worker Representation*. New York: Palgrave Macmillan.

Heery, Edmund, and Mike Noon. 2008. "Job Regulation." In *A Dictionary of Human Resource Management*. Oxford: Oxford University Press. https://www.oxfordreference.com/view/10.1093/oi/authority.20110803100021265.

Helleiner, Eric. 1995. "Explaining the Globalization of Financial Markets: Bringing States Back." *Review of International Political Economy* 2, no. 2: 315–41. https://doi.org/10.1080/09692299508434322.

Hester, Blake. 2017. "The Costs of Developing Easter Eggs." *Polygon*, January 19. https://www.polygon.com/features/2017/1/19/14318984/the-costs-of-developing-easter-eggs.

———. 2018. "IGDA: Interest in Diversity, but Not Actual Diversity on the Rise in Game Industry." Reddit. https://www.reddit.com/r/GGdiscussion/comments/7pi2dx/igda_interest_in_diversity_but_not_actual.

Hindess, Barry. 2002. "Neo-Liberal Citizenship." *Citizenship Studies* 6, no. 2: 127. https://doi.org/10.1080/13621020220142932.

Hirshfield, Laura E. 2010. "'She Won't Make Me Feel Dumb': Identity Threat in a Male-Dominated Discipline." *International Journal of Gender, Science and Technology* 2, no. 1: 6–24. http://genderandset.open.ac.uk/index.php/genderandset/article/view/60.

Hirschman, Albert. 1970. *Exit, Voice, and Loyalty: Responses to Decline in Firms, Organizations, and States*. Cambridge: Harvard University Press.

Hjorth, Larissa, and Dean Chan. 2009. *Gaming Cultures and Place in Asia-Pacific*. New York: Routledge.

Hobday, Mike. 2000. "The Project-Based Organisation: An Ideal Form for Managing Complex Products and Systems?" *Research Policy* 29: 871–93. https://doi.org/10.1016/S0048-7333(00)00110-4.

Hochschild, Arlie R., and Anne Machung. 1989. *The Second Shift: Working Parents and the Revolution at Home*. New York: Viking.

Hodgkinson, Gerard P., and William H. Starbuck, eds. 2008. "Organizational Decision Making: Mapping Terrains on Different Planets." Free hand-out. *The Oxford Handbook of Organizational Decision Making*. https://www.oxfordhandbooks.com/view/10.1093/oxfordhb/9780199290468.001.0001/oxfordhb-9780199290468-e-1.

Hodgson, Damian. 2004. "Project Work: The Legacy of Bureaucratic Control in the Post-bureaucratic Organization." *Organization* 11, no. 1: 81–100. https://doi.org/10.1177/1350508404039659.

Hodgson, Damian, and Louise Briand. 2013. "Controlling the Uncontrollable: 'Agile' Teams and Illusions of Autonomy in Creative Work." *Work, Employment, and Society* 27, no. 2: 308–25. https://doi.org/10.1177/0950017012460315.

———. 2015. "The Re-regulation of Control in the Context of Project-Based Work." *International Journal of Work Innovation* 1, no. 3: 287–304. https://doi.org/10.1504/IJWI.2015.074170.

Hon, Dee. 2009. "Rough Play in Vancouver Video Games." *BC Business*, June 3. https://www.bcbusiness.ca/rough-play-in-vancouver-video-games.

Hossfeld, Karen. 1995. "Why Aren't High-Tech Workers Organized?: Lessons in Gender, Race, and Nationality from Silicon Valley." In *Working People of California*, edited by Danial Cornford, 405–32. California: University of California Press. https://publishing.cdlib.org/ucpressebooks/view?docId=ft9x0nb6fg&chunk.id=d0e13046&toc.depth=1&toc.id=d0e13046&brand=ucpress.

Hotho, Sabine, and Katherine Champion. 2011. "Small Businesses in the New Creative Industries: Innovation as a People Management Challenge." *Management Decision* 49, no. 1: 29–54.

Huard Pelletier, Vincent, Arianne Lessard, Florence Piché, Charles Tétreau, and Martin Descarreaux. 2020. "Video Games and Their Associations with Physical Health: A Scoping Review." *British Medical Journal BMJ Open Sport, and Exercise Medicine* 6, no. 1. https://bmjopensem.bmj.com/content/6/1/e000832.

Huber, Evelyn, and John D. Stephens. 2015. *Power, Markets, and Top Income Shares*. Working paper 404, The Kellogg Institute for International Studies, University of Notre Dame. http://dx.doi.org/10.2139/ssrn.2574544.

Hui, Stephen. 2012. "Ubisoft Shuts Down Vancouver Video Game Studio." *Georgia Straight*, January 17. https://www.straight.com/blogra/ubisoft-shuts-down-vancouver-video-game-studio.

Huntemann, Nina B., and Ben Aslinger. 2013. *Gaming Globally: Production, Play, and Place*. New York: Palgrave MacMillan.

Hurd, Richard W., and John Bunge. 2004. "Unionization of Professional and Technical Workers: The Labor Market and Institutional Transformation." In *Emerging Labor Market Institutions for the Twenty-First Century*, 3rd ed, edited by Richard B. Freeman, Joni Hersch, and Lawrence Mishel, 179–206. Chicago: University of Chicago Press. https://www.nber.org/books-and-chapters/emerging-labor-market-institutions-twenty-first-century.

Hutchins, Aaron. 2012. "Better Tax Credits Lure BC Video Game Makers to Ontario." *MacLean's*, July 26. https://www.macleans.ca/economy/business/better-tax-credits-lure-b-c-video-game-makers-to-ontario.

Huws, Ursula. 2011. "Expression and Expropriation: The Dialectics of Autonomy and Control in Creative Labor." *Ephemera: Theory and Politics in Organisation* 10, no. 3/4: 504–21. http://www.ephemeraweb.org.

—. 2014. *Labor in the Global Digital Economy: The Cybertariat Comes of Age*. New York: Monthly Review Press. http://digamo.free.fr/huws14.pdf.

Hyman, Jeff. 2008. "Quality of Life: Does Anyone Still Give a Damn?" *Gamasutra*, May 12. https://www.gamedeveloper.com/business/quality-of-life-does-anyone-still-give-a-damn-

Hyman, Jeffrey, Cliff Lockyer, Abigail Marks, and Dora Scholarios. 2004. "Needing a New Programme: Why Is Union Membership So Low among Software Workers?" In *The Future of Worker Representation*, edited by Geraldine Healy, Edmund Heery, Phil Taylor, and William Brown, 37–61. Future of Work series. London: Palgrave Macmillan.

Hyman, Paul. 2007. "Outsourcing: Video Game Art Is Increasingly 'To Go.'" *Hollywood Reporter*, March 29. https://www.hollywoodreporter.com/news/video-game-art-is-increasingly-132990.

Iantorno, Michael and Marie LeBlanc Flanagan. 2023. "If you don't like the game change the rules," Game Arts International Network, September 22. https://gameartsinternational.network/if-you-dont-like-the-game-change-the-rules.

IBISWorld. 2022. "Video Games in the US: Employment Statistics 2005–2028." Industry statistics—United States. https://www.ibisworld.com/industry-statistics/employment/video-games-united-states.

Industrial Welfare Commission (IWC). 2002. "Order No. 4-2001 Regulating Wages, Hours and Working Conditions in the Professional, Technical, Clerical, Mechanical and Similar Occupations." Department of Industrial Relations, State of California. http://www.dir.ca.gov/IWC/IWCArticle4.pdf.

Industrial Workers of the World (IWW). 2019. "A Year of Organizing Freelance Journalists: The Industrial Workers of the World Freelance Journalists Union Is One Year Old. A Member-Organizer Describes the Campaign." Portside

Labor, August 26. https://portside.org/2019-08-26/year-organizing-freelance-journalists.

Institut de la statistique du Québec (ISQ). 2013. *Les pratiques de conciliation travail et vie personnelle: Un outil pour atténuer la détresse psychologique des salariés du Québec*. Quebec: Government of Quebec. http://collections.banq.qc.ca/ark:/52327/bs2322810.

Interactive Digital Media Tax Credit. n.d. "Alberta Business Grants." https://albertabusinessgrants.ca/grants/interactive-digital-media-tax-credit.

Interactive Games and Entertainment Association (IGEA). 2021. "IGEA's response to Queensland Government taking game development funding to the next level." Press release, Interactive Games and Entertainment Association. October 28. https://igea.net/2021/10/igea-response-queensland-government-taking-game-development-funding-to-the-next-level.

International Game Developers Association (IGDA). 2004. *Quality of Life in the Game Industry: Challenges and Best Practices*. International Game Developers Association. https://igda.org/resources-archive/quality-of-life-in-the-game-industry-challenges-and-best-practices-2004.

—. 2005. *Game Developer Demographics: An Exploration of Workforce Diversity*, commissioned by the International Game Developers Association (IGDA). https://gamesindustryskills.files.wordpress.com/2009/11/igda_developer demographics_oct05.pdf.

International Game Developers Association (IGDA) Foundation. 2015. *Intel Scholars in Action*. International Game Developers Association Foundation, July 16. http://igdafoundation.org/2015/07/intel-scholars-in-action.

Ito, Kenji. 2007. "Possibilities of Non-commercial Games: The Case of Amateur Role-Playing Games Designers in Japan." In *Worlds in Play: International Perspectives on Digital Games Research*, edited by Suzanne de Castell and Jennifer Jenson, 129–42. New York: Peter Lang Publishing.

Ivory, James D. 2006. "Still a Man's Game: Gender Representation in Online Reviews of Video Games." *Mass Communication, and Society* 9, no. 1: 103–14. https://doi.org/10.1207/s15327825mcs0901_6.

Ivory, James D., and Adrienne Holz Ivory. 2016. "Playing Around with Causes of Violent Crime: Violent Video Games as a Diversion from the Policy Challenges Involved in Understanding and Reducing Violent Crime." In *Video Game Policy Production, Distribution, and Consumption*, edited by Steven Conway and Jennifer deWinter, 146–60. London: Routledge.

Izushi, Hiro, and Yuko Aoyama. 2006. "Industry Evolution and Cross-Sectoral Skill Transfers: A Comparative Analysis of the Video Game Industry in Japan, the United States, and the United Kingdom." *Environment and Planning A: Economy and Space* 38, no. 10: 1,843–61. https://doi.org/10.1068/a37205.

Jacobs, Jerry A., and Kathleen Gerson. 2001. "Overworked Individuals or Overworked Families? Explaining Trends in Work, Leisure and Family Time." *Work and Occupations* 28, no. 1: 40–63. https://doi.org/10.1177/0730888401028001004.

Jarvis, Helen, and Andy C. Pratt. 2006. "Bringing It All Back Home: The Extensification and 'Overflowing' of Work. The Case of San Francisco's New Media Households." *Geoforum* 37, no. 3: 331–39. https://doi.org/10.1016/j.geoforum.2005.06.002.

Jensen, Anders, Christian Thuesen, and Joana Geraldi. 2016. "The Projectification of Everything: Projects as a Human Condition." *Project Management Journal* 47, no. 3: 21–34. https://doi.org/10.1177/875697281604700303.

———. 2010a. "Gender, Simulation and Gaming: Research Review and Redirections." *Simulation and Gaming* 41, no. 1: 51–71.
———. 2010b. "Girls@play: Gender and Digital Gameplay." In *Handbook of Research in the Social Foundations of Education*, edited by Steven E. Tozer, Bernardo P. Gallegos, and Annette M. Henry, 504–14. New York: Routledge. https://doi.org/10.4324/9780203874837.ch39.
———. 2005. "Her Own Boss: Gender and the Pursuit of Incompetent Play." In *Proceedings of DiGRA International Conference, Changing Views: World in Play*, edited by Suzanne de Castell and Jennifer Jenson. Vancouver: University of Vancouver. http://www.digra.org/dl/db/06278.27455.pdf.
———. 2018. "'The Entrepreneurial Gamer': Regendering the Order of Play." *Games and Culture* 13, no. 7: 728–46. https://doi.org/10.1177/1555412018755913.
Jenson, Jennifer, Stephanie Fisher, and Suzanne de Castell. 2011. "Disrupting the Gender Order: Leveling Up and Claiming Space in an After-School Video Game Club." *International Journal of Gender, Science and Technology* 3, no. 1: 148–69. http://genderandset.open.ac.uk/index.php/genderandset/article/view/129.
Ji-hye, Jun. 2019. "Game Firms Struggle with Increasingly Aggressive Unions." *Korea Times*, September 11. https://www.koreatimes.co.kr/www/tech/2019/09/134_275490.html.
Jin, Dal Yong. 2010. *Korea's Online Gaming Empire*. Cambridge: MIT Press.
Johns, Jennifer. 2006. "Video Games Production Networks: Value Capture, Power Relations and Embeddedness." *Journal of Economic Geography* 6: 151–80. https://doi.org/10.1093/jeg/lbi001.
Johnson, Robin. 2018. "Technomasculinity and Its Influence in Video Game Production." In *Masculinities in Play*, edited by Nicholas Taylor, and Gerald Voorhees, 249–62. Palgrave Macmillan. https://doi.org/10.1007/978-3-319-90581-5_14.
Kafai, Yasmin B., Carrie Heeter, Jill Denner, and Jennifer Y. Sun, eds. 2008. *Beyond Barbie and Mortal Kombat: New Perspectives on Gender and Gaming*. Cambridge, London: MIT Press.
Kalleberg, Arne, Jeremy Reynolds, and Peter V. Marsden. 2003. "Externalizing Employment: Flexible Staffing Arrangements in US Organizations." *Social Science Research* 32, no. 4: 525–52. https://doi.org/10.1016/S0049-089X(03)00013-9.
Kanai, Atsuko. 2009. "'Karoshi (Work to Death)' in Japan." *Journal of Business Ethics* 84: 209–16. https://link.springer.com/article/10.1007/s10551-008-9701-8.
Kanter, Rosabeth Moss. 1977. *Men and Women of the Corporation*. New York: Basic Books.
Karasek, Robert, and Töres Theorell. 1990. *Healthy Work: Stress, Productivity and the Reconstruction of Working Life*. New York: Basic Books.
Kasurinen, Jussi, Risto Laine, and Kari Smolander. 2013. "How Applicable Is ISO/IEC 29110 in Game Software Development?" In *Product-Focused Software Process Improvement*, edited by Jens Heidrich, Markku Oivo, Andreas Jedlitschka, and Maria Teresa. PROFES 2013, 14th international conference, Paphos, Cyprus, June 12–14, 2013. Baldassarre Proceedings. https://link.springer.com/chapter/10.1007/978-3-642-39259-7_4.
Kasurinen, Jussi, Andrew Maglyas, and Kari Smolander. 2014. "Is Requirements Engineering Useless in Game Development?" In *Lecture Notes in Computer Science* book series (LNCS, vol. 8,396) (including subseries *Lecture Notes in*

Artificial Intelligence and Lecture Notes in Bioinformatics). https://link.springer.com/chapter/10.1007/978-3-319-05843-6_1.

Kasurinen, Jussi, and Kari Smolander. 2014. "What Do Game Developers Test in Their Products?" In *Proceedings of the 8th ACM/IEEE International Symposium on Empirical Software Engineering and Measurement*. https://dl.acm.org/doi/10.1145/2652524.2652525.

Kaufman, Bruce E. 2004. "Industrial Relations: Retrospect and Prospect." In *The Global Evolution of Industrial Relations: Events, Ideas and the IIRA*, edited by Bruce E. Kaufman, 583–631. Geneva: International Labor Office.

—. 2014. "Employee Voice before Hirschman: Its Early History, Conceptualization and Practice." In *Handbook of Research on Employee Voice*, edited by Adrian Wilkinson, Jimmy Donaghey, Tony Dundon, and Richard Freeman, 17–35. Cheltenham, UK: Edward Elgar Publishing.

Kaufman, Bruce E., and David Levine. 2000. "An Economic Analysis of Employee Representation." In *Nonunion Employee Representation: History, Contemporary Practice and Policy*, edited by Bruce E. Kaufman and Daphne Gottlieb Taras, 149–76. Armonk, New York: M. E. Sharpe.

Kazemi, Darius. 2013. "Some Thoughts on the IGDA (or: Why I Quit)." *Tiny Subversions* (blog), September 3. http://tinysubversions.com/2013/09/some-thoughts-on-the-igda-or-why-i-quit/index.html.

Kelly, John. 1998. *Rethinking Industrial Relations: Mobilization, Collectivism, and Long Waves*. London: Routledge.

Kelly, Stephen, Vojtech Klézl, John Israilidis, Neil Malone, and Stuart Butler. 2021. "Digital Supply Chain Management in the Videogames Industry: A Systematic Literature Review." *Computer Games Journal* 10: 19–40. https://doi.org/10.1007/s40869-020-00118-0.

Kennedy, Helen. 2008. "Going the Extra Mile: Emotional and Commercial Imperatives in New Media Work." *Convergence: International Journal of Research into New Media* 15, no. 2: 177–96. https://doi.org/10.1177/1354856508101582.

Keogh, Brendan. 2018. "From Aggressively Formalised to Intensely In/Formalised: Accounting for a Wider Range of Videogame Development Practices." *Creative Industries Journal* 12, no. 1: 14–33. https://doi.org/10.1080/17510694.2018.1532760.

—. 2021. "The Cultural Field of Video Game Production in Australia." *Games and Culture* 16, no. 1: 116–135. https://journals.sagepub.com/doi/10.1177/1555412019873746.

—. 2023. *The Videogame Industry Does Not Exist: Why We Should Think beyond Commercial Game Production*. Cambridge: MIT Press.

Keogh, Brendan, and Benjamin Abraham. 2022. "Challenges and Opportunities for Collective Action and Unionization in Local Games Industries." *Organization*, OnlineFirst. https://doi.org/10.1177/13505084221082269.

Kerr, Aphra. 2006. "Spilling Hot Coffee?: Grand Theft Auto as Contested Cultural Product." In *A Strategy Guide for Studying the Grand Theft Auto Series*, edited by Nathan Garretts. Jefferson, North Carolina: McFarland Press. https://mural.maynoothuniversity.ie/436.

—. 2011. "The Culture of Gamework." In *Managing Media Work*, edited by Mark Deuze, 225–36. Los Angeles: Sage.

—. 2017. *Global Games: Production, Circulation and Policy in the Networked Era*. London: Routledge.

Keune, Maarten, Noëlle Payton, Wike Been, Anne Green, Chris Mathieu, Dominik Postels, Filip Rehnström, Chris Warhurst, and Sally Wright. 2018.

"Innovation and Job Quality in the Games Industry in Germany, the Netherlands, Sweden and the UK." In *Virtuous Circles between Innovations, Job Quality and Employment in Europe?: Case Study Evidence from the Manufacturing Sector, Private and Public Service Sector*, edited by Karen Jaehrling. European Commission's Horizon 2020 Programme "EURO-2-2014: The European Growth Agenda." https://www.iaq.uni-due.de/aktuell/veroeff/2018/QiInne_wp6_3_2018.pdf.

Kilkenny, Katie. 2022. "Why Writers' Guild West Shuttered Programs for Emerging Writers." *Hollywood Reporter*, August 5. https://www.hollywoodreporter.com/business/business-news/writers-guild-west-shuttered-programs-for-emerging-screenwriters-1235192248.

Kim, Changwook, and Sangkyu Lee. 2020. "Fragmented Industrial Structure and Fragmented Resistance in Korea's Digital Game Industry." *Global Media and China* 5, no. 4: 354–71. https://doi.org/10.1177/2059436420932518.

Kim, Matt. 2018. "EA DICE Has Reportedly Lost 10 Percent of Employees amid Battlefront 2's Struggles." *USgamer*, October 19. https://www.usgamer.net/articles/report-ea-dice-lost-10-percent-of-employees-this-year-over-battlefront-2-and-increasing-competition-in-sweden-game-industry.

Kirkpatrick, Graeme. 2013. *Computer Games and the Social Imaginary*. Cambridge: Polity Press.

Klare, Karl. 2000. "The Horizons of Transformative Labour and Employment Law." In *Labour Law in an Era of Globalization: Transformative Practices and Possibilities*, edited by Joanne Conaghan, Richard Michael Fischl, and Karl Klare, 3–29. Oxford: Oxford University Press.

Klepek, Patrick. 2020. "Video Game Layoffs Are So Common, This Person Built a Website to Track Them." *VICE Magazine*, January 15. https://www.vice.com/en/article/dygp3a/video-game-layoffs-are-so-common-this-person-built-a-website-to-track-them.

Kline, Stephen, Nick Dyer-Witheford, and Greig de Peuter. 2003. *Digital Play: The Interaction of Technology, Culture, and Marketing*. Montreal and Kingston: McGill-Queen's University Press.

Ko, Jaekwon, and SeungUk Hur. 2014. "The Impacts of Employee Benefits, Procedural Justice and Managerial Trustworthiness on Work Attitudes: Integrated Understanding Based on Social Exchange Theory." *Public Administration Review* 74, no. 2: 176–87. https://doi.org/10.1111/puar.12160.

Koch, Cameron. 2014. "Crytek Closes UK Studio, Sells Upcoming Game 'Homefront: The Revolution.'" *Tech Times*, July 30. https://www.techtimes.com/articles/11689/20140730/crytek-closes-uk-studio-sells-upcoming-game-homefront-revolution.htm.

Kocurek, Carly A. 2016. "Against the Arcade: Video Gaming Regulation and the Legacy of Pinball." In *Video Game Policy: Production, Distribution and Consumption*, edited by Steven Conway and Jennifer deWinter, 206–16. London: Routledge.

Kollmeyer, Christopher, and John Peters. 2018. "Financialization and the Decline of Organized Labor: A Study of 18 Advanced Capitalist Countries, 1970–2012." *Social Forces* 98, no. 1: 1–30. https://doi.org/10.1093/sf/soy105.

Komulainen, Lauri, and Olli Sotamaa. 2020. "IGDA Finland Hubs as Their Role in Local Game Development." In *Proceedings of the 23rd International Conference on Academic Mindtrek*. New York: Association for Computing Machinery. https://dl.acm.org/doi/10.1145/3377290.3377294.

Konovsky, M. A. 2000. "Understanding Procedural Justice and Its Impact on Business Organizations." *Journal of Management* 26, 489–511. https://doi.org/10.1177/014920630002600306.

Kotamraju, Nalini P. 2002. "Keeping Up: Web Design Skill and the Reinvented Worker." *Information, Communication, and Society* 5, no. 1: 1–26. https://doi.org/10.1080/13691180110117631.

Krotoski, Aleks. 2004. "Chicks and Joysticks: An Exploration of Women and Gaming." *Entertainment and Leisure Software Publishers Association* (ELSPA). White paper. https://www.semanticscholar.org/paper/Chicks-and-Joysticks%3A-an-exploration-of-women-and-Krotoski/96243b0996c90b4ddc4f301607c8b04d79ef4469.

Kücklich, Julian. 2005. "Precarious Playbour: Modders and the Digital Games Industry." *Fibreculture Journal* 5, no. 1: http://five.fibreculturejournal.org/fcj-025-precarious-playbour-modders-and-the-digital-games-industry.

Kuehn, Kathleen, and Thomas Corrigan. 2013. "Hope Labor: The Role of Employment Prospects in Online Social Production." *Political Economy of Communication* 1, no. 1: 9–25. http://www.polecom.org/index.php/polecom/article/view/9.

Kyle, Linda K., and Jo Bryce. 2012. "Putting the 'Fun Factor' into Gaming: The Influence of Social Contexts on Experiences of Playing Videogames." *International Journal of Internet Science* 7, no. 1: 23–36. https://research.edgehill.ac.uk/en/publications/putting-the-fun-factor-into-gaming-the-influence-of-social-contex-2.

Lalande, André. 1926. *Vocabulaire technique et critique de la philosophie*. Paris: PUF.

Land, Susan K., and Bret Wilson. 2006. "Using IEEE Standards to Support America's Army Gaming Development." *Computer* 39, no. 11: 105–7. https://ieeexplore.ieee.org/abstract/document/4014781.

Laramee, Francois Dominic. 2005. *Secrets of the Game Business*. Boston: Charles River Media.

Lapavitsas, Costas. 2014. *Profiting without Producing: How Finance Exploits Us All*. New York: Verso.

Lê, Patrick L., David Massé, and Thomas Paris. 2013. "Technological Change at the Heart of the Creative Process: Insights from the Videogame Industry." *International Journal of Arts Management* 15, no. 2: 45–59. http://researchgate.net/publication/252322671.

Lee, Kyungjin, Chunhui Suh, Jong-Eun Kim, and Jae Oh Park. 2017. "The Impact of Long Working Hours on Psychosocial Stress Response among White-Collar Workers." *Industrial Health* 55, no. 1: 46–53. https://doi.org/10.2486/indhealth.2015-0173.

Lee, Sangheon, Deirdre McCann, and Jon C. Messenger. 2007. *Working Time around the World: Trends in Working Hours, Laws and Policies in a Global Comparative Perspective*. New York: International Labour Organization (ILO), Routledge.

Lees, Matt. 2016. "What Gamergate Should Have Taught Us about the 'Alt-Right.'" *Guardian*, December 1.

Legault, Marie-Josée. 2005a. "Droits de la personne, relations de travail et défis pour les syndicats contemporains." *Relations industrielles/Industrial Relations* 60, no. 4: 683–708. https://doi.org/10.7202/012340ar.

———. 2005b. "Differential Gender Effects of Project Management and Management by Project on Skilled Professionals." In *Reformulating Industrial Relations in Liberal Market Economies/Reformuler les relations industrielles dans une* économie *de marché libérale*, edited by Kay S. Devine and Jean-Noel Grenier, 105–24. Concord, ON: CIRA/ACRI and Captus Press.

———. 2008. "Social Relations and Knowledge Management Theory and Practice." In *Management Practices in High Tech Environments*, edited by Dariusz Jemielniak and Jerzy Kociatkiewicz, 167–90. Hershey, Pennsylvania: IGI Global, Information Science Reference. http://www.igi-global.com/reference/details.asp?id=7443.

———. 2013. "IT Firms' Working Time (De)regulation Model." *Work, Organization, Labour and Globalisation* 7, no. 1: https://doi.org/10.13169/workorgalaboglob.7.1.0076.

———. 2015. "Les ententes restrictives d'emploi en droit québécois." A case law synthesis on NCAs and NDAs, in the course ADM 6506 Gestion des conflits en contexte de projet, TÉLUQ University, Quebec.

———. 2017. *Équité en emploi—Équité salariale*, 2nd ed. Quebec: Presses de l'Université du Québec.

Legault, Marie-Josée, and Hind Belarbi-Basbous. 2006. "Gestion par projets et santé mentale au travail dans la nouvelle économie." *Perspectives interdisciplinaires sur le travail et la santé (PISTES)* 8, no. 1. https://doi.org/10.4000/pistes.3086.

Legault, Marie-Josée, and Stéphanie Chasserio. 2009. "Le client et l'équipe, importantes sources de régulation dans la gestion par projets." In *Restructurations, précarisation, valeurs*, edited by Béatrice Appay and Steve Jefferys, 143–56. Toulouse: Octares.

———. 2010. "La domination dans le modèle de production de haute performance dans la gestion de projets." In *La domination au travail: des conceptions totalisantes à la diversification des formes de domination*, edited by Romaine Malenfant and Guy Bellemare, 99–124. Quebec: PUQ.

———. 2012. "Professionalization, Risk Transfer, and the Effect on Gender Gap in Project Management." *International Journal of Project Management* 30, no. 6: 697–707. http://dx.doi.org/10.1016/j.ijproman.2011.11.004.

———. 2014. "Gestion par projets/ou organisation du travail par projets." In *Dictionnaire des risques psycho-sociaux*, edited by Philippe Zawieja and Franck Guarnieri, 339–43. Paris: Éditions du Seuil. http://r-libre.teluq.ca/270.

Legault, Marie-Josée, and Martine D'Amours. 2011. "Représentation collective et citoyenneté au travail en contexte de projet: Les cas des artistes interprètes et des concepteurs de jeux vidéo." *Relations industrielles/Industrial Relations* 66, no. 4: 655–77. http://www.erudit.org/revue/ri/2011/v66/n4/index.html.

Legault, Marie-Josée, and Kathleen Ouellet. 2012. "So into It They Forget What Time It Is?: Video Game Designers and Unpaid Overtime." In *Managing Dynamic Technology-Oriented Business: High-Tech Organizations and Workplaces*, edited by Dariusz Jemielniak and Abigail Marks, 82–102. Hershey, Pennsylvania: IGI Global, Information Science Reference. http://www.igi-global.com/book/managing-dynamic-technology-oriented-businesses/62632.

Legault, Marie-Josée, and Johanna Weststar. 2009. *Report of the Quality of Life Survey 2009*, commissioned by the International Game Developers' Association (IGDA).

———. 2012. *Report of the Quality of Life Survey 2009*, commissioned by the International Game Developers' Association. http://www.gameqol.org/igda-qol-survey.

—. 2013. "Are Game Developers Standing Up for Their Rights?" *Gamasutra*, January 8. https://www.gamedeveloper.com/business/are-game-developers-standing-up-for-their-rights-.

—. 2014. "Comment jouer la régulation dans l'industrie du jeu vidéo?" *Relations industrielles/Industrial Relations* 69, no. 1: 136–58. https://doi.org/10.7202/1024210ar.

—. 2015a. *Working Time among Video Game Developers, 2004–2014: Summary Report*. http://www.gameqol.org/igda-qol-survey.

—. 2015b. "The Capacity for Mobilization in Project-Based Cultural Work: A Case of the Video Game Industry." *Canadian Journal of Communication* 40, no. 2: 203–21. https://doi.org/10.22230/cjc.2015v40n2a2805.

—. 2017. "Videogame Developers among 'Extreme Workers': Are Death Marches Over?" *E-journal of International and Comparative Labour Studies* 6, no. 3: 1–29. http://ejcls.adapt.it/index.php/ejcls_adapt/article/view/167/711.

—. 2021. "Organizing Challenges in the Era of Financialization: The Case of Videogame Workers." *Work, Organisation, Labour, and Globalisation* 15, no. 2: 7–24. https://doi.org/10.13169/workorgalaboglob.15.2.0007.

Legge, Karen. 2005. *Human Resource Management: Rhetorics and Realities*. Houndmills, UK: Palgrave Macmillan Education.

Lemière, Séverine. 2006. "Un salaire égal pour un emploi de valeur comparable." *Travail, genre et sociétés* 1, no. 15: 83–100. https://www.cairn.info/revue-travail-genre-et-societes-2006-1-page-83.htm.

Levchak, Charisse C. 2018. "Microaggressions, Macroaggressions, and Modern Racism in the Workplace." In *Microaggressions and Modern Racism: Endurance and Evolution*, edited by Charisse Levchak, 105–212. Cham, Switzerland: Palgrave Macmillan.

Liao, Shannon. 2021. "Over 100 Activision Blizzard Employees Stage Walkout, Demand CEO Step Down." *Washington Post*, November 16. https://www.washingtonpost.com/video-games/2021/11/16/activision-blizzard-kotick-walkout.

Lillie, Nathan, and Ian Greer. 2007. "Industrial Relations, Migration and Neoliberal Politics: The Case of the European Construction Sector." *Politics and Society* 35, no. 4: 551–81. https://doi.org/10.1177/0032329207308179.

Limelight Networks. 2020. *The State of Online Gaming: 2019*. White paper. https://www.limelight.com/resources/white-paper/state-of-online-gaming-2019/#spend.

Lindgren, Monica, and Johann Packendorff. 2006. "What's New in New Forms of Organizing?: On the Construction of Gender in Project-Based Work." *Journal of Management Studies* 43, no. 4: 841–66. https://doi.org/10.1111/j.1467-6486.2006.00613.x.

L'Italien, François. 2012. *Béhémoth capital: Contribution à une théorie dialectique de la financiarisation de la grande corporation*. PhD thesis, Laval University, Quebec. https://corpus.ulaval.ca/jspui/handle/20.500.11794/23427.

Llerena, Patrick, Thierry Burger-Helmchen, and Patrick Cohendet. 2009. "Division of Labor and Division of Knowledge: A Case Study of Innovation in the Video Game Industry." In *Schumpeterian Perspectives on Innovation, Competition and Growth*, edited by Uwe Cantner, Jean-Luc Gaffard, and Lionel Nesta, 315–33. Berlin: Springer. https://link.springer.com/chapter/10.1007/978-3-540-93777-7_18.

Lodemel, Ivar, and Amilcar Moreira, eds. 2014. *Activation or Workfare?: Governance and the Neo-Liberal Convergence*, Oxford: Oxford University Press.

Long, Brandon S. 2005. "Protecting Employer Investment in Training: Noncompetes vs. Repayment Agreements." *Duke Law Journal* 54, no. 5: 1,295–320. https://www.jstor.org/stable/40040471.

López-Bohle, Sergio, P. Matthijs Bal, Paul G. W. Jansen, Pedro I. Leiva, and Antonia Mladinic Alonso. 2017. "How Mass Layoffs Are Related to Lower Job Performance and OCB among Surviving Employees in Chile: An Investigation of the Essential Role of Psychological Contract." *International Journal of Human Resource Management* 28, no. 20: 2,837–60. https://doi.org/10.1080/09585192.2016.1138988.

Larusso, Silvio. 2019. *Entreprecariat*. Eindhoven, The Netherlands: Onomatopee.

Lundin, Rolf A., Niklas Arvidsson, Tim Brady, Eskil Ekstedt, Christophe Midler, and Jörg Sydow. 2015. *Managing and Working in Project Society: Institutional Challenges of Temporary Organizations*. Cambridge: Cambridge University Press.

Lupton, Deborah. 1999. *Risk*. London: Routledge.

MacDonald, Ian, and Manek Kolhatkar. 2021. "An Experimental Organization of Precarious Professionals: The Two-Step Unionization of Québec Archaeologists." *Labour/Le Travail* 88 (fall), 27–51. https://doi.org/10.52975/llt.2021v88.0004.

Make Games South Africa (MGSA). 2016. "Association News: Launch of IESA. Make Games SA." http://makegamessa.com/discussion/3768/launch-of-iesa.

Manson, Bonita J. 2014. *Downsizing Issues: The Impact on Employee Morale and Productivity—Studies on Industrial Productivity*. New York: Routledge.

Marculewicz, Stefan, Alan Model, and Tanja Thompson. 2021. "Minority Unions: A Major Concern for Employers in 2021 and Beyond?" *Littler Publications*, January 12. https://www.jdsupra.com/legalnews/minority-unions-a-major-concern-for-6920760.

Marklund, Bjorn Berg, Henrik Engström, Marcus Hellkvist, and Per Basklund. 2019. "What Empirically Based Research Tells Us about Game Development." *Computer Games Journal* 8: 179–98. https://doi.org/10.1007/s40869-019-00085-1.

Marshall, Thomas Humphrey. 1950. *Citizenship and Social Class: And Other Essays*. Cambridge: Cambridge University Press.

—. 1964. "Citizenship and Social Class." In *Class, Citizenship and Social Development*, edited by Thomas H. Marshall, 65–122. Garden City, New York: Double Day.

Martins, Nicole, Dmitri C. Williams, Kristen Harrison, and Rabindra A. Ratan. 2009. "A Content Analysis of Female Body Image in Video Games." *Sex Roles* 61: 824–86. https://doi.org/10.1007/s11199-009-9682-9.

Maxwell, Richard, and Toby Miller. 2012. "'Warm and Stuffy': The Ecological Impact of Electronic Games." In *The Video Game Industry: Formation, Present State, and Future*, edited by Peter Zackariasson and Timothy L. Wilson, 179–97. New York and Abingdon: Routledge.

McAlevey, Jane. 2020. *A Collective Bargain: Unions, Organizing and the Fight for Democracy*. New York: Ecco/Harper Collins.

McAllister, Graham, and Gareth R. White. 2015. "Video Game Development and User Experience." In *Game User Experience Evaluation*, edited by Regina Bernhaupt, 11–35. Cham, Switzerland: Springer International Publishing. https://link.springer.com/chapter/10.1007/978-3-319-15985-0_2.

McCluskey, Martha T. 2002. "The Rhetoric of Risk and the Redistribution of Social Insurance." In *Embracing Risk: The Changing Culture of Insurance and Responsibility*, edited by Tom Baker and Jonathan Simon, 146-70. Chicago: University of Chicago Press. https://doi.org/10.7208/chicago/9780226035178.003.0007.

McEwan, Travis. 2019. "'I Felt Betrayed': Gaming Companies Unsure of Future in Alberta after Tax Credit Axed." *CBC News*, October 25. https://www.cbc.ca/news/canada/edmonton/gaming-tax-credit-alberta-1.5336579.

McKinlay, Alan, and Chris Smith. 2009. *Creative Labour: Working in the Creative Industries*. Houndmills, UK: Palgrave Macmillan.

McMillen, Andrew. 2011. "The Emails behind the Whistle Blowing at Team Bondi." *Gamesindustry.biz*, July 5. https://www.gamesindustry.biz/articles/2011-07-05-revealed-the-internal-emails-that-provoked-whistle-blowing-at-team-bondi-blog-entry.

———. 2012. "Why Did LA Noire Take Seven Years to Make?" *IGN*, May 5. https://ca.ign.com/articles/2011/06/24/why-did-la-noire-take-seven-years-to-make.

McRobbie, Angela. 2002. "From Holloway to Hollywood: Happiness at Work in the New Cultural Economy." In *Cultural Economy: Cultural Analysis and Commercial Life*, edited by Paul du Gay and Michael Pryke, 97-114. London: Sage.

———. 2003. "Clubs to Companies: Notes on the Decline of Political Culture in Speeded Up Creative Worlds." *Cultural Studies* 16, no. 4: 516-31. https://doi.org/10.1080/09502380210139098.

———. 2016. *Be Creative: Making a Living in the New Culture Industries*. Cambridge: Polity Press.

———. 2018. "The Creativity Dispositive: Labor Reform by Stealth—Interview with Angela McRobbie." In *Critical Theory at a Crossroads*, edited by Stijn De Cauwer, 146-58. New York: Columbia University Press.

Meyer, John P., and Natalie J. Allen. 1997. *Commitment in the Workplace: Theory, Research and Application*. Thousand Oaks: Sage.

Miller, Linda, Fiona Neathey, Emma Pollard, and Darcy Hill. 2004. *Occupational Segregation, Gender Gaps and Skill Gaps*, Equal Opportunities Commission Working paper series 15. https://citeseerx.ist.psu.edu/viewdoc/download?doi=10.1.1.465.8928&rep=rep1&type=pdf.

Miller, Monica K., and Alicia Summers. 2007. "Gender Differences in Videogame Characters' Roles, Appearances, and Attire as Portrayed in Video Game Magazines." *Sex Roles* 57: 733-42. https://doi.org/10.1007/s11199-007-9307-0.

Miller, Susan J., and David C. Wilson. 2006. "Perspectives on Organizational Decision-Making." In *The SAGE Handbook of Organization Studies*, edited by Stewart R. Clegg, Cynthia Hardy, Tom Lawrence, and Walter R. Nord, 469-84. London: Sage.

Milner, David. 2018. "Crunch: The Video Game Industry's Notorious Labor Problem." *Game Informer*, January 16. https://www.gameinformer.com/b/features/archive/2018/01/16/crunch-the-video-game-industrys-notorious-labor-problem.aspx.

Minotti, Mike. 2019. "US Presidential Candidate Bernie Sanders Supports Video Game Workers Unions." *Venture Beat*, June 18. https://venturebeat.com/2019/06/18/u-s-presidential-candidate-bernie-sanders-supports-video-game-workers-unions.

Mizunoya, Takeshi. 2002. "An International Comparison of Unpaid Overtime Work among Industrialized Countries." *Journal of the Society of Economic*

Statistics 81. http://www.ilo.org/public/english/bureau/stat/download/articles/2002-3.pdf.

Monneuse, Denis. 2013. *Le surprésentéisme: Travailler malgré la maladie*. Brussels: de Boeck.

Moody, Joshua, and Aphra Kerr. 2020. "What's the Score? Surveying Game Workers in Ireland." Project Report, GWU Ireland-FSU. https://doi.org/10.31235/osf.io/zshk5.

Moore, Sarah, Leon Grunberg, and Edward Greenberg. 2004. "Repeated Downsizing Contact: The Effects of Similar and Dissimilar Layoff Experiences on Work and Well-Being Outcomes." *Journal of Occupational Health Psychology* 9, no. 3: 247–57. https://doi.org/10.1037/1076-8998.9.3.247.

Moralde, Oscar. 2018. "From Passion to Power: Game Unions and Historical Lessons from Media Labor." *First Person Scholar*, September 12. http://www firstpersonscholar.com/from-passion-to-power.

Morrison, Elisabeth. 2011. "Employee Voice Behavior: Integration and Directions for Future Research." *Academy of Management Annals* 5, no. 10: 373–412. http://dx.doi.org/10.1080/19416520.2011.574506.

Mosca, Marco. 2018. "Crunch, droit du travail, sexisme... Les combats du STJV dans le jeu vidéo." *Les Numériques*, March 6. https://www.lesnumeriques.com/loisirs/stjv-dans-jeu-video-on-doit-cruncher-a3599.html.

Mosco, Vincent. 2009. *Political Economy of Communication*. London: Sage.

Moses, Yolanda. 2016. "Is the Term 'People of Color' Acceptable in This Day and Age?" *Sapiens Anthropology*, December 7. https://www.sapiens.org/column/race/people-of-color.

Mowday, Richard T., Richard M. Steers, and Lyman W. Porter. 1979. "The Measurement of Organizational Commitment." *Journal of Vocational Behavior* 14: 224–47. https://doi.org/10.1016/0001-8791(79)90072-1.

Moyser, Melissa, and Amanda Burlock. 2018. "Time Use: Total Work Burden, Unpaid Work and Leisure." In *Women in Canada: A Gender-Based Statistical Report*, Statistics Canada, Cat. no 89-503-X. https://www150.statcan.gc.ca/n1/en/pub/89-503-x/2015001/article/54931-eng.pdf?st=pvNlQSTs.

Mudhar, Raju. 2012. "Rockstar Games Expands in Ontario." *Toronto Star*, July 11. https://www.thestar.com/entertainment/2012/07/11rockstar_games _expands_in_ontario.html.

Mueller, Eleanor. 2020. "What the Workplace Will Look like under a Biden White House." *Politico*, November 9. http://politico.com/newsletters/weekly -shift/2020/11/09/what-the-workplace-will-look-like-under-a-biden-white -house-791482.

Muriel, Daniel, and Garry Crawford. 2018. "Video Games as Culture." *Considering the Role and Importance of Video Games in Contemporary Society*. London: Routledge.

Murphy-Hill, Emerson, Thomas Zimmermann, and Nachiappan Nagappan. 2014. "Cowboys, Ankle Sprains, and Keepers of Quality: How Is Video Game Development Different from Software Development?" In *Proceedings of the 36th International Conference on Software Engineering, Hyderabad, India*. https://dl.acm.org/doi/abs/10.1145/2568225.2568226.

Murray, Gregor, and Pierre Verge. 1999. *La représentation syndicale: Visage juridique actuel et futur*. Quebec: Presses de l'Université Laval.

Musial, Monica, Antti Kauppinen, and Vesa Puhakka. 2015. "Recognised Creativity: The Influence of Process, Social Needs, and the Third Drive on Creative

Individuals' Work through Social Media." In *Social Media and Networking: Concepts, Methodologies, Tools, and Applications*, edited by Monica Musial, Antti Kauppinen, and Vesa Puhakka, 1,249–80. https://www.igi-global.com/book/social-media-networking/125529.

Myllärniemi, Varvana, Mikko Raatikainen, and Tomi Männistö. 2006. "Interorganisational Approach in Rapid Software Product Family Development: A Case Study." In *Reuse of Off-the-Shelf Components*, edited by Maurizio Morisio, 73–86. Ninth international conference on software reuse, ICSR 2006 proceedings. https://link.springer.com/chapter/10.1007/11763864_6.

Nadal, Kevin, Chassitty Whitman, Lindsey Davis, Tanya Erazo, and Kristin Davidoff. 2016. "Microaggressions toward Lesbian, Gay, Bisexual, Transgender, Queer, and Genderqueer People: A Review of the Literature." *Journal of Sex Research* 53, nos. 4–5, 488–508. https://doi.org/10.1080/00224499.2016.1142495.

Neff, Gina. 2012. *Venture Labor: Work and the Burden of Risk in Innovative Industries*. Cambridge: MIT Press.

Neff, Gina, Elisabeth Wissinger, and Sharon Zukin. 2005. "Entrepreneurial Labour among Cultural Producers: 'Cool' Jobs in 'Hot' Industries." *Social Semiotics* 15, no. 3: 307–34. https://doi.org/10.1080/10350330500310111.

Neyfakh, Leon. 2014. "Not Your Grandpa's Labor Union: As 'Employee' and 'Employer' Become Hazy Categories, Experiments in Worker Advocacy Are Replacing Unions as We've Known Them." *Boston Globe*, April 6.

Nichols, Randall James. 2005. *The Games People Play: A Political Economic Analysis of Video Games and Their Production*, PhD dissertation, School of Journalism and Communication, University of Oregon.

———. 2013. "Who Plays, Who Pays?: Mapping Video Game Production and Consumption Globally." In *Gaming Globally*, edited by Nina Huntemann and Ben Aslinger, 19–40. New York: Palgrave MacMillan. https://doi.org/10.1057/9781137006332_2.

———. 2016. "Curt Schilling's Gold Coins: Lessons for Creative Industry Policy in Light of the 38 Studios Collapse." In *Video Game Policy: Production, Distribtion and Consumption*, edited by Steven Conway and Jennifer deWinter, 217–29. London: Routledge.

Nieborg, David. 2021. "How to Study Game Publishers: Activision Blizzard's Corporate History." In *Game Production Studies*, edited by Olli Sotamaa and Jan Švelch, 179–95. Amsterdam: Amsterdam University Press.

Nieborg, David, and Jeroen de Kloet. 2016. "A Patchwork of Potential: A Survey of the European Game Industry." In *Global Game Industries and Cultural Policy*, edited by Anthony Fung, 201–26. London: Palgrave.

Nienhüser, Werner. 2014. "Works Councils." In *Handbook of Research on Employee Voice*, edited by Adrian Wilkinson, Jimmy Donaghey, Tony Dundon, and Richard Freeman, 247–62. Cheltenham, UK: Edward Elgar Publishing.

Nieva, Richard. 2021. "Google AI Chief Says Reputation Hit to Unit Is 'Real' after Turmoil." *CNET*, May 18. https://www.cnet.com/news/google-ai-chief-says-reputation-hit-to-unit-is-real-after-turmoil.

Nordicity. 2013. *2012 Canadian Interactive Industry Profile*, commissioned for the Canadian Interactive Alliance/L'Alliance Interactive Canadienne (CIAIC). https://ciaic.files.wordpress.com/2012/11/ciip-report-_english-r5-final.pdf.

———. 2019. "The Canadian Video Game Industry 2019." Entertainment Software Association of Canada. http://theesa.ca/wp-content/uploads/2019/11/CanadianVideoGameSector2019_EN.pdf.

NorthBridge Consultants. n.d. *SR&ED and Digital Media Tax Credits for the Digital Gaming Industry*. https://www.northbridgeconsultants.com/fund/scientific-research-and-experimental-development-sred/sred-and-digital-media-tax-credits-for-the-digital-gaming-industry.

Nova Scotia Department of Finance. 2011. "Overview of the Nova Scotia Tax System." https://www.novascotia.ca/finance/site-finance/media/finance/Overview_of_NS_Tax_System_2011-04-04.pdf.

Nova Scotia Department of Finance and Treasury Board. 2018. "Nova Scotia Digital Media Tax Credit Guidelines." https://www.novascotia.ca/finance/en/home/taxation/tax101/businesstax/corporateincometax/digitalmediataxcredit.aspx.

Nussenbaum, Evelyn. 2004. "Video Game Makers Go Hollywood. Uh-Oh." *New York Times*, August 22.

O'Brady, Sean. 2014. "Review of *The Fissured Workplace: Why Work Became So Bad for So Many and What Can Be Done to Improve It* by David Weil." *Relations industrielles/Industrial Relations* 69, no. 3: 655–57. https://doi.org/10.7202/1026766ar.

O'Brien, Ciara. 2015. "Games Association Offers 'Scholarship' to Irish Developers." *Irish Times*, December 8.

O'Carroll, Aileen. 2015. *Working Time, Knowledge Work and Post-industrial Society: Unpredictable Work*. London: Palgrave.

O'Doherty, Damian, and Hugh Willmott. 2009. "The Decline of Labour Process Analysis and the Future Sociology of Work." *Sociology* 43, no. 5: 931–51. https://doi.org/10.1177/0038038509340742.

O'Donnell, Casey. 2014. *Developer's Dilemma: The Secret World of Videogame Creators*. Cambridge: MIT Press.

———. 2019. "Making Media: Reflections on the Shifts and Swerves of the Global Games Industry." In *Making Media: Production, Practices and Professions*, edited by Mark Deuze and Mirjam Prenger. Amsterdam: Amsterdam University Press.

O'Hagan, Ann O., and Rory V. O'Connor. 2015. "Towards an Understanding of Game Software Development Processes: A Case Study." In *Communications in Computer and Information Science* book series (CCIS), vol. 543. https://link.springer.com/chapter/10.1007/978-3-319-24647-5_1.

O'Malley, Patrick. 2004. *Risk, Uncertainty and Government*. London: GlassHouse Press.

O'Reilly, Dermot, and Michael Rosato. 2013. "Worked to Death?: A Census-Based Longitudinal Study of the Relationship between the Numbers of Hours Spent Working and Mortality Risk." *International Journal of Epidemiology* 42, no. 6: 1,820–30. https://doi.org/10.1093/ije/dyt211.

O'Riain, Sean. 2000. "Net-Working for a Living: Irish Software Developers in the Global Workplace." In *The Critical Study of Work: Labor, Technology and Global Production*, edited by Rick Baldoz, Charles Koeber, and Philip Kraft, 258–82. Philadelphia: Temple University Press.

Okoro, Catherine A., NaTasha D. Hollis, Alissa C. Cyrus, and Shannon Griffin-Blake. 2018. "Prevalence of Disabilities and Health Care Access by Disability Status and Type among Adults: United States, 2016." *Morbidity and Mortality Weekly Report* 67, no. 32: 882–87. http://dx.doi.org/10.15585/mmwr.mm6732a3.

Ontario Creates. 2020. "Ontario Interactive Digital Media Tax Credit (OIDMTC)." April. https://ontariocreates.ca/tax-incentives/oidmtc.

Ontario Ministry of Colleges and Universities. n.d. "Canada-Ontario Job Grant." Government of Ontario. http://www.tcu.gov.on.ca/eng/eopg/cojg.

Ontiveros, Maria L. 2000. "A New Course for Labour Unions: Identity-Based Orgnizing as a Response to Globalization." In *Labour Law in an Era of Globalization: Transformative Practices and Possibilities*, edited by Joanne Conaghan, Richard Michael Fischl, and Karl Klare, 417–28. Oxford: Oxford University Press.

Organ, Dennis W. 1997. "Organizational Citizenship Behavior: It's Construct Cleanup Time." *Human Performance* 10, no. 2: 85–97. https://doi.org/10.1207/s15327043hup1002_2.

Organ, Dennis W., Phillip M. Podsakoff, and Scott MacKenzie. 2006. *Organizational Citizenship Behavior: Its Nature, Antecedents, and Consequences*, London: Sage.

Organ, Dennis W., and Katherine Ryan. 1995. "A Meta-Analytic Review of Attitudinal and Dispositional Predictors of Organizational Citizenship Behavior." *Personnel Psychology* 48, no. 4: 775–802. https://doi.org/10.1111/j.1744-6570.1995.tb01781.x.

Organisation for Economic Co-operation and Development (OECD). n.d. "Employment by activities and status (ALFS)." *OECD.stat*. Data extracted on 6 June 2020. https://stats.oecd.org/Index.aspx?DataSetCode=ALFS_EMP.

———. 2017a. "How Technology and Globalisation Are Transforming the Labour Market." In *OECD Employment Outlook 2017*. Paris: OECD Publishing. http://dx.doi.org/10.1787/empl_outlook-2017-7-en.

———. 2017b. *Future of Work and Skills*. Paper presented at the second meeting of the G20 Employment working Group, February 15–17. https://www.oecd.org/els/emp/wcms_556984.pdf.

———. 2019. *The Future of Work: OECD Employment Outlook 2019—Highlights*. http://www.oecd.org/employment/outlook.

Osterman, Paul, Thomas Kochan, Richard Locke, and Michael J. Piore. 2001. *Working in America: A Blueprint for the New Labor Market*. Cambridge: MIT Press.

Ozimek, Anna M. 2019a. "The 'Grey Area' of Employment Relations in the Polish Videogame Industry." *International Journal of Cultural Studies* 22, no. 2: 298–314. https://doi.org/10.1177/1367877918821238.

———. 2019b. "Outsourcing Digital Game Production: The Case of Polish Testers." *Television, and New Media* 20, no. 8: 824–35. https://doi.org/10.1177/1527476419851088.

Paaßen, Benjamin, Thekla Morgenroth, and Michelle Stratemeyer. 2017. "What Is a True Gamer?: The Male Gamer Stereotype and the Marginalization of Women in Video Game Culture." *Sex Roles* 76: 421–35. https://doi.org/10.1007/s11199-016-0678-y.

Palley, Thomas I. 2004. "From Keynesianism to Neoliberalism: Shifting Paradigms in Economics." *Foreign Policy in Focus*. https://fpif.org/from_keynesianism_to_neoliberalism_shifting_paradigms_in_economics.

Palm, Kristina, and Marcus Lindahl. 2015. "A Project as a Workplace: Observations from Project Managers in Four R&D and Project-Intensive Companies." *International Journal of Project Management* 33: 828–38. https://doi.org/10.1016/j.ijproman.2014.10.002.

Paprocki, Matt. 2018. "EA Spouse 14 Years Later: How One Person Tried Correcting EA Culture." *Rolling Stone*, February 27.

Parker, Felan, Jennifer R. Whitson, and Bart Simon. 2018. "Megabooth: The Cultural Intermediation of Indie Games." *New Media and Society* 20, no. 5: 1,953–72. https://doi.org/10.1177/1461444817711403.

Parrish, Ash. 2021a. "Activision Blizzard Sued Again, This Time for Labor Violations." *Verge*, September 14. https://www.theverge.com/2021/9/14/22674269/activision-blizzard-sued-nlrb-labor-violations.

—. 2021b. "ActivisiOn Blizzard Ends Forced Arbitration as CEO Takes a Massive Pay Cut." *Verge*, October 28. https://www.theverge.com/2021/10/28/22750450/activision-blizzard-ends-forced-arbitration-bobby-kotick-paycut.

Parvini, Sarah. 2023. "Activision Blizzard to Pay $35 Million to Settle SEC Charges on Workplace Disclosures." *Los Angeles Times*, February 3.

Paul, Christopher A. 2018. *The Toxic Meritocracy of Video Games: Why Gaming Culture Is the Worst*. Minnesota: University of Minnesota Press.

Paul, Kari. 2022. "Judge Approves Activision Blizzard's $18M Settlement over Sexual Harassment Suit." *Guardian*, March 29.

Pemsel, Sofia, Ralf Müller, and Jonas Söderlund. 2016. "Knowledge Governance Strategies in Project-Based Organizations." *Long Range Planning* 49: 648–60. https://doi.org/10.1016/j.lrp.2016.01.001.

Pereira, Richard. 2009. "The Costs of Unpaid Overtime Work in Canada: Dimensions and Comparative Analysis." Integrated Studies Project, Master of Arts, Integrated Studies, University of Athabasca.

Pérez-Zapata, Oscar, Amparo Serrano Pascual, Gloria Álvarez-Hernández, and Cecilia Castaño Collado. 2016. "Knowledge Work Intensification and Self-Management: The Autonomy Paradox." *Work, Organisation, Labour, and Globalisation* 10, no. 2: 27–49. https://www.jstor.org/stable/10.13169/workorgalaboglob.10.issue-2.

Perks, Matthew. 2021. "Regulating In-Game Monetization: Implications of Regulation on Games Production." In *Game Production Studies*, edited by Olli Sotamaa and Jan Švelch, 217–33. Amsterdam: Amsterdam University Press.

Perks, Matthew, and Jennifer R. Whitson. 2022. "Inclusion, Access, and Equity: Diversity Initiatives in Canada's Game Industry." in *Creative Industries in Canada*, edited by Miranda Campbell and Cheryl Thompson, 1–34. Toronto: Canadian Scholars Press.

Perlow, Leslie A. 2012. "Sleeping with Your Smartphone: How to Break the 24/7 Habit and Change the Way You Work." *Harvard Business Review Press*.

Perlow, Leslie A., and Erin L. Kelly. 2014. "Toward a Model of Work Redesign for Better Work and Better Life." *Work and Occupations* 41, no. 1: 111–34. https://doi.org/10.1177/0730888413516473.

Perlow, Leslie A., Melissa Mazmanian, and Elisabeth Hansen. 2017. "Shifting towards a Collective Temporal Orientation: Enabling a Sustainable Performance Culture." Conference of the Annual Academy of Management Meeting, Vancouver, Canada. https://doi.org/10.5465/ambpp.2015.15568abstract.

Perlow, Leslie A., and Jessica L. Porter. 2009. "Making Time Off Predictable and Required." *Harvard Business Review* 87, no. 10: 102–9. https://europepmc.org/article/med/19839447.

Perret, Michael. 2016. "Banning Violent Video Games in Switzerland: A Public Problem Going Unnoticed." In *Video Game Policy: Production, Distribution and Consumption*, edited by Steven Conway and Jennifer deWinter, 161–75. London: Routledge.

Perrons, Diane. 2002. "Gendered Divisions in the New Economy: Risks and Opportunities." *GeoJournal* 56, no. 4: 271–80. https://doi.org/10.1023/A:1025955420257.

———. 2003. "The New Economy and the Work-Life Balance: Conceptual Explorations and a Case Study of New Media." *Gender, Work and Organization* 10, no. 1: 65–93. https://doi.org/10.1111/1468-0432.00004.

———. 2007. "Living and Working Patterns in the New Knowledge Economy: New Opportunities and Old Social Divisions in the Case of New 37 Media and Care Work." In *Gender Divisions in the New Economy: Changing Patterns of Work, Care and Public Policy in Europe and North America*, edited by Diane Perrons, Colette Fagan, Linda McDowell, Kath Ray, and Kevin Ward, 188–206. London: Edward Elgar Publishing.

Peters, Thomas J., and Robert H. Waterman. 1982. *In Search of Excellence*. New York: Harper and Row.

Peticca-Harris, Amanda, Johanna Weststar, and Steve McKenna. 2015. "The Perils of Project-Based Work: Attempting Resistance to Extreme Work Conditions in Video Game Development." *Organization* 22, no. 4: 570–87. https://doi.org/10.1177/1350508415572509.

Petrillo, Fabio, Marcelo Pimenta, Francisco M. Trindade, and Carlos A. Dietrich. 2009. "What Went Wrong?: A Survey of Problems in Game Development." *Computers in Entertainment* 7, no. 1: 13. https://dl.acm.org/doi/10.1145/1486508.1486521.

Pfeffer, Jeffrey. 2017. "Building Sustainable Organizations: The Human Factor." *Academy of Management Perspectives* 24, no. 1: 34–45. https://doi.org/10.5465/amp.24.1.34.

Pfeiffer, Sabine, Stefan Sauer, and Tobias Ritter. 2019. "Agile Methods as Stress Management Tools?: An Empirical Study." *Work Organisation, Labour, and Globalisation* 13, no. 2. https://www.jstor.org/stable/pdf/10.13169/workorgalaboglob.13.2.0020.pdf?refreqid=excelsior%3Aa3b0991f549ee829395779598394bbd7.

Phelps, Nicole. 2022. "The Model Alliance announces the Fashion Workers Act, A New Pro-labor Bill to Protect Models and Other Industry Creatives." *Vogue*, March 25. https://www.vogue.com/article/fashion-workers-act-model-alliance.

Philipupillai, Kevin. 2021. "Alphabet Workers Go Wall-to-Wall." *Monitor*, May 1. https://monitormag.ca/articles/alphabet-workers-go-wall-to-wall.

Picq, Thierry, Alain Asquin, and Gilles Garel. 2007. "Le côté sombre des projets: Quand les individus et les collectifs sociaux sont mis en danger par le travail en projet." *Gérer et Comprendre* 90: 43–54. https://halshs.archives-ouvertes.fr/halshs-00687924.

Pina e Cunha, Miguel. 2002. "The Best Place to Be: Managing Control and Employee Loyalty in a Knowledge-Intensive Company." *Journal of Applied Behavioral Science* 38, no. 4: 481–95. https://doi.org/10.1177/002188602237793.

Pinto, Jeffrey K., Shariffah Dawood, and Mary Beth Pinto. 2014. "Project Management and Burnout: Implications of the Demand–Control–Support Model on Project-Based Work." *International Journal of Project Management* 32: 578–89. https://doi.org/10.1016/j.ijproman.2013.09.003.

Plant, Raymond. 2012. *The Neo-Liberal State*. Oxford: Oxford University Press.

Platman, Kerry, and Philip Taylor. 2004. "Workforce Ageing in the New Economy: A Comparative Study of Information Technology Employment." University of Cambridge, Cambridge Interdisciplinary Research Centre on Ageing. https://doi.org/10.1007/0-387-34588-4_11.

Plunkett, Luke. 2012. "Every Game Studio That's Closed Down since 2006." *Kotaku Australia*, January 16. https://kotaku.com/every-game-studio-thats-closed-down-since-2006-5876693.

Politowski, Cristiano, Daniel de Vargas, Antonio A. Foletto, and Lisandra Fontoura. 2016. "Software Engineering Processes in Game Development: A Survey about Brazilian Developers' Experiences." SBC. Proceedings of the 14th SB Games Conference. http://www.sbgames.org/sbgames2016/downloads/anais/157812.pdf.

Postigo, Hector. 2003. "From Pong to Planet Quake: Post-industrial Transitions from Leisure to Work." *Information, Communication and Society* 6, no. 4: 593–607.

Powell, Gary N., and D. Anthony Butterfield. 2003. "Gender, Gender Identity, and Aspirations to Top Management." *Women in Management Review* 18, no. 1/2: 88–96.

Powell, Kendall. 2017. "Work–Life Balance: Break or Burnout." *Nature* 545, no. 7,654: 375–77. https://www.nature.com/articles/nj7654-375a.pdf.

Prescott, Julie, and Jan Bogg. 2010. "The Computer Games Industry: Women's Experiences of Work Role in a Male Dominated Environment." In *Women in Engineering, Science and Technology: Education and Career Challenges*, edited by Aileen Cater-Steel and Emily Cater, 138–58. Hershey, Pennsylvania: IGI Global.

—. 2011a. "Segregation in a Male-Dominated Industry: Women Working in the Computer Games Industry." *International Journal of Gender, Science and Technology*, Women in Games Special Issue, 3, no. 1: 206–27. http://genderandset.open.ac.uk/index.php/genderandset/issue/view/8.

—. 2011b. "Career Attitudes of Men and Women Working in the Computer Games Industry." *Eludamos: Journal for Computer Game Culture* 5, no. 1: 7–28. https://eludamos.org/index.php/eludamos/article/view/vol5no1-2.

—. 2013. "The Gendered Identity of Women in the Games Industry." *Eludamos: Journal for Computer Game Culture* 7, no. 1: 55–67. https://eludamos.org/index.php/eludamos/article/view/vol7no1-3/7-1-3-html.

Project Management Institute (PMI). 2019. *A Guide to the Project Management Body of Knowledge (PMBoK Guide)*, 6th ed., Newton Square, PMI inc. https://www.pmi.org/pmbok-guide-standards/foundational/pmbok.

Quilgars, Deborah, and David Abbott. 2000. "Working in the Risk Society: Families Perceptions of, and Responses to, Flexible Labour Markets and the Restructuring of Welfare." *Community, Work, and Family* 3, no. 1: 15–36. https://doi.org/10.1080/713658900.

Quinn, Zoë. 2017. *Crash Override: How Gamergate (Nearly) Destroyed My Life, and How We Can Win the Fight against Online Hate*. New York: Public Affairs Books.

Rainey, Rebecca. 2020. "Trump's Workplace Watchdog Assailed for Lenient Penalties on COVID Safety Violators." *Politico*, October 6. https://www.politico.com/news/2020/10/06/osha-coronavirus-penalties-426828.

Ramos, Mario J. 2018. "Riot Games répond aux allégations de sexisme et harcèlement sexuel." RDS Jeux vidéo, September 4. https://jeuxvideo.rds.ca/riot-games-repond-aux-allegations-de-sexisme-et-harcelement-sexuel.

Reay, Diane. 2004. "Gendering Bourdieu's Concepts of Capitals?: Emotional Capital, Women and Social Class." In *Feminism after Bourdieu*, edited by Lisa Adkins and Beverley Skeggs, 57–75. Oxford: Oxford University Press.

Reed, Michael. 2005. "Beyond the Iron Cage?: Bureaucracy and Democracy in the Knowledge Economy and Society." In *The Values of Bureaucracy*, edited by Paul DuGay, 115–40. Oxford: Oxford University Press.

Reid, Erin. 2015. "Embracing, Passing, Revealing, and the Ideal Worker Image: How People Navigate Expected and Experienced Professional Identities." *Organization Science* 26, no. 4: 997–1,017. https://doi.org/10.1287/orsc.2015.0975.

Robertson, Maxine, and Geraldine O'Malley Hammersley. 2000. "Knowledge Management Practices within a Knowledge-Intensive Firm: The Significance of the People Management Dimension." *Journal of European Industrial Training* 24, no. 2–4: 241–53. https://doi.org/10.1108/03090590010321205.

Robertson, Maxine, Harry Scarbrough, and Jacky Swan. 2003. "Knowledge Creation in Professional Service Firms: Institutional Effects." *Organization Studies* 24, no. 6: 831–57. https://doi.org/10.1177/0170840603024006002.

Robinson, Judith, and Sébastien Jetté. 2003. "La protection des secrets commerciaux en dehors de la relation employeur-employé." In *Développements récents en droit de la propriété intellectuelle*, vol. 197, 1–41. Service de la formation continue du Barreau du Québec. Cowansville: Éditions Yvon Blais.

Rockstar Spouse. 2010. "Wives of Rockstar San Diego Employees Have Collected Themselves." Web log comment. January 7. https://www.gamedeveloper.com/business/wives-of-rockstar-san-diego-employees-have-collected-themselves.

Rodino-Colocino, Michelle. 2007. "High-Tech Workers of the World, Unionize!: A Case Study of WashTech's New Model of Unionism." In *Knowledge Workers in the Information Society*, edited by Catherine McKercher and Vincent Mosco, 209–28. Lanham, Maryland: Lexington Books.

Rollings, Andrew, and Dave Morris. 2004. *Game Architecture and Design*. Berkeley, California: New Riders.

Rose, Emily. 2016. "Workplace Temporalities: A Time-Based Critique of the Flexible Working Provisions." *Industrial Law Journal*: 245–67. https://doi.org/10.1093/indlaw/dww039.

Roseboro, Angela. 2021. "Annual Diversity and Inclusion (D&I) Progress Report." *Riot Games*, September 7. https://www.riotgames.com/en/news/annual-diversity-and-inclusion-di-progress-report-august-2021.

Ross, Andrew. 2003. *No-Collar: The Humane Workplace and Its Hidden Costs*. New York: Basic Books.

—. 2009. *Nice Work If You Can Get It: Life and Work in Precarious Times*. New York: New York University Books.

Rothfeld, Becca. 2020. "At-Will Employment Is the Real 'Cancel Culture.'" *Jacobin*, October 23. https://www.jacobinmag.com/2020/10/at-will-employment-twitter-cancel-culture-academic-workers-fired-students.

Rubery, Jill, Kevin Ward, Damian Grimshaw, and Hum Beynon. 2005. "Working Time, Industrial Relations and the Employment Relationship." *Time and Society* 14, no. 1: 89–111. https://doi.org/10.1177/0961463X05050300.

Ruffino, Paolo. 2018. *Future Gaming: Creative Interventions in Video Game Culture*. London: Goldsmiths Press.

Ruffino, Paolo, ed. 2021. *Independent Videogames: Cultures, Networks, Techniques and Politics*. London: Routledge.

Ruggill, Judd Ethan, and Ken S. McAllister. 2016. "E(SRB) Is for Everyone: Game Ratings and the Practice of Content Evaluation." In *Video Game Policy: Production, Distribution and Consumption*, edited by Steven Conway and Jennifer deWinter, 71–84. London: Routledge.

Salaman, Graeme. 2005. "Bureaucracy and Beyond: Managers and Leaders in the 'Post-bureaucratic' Organization." In *The Values of Bureaucracy*, edited by Paul DuGay, 141–63. Oxford: Oxford University Press.

Sandqvist, Ulf. 2012. "The Development of the Swedish Game Industry: A True Success Story?" In *The Video Game Industry: Formation, Present State, and Future*, edited by Peter Zacakriasson and Timothy L. Wilson, 134–56. New York: Routledge.

Sarkeesian, Anita. 2013. "Tropes versus Women in Video Games." Video series. https://www.youtube.com/playlist?list=PLn4ob5ttEaAvc8F3fjzE62esf9yP61.

Sato, Kaori, Sachiko Kuroda, and Hideo Owan. 2020. "Mental Health Effects of Long Work Hours, Night and Weekend Work, and Short Rest Periods." *Social Science, and Medicine* 246: 1–11. https://doi.org/10.1016/j.socscimed.2019.112774.

Scarbrough, Harry. 1999. "Knowledge as Work: Conflicts in the Management of Knowledge Workers." *Technology Analysis and Strategic Management* 11, no. 1: 5–16. https://doi.org/10.1080/095373299107546.

Scarbrough, Harry, and Nicholas Kinnie. 2003. "Barriers to the Development of Team Working in UK Firms." *Industrial Relations Journal* 34, no. 2: 135–49. https://doi.org/10.1111/1468-2338.00264.

Schiffer, Zoe. 2021a. "Here's What We Know about the Google Union So Far." *Verge*, January 5. https://www.theverge.com/2021/1/5/22215171/google-alphabet-union-cwa-organizers-goals-explainer.

—. 2021b. "Google Union In Turmoil Following Global Alliance Announcement." *Verge*, January 31. https://www.theverge.com/2021/1/30/22256577/alphabet-workers-union-turmoil-global-alliance-announcement-google-cwa.

Schiller, Ben. 2015. "Where There Aren't Unions, Can Online Platforms Organize Workers?" *Fast Company*, July 6. https://www.fastcompany.com/3047759/where-there-arent-unions-can-online-platforms-organize-workers.

Schmalz, Marc, Aimee Finn, and Hazel Taylor. 2014. "Risk Management in Videogame Development Projects." *Hawaii International Conference on System Science*. https://ieeexplore.ieee.org/stamp/stamp.jsp?tp=&arnumber=6759136.

Schreier, Jason. 2013a. "Investigation: A Video Game Studio from Hell." *Kotaku*, June 7. https://kotaku.com/investigation-a-video-game-studio-from-hell-511872642.

—. 2013b. "Shake-Up at Studio from Hell." *Kotaku*, June 8. https://kotaku.com/shake-up-at-studio-from-hell-512135529.

—. 2013c. "The Video Game Studio from Hell: Four Months Later." *Kotaku*, October 17. https://kotaku.com/the-video-game-studio-from-hell-four-months-later-1447281005/all.

—. 2014a. "Sources: Crytek's UK Staff No Longer Going to Work." *Kotaku*, July 3. https://kotaku.com/sources-crytek-uks-staff-are-currently-on-leave-1599923133.

—. 2014b. "Why Game Developers Keep Getting Laid Off." *Kotaku*, June 5. https://kotaku.com/why-game-developers-keep-getting-laid-off-1583192249.

—. 2015. "Crunch Time: Why Developers Work Such Insane Hours." *Kotaku*, May 16. https://www.kotaku.com.au/2015/05/crunch-time-why-game-developers-work-such-insane-hours.

—. 2018. "It's Time for Game Developers to Unionize." *Kotaku*, March 22. https://kotaku.com/it-s-time-for-game-developers-to-unionize-1823992430.

Scott, Sean R. 2014. "Maintaining Quality of Life as a Game Developer, Entrepreneur, and Parent." *IGDA Perspectives Newsletter*, August 31. http://newsletter

.igda.org/2014/08/31/maintaining-quality-of-life-as-a-game-developer-entrepreneur-and-parent.

Selwyn, Neil. 2007. "Hi-Tech = Guy-Tech?: An Exploration of Undergraduate Students' Perceptions of Information and Communication Technologies." *Sex Roles* 56, 525–36. https://doi.org/10.1007/s11199-007-9191-7.

Semuels, Alana. 2019. "'Every Game You Like Is Built on the Backs of Workers': Video Game Creators Are Burned Out and Desperate for Change." *Time*, June 11. https://time.com/5603329/e3-video-game-creators-union.

Sennet, Richard. 1998. *The Corrosion of Character: The Personal Consequences of Work in the New Capitalism*. London: Norton and Company.

Shane, Scott, and Daisuke Wakabayashi. 2018. "'The Business of War': Google Employees Protest Work for the Pentagon." *New York Times*, April 4.

Shapiro, Debra L., and Jeanne M. Brett. 2005. "What Is the Role of Control in Organizational Justice?" In *Handbook of Organizational Justice*, edited by Jerald Greenberg and Jason A. Colquitt, 155–78. Mahwah, New Jersey: Lawrence Erlbaum Associates.

Sheffield, Brandon. 2009. "GDC: Gears of War 2 Producer Fergusson Talks 'Necessary Crunch.' *Gamasutra*, March 26. https://www.gamedeveloper.com/game-platforms/gdc-gears-of-war-2-producer-fergusson-talks-quot-necessary-crunch-quot-.

Scheiber, Noam, and Kellen Browning. 2022. "Video Game Workers at Microsoft and Activision Take Steps to Unionize." *New York Times*, December 5.

Shirky, Clay. 2008. *Here Comes Everybody: The Power of Organizing Without Organizations*. New York: Penguin.

Shuler, Liz. 2019. "An Open Letter to Game Developers from America's Largest Labor Organization." *Kotaku*, February 15. https://kotaku.com/an-open-letter-to-game-developers-from-americas-largest-1832652654.

Simon, Laurent. 2006. "Managing Creative Projects: An Empirical Synthesis of Activities." *International Journal of Project Management* 24, no. 2: 116–26. https://www.sciencedirect.com/science/article/pii/S0263786305000967.

Simpson, Ruth. 1998. "Presenteeism, Power and Organisational Change: Long Hours as a Career Barrier and the Impact on the Working Lives of Women Managers." *British Journal of Management Communication Quarterly* 9, no. 1: 37–50. https://doi.org/10.1111/1467-8551.9.s1.5.

Sinclair, Brendan. 2013. "Ex-IGDA Director: Devs Would Be Better Off If IGDA Didn't Exist." *Gamesindustry.biz*, September 4. https://www.gamesindustry.biz/articles/2013-09-04-ex-igda-director-devs-would-be-better-off-if-igda-didnt-exist.

—. 2020. "Nexon Korea and Union Agree on Pay Raises." *Gamesindustry.biz*, February 6. https://www.gamesindustry.biz/articles/2020-02-06-nexon-korea-and-union-agree-on-wage-boost.

—. 2021. "French Union Files Collective Lawsuit against Ubisoft." *Gamesindustry.biz*, July 16. https://www.gamesindustry.biz/articles/2021-07-16-french-union-files-collective-lawsuit-against-ubisoft.

—. 2022. "Microsoft Acquires Activision Blizzard." *Gamesindustry.biz*, January 18. https://www.gamesindustry.biz/articles/2022-01-18-report-microsoft-to-acquire-activision-blizzard.

Singh, Val, and Susan Vinnicombe. 2000. "What Does 'Commitment' Really Mean?: Views of UK and Swedish Engineering Managers." *Personnel Review* 29, no. 2: 228–58. https://doi.org/10.1108/00483480010296014.

Skerrett, Kevin, Johanna Weststar, Simon Archer, and Chris Roberts, eds. 2018. *The Contradictions of Pension Fund Capitalism*. Ithaca: Cornell University Press.

Skillsearch. 2021. *Games and Interactive Salary and Satisfaction Survey Results*. https://www.skillsearch.com/assets/Games_and_Interactive_Salary_and_Satisfaction_Survey_2021.pdf.

Slattery, Laura. 2021. "Ireland Presses Start Button on Video Games Tax Credit." *Irish Times*, October 18.

Sloper, Tom. 2017. "Working as a Tester FAQ5: The Unsung Heroes of Games." Sloperama Productions. http://www.sloperama.com/advice/lesson5.htm.

Smith, Andrew. 2020. "Game Workers Unite Calls for Greater Aid for Industry Workers Impacted by COVID-19." *IGN.com*, March 22. https://www.ign.com/articles/game-workers-unite-calls-for-greater-aid-for-industry-workers-impacted-by-covid-19.

Smith, Chris, and Alan McKinlay. 2009. "Creative Labor: Content, Contract and Control." In *Creative Labour: Working in the Creative Industries*, edited by Alan McKinlay and Chris Smith, 29–50. New York: Palgrave Macmillan.

Social Security Association. 2018a. *Social Security Programs throughout the World: Europe, 2018*. International Social Security Association. https://ww1.issa.int/sites/default/files/documents/2020-05/ssptw18europe.pdf.

———. 2018b. *Social Security Programs throughout the World: Asia and the Pacific, 2018*. International Social Security Association. https://ww1.issa.int/sites/default/files/documents/2020-05/ssptw18asia.pdf.

———. 2019a. *Social Security Programs throughout the World: Africa, 2019*. International Social Security Association. https://ww1.issa.int/sites/default/files/documents/2020-05/ssptw19africa.pdf.

———. 2019b. *Social Security Programs throughout the World: The Americas, 2019*. International Social Security Association. https://ww1.issa.int/sites/default/files/documents/2020-05/ssptw19americas.pdf.

Sotamaa, Olli, Kristine Jørgensen, and Ulf Sandqvist. 2020. "Public Game Funding in the Nordic Region." *International Journal of Cultural Policy* 26, no. 5: 617–32. https://doi.org/10.1080/10286632.2019.1656203.

Sotamaa, Olli, and Jan Švelch. 2021. *Game Production Studies*. Amsterdam: Amsterdam University Press. https://library.oapen.org/bitstream/handle/20.500.12657/47043/9789048551736.pdf?sequence=1#page=198.

Srauy, Sam. 2019. "Professional Norms and Race in the North American Video Game Industry." *Games and Culture* 14, no. 5: 478–97. https://doi.org/10.1177/1555412017708936.

Stacey, Patrick, Andrew Brown, and Joe Nandhakumar. 2007. "Making Sense of Stories: The Development of a New Mobile Computer Game." In *Proceedings of the Annual Hawaii International Conference on System Sciences*. https://ieeexplore.ieee.org/abstract/document/40764.

Stacey, Patrick, and Joe Nandhakumar. 2008. "Opening Up to Agile Games Development." *Communications of the ACM* 51, no. 12: 143–46. https://doi.org/10.1145/1409360.1409387.

———. 2009. "A Temporal Perspective of the Computer Game Development Process." *Information Systems Journal* 19, no. 5: 479–97. https://onlinelibrary.wiley.com/doi/full/10.1111/j.1365-2575.2007.00273.x.

Stanford Encyclopedia of Philosophy. 2017. "Citizenship." https://plato.stanford.edu/entries/citizenship/#FemiCrit.

Steinfeldt, Jesse A., Ellen L. Vaughan, Julie R. LaFollette, and Matthew C. Steinfeldt. 2012. "Bullying among Adolescent Football Players: Role of Masculinity and Moral Atmosphere." *Psychology of Men and Masculinity* 13, no. 4: 340–53. https://doi.org/10.1037/a0026645.

Strickland, Derek. 2020. "2019's Top-Earning Video Game Companies: Sony Conquers the Charts." *TweakTown*, May 22. https://www.tweaktown.com/news/72703/2019s-top-earning-video-game-companies-sony-conquers-the-charts/index.html.

Supiot, Alain. 2001. *Beyond Employment: Changes in Work and the Future of Labour Law in Europe*. Oxford: Oxford University Press.

Surette, Tim. 2006. "EA Settles OT Dispute, Disgruntled 'Spouse' Outed." *Gamespot*, April 26. https://www.gamespot.com/articles/ea-settles-ot-dispute-disgruntled-spouse-outed/1100-6148369.

Swan, Jackie, Harry Scarbrough, and Maxine Robertson. 2002. "The Construction of 'Communities of Practice' in the Management of Innovation." *Management Learning* 33, no. 4: 477–96. https://doi.org/10.1177/1350507602334005.

Tarnoff, Ben. 2018. "Coding and Coercion: An Interview with Björn Westergard." *Jacobin*, April 11. https://www.jacobinmag.com/2018/04/lanetix-tech-workers-unionization-campaign-firing.

Taylor, Allan, and James Robert Parish. 2007. *Career Opportunities in the Internet, Video Games and Multimedia*. Infobase Publishing.

Taylor, Catherine J. 2010. "Occupational Sex Composition and the Gendered Availability of Workplace Support." *Gender and Society* 24, no. 2: 189–212. https://doi.org/10.1177/0891243209359912.

Taylor, Haydn. 2019. "Gender Pay Gap Widens in UK Games Industry." *Gamesindustry.biz*, April 8. https://www.gamesindustry.biz/articles/2019-04-08-gender-pay-gap-widens-in-uk-games-industry.

Taylor, Nicholas, and Gerald Voorhees. 2018. *Masculinities in Play*, London: Palgrave Macmillan.

Taylor, Nicholas, Jennifer Jenson, and Suzanne de Castell. 2009. "Cheerleaders, Booth Babes, Halo Hoes: Pro-gaming, Gender and Jobs for the Boys." *Digital Creativity* 20, no. 4: 239–52. https://doi.org/10.1080/14626260903290323.

Taylor, Stephanie, and Karen Littleton. 2008. "Art Work or Money: Conflicts in the Construction of a Creative Identity." *Sociological Review* 56: 275–92. https://doi.org/10.1111/j.1467-954X.2008.00788.x.

Taylor-Gooby, Peter. 2004. "New Social Risks in Post-industrial Society: Some Evidence on Responses to Active Labour Market Policies from Eurobarometer." *International Social Security Review* 57, no. 3: 45–64. https://doi.org/10.1111/j.1468-246X.2004.00194.x.

Teipen, Christina. 2008. "Work and Employment in Creative Industries: The Video Games Industry in Germany, Sweden and Poland." *Economic and Industrial Democracy* 29, no. 3: 309–35. https://doi.org/10.1177%2F0143831X08092459.

—. 2015. "The Implications of the Value Chain and Financial Institutions for Work and Employment: Insights from the Video Game Industry in Poland, Sweden and Germany." *British Journal of Industrial Relations* 54, no. 2: 311–33. https://doi.org/10.1111/bjir.12144.

Ter Minassian, Hovig, and Vinciane Zabban. 2021. "Should I Stay or Should I Go?: The Circulations and Biographies of French Game Workers in a 'Global

Games' Era." In *Game Production Studies*, edited by Olli Sotamaa and Jan Švelch, 65–82, Amsterdam: Amsterdam University Press.

Thang, Jimmy. 2012. "The Tough Life of a Games Tester." *IGN.com*, April 2. http://www.ign.com/articles/2012/03/29/the-tough-life-of-a-games-tester.

Thomas, Janice Lynne, and Pamela Buckle-Henning. 2007. "Dancing in the White Spaces: Exploring Gendered Assumptions in Successful Project Managers' Discourse about Their Work." *International Journal of Project Management* 25, no. 6: 552–59. https://doi.org/10.1016/j.ijproman.2007.05.001.

Thompson, Paul, and Mats Alvesson. 2005. "Bureaucracy at Work." In *The Value of Bureaucracy*, edited by Paul DuGay, 89–114. Oxford: Oxford University Press.

Thompson, Paul, Rachel L. Parker, and Stephen D. Cox. 2016. "Interrogating Creative Theory and Creative Work: Inside the Games Studio." *Sociology* 50, no. 2: 316–32. https://doi.org/10.1177/0038038514565836.

Thompson, Paul, and Diane Van den Broek. 2010. "Managerial Control and Workplace Regimes: An Introduction." *Work, Employment and Society* 24, no. 3: 1–12. https://doi.org/10.1177/0950017010384546.

Thuderoz, Christian. 2010. "Citoyens au travail," "entreprises citoyennes," and "Les motifs d'une convergence inédite." In *Travail et citoyenneté: Quel avenir?*, edited by Michel Coutu and Gregor Murray, 197–228. Quebec: Presses de l'Université Laval.

Tison, Florence. 2019. "Retour sur nos entrevues marquantes de 2019: les gameuses systématiquement harcelées." *Espresso-Jobs*, December 12. https://espresso-jobs.com/conseils-carriere/les-gameuses-du-Québec-systematiquement-harcelees-en-ligne.

Tô, Laurence, Marie-Josée Legault, and Johanna Weststar. 2016. *Collective Action and Representation Gap among Videogame Developers, 2004–2014*. Summary Report, commissioned by the International Game Developers Association (IGDA). http://www.gameqol.org/igda-qol-survey.

Tokumitsu, Miya. 2015. *Do What You Love: And Other Lies about Success and Happiness*. New York: Regan Arts.

Tòth, Istvan G. 2014. "Revisiting Grand Narratives of Growing Income Inequalities: Lessons from 30 Country Studies." In *Changing Inequalities and Societal Impacts in Rich Countries: Thirty Countries' Experiences*, edited by Brian Nolan, Wiemer Salverda, Daniele Checchi, Ive Marx, Abigail McKnight, Istvan G. Tòth, and Herman G. Van de Werfhorst, 11–47. Oxford: Oxford University Press. 10.1093/acprof:oso/9780199687428.003.0002.

Tran, Minh Quang, and Robert Biddle. 2008. "Collaboration in Serious Game Development: A Case Study." In *Proceedings of the 2008 Conference on Future Play: Research, Play, Share*: 49–56. https://dl.acm.org/doi/10.1145/1496984.1496993.

Tschang, F. Ted, and Janusz Szczypula. 2006. "Idea Creation, Constructivism and Evolution as Key Characteristics in the Videogame Artifact Design Process." *European Management Journal* 24, no. 4: 270–87. https://doi.org/10.1016/j.emj.2006.05.003.

Turcev, Nicolas. 2018. "Pour la première fois en sept ans, un studio de jeu vidéo français se met en grève." *Gamekult Premium*, February 15. https://www.gamekult.com/actualite/pour-la-premiere-fois-en-sept-ans-un-studio-de-jeu-video-francais-se-met-en-greve-3050802527.html.

Turner, J. Rodney, Martina Huemann, and Anne Keegan. 2018. *Human Resource Management in the Project-Oriented Organization*, Newtown Square, Pennsylvania: Project Management Institute.

United States Census. n.d. "QuickFacts: United States." United States Census Bureau. https://www.census.gov/quickfacts/fact/table/US/LFE046219.

United States Department of Labor. 2008. *Fact Sheet #17E: Exemption for Employees in Computer-Related Occupations under the Fair Labor Standards Act (FLSA).* US Wage and Hour Division. http://www.dol.gov/whd/overtime/fs17e_computer.pdf.

Valenduc, Gérard, Patricia Vendramin, Caroline Guffens, Anna M. Ponzelli, Adele Lebano, Laurence d'Ouville, Isabelle Collet, Ina Wagner, Andrea Birbaumer, Marianne Tolar, and Juliet Webster. 2004. *Widening Women's Work in Information and Communication Technology.* European Commission. http://www.ftu-namur.org/www-ict.

Valentine, Rebekah. 2019. "Nexon Korea Union Holds Demonstration One Year after Formation." *Gamesindustry.biz*, September 5. https://www.gamesindustry.biz/articles/2019-09-05-nexon-korean-union-holds-demonstration-one-year-after-formation.

Van der Bos, Kees. 2005. "What Is Responsible for the Fair Process Effect." In *Handbook of Organizational Justice*, edited by Jerald Greenberg and Jason A. Colquitt, 273–300. Mahwah, New Jersey: Lawrence Erlbaum Associates.

van Jaarsveld, Danielle. 2004. "Collective Representation among High-Tech Workers at Microsoft and Beyond: Lessons from WashTech/CWA." *Industrial Relations* 43, no. 2: 364–85. https://papers.ssrn.com/sol3/papers.cfm?abstract_id=524276.

van Roessel, Lies, and Jan Švelch. 2021. "Who Creates Microtransactions: The Production Context of Video Game Monetization." In *Game Production Studies*, edited by Olli Sotamaa and Jan Švelch, 197–215. Amsterdam: Amsterdam University Press.

Vézina, Michel, Esther Cloutier, Susan Stock, Katherine Lippel, Éric Fortin, Alain Delisle, Marie St-Vincent, Amélie Funes, Patrice Duguay, Samuel Vézina, and Pascale Prud'homme. 2011. *Enquête québécoise sur des conditions de travail, d'emploi et de santé et de sécurité du travail (EQCOTESST).* Rapport R-691, Government of Quebec, Institut national de santé publique du Québec, Institut de la statistique du Québec et Institut de recherche Robert-Sauvé en santé et en sécurité du travail. https://www.irsst.qc.ca/publications-et-outils/publication/i/100592/n/enquete-Québecoise-conditions-travail-emploi-sst-eqcotesst-r-691.

Virtanen, Marianna, Jane E. Ferrie, Archana Singh-Manoux, Martin J. Shipley, Stephen A. Stansfeld, Michael G. Marmot, Kirsi Ahola, Jussi Vahtera, and Mika Kivimaki. 2011. "Long Working Hours and Symptoms of Anxiety and Depression: A 5-Year Follow-Up of the Whitehall II Study." *Psychological Medicine* 41, no. 12: 2,485–94, 10.1017/S0033291711000171.

Virtanen, Marianna, Katriina Heikkilä, Markus Jokela, Jane E. Ferrie, G. David Batty, Jussi Vahtera, and Mika Kivimäki. 2012. "Long Working Hours and Coronary Heart Disease: A Systematic Review and Meta-Analysis." *American Journal of Epidemiology* 176, no. 7: 586–96. https://doi.org/10.1093/aje/kws139.

Vosko, Leah, and the Closing the Enforcement Gap Research Group. 2020. *Closing the Enforcement Gap: Improving Employment Standards Protections for People in Precarious Jobs.* Toronto: University of Toronto Press.

Vosko, Leah, Andrea Noack, and Eric Tucker. 2016. *Employment Standards Enforcement: A Scan of Employment Standards Complaints and Workplace Inspections and Their Resolution under the Employment Standards Act, 2000.* Report for the Ontario Ministry of Labour to support the Changing Workplaces Review of 2015. Queen's Printer for Ontario. http://closeesgap.ca/download/750.

Wajcman, Judy. 1991. *Feminism Confronts Technology*. Cambridge: Polity Press.

Walby, Sylvia. 2011. "Is the Knowledge Society Gendered?" *Gender, Work and Organization* 18, no. 1: 1–29. https://doi.org/10.1111/j.1468-0432.2010.00532.x.

Walfisz, Martin, Peter Zackariasson, and Timothy L. Wilson. 2006. "Real-Time Strategy: Evolutionary Game Development." *Business Horizons* 49, no. 6: 487–98. https://doi.org/10.1016/j.bushor.2006.04.001.

Wang, Alf Inge, and Njål Nordmark. 2015. "Software Architectures and the Creative Processes in Game Development." In *Entertainment Computing-ICEC 2015: 14th International Conference, ICEC 2015, Proceedings*, edited by Konstantinos Chorianopoulos, Monica Divitini, Janinicke Baalsrud Hauge, Letizia Jaccheri, and Rainer Malaka, 272–85. Cham, Switzerland: Springer International Publishing. https://link.springer.com/chapter/10.1007/978-3-319-24589-8_21.

Warren, Tom. 2021. "Microsoft Completed Bethesda Acquisition, Promised Some Xbox and PC Exclusives." *Verge*, March 9. https://www.theverge.com/2021/3/9/22319124/microsoft-bethesda-acquisition-complete-finalized.

Watts, Jacqueline H. 2009. "'Allowed into a Man's World' Meanings of Work-Life Balance: Perspectives of Women Civil Engineers as 'Minority' Workers in Construction." *Gender, Work and Organization* 16, no. 1: 37–57. https://doi.org/10.1111/j.1468-0432.2007.00352.x.

Weaver, Ryan. 2014. "Government Grants, Loans, and Tax Credits for Digital Media Projects." *Mentor Works*. September 12. https://www.mentorworks.ca/blog/government-funding/funding-for-digital-media-09-2014.

Weber, Maximilian Karl Emil. 1978 (1921). *Economy and Society: An Outline of Interpretive Sociology*. Translated by Ephraim Fischoff. Berkeley, California: University of California Press.

Weil, David. 2014. *The Fissured Workplace: Why Work Became So Bad for So Many and What Can Be Done to Improve It*. Cambridge: Harvard University Press.

Wenell, Torbjörn, Eskil Ekstedt, and Rolf A. Lundin. 2017. "On the Road to Project Society: A Swedish Story." *PM World Journal* 6, no. 1: 1–6. https://www.wenellse.cdn.triggerfish.cloud/uploads/2017/01/on-the-road-to-project-society-wenell-ekstedt-lundin-pm-world-journal-jan-2017.pdf.

Westecott, Emma, Suzanne Stein, Hsu Cheryl, and Kashfia Rahman. 2019. "In Situ: Researching Corporate Diversity Initiatives with Game Developers." In *DiGRA '19—Proceedings of the 2019 DiGRA International Conference: Game, Play and the Emerging Ludo-Mix DiGRA, August 6–10, Kyoto*. http://openresearch.ocadu.ca/id/eprint/2793.

Weststar, Johanna. 2015. "Understanding Video Game Developers as an Occupational Community." *Information, Communication and Society* 18, no. 10: 1,238–52. https://doi.org/10.1080/1369118X.2015.1036094.

Weststar, Johanna, and Louis-Étienne Dubois. 2022. "From Crunch to Grind: Adopting Servitization in Project-Based Creative Work." *Work, Employment and Society*, OnlineFirst. https://doi.org/10.1177/09500170211061228.

Weststar, Johanna, and Marie-Josée Legault. 2012. "Facts and Discussion about Hours of Work in the Video Game Industry." In *Cultural Perspectives of Video Games: From Designer to Player*, edited by Adam L. Bracken and Natacha Guyot, 187–97. Oxford: Interdisciplinary Press.

—. 2014. *Developer Satisfaction Survey 2014: Employment Report*, commissioned by the International Game Developers' Association (IGDA). https://www.gameqol.org/igda-qol-survey.

—. 2015. *2015 Developer Satisfaction Survey: Summary Report*, commissioned by the International Game Developers' Association. https://www.gameqol.org/igda-qol-survey.

—. 2016. *Developer Satisfaction Survey 2016: Summary Report*, commissioned by the International Game Developers' Association. https://www.gameqol.org/igda-qol-survey.

—. 2017. "Why Might a Videogame Developer Join a Union?" *Labor Studies Journal* 42, no. 4: 295-321. https://doi.org/10.1177/0160449X17731878.

—. 2018. "Women's Experiences on the Path to a Career in Game Development." In *Feminism in Play*, edited by Kishonna L. Gray, Gerald Voorhees, and Emma Vossen, 105-23. London: Palgrave Macmillan. https://r-libre.teluq.ca/1656.

—. 2019. "Building Momentum for Collectivity in the Digital Game Community." *Television and New Media* 20, no. 8: 848-61. https://doi.org/10.1177/1527476419851087.

Weststar, Johanna, Marie-Josée Legault, Chandell Gosse, and Victoria O'Meara. 2016. *Developer Satisfaction Survey 2014, and 2015: Diversity in the Game Industry Report*, commissioned by the International Game Developers Association (IGDA). https://www.gameqol.org/igda-qol-survey.

Weststar, Johanna, Victoria O'Meara, Chandell Gosse, and Marie-Josée Legault. 2017. *Diversity among Videogame Developers: 2004-2015*, commissioned by the International Game Developers Association (IGDA). http://www.gameqol.org/igda-qol-survey.

Weststar, Johanna, Victoria O'Meara, and Marie-Josée Legault. 2017. *Developer Satisfaction Survey 2017: Summary Report*, commissioned by the International Game Developers Association (IGDA). https://www.gameqol.org/igda-qol-survey.

—. 2018. *Developer Satisfaction Survey 2015, and 2016: Employment Report*, commissioned by International Game Developers Association (IGDA). http://www.gameqol.org/igda-qol-survey.

Weststar, Johanna, Eva Kwan, and Shruti Kumar. 2019. *Developer Satisfaction Survey 2019: Summary Report*, commissioned by the International Game Developers Association (IGDA). http://www.gameqol.org/igda-qol-survey.

Whitson, Jennifer. 2013. "The 'Console Ship Is Sinking' and What This Means for Indies." *Loading...: Journal of the Canadian Game Studies Association* 7, no. 11: 122-29. https://journals.sfu.ca/loading/index.php/loading/article/view/125.

Whitson, Jennifer R., Bart Simon, and Felan Parker. 2021. "The Missing Producer: Rethinking Indie Cultural Production in Terms of Entrepreneurship, Relational Labour, and Sustainability." *European Journal of Cultural Studies* (December), OnlineFirst. https://doi.org/10.1177/1367549418810082.

Wilkinson, Adrian, Jimmy Donaghey, Tony Dundon, and Richard Freeman. 2014. *Handbook of Research on Employee Voice*. Cheltenham, UK: Edward Elgar Publishing.

Williams, Dmitri, Nicole Martins, Mia Consalvo, and James D. Ivory. 2009. "The Virtual Census: Representations of Gender, Race and Age in Video Games." *New Media, and Society* 11, no. 5: 815-34. https://doi.org/10.1177/1461444809105354.

Williams, Ian. 2015. "Crunched: Has the Games Industry Really Stopped Exploiting Its Workforce?" *Guardian*, February 18.

Wilson, Daniel J. 2009. "Beggar Thy Neighbor?: The In-State, Out-of-State, and Aggregate Effects of R&D Tax Credits." *Review of Economics and Statistics* 91, no. 2: 431–36. https://doi.org/10.1162/rest.91.2.431.

Wingfield, Nick. 2015. "Intel Allocated $300 Million for Workplace Diversity." *New York Times*, January 6.

Wolf, Mark, and Bernard Perron, eds. 2003. *The Video Game Theory Reader*. New York: Routledge.

Women in Games (WIG). 2021. "New League for Riot Games as Studio Becomes Latest Corporate Ambassador." Women in Games, press release, October 28. https://www.womeningames.org/new-league-for-riot-games-as-studio-becomes-latest-corporate-ambassador.

Women in Games International (WIGI). 2021. "Women in Games International is Partnering with Activision Blizzard through a Landmark $1M Grant to Advance the Success of Women in the Global Games Industry." Women in Games International, press release, November 2. https://www.getwigi.com/wigiactivisionblizzardgrant.

Woodcock, Jamie. 2016. "The Work of Play: Marx and the Video Games Industry in the United Kingdom." *Journal of Gaming, and Virtual Worlds* 8, no. 2: 131–43. https://doi.org/10.1386/jgvw.8.2.131_1.

——. 2020. "Organizing in the Game Industry: The Story of Game Workers Unite UK." *New Labor Forum* 29, no. 1: 50–57.

Woodfield, Ruth. 2002. "Woman and Information Systems Development: Not Just a Pretty (Inter)face?" *Information, Technology and People* 15, no. 2: 119–38. https://doi.org/10.1108/09593840210430561.

WorkBC. n.d. "What is the B.C. Employer Training Grant Program?" Government of British Columbia. https://www.workbc.ca/Employer-Resources/BC-Employer-Training-Grant/What-is-the-B-C-Employer-Training-Grant.aspx.

Workplace Gender Equality Agency. 2016. *UnPaid Care Work and the Labour Market: Insight Paper*. Workplace Gender Equality Agency, Government of Australia. https://www.wgea.gov.au/publications/unpaid-care-work-and-the-labour-market.

Wong, Kapo, Alan H. S. Chan, and S. C. Ngan. 2019. "The Effect of Long Working Hours and Overtime on Occupational Health: A Meta-Analysis of Evidence from 1998 to 2018." *International Journal of Environmental Research and Public Health* 16, no. 12: 1–22. https://doi.org/10.3390/ijerph16122102.

Yahya, Salleh, and Wee-Keat Goh. 2002. "Managing Human Resources toward Achieving Knowledge Management." *Journal of Knowledge Management* 6, no. 5: 457–68. https://doi.org/10.1108/13673270210450414.

Yarwood, Jack. 2016. "Easter Eggs: The Hidden Secrets of Videogames." *Paste Magazine*, March 27. https://www.pastemagazine.com/articles/2016/03/easter-eggs-the-hidden-secrets-of-videogames.html.

Yee, Nick. 2008. "Maps of Digital Desires: Exploring the Topography of Gender and Play in Online Games." In *Beyond Barbie and Mortal Kombat: New Perspectives on Gender and Gaming*, edited by Yasmin B. Kafai, Carrie Heeter, Jill Denner, and Jennifer Y. Sun, 83–96. Cambridge: MIT Press.

Yeuk-Mui May, Tam, Marek Korczynski, and Stephen J. Frenkel. 2002. "Organizational and Occupational Commitment: Knowledge Workers in Large Corporations." *Journal of Management Studies* 39: 775–801. https://doi.org/10.1111/1467-6486.00311.

Yin-Poole, Wesley. 2021. "Activision Blizzard Boss Bobby Kotick's $155M Pay Package Approved by Shareholders." *Eurogamer*, June 22. https://www.eurogamer.net/articles/2021-06-22-activision-blizzard-boss-bobby-koticks-usd155m-pay-package-approved-by-shareholders.

Yoon, Yeogyeong, Jia Ryu, Hyunjoo Kim, Chung won Kang, and Kyunghee Jung-Choi. 2018. "Working Hours and Depressive Symptoms: The Role of Job Stress Factors." *Annals of Occupational and Environmental Medicine* 30, no. 46. https://doi.org/10.1186/s40557-018-0257-5.

Young, Christopher J. 2018. "Game Changers: Everyday Gamemakers and the Development of the Video Game Industry." PhD dissertation, University of Toronto. https://www.proquest.com/docview/2087728878?pq-origsite=gscholar&fromopenview=true.

Yourdon, Edward. 2004. *Death March*, 2nd ed. Upper Saddle River, New Jersey: Prentice Hall.

Zackariasson, Peter, Martin Walfisz, and Timothy L. Wilson. 2006. "Management of Creativity in Video Game Development: A Case Study." *Services Marketing Quarterly* 27, no. 4: 73–97. https://www.tandfonline.com/doi/abs/10.1300/J396v27n04_05.

Zampolini, Pauline. 2018a. "Les représentations féminines dans les jeux vidéo: Entrevue avec Elodie Simard." *RDS Jeux vidéo*, December 12. https://jeuxvideo.rds.ca/les-representations-feminines-dans-les-jeux-video-entrevue-avec-elodie-simard.

—. 2018b. "Le sport électronique et les femmes: Un rapport encore conflictuel." *FMC veille*, January 26. https://trends.cmf-fmc.ca/fr/le-sport-electronique-et-les-femmes-un-rapport-encore-conflictuel.

DATA APPENDIX

Introduction

Table 0.1
Membership and Participation in the IGDA (% of respondents) (whole sample: 2014, 2015, 2016, 2017, 2019)

Membership	2014	2015	2016	2017	2019
Member of the IGDA	36	23	40	33	41
Not a member, but plan to become one	14	9	9	14	8
Not a member, but have been in the past	22	14	15	16	22
Never been a member	28	52	36	37	28
Participation					
There is an IGDA chapter in their area	—	47	60	59	57
Attended an IGDA event in their area	53	34	45	45	43
Attended an IGDA event at conferences	—	31	41	37	43

Source: Original data from IGDA DSS 2014, 2015, 2016, 2017, 2019

Chapter 4

Figure 4.3
What is your current view of job opportunities in the game industry? (2014-19)

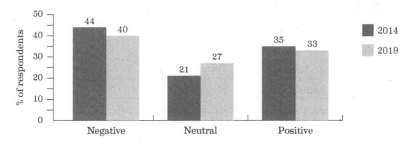

Source: Original data from IGDA DSS 2014, 2019

Table 4.3
Distribution of VGDs (% of respondents) according to sexual orientation, 2015–19

Reporting being	2015	2019
Heterosexual	81	79
Gay or lesbian	4	4
Bisexual	13	12
Other	3	5

Source: Weststar, Legault, Gosse, and O'Meara 2016, 10; Weststar, Kwan, and Kumar 2019, 12

Table 4.4
Distribution of VGDs (% of respondents) according to ethnic origin, 2015–19

Reported being	2015	2019
White/Caucasian/European	76	81
East/South East Asian	9	8
Hispanic, Latino, Latina, Latinx	7	7
Black/African American/African/Afro-Caribbean	3	2
Aboriginal/Indigenous	2	5
South Asian	2	4
Arab or West Asian	2	2
Pacific Islander	1	—
Other	1	5

Source: Weststar, Legault, Gosse, and O'Meara 2016, 8; Weststar, Kwan, and Kumar 2019, 13
Note: Totals do not add to 100% because respondents could select multiple categories

Table 4.8
Distribution of answers (% of respondents) to the question: "In general, how important would you rate the following?" (2015–19)

(Somewhat and very important)	2015	2019
Diversity in the workplace	62	83
Diversity in the game industry	66	85
Diversity in game content	72	87

Source: Weststar, Legault, Gosse, and O'Meara 2016; Weststar, Kwan, and Kumar 2019

Table 4.10
Distribution of answers (% of respondents) to the question: "Do you have any children?" (2004–19)

	2004	2009	2015	2019
No	77	73	78	65
Yes	23	27	22	35

Source: Legault and Weststar 2012b; Weststar, Legault, Gosse, and O'Meara 2016; Weststar, Kwan, and Kumar 2019

Table 4.11
Distribution of answers (% of respondents) according to age categories of children (2014 and 2019)

	2014	2019
No children	73	71
Preschool children	16	15
School-aged children	13	13
Adult children	2	5

Source: Original data from IGDA DSS 2014, 2019

Table 4.12
Distribution of answers (% of respondents) to the question: "I feel that I'm constantly behind at work and at home and never have enough time for either" (2009–19)

	2009	*Aggregated*	2014	*Aggregated*	2019	*Aggregated*
Strongly agree	11	41	12	40	15	44
Agree	30		28		29	
Neutral	22		24		21	
Disagree	31	37	27	36	26	34
Strongly disagree	6		9		8	

Source: Original data from IGDA QoL 2009; DSS 2014, 2019

DATA APPENDIX 357

Chapter 7

Table 7.1
Distribution of answers (% of respondents) to the question: "Management seeks my input and acts on it" (2009, 2014, 2019)

	2009	2014	2019
Strongly agree	11	11	24
Agree	37	35	33
Neither agree nor disagree	29	28	25
Disagree	15	15	11
Strongly disagree	8	10	7

Source: Original data from IGDA QoL 2009; DSS 2014, 2019

Table 7.5
Distribution of answers (% of respondents) to the question: "If a vote were held today to form a union at your company/studio, how would you vote? (2014–19)

	Managers		Developers (from Table 9.6)	
	2014	2019	2014	2019
For	45	40	48	52
Against	32	21	25	9
No opinion or prefer not to say*	9	35	14	37
I would not vote at all	13	3	14	2

Source: Adapted from Tô, Legault, and Weststar 2016, 33; with original data from IGDA DSS 2014, 2019

* The wording for this response option changed across the three surveys. Actual language pursuant to each survey was "no opinion or prefer not to say" (2009), "prefer not to say" (2014), "don't know or need more information" (2019).

Chapter 8

Table 8.2
Tax Credit Regimes across Canada/Other Provinces

Year	Credit Amount and Details
Nova Scotia: Digital Media Tax Credit	
2008–2021	• The lesser of 50% of eligible Nova Scotia labour expenses or 25% of total expenditures made in Nova Scotia • Plus regional bonuses—products developed outside the Halifax Regional Municipality yield a 10% bonus credit on labour expenditure or a 5% bonus credit on total expenditures • Cannot stack with federal SR&ED
2007	• 17.5%
Manitoba: Interactive Digital Media Tax Credit	
2008–2022	• 40% when a corporation pays at least 25% of the salary and wages to employees who are Manitoba residents for the project period • As of June 30, 2016, 35% when a corporation that pays less than 25% of its wages to Manitoba employees, still incurs labour expenses of at least $1 million more than government assistance related to those expenses • Stacking allowed subject to certain rules
Prince Edward Island: Innovation and Development Labour Rebate Program	
Present	• Rebate of 25% of eligible labour expenses to a maximum of one year of eligible expenses
Newfoundland and Labrador: Interactive Digital Media Tax Credit	
2015–Present	• 40% • Cannot stack with federal SR&ED
Alberta: Interactive Digital Media Tax Credit	
April 2018–2019	• Was 25%; program cut in 2019 budget • Cannot stack with federal SR&ED

Sources: Avery and Cornell 2016; Canada Revenue Agency 2019; Dryden 2019; email correspondence with Erin Dalton, Audit Manager, Alberta Department of Finance (July 22, 2019); Government of Prince Edward Island (n.d.); Interactive Digital Media Tax Credit Regulations (n.d.); Newfoundland and Labrador *Income Tax Act*[*]; Nova Scotia Department of Finance 2011; Nova Scotia Department of Finance and Treasury Board 2018

[*] Legislative Assembly of Newfoundland and Labrador: Income Tax Act, 2000, Regulation 84/15—Interactive Digital Media Tax Credit, www.assembly.nl.ca/legislation/sr/regulations/rc150084.htm

Table 8.3
Distribution of answers (% of respondents) to the question: "What is the role of the IGDA?" (whole sample: 2014, 2015, 2016, 2017, 2019)

	2014	2015	2016	2017	2019
Networking and community	78	68	77	75	78
Professional development	45	41	48	44	49
Advocacy	41	44	53	52	52
International outreach	21	22	29	37	31
Don't know	16	17	12	14	13
Other	3	8	6	2	4

Source: Original data from IGDA DSS 2014, 2015, 2016, 2017, 2019

Figure 8.1
Distribution of answers (% of respondents) to the question: "How would you rate the overall effectiveness of the IGDA?" (whole sample: 2014, 2015, 2016 2017, 2019)

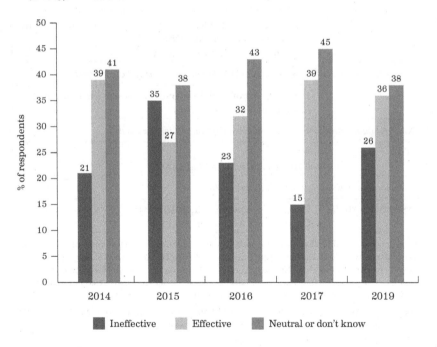

Source: Original data from IGDA DSS 2014, 2015, 2016, 2017, 2019

Chapter 9

Table 9.1
Distribution of answers (% of respondents) to the question: "Have you experienced crunch time in the past two years?" (2014 and 2019)

	2014	Aggregated	2019	Aggregated
No	21	21	36	36
Once	19		17	
Twice	19	80	11	64
More than twice	42		36	

Source: Legault and Weststar 2015a, 16; original data from IGDA DSS 2019

Figure 9.2
Distribution of answers to the question: "How many hours per week on average do you actually work when in crunch time?" (2004–19)

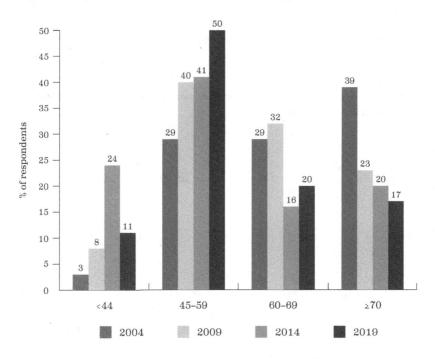

Source: modified from Legault and Weststar 2015a, 22–23; original data from IGDA DSS 2019

DATA APPENDIX 361

Figure 9.3
Distribution of answers to the question: "On average how many weeks per year do you crunch?" (2009–14)

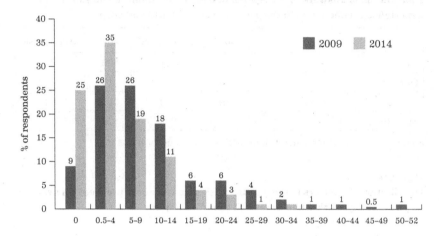

Source: modified from Legault and Weststar 2015a, 25

Figure 9.4
Distribution of answers to the question: "On average how many weeks in a row do you crunch?" (2004–14)

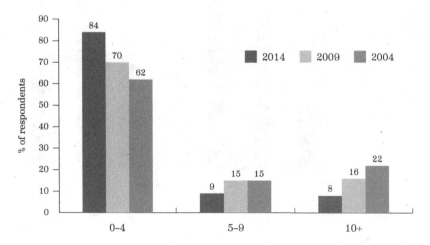

Source: Legault and Weststar 2015a, 27

Table 9.5
Distribution of answers (% of respondents) to the question: "Do you feel that crunch time is expected at your workplace as a normal part of your job?" (2014–19)

	2014	2019
No	35	41
Yes	54	44
Not sure	11	15

Source: Legault and Weststar 2015a, 17; original data from IGDA DSS 2019

Table 9.6
Distribution of answers (% of respondents) to the question: "What are the top three reasons that crunch happens at your company?" (2014 and 2019)

	2014	2019
Poor/unrealistic scheduling	62	65
Feature creep	44	—
Unclear expectations	40	31
Inexperienced management	31	25
Not enough people on the team	30	30
People do it voluntarily	27	28
Changes from external stakeholders (i.e., publisher, head office)	26	17
Inexperienced team	17	11
Changes from within the studio	16	9
Software problems (i.e., slowness, not having the needed tools)	14	14
It is mandated as part of the schedule	12	3
Changes from within the team	11	12
Turnover within the team	6	5
Turnover among managers	4	—
Physical problems (infrastructure, computer hardware)	4	4

Source: Original data from IGDA DSS 2014, 2019

Table 9.8
Distribution of answers (% of respondents) to the statement: "I am judged more by the hours I put in than by the quality of my work." (2009–19)

	2009	Aggregated	2014	Aggregated	2019	Aggregated
Strongly agree	7	20	11	22	6	15
Agree	13		11		9	
Neutral	22	22	18	18	18	18
Disagree	39	57	32	60	31	67
Strongly disagree	18		28		36	

Source: Original data from IGDA DSS 2009, 2014, 2019

Table 9.9
Distribution of answers (% of respondents) to the statement: "I worry that the time I spend with my family diminishes my chances of promotion/advancement." (2009–19)

	2009	Aggregated	2014	Aggregated	2019	Aggregated
Strongly agree	6	21	8	31	7	25
Agree	15		23		18	
Neutral	20	20	18	18	20	20
Disagree	37	58	30	50	32	56
Strongly disagree	21		20		24	

Source: Original data from IGDA DSS 2009; DSS 2014; DSS 2019

Table 9.10
Distribution of answers (% of respondents) to the question: "Have you ever been denied a vacation/been asked to cancel a vacation you'd already scheduled?" (2009–19)

	2009	2014	2019
Been denied a vacation	22	21	—
Been asked to cancel a vacation you'd already scheduled	24	15	59*
Been denied promised time off *in lieu*	—	20	19

Source: Original data from IGDA QoL 2009; DSS 2014, 2019

* In 2019 the self-employed were asked: "Have you ever had to cancel or reschedule a vacation or other time-off because of project demands?" Their responses are included here.

Chapter 10

Table 10.1
Distribution of answers (% of respondents) to the question: "Does your company/studio/school have any of the following equality and diversity related policies and procedures?" (2015–19)

Policies and procedures	2015	2019
General non-discrimination policy	58	70
Sexual harassment policy	51	62
Equal opportunity hiring policy	52	59
Formal complaint procedure	29	36
Formal disciplinary process related to equality and diversity policies	24	30
Safe space	—	21
Retention measurement process	13	13
None	11	8
Don't know	22	22

Source: Weststar, Legault, Gosse, and O'Meara 2016, 31; original data from DSS 2019
Note: Columns do not total 100% due to multiple response allowances

Table 10.2
"Does your company/studio/school have any of the following equality and diversity related programs?" (2015–19) (% of respondents)

Programs	2015	2019
Partnerships with community colleges, groups, or nonprofits to foster a pipeline of diverse candidates	12	17
Partnerships with community colleges, groups, or nonprofits to foster game developer skills and competencies among diverse candidates	11	16
Retention measures or programs such as on-boarding, mentoring, or professional development programs to retain diverse talent	11	16
Targeted marketing or advertising to diverse demographics	6	12
Programs or partnerships to foster new product or service ideas and innovations from diverse groups	6	7
None	33	38
Don't know	33	27
Not applicable/decline to answer	13	7

Source: Weststar, Legault, Gosse, and O'Meara 2016, 31; original data from DSS 2019
Note: Columns do not total 100% due to multiple response allowances

Figure 10.2
Distribution of income by gender, 2015

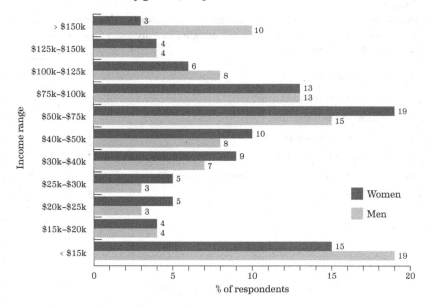

Source: Weststar, O'Meara, Gosse, and Legault 2017, 21

Figure 10.3
Distribution of income by gender, 2019

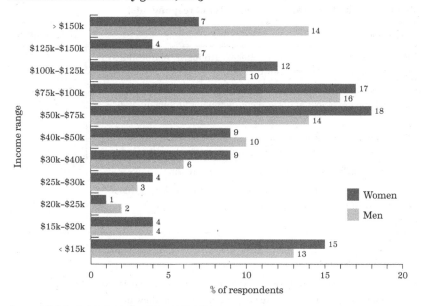

Source: Original data from the IGDA DSS 2019

Figure 10.4
Distribution of income by ethnic group, 2015

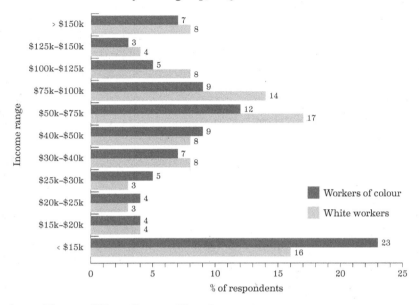

Source: Weststar, O'Meara, Gosse, and Legault 2017, 21

Figure 10.5
Distribution of income by ethnic group, 2019

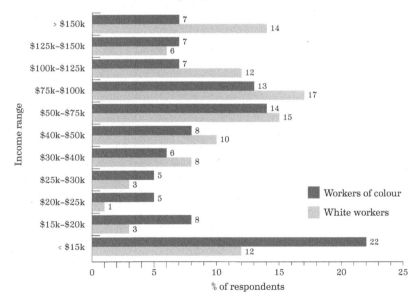

Source: Original data from the IGDA DSS 2019

DATA APPENDIX 367

Table 10.4
VGDs' dependents, 2019 (% of respondents)

	Men	*Women*
No children	65	78
Pre-school children	14	9
School-age children	19	11
Adult children	7	7
Responsible for an elderly parent/relative	11	15

Source: Original data from IGDA DSS 2019

INDEX

#1ReasonToBe (hashtag), 254

AAA (triple A) studios, 37, 58, 224, 283, 295
ABK (Activision Blizzard King) Workers Alliance, 174, 213
absenteeism, 170
active citizenship, 5, 23, 127, 293
Activision Blizzard, 43, 47, 174–75, 212, 221, 255, 260, 275
Activision Blizzard King (ABK) Workers Alliance, 174, 213
affirmative action, 261
AFL-CIO (US), 184–85
Agile programming method, 41
Alphabet Workers Union (Google), 185, 187, 213, 298
angel investor, 50
Anti-Censorship and Social Issues (issue-based group), 208, 216
Apple, 50
arbitrariness. See workers, arbitrary treatment
Arthurs, Harry, xiii, 3–5
at-will employment, 70–73, 105, 139
awards, 188–89, 210

BAME (Black, Asian, and Minority Ethnic) in Games (now BiG), 220–21
Beck, Ulrich, 70
Bellini, Andrea, 177–78, 183
belonging: game relatability, 286–88; heard and valued, 284–86; and IGDA, 215; as part of diversity, inclusion, and belonging framework, 256–58, 257f, 288. See also diversity; gender issues; harassment; inequities; sexism
benefits, state or employer, 107–10
Bethesda Softworks, 47

A Better Ubisoft (issue-based group), 213
BiG (formerly BAME in Games), 220–21
BioWare, 185
Black communities: BiG (was BAME in games), 220–21; BIPOC communities, 79n2, 200; Black in Games (issue-based group), 216; #BlackLivesMatter, 289; demographics, 75; pay issues, 265; racism, 80–82, 81f; systemic discrimination, 12–14. See also diversity; inequities; persons of colour; racialized groups
bonuses, 163–64, 231, 233, 234
Bosniak, Linda, 16, 292
British Columbia, 205, 234
Budd, John W., 9–10
bugs, 42
bullying, 269–70
Bulut, Ergin: about, xiv; case study of acquired studio, 53, 60; cruel optimism, 88; crunch time, 237; economic forces on videogame industry, 126; flexible employment, 65–66; gender issues, 95, 267; meritocracy as systemic sexism, 282
bureaucracy, 10, 130, 131
burnout, 84, 89, 90, 92, 115–17, 173, 247

California Department of Fair Employment and Housing, 260
Campaign to Organize Digital Employees (CODE), 185–86, 213, 298
Canada: and Charter of Rights and Freedoms, 212n17; and diversity and inclusion policies, 259; as one of main hosts for videogame industry, 45; and salaries, 261; and tax credits, 196f, 359f
Canada Media Fund (CMF), 198–200

Canadian Interactive Alliance/
  L'Alliance interactive canadienne
  (CIAIC), 204–205
Capcom, 45
career advancement, 121–22, 122*f*
Cassell, Justine, 253
casualization of labour, 70–73
censorship, 205, 208, 216
children/childcare, 94–96, 259, 267,
  268, 357*f*, 368*f*
China, 194
Chinese in Games (issue-based group),
  216
citizenship at work, 3–21; about, xiii,
  xv, 3; distribution of power, 8–10;
  domain of citizenship, 18–20, 21*f*, 77,
  165*f*, 166, 209, 250–51, 299–301; fair
  procedures, 131–33; four components
  of, 3–4, 5*f*, 16, 20, 291–95; inclusion,
  16–20; industrial citizenship, xiii,
  3–8, 12–16, 292, 299, 300; object of
  citizenship, 17–18, 21*f*, 165*f*, 166, 194,
  299–301; post-industrial landscape,
  10–12; subject of citizenship, 16–17,
  20, 21*f*, 165*f*, 166, 194, 208, 299–301
civil citizenship, 7*f*
civil rights, 7*f*
clients, 31–33, 34, 46, 51–55
CODE—the Campaign to Organize
  Digital Employees, 185–86, 213, 298
collective bargaining, 7*f*, 8, 17–18, 23
collective short-term mobilizations,
  173–77
Communications Workers of America
  (CWA), 175, 185
compensation systems: bonuses,
  163–64, 231, 233, 234; discretionary, 33, 161–64, 162*f*, 245–47; Equal
  Pay Act (California), 175; and
  evaluations, 156–61, 165*f*, 243, 294;
  inequities, 261–62, 263, 265, 367*f*;
  pension plans, 19, 125, 126*f*, 299, 302;
  promotion, 156–61; seniority, 17, 23,
  68; severance packages, 108–9; state
  or employer benefits, 107–10
conferences, 119
conflicts, 97, 171–72, 172*f*
Consalvo, Mia, 255
contracts, open-ended, 68
Corrigan, Thomas, 88
Côté, Amanda C., 237

COVID-19, 113–14, 259. *See also*
  pandemic
Coworker.org, 212
Crane, Luke, 254
creative class, 64–65, 82, 97
Creative Technology Association of
  British Columbia, 205
crediting practices, 148–51, 149*f*, 165*f*,
  170–71, 174, 216, 294
cruel optimism, 88–89
crunch time: about, xxiv, 220n22, 227;
  compensation for, 162, 164; culture
  of, 85, 89–90, 169, 176, 250; measuring of, 229–30, 361–63*f*; and parents,
  74, 266–69; pervasiveness of, 241–44;
  project management constraints,
  58, 102, 236–40, 238*f*, 240*f*, 241–44;
  refusal, 32, 87, 247–50
Crytek UK studio, 174

Dames Making Games, 222
D'Anastasio, Cecilia, 174
dancers, 302
deadlines, 26, 51–53, 237
death march, 227
de Castell, Suzanne, 281
decision-making processes, 132*f*. *See
  also* crunch time
de Kloet, Jeroen, 200, 211, 301
Denmark, 183–84, 203
de Peuter, Grieg, xv, 37, 88
Developer Credits (issue-based group),
  216
Devs with Kids (issue-based group), 216
DICE (Digital Illusions Creative
  Entertainment), 183
DigiBC, 205
Digital Mentorship Program, 221
disabilities, 76, 116
discipline and dismissals, 134–41;
  about, 165*f*; layoffs, 66–70, 68*f*, 84,
  136, 174, 200. *See also* firings
discrimination, systemic, 13–14
diversity: about, 73–76, 214–15, 220–22,
  256–58, 257*f*, 261*f*, 356*f*; disabilities,
  76, 116; racialized groups, 79n2,
  193–94, 200, 217, 265, 287; racism,
  80–82, 81*f*. *See also* Black communities; persons of colour; women in
  the workforce

domain of citizenship, 18–20, 21f, 77, 165f, 166, 209, 250–51, 299–301
Dyer-Witheford, Nick, xiv, xv

EA Spouse (blog), 173
Easter eggs, 170–71
education. *See* professional development
Electronic Arts (EA), 45, 54, 113–14, 173, 175–77, 180, 183. *See also EA Spouse* (blog)
employment risks, 105–27; health risks, 115–18; obsolescence, 118–24; old age, 124–26; protections against, 107–15; risk transfer, 105–7
engineers, 183
Entertainment Software Association (ESA), 202, 204, 206, 207
Entertainment Software Rating Board (ESRB), 206, 207
Equal Employment Opportunity Commission (US), 175
Equal Pay Act (California), 175
ethnicity. *See* diversity; persons of colour; racialized groups
Eugen Systems, 184
Europe, 45, 67, 194, 202, 211, 261
European Game Development Federation (EGDF), 203–204
evaluations, 156–61, 157f, 165f, 243, 294
events, 123, 209, 211, 214, 223, 355f
Extreme programming method, 41

Fair Play Alliance, 210, 220, 222
fair procedure, 131–33
fast-food workers, 302
feature creep, 239
FedEx, 11n3
feelgood teams, 180
Ferraras, Isabelle, xv
financialization of videogame industry, 12, 56–58, 63, 106, 126, 292–94, 302
Financial Services Union (FSU), 184, 198
Finland, 183, 199, 207
firings: and employment flexibility, 105–6, 169; examples of, 116, 123, 135–36, 140, 298; and fair procedure, 133, 139; motives for, 138f; or sidelined, 137; risk of project-based work, 58, 292; threat/consequence of, 242, 248
Fisher, Stephanie, 281
flexploitation, 88
Florida, Richard, 66
France, 184, 194
franchises, 54, 58
free labour/playbour, xii, 64–65, 89, 101, 237. *See also* passion/play
freemium games, 216, 237
From Barbie to Mortal Kombat (Cassell and Jenkins), 253
Full Indie in Vancouver, 222–23
funding, 27, 43–51, 106, 120, 198–201. *See also* tax credits
fun factor, 39–40, 42–43

Gamasutra. *See Game Developer*
gambling, 81f, 205, 207
Game Developer (formerly *Gamasutra*), 209–10, 215, 239, 249, 261
Game Developers Choice Awards, 210
Game Developers Conference (GDC), 47–50, 119, 180, 209, 254, 275
game jams, 123
GameLoop, Boston, 119
Game Makers of Finland, 183
gameplay goals, 39–40
game rating systems, 38, 208, 213
Gamergate, 81, 215, 255, 283, 289
GameStop, 114
Gamewatch.org, 173
Game Workers Alliance, 175, 185, 186
Game Workers Australia, 212
Game Workers Unite (GWU), 113–14, 184–85, 211, 212
gender issues: masculinity, 253, 274; occupational segregation, 19, 77–80, 78ff; sexual orientation, 74–75, 356f; transgender population, 74–75, 215f; white, male, and cisgender, 12, 20, 253, 256, 264, 274, 280, 288, 294, 295. *See also* diversity; harassment; sexism; women in the workforce
Germany, 68, 202
Gill, Rosalind, 63, 95
Global Value Chain approach, 45
Goodgame Studios, 180
Google (Alphabet Workers Union), 185, 187, 213, 298

Guide to the Project Management Body of Knowledge (PMBOK), 26

hackers, xii
Hammar, Emil, 289
Handy, Jocelyn, 282
harassment: exclusionary effect of, 14–15, 274–75; Fair Play Alliance, 210, 220, 222; Gamergate, 81, 215, 255, 283, 289; HR policies on, 259–60, 290, 300; motive for firing, 138; of non-dominant group, 18, 73, 101, 269, 283; sexual harassment, 174–75, 184, 213, 221, 255, 275–76. *See also* gender issues; sexism
Harris, Brandon C., 237
Harvey, Alison, 278
health issues, 7*f*, 84–88, 115–18, 118*f*, 293
Hirschman, Albert, 168
Hochschild, Arlie R., 266
"Hot Coffee" affair, 206n11, 207
HTML Writers Guild, 177
human resource management (HRM): about, 3n1, 23; decision making, 9, 129–34; employees on demand, 28; long-term *versus* short-term, 99; policies, xiv, 133–34; post-bureaucratic conditions, 33; and project management, 25

IGDA (International Game Developers Association): about, xviii–xix, 213–20, 360*f*; effectiveness of, 218*f*, 360*f*; and GDC, 210; membership and participation in, 203, 355*f*; Quality of Life (QoL) survey, xi–xii, xix–xx, 67, 73, 75–76, 77–80, 173, 217, 228; and unions, 220; YetiZen party, 255
inclusion, 16–20, 257*f*, 258
independent contracting, 236
Independent Games Festival, 210
Independent Workers' Union of Great Britain (IWGB), 184
India, 67
Indigenous Peoples, 200
individual bargaining, 17–18
industrial citizenship, xiii, 3–8, 12–16, 292, 299, 300
inequities: compensation systems, 261–62, 263, 265, 367*f*; experiences of, 269–74, 271*f*; women in the workforce, 269–74. *See also* Black communities; gender issues; harassment; persons of colour; racialized groups; women in the workforce
Informa, 209
information technology (IT) services, xiv, 234
insurance plans, 6, 7*f*, 117
Intel, 215
intellectual property (IP), 38, 46, 47, 98, 141, 148, 170, 174, 209, 294. *See also* crediting practices
Interactive Entertainment South Africa (IESA), 203
Interactive Ontario, 204
Interactive Software Federation of Europe (ISFE), 202
International Game Developers Association. *See* IGDA
International Game Summit, Montréal, 119
Ireland, 198
iron triangle (budget, deadline, scope): client as constraint, 25–26; closed budget envelope, 34, 52, 90; as evaluation criteria, 25–26, 44; and project managers, 33, 106, 302; workers unable to affect, 30, 115, 293
issue-based groups, 210, 220–22

Japan, 45, 194
Jenkins, Henry, 253
Jenson, Jennifer, 281
Jewish Game Developers (issue-based group), 216
job actions, 173–75
job control/insecurity, 58, 70, 84–88, 90–92, 91*f*, 355*f*
job titles, 77, 78*f*, 150–51
Johns, Jennifer, 54

Kazemi, Darius, 218, 254–55
Keogh, Brendan, 225, 298
Kerr, Aphra, 202, 203, 204, 205, 211
Keune, Maarten, 202
Keynesian economic theory, 11–12
Keywords Studios, 185
knowledge workers, xv, 16–17, 24, 56–57, 65, 97–98
Korea, 63

Kotick, Bobby, 212
Kücklich, Julian, xii
Kuehn, Kathleen, 88

labour laws, 23
La Guilde du jeu vidéo du Québec, 204
Lanetix, 137
Latinx in Games (issue-based group), 216
lawsuits, 174, 175-77
layoffs, 66-70, 68f, 84, 136, 174, 200
Legault, Marie-Josée, 291
licensing, 50-51
live games, 54
loot boxes, 207

Machung, Anne, 266
Make Games South Africa (MGSA), 203
Marshall, Thomas Humphrey, xiii, 3-5, 295
Marxism, 267
masculinity, 253, 274
McAllister, Ken S., 207
McRobbie, Angela, 63
meetups and informal groups, 222-25
#MeToo, 289
Mexico, 208
microaggressions, 269
Microsoft, 44, 47, 175
middleware, 44
migrant workers, 17, 19, 108
mobbing, 270
mobility, employment, 27-30, 38, 58-59, 69-71, 95, 106, 293
modders/modding, xii, xiv, 206n11
Model Alliance, 303
Montréal International, 204
Mont Royal Gaming Society in Montreal, 222
Mosco, Vincent, 301
musicians, 302

National Guestworker Alliance, 303
Neff, Gina, 101, 124
neoliberalism, 11, 12
Netherlands, 199, 202
networking, 110-14, 122-23, 213-14
NewsGuild-CWA (Communications Workers of America), 137
New York Fashion Workers, 303

Nexon, 184
Nichols, Randall, xi-xii
Nieborg, David, 48, 200, 211, 301
Nintendo, 38, 44, 47
non-binary population, 215f
non-compete agreements (NCAs), 141-48, 165f, 170, 223, 294
non-disclosure agreements (NDAs), 141-48, 165f, 170, 194, 209, 294
non-union employee representation (NER), 172
Norway, 198

object of citizenship. See citizenship at work
obsolescence, 118-24
occupational segregation, 19, 77-80
OECD (Organisation for Economic Co-operation and Development), 263
old age/aging, 100-101, 124-26
Ontario, 204, 234
open-door policies, 136, 296
organizational democracy, 9, 131, 291, 295-99
outsourcing, 67
overtime: legal regulations, 233-36, 244, 245; modes of compensation, 232f, 233; overpresenteeism, 85-86; paid, 246-47; time off in lieu, 245, 247; voluntary, 32, 34, 138f, 139, 164, 173, 230-36. See also crunch time
Ozimek, Anna M., 83, 170

pandemic, 113-14, 259. See also COVID-19
Pan-European Game Information (PEGI) system, 208
Paradox Interactive, 183
parental leave, 93-94, 114-15, 115f, 267
part-time employees, 72, 108, 228, 263n3, 268-69, 293
passion/play: and crunch time, 241-42; gender issues, 268, 274; and intellectual property, 148; normalizing overwork, 102, 243; playbour/free labour, xii, 64-65, 89, 101, 237; work as labour of love, 89-90, 281, 302. See also free labour/playbour
passive citizenship, 5, 127, 133, 259, 289, 293
paternity leave, 267

INDEX 373

pay. *See* compensation system
PC games, 38
peers, 31–33, 160–61, 244–45
pension plans, 19, 125, 126*f*, 299, 302
Perks, Matthew, 199, 205–6, 207
persons of colour: about, 79n2, 200n2; and crunch time, 266; and diverse work environment, 81–82, 261; and IGDA, 217, 218*f*; and inequities, 270, 272, 272*f*, 273*f*; occupational segregation, 79; representation opportunities, 200; and salary, 263, 265, 367*f*; and work-life balance, 268. *See also* Black communities; diversity; inequities; racialized groups
piracy, 44
playbour/free labour, xii, 64–65, 89, 101, 237. *See also* passion/play
PlayStation, 44
Poland, 68, 83
political citizenship, 7*f*, 108
post-bureaucratic environments. *See* project-based working conditions
post-industrial landscape, 10–12
Pratt, Andy C., 63, 95
pregnancy, 93, 114–15, 115*f*
presenteeism, 31, 85, 115
problem resolution, 171–72, 172*f*
procedural justice, 130–31, 140
professional associations, 177–79, 194, 201–5. *See also* IGDA
professional development, 7*f*, 29, 110, 118–21, 119*f*, 121–24, 152–53, 165*f*
Professionals Australia union, 212
project-based working conditions, 24–33; compensation, 33; deadlines, 26; funding, 27; nomadic careers, 27–30; teamwork, 31–33; unpredictable working time, 30–31. *See also* harassment; risks
project management, 23–34; about, xv; crunch time, 58, 102, 236–40, 238*f*, 240*f*, 241–44; *Guide to the Project Management Body of Knowledge* (PMBoK), 26; and HRM, 25, 133–34; and iron triangle, 33, 106, 302; project assignment, 153–56; Project Management Institute, 24; and risk, 106–107
promotion, 156–61

quality assurance (QA), 8–10, 82–84, 112, 174, 185, 186, 213. *See also* testers
Quality of Life (QoL) survey (IGDA), xix–xx, 217, 228
Quantic Dream, 184
Quebec, 118, 196*f*, 197, 204, 234
Quinn, Zoë, 255
quitting, 168–70

racialized groups, 79n2, 193–94, 200, 217, 265, 287. *See also* Black communities; diversity; inequities; persons of colour
racism, 80–82, 81*f*
Raven Software, 174–75, 185, 186, 213
reputation, 85–86, 110–14, 137, 140, 144, 153, 170
Resilience Force, 303
Riot Games, 174–77, 213, 221, 255, 260, 282
risks, 63–102; at-will employment, 70–73, 105, 139; of failure, 25–26, 34, 43–51; to health, 84–88, 90–93; limited by, 105; obsolescence, 118–24; occupational segregation, 77–80; racism, 80–82, 81*f*; responsibility for, 54, 293; risk aversion, 287; to social health, 93–96; temporary status of employment, 82–84; transfer of, 31, 105–7; unemployment, 66–70. *See also* gender issues; harassment; sexism
Rockstar, 113–14
Rockstar Spouse (blog), 239
Romero, Brenda, 254–55
Rowlands, Lorraine, 282
Ruffino, Paolo, 209
Ruggill, Judd Ethan, 207

sabotage, 170
Sarkeesian, Anita, 254
Scientific Research and Experimental Development (SR&ED) tax incentive program, 197
scope creep, 42, 239
Screen Actors Guild–American Federation of Television and Radio Artists (SAG-AFTRA), 180, 187
Scrum programming method, 41
segregation, occupational, 19, 77–80

seniority, 17, 23, 68
severance packages, 108–9
sex in videogames, 205–6, 206n11, 287
sexism: accusations of, 174–76, 260; culture of, 20, 74, 267, 274–78, 282, 290; Gamergate, 254–55; increase of, 80–82, 81*f*; motive for firing, 138. *See also* gender issues; harassment; inequities; women in the workforce
SG Guild, 184
Shepherd, Tamara, 278
skills: about, 32, 82–84; soft skills, 32, 264–65, 271; technical skills, 32, 97
Skillsearch, 261
Smilegate, 184
social media, 111, 193–94
social regulation of work, 193–226; events, 209–11; game content, 205–9; industry associations, 201–5; issue-based groups, 220–22; lobbying and direct state involvement, 194–201; meetups and informal groups, 222–25; non-compete agreements (NCAs), 223
social security systems, 107–10
soft skills. *See* skills, soft skills
Solidaires Informatique, 184, 212
Soni, Saket, 303
Sony, 44, 48, 175
Sotamaa, Olli, 194
South Africa, 203
South Korea, 184, 194
special interest groups (SIGs), 208, 215–16. *See also* individual groups
Starbreeze, 183
Starting Point (union), 184
state or employer benefits, 107–10
stress, 31, 90
Studio Affiliate Program, 203
studios, 37–61; bureaucracy, 10, 130, 131; client control over the development process, 51–55; financialization of, 55–58; flexibility of employment, 58–61; and job stability, 60; numbers of, 71*f*f; risk of failure, 43–51; uncertainty, 38–43. *See also* individual studios; videogame industry (VGI); workers
subject of citizenship. *See* citizenship at work

Švelch, Jan, 151, 194, 216
Sweden, 68, 182–83, 202
Switch, 38, 44
Syndicat des Travailleurs et Travailleuses du Jeu Vidéo (STJV), 184

Take This, 210, 220, 221–22
Take Two, 45
tax credits, 57, 60, 110, 194–98, 196*f*, 251, 297–98, 359*f*
teamwork, 31–33, 38–39, 42, 96–98; multidisciplinary teams, 31
Teipen, Christina, 67–68, 180, 183
Tekes, 199
temporary employment, 19, 72, 112
Ter Minassian, Hovig, 58–59
testers, 82–84, 89, 112, 142, 170. *See also* quality assurance (QA)
THQ, 45
time off, 231, 234, 246–47
Torontaru in Toronto, 222
training, 118–21, 119*f*, 152–53, 165*f*. *See also* professional development
transgender population, 74–75, 215*f*
Trendy Entertainment, 176
turnover/churn, 66–67, 168
Twitter (now X). *See* X (formerly Twitter)

Ubifree (anonymous virtual union), 182
Ubisoft: A Better Ubisoft (issue-based group), 213; in-house development, 47; lawsuit against, 212; representatives on boards, 204; and sexual misconduct, 176, 184, 255, 260, 275; Ubifree (virtual union), 182; and Women in Games International, 221; worker groups at, 174
unemployment, 66–70, 70*f*, 108–9, 138*f*, 168–70. *See also* discipline and dismissals
unionization/unions, 179–90; about, 294, 297, 299, 358*f*; Alphabet Workers Union (Google), 185, 187, 213, 298; bargaining agents, 23, 179, 211–13; Financial Services Union (FSU), 184, 198; Independent Workers' Union of Great Britain (IWGB), 184; non-union employee

INDEX 375

representation (NER), 172; positive views toward, 180–82; Professionals Australia union, 212; representation gaps, 182–85; in Sweden, 67–68, 182–83; Ubifree (anonymous virtual union), 182; various models of, 185–87; voting propensity for, 180–82, 181*f*

United Kingdom, 194, 202, 261

United States: AFL-CIO (US), 184–85; California Department of Fair Employment and Housing, 260; Equal Employment Opportunity Commission, 175, 255–56; Equal Pay Act (California), 175; Fair Labor Standards Act, 233–34; as main host, 45; New York Fashion Workers, 303; salaries, 261; Securities Exchange Commission, 255–56; and tax credits, 197; United Food and Commercial Workers (UFCW), 185; Workplace Bullying Institute, 269

Unity (game development tool), 222–23

unlimited, unpaid overtime (UUO). *See* crunch time

value chain, 43–51

Vanedge Capital, 49

Van Roessel, Lies, 151, 216

venture capital, 27, 106, 120

venture labour, 101, 124

Vézina, Michael, 85

videogame developers. *See* workers

videogame industry (VGI): about, 12, 47, 64; financialization of, 12, 56–58, 63, 106, 126, 292–94, 302; intellectual property (IP), 38, 46, 47, 98, 141, 148, 170, 174, 209, 294; profits/sales figures, xi, 43–44, 47; self-regulation, 207–8; study, xviii–xxii; turnover/churn, 66–67, 168. *See also* citizenship at work; human resource management (HRM); iron triangle; project management; social regulation of work; studios; workers

Videogame Writers Caucus, 188

Video Software Dealers Association, 206

violence, 81*f*, 193–94, 205–6, 208, 213, 287

Vivendi, 175

Vodeo Games, 185
Vodeo Workers United, 185
Voltage Entertainment, 185

Weil, David, 57
wellness programs, 117–18
Westecott, Emma, 256, 268, 288
WGA (Writer's Guild of America), 187–88
whistleblowers, 172, 175
white, male, and cisgender, 12, 20, 253, 256, 264, 274, 280, 288, 294, 295
whiteness, 261
Whitson, Jennifer R., 199
Women in Games International (WIGI), 220–22, 225
women in the workforce, 253–90; and crunch time, 266–69; Dames Making Games, 222; historical data, 73–74; HR policies and programs, 258–61, 365*f*; in leadership positions, 199; occupational segregation, 19, 77–79; and overtime culture, 87–88; pregnancy, 93, 114–15, 115*f*; and role of IGDA, 214–15, 215*f*, 217; scarcity of, 31; stereotyped profiling, 278–84; Women in Games group, 179, 216, 220–21, 223, 278; Women in Games International (WIGI), 220–21. *See also* diversity; gender issues; harassment; inequities; sexism
Woodfield, Ruth, 264–65
workers, arbitrary treatment, 129–34; compensation, 161–64; evaluation and promotion, 156–61; fair procedure, 131–33; non-compete agreements (NCAs), 141–48, 165*f*, 170, 223, 294; non-disclosure agreements (NDAs), 141–48, 165*f*, 170, 194, 209, 294; procedural justice, 130–31; project assignment, 153–56; training, 152–53. *See also* crediting practices; discipline and dismissals; human resource management (HRM); studios
workers, developers: and autonomy, 53–54; burnout, 84, 89, 90, 92, 115–17, 173, 247; career advancement, 121–22, 122*f*; casualization of labour, 70–73; characteristics of, 40–41; contract replacing long-term, 57; on demand, 27–30; demographics, 75*f*f;

events, 123, 209, 211, 214, 223, 355*f*;
fair treatment of, 178*f*; health issues,
7*f*, 84–88, 115–18, 118*f*, 293; job control/insecurity, 58, 70, 84–88, 90–92,
91*f*, 355*f*; knowledge workers, xv,
16–17, 24, 56–57, 65, 97–98; migrant
workers, 17, 19, 108; mobility, employment, 27–30, 38, 58–59, 69–71,
95, 106, 293; opinion of problem
resolution, 172*f*; part-time employees, 72, 108, 228, 263n3, 268–69, 293;
physical health, 90–93; reputation,
85–86, 110–14, 137, 140, 144, 153;
social health, 93–96; Videogame
Writers Caucus, 188; work neglect,
170–71. *See also* belonging; diversity;
inequities; passion/play; project-based working conditions; risks;
social regulation of work; studios;
unemployment; videogame industry
(VGI); women in the workforce
workers, time regulation of, 227–51;
peers as regulators, 244–45; working
hours, 228–29, 229*f*, 246; work-life
balance, 64, 93–94, 268*f*. *See also*
compensation systems; crunch time;
overtime
workers, voice of, 167–91, 194, 201–5;
collective short-term mobilizations,
173–77; employee exit, 168–70;
employee neglect, 170–71; individual
employee voice, 171–73; professional
associations, 177–79, 194, 201–5;
representation gaps, 182–85. *See also*
IGDA; unionization/unions
Workforce Skills Development and
Recognition Fund (Quebec), 118
works councils (Europe), 179–80
Writer's Guild of America (WGA),
187–88

X (formerly Twitter), 111
Xbox, 44

YetiZen party, 255
Young, Christopher J., 225

Zabban, Vinciane, 58–59
ZeniMax Media, 47, 185